Oskar Kokoschka: *the Artist and his Time*

OSKAR KOKOSCHKA

THE ARTIST AND HIS TIME

a Biographical Study by J. P. Hodin

NEW YORK GRAPHIC SOCIETY

*First published in London 1966 by Cory, Adams & Mackay Ltd, 37 Museum Street, WC1
and in the U.S.A. by New York Graphic Society, Greenwich, Connecticut.
Library of Congress Catalogue No. 66–15797. All rights reserved.
The text is set in 'Monotype' Ehrhardt; printed and bound in England
by W. & J. Mackay and Co. Ltd, Chatham, Kent.*

CONTENTS

LIST OF ILLUSTRATIONS

COLOUR PLATES

BLACK AND WHITE ILLUSTRATIONS

TO THE MEMORY OF KATHLEEN, COUNTESS OF DROGHEDA

PREFACE

In my essay *Larenopfer** I stated what Oskar Kokoschka means to me and to my generation. The present work is more than a personal confession; it is an historical assessment.

When I moved to London from Stockholm in 1944 the war was still at its height, but I immediately began to collect the material for a comprehensive biography of the artist that I had been planning since 1938, and Kokoschka's presence in England enabled me to have very frequent conversations with him, to assemble, check and interpret the main events and details of his rich, creative life. This work is built up entirely on those meetings and conversations; they shed light on the artist's character, but also illumine the times through which he was destined to live, and which tempered his activity. However, Kokoschka's attitude to life and to art would seem to be only one aspect of an organically determined and unified, if contradictory, whole, were it not for his attitude to contemporary political and economic thought, to scientific and technical problems, to philosophy, psychology, music and literature, to the plight of the visual arts and, above all, his personal understanding of the evolving historical-cultural picture. For he was never a passive observer, no stoic. He plunged headlong into the fray, criticizing and ratifying fearlessly, at the same time separating the essential from the transient, the sick and perverted from the healthy and upright. His life was a pattern of integrity; his work reveals a man of noble presence and rare unity, who was both a landmark and an example for the future. One thing is assured: the significance of his work. The future alone will assess fully the influential grandeur of the man, and only then will his real stature be revealed.

The artist's experiences which he related to me, all that I had observed and noted for over thirty years, had to be analysed and rearranged in tangible form. Kokoschka's own account would have appeared one-sided, even sometimes distorted by the mood of the moment, had it not been balanced by another aspect, of which he was unaware; his subconscious self and the effect he had upon his contemporaries.

Such values are essential for the completion of a biography in an era characterized by the advent of depth psychology, in which, it may be added, Kokoschka places as little faith as he does in time. I have therefore brought in witnesses who knew Kokoschka at different periods in his life; some of this material appeared in *Bekenntnis zu Kokoschka*,† but it is otherwise published here for the first time in this, his life-story. For it *is* a story even if nothing in it is invented, only perhaps altered slightly by circumstance and memory, in the way that truth and poetry are interchangeable in the mind of an imaginative artist. I have turned to the psychologists for guidance and have drawn on the auxiliary sciences of graphology, physiognomy, Gestalt-psychology (so closely connected

* *Larenopfer*: Sacrifice to the Household Gods.
† *Bekenntnis zu Kokoschka*: Acknowledgement to Kokoschka.

with art and artists), chirology and even astrology in its new Jungian guise. All this has been evoked and used for the first time in the examination of a personality, so that by analysis of all the 'graphic' elements (excluding his actual work) the artist's unconscious strivings and failings should be revealed. For are not the graphic elements—hand-writing, and its similarity to brush-work, the changing lines on face and palm—the equivalent of form in the work and person of the artist, just as the paths of the planets outline the structure of an astrology which Jung believed to embody the earliest form of human typology?

I have thus attempted to elucidate things of which Kokoschka remained unaware, things which he suppressed or altered in the process of work and the search for under-standing. There was no question of analysis for its own sake—that would have been pointless—but only of its use as an intermediary in the metamorphosis of the artist's own story into a biography. This part is to be published under a separate title: *The Psycho-graphy of an Artist. A Depth-Psychological Study of Oskar Kokoschka*, and will soon appear. Thus two books have been completed as off-shoots of the main work, but all three are testimonies of our era and of one of the rarest and most talented artists in the history of modern art. In future Kokoschka's name will be added to those of the great masters of Expressionist vision: Grünewald, Rembrandt, Goya and Munch. Vision and imagina-tion are thus carried on from generation to generation, forging a chain that links the past with the future like a tree with its roots deep underground that brings forth flowers and fruit though storm and wind may lash its crown.

I am deeply grateful, first and foremost, to the artist; not only has he never refused me the chance of being with him and has always readily answered what must, on occasion, have been irritating questions, but for the immense task of reading and annotating both versions of my manuscript. That he also allowed me the freedom to decide whether or not his suggestions were to be adopted is deeply appreciated. His friendship has been an incalculable support in my task and an unforgettable spiritual experience. Munch had revealed to me man's potential, but to be with Kokoschka was to walk in a garden, to experience the miracle of creation and the changing seasons. The whole panorama could be glimpsed from there—the broad plain of history, man's daring and destiny.

I am very indebted to my wife Pamela for the peace she secured for me in which I could work and mature. She, like my mother, never doubted that I would fulfil my literary task even when conditions often proved unfavourable and most difficult.

I am also thankful to Mr Anthony Adams, who realized the international nature of the work and put all his energies into producing English and American editions.

My thanks are also due to Frau Olda, the artist's wife, who has been helpful and ready with answers over the years; to Diana Imber for her translation; and also the artist and Herr Norbert Kletterer for permission to print the illustrations. Nor must the many public and private owners of Kokoschka's work be forgotten for they have gladly allowed their treasures to be reproduced.

J. P. HODIN

THE THREE FACES OF KOKOSCHKA

The time is February 1944. Oskar Kokoschka's studio was at No. 99a Park Lane, London; a big quiet room with a skylight where he could be alone with his painting. The easel held a canvas which the artist had been working on for some time, and a delicate smell of oil paint and turpentine hung in the air. The big sofa on which I was sitting was covered with a patchwork quilt; a tall screen decorated with figures cut off the head of this sofa from a corner where paintings and unused canvases were stacked. The table on the left was full of a conglomeration of tubes, brushes, and palettes, and next to it was a high-backed chair standing on a wooden frame with steps. It looked like a throne and was intended for portrait sitting. Heavy and medieval in appearance, it was covered with velvet drapery.* Hanging from the ceiling was a ring with a celluloid parrot and a multi-coloured electric-light bulb.

On the chimney-piece to the right I saw some crinkled silver and gold paper, a few dried-up flowers, a porcelain partridge, a piece of rock-crystal and some pink shells. I smiled. That was his landscape, explained Kokoschka, to help him forget that he was in a city. Opposite were two blacked-out windows. It was late afternoon.

My eyes wandered from these things to the picture on the easel. In the foreground and slightly to the right I saw the head and shoulders of a woman. She had a penetrating but warm gaze and a strange smile played round her half-open lips. There was something indefinable, an unreal reality, enhanced by the realism with which the face was portrayed. From time to time the mouth seemed to me to open as if to speak, like Pythia, giving utterance to a riddle, while the eyes kept looking round into the landscape swarming with small figures which surrounded her in a luminous, sharp green. Her right hand touched the flower on her breast with two fingers. She was the Madonna and Pomona, Maria and Demeter in one, set in a Baroque landscape calling forth religious associations.

Who is this woman? I asked.

The Goddess, was his reply.

I looked towards the picture again. The small figures on the left were crowded in upon each other. In front a wilful mule bared its teeth in frustration. On it sat the devil. Red. A whore kicked up her leg, hiding the figure of Christ on the cross. There were graves, and a corpse swung on the gallows.

* (*Note by Kokoschka*: The room was like that when I took it and I was too disinterested to change anything. I never do, not in hotels or anywhere. I never stay in one place long enough, am always on the move.)

Look how the filthy creature dances—I still seem to hear the echo of Kokoschka's voice—she sells herself for food, the slut.

On the right of the Goddess is a small fleeing figure. It is the mother with the only child to be rescued from the chaos. Kokoschka's blue eyes flashed when he told me that he would like to reinstate the devil. His eyes moved like those of a bird, turning inwards and showing the whites. Crossing the studio silently, he came up to me. He had a powerful face with a long head and short hair combed flat to his skull. When he talked he would become excited and then one felt as though a bridled passion formed his words: they were like a volcano.

He believed that mankind must learn the meaning of fear again. The symbol of hell had been put aside while hell itself was being created on earth. Scientists had laughed at the devil and called him an old wives' tale, till present-day man no longer recognized any moral law, only police rule. But when he becomes afraid of himself, then, and only then, will it be possible to expect a change in the structure of society. Man is and always will be a primitive; reason cannot alter that. The devil, the principle of evil, with his horns, goat's hooves and tail, the picture of a creature, half-man, half-beast, and at the same time a chthonic god, was there before my eyes as a living being; it reminded me of Jung's theory of an archaic personification of the sinister, unbalanced aspect of the unconscious, which one can never lay hold of and which remains, therefore, for ever trapped in its original state of untamed savagery. In this painting the artist had attained the same position as the philosopher; this devil was primarily a psychological invention conjured out of the evil of the times, from humanity's unrestrained, primitive drives, and spell-bound in tangible form by the artist.

Kokoschka stood close beside me. He had put on the blue and white striped apron which he used for working. He looked tired. His mouth was hard and bitter, his forehead lined, but his eyes were calm as though they saw through a veil of sorrow. The whole face was imbued with intense vitality, every muscle in the cheeks moving, like those of an actor, and reflecting the slightest emotion. This expressive face, together with the gestures and the modulation of his voice, gave his words meaning and spiritual richness. Like listening to an actor, one followed him with hope out of the fearful present into a distant prospect; but sometimes one was abandoned in a sea of darkness, because he, too, for the moment had lost his way.

Kokoschka offered me a cigarette from his long flat case, lighting his own with an old-fashioned wick which he had treasured since the days of the first war (it works better in a wind, all the others go out); for moral collapse, war, postwar and another war had been the essential if not the determining features of Kokoschka's life. It is strange that the work of his early youth, surging with new power, had been destructive and analytical, strange the unalterable fact that he belonged to the group of artists who foresaw and depicted the collapse, thereby preparing the way for the catastrophes which finally buried the nobility and the *bourgeoisie* who despite all their criticism had understood and supported him, the very class which he admitted to be his own. But we often find the most glaring defects in those whom we ought to love the most. And when his fresh and fearless

TIGON, 1926

mind first penetrated into the putrescence of the age its effect was to destroy even further.

That is the first face of Kokoschka. It is the face of a revolutionary idealist, a fighter belonging to that spiritual underground movement which for centuries past has always had to flee into the dark for safety when the dead hand of political reality forces it to cling to life for the sake of an ancient moral law and mystic understanding.

Unconsciously at first, and with a mixture of shyness and anxiety, he tried to indicate the fearful cancer which was gnawing away at men's souls; there in pre-war Vienna he tried to show the real face of his contemporaries, tearing away their masks in his portraits. Art for him then was a means of accusation and exposure, a rejection of the times, rather than an expression of amazement at the wonder of existence, at the beauty and power of life. Later on he began to write and there too followed a relentless uncovering of the truth as he poured rebellious irony into his savage speeches, essays, and articles. Every single opportunity—the foreword to a catalogue, a letter, or an essay on a work of art—was used to attack the evils of the times. And in a collection of drawings made during the first world war and a series of wartime paintings from the second, he expressed the tragedy and irony, the lesson for his contemporaries, in the manner of Hieronymus Bosch, Breughel the Elder, and Goya and Ensor in their time.

And the second face? When Kokoschka finished talking about the devil I could see that he had much more to say, but that he would never be able to describe the evil in words. Everyone believed in progress. They were deceived, he thought. He was a believer too, and truth is only what one believes. He had never believed in progress, which results in a misuse of the intellect, but rather in reason, in the Goddess, the return of the matriarchy. For years he had carried the image of the Goddess within himself until she seemed to be more real than the physical world about him but sometimes when he was tired the vision left him. Then suddenly she was there again and he would discover new, important features only discernible with heightened perception and an unclouded eye. Then he would scrape away the old paint from the canvas: his vision was realised again. The face was so real that then, and only then, was he in the presence of something living. The vision crystallizes in rational form. It happens in Buddhism, he told me, and formerly this had puzzled him. There is also a passage in the Upānishād which defines painted form as a spirit in the Mayan hierarchy in the physical world, and possessed therefore of body and soul. His painting, he said, resembled the magic of an ancient priesthood. Time was of no importance as long as one did not have it shoved under one's nose. The times revealed nothing to him; it had to come from oneself. A bomb or two did not mean much. Nor was he curious to know the future and never looked at the war damage. So far he had escaped and he had been in London during the worst of the bombing. Once he had seen it; cats crouching in a burning house. And the small Benedictine monk, Macnab, with his hungry, thin little face, climbing over the wreckage with an open umbrella; he was always smiling, making things easy, helping everyone, and he was greatly loved. That was the kind of humanity that wrought miracles. He knew all the time that in two or three weeks he would die. He was fatally ill with cancer of the tongue, could eat nothing and must perforce die of hunger. . . .

No, cried Kokoschka in his excitement, as long as he held the vision in his mind he had been able to feed upon it. What else was left but to cling to the few roots he possessed?

He had always been fascinated by inner creative processes, he told me, and often felt an emptiness; that was why he was so egocentric, because he had to confine himself to his own path.

Today I feel renewed, but often I feel empty, dry, and then I write about the education of children. Today the old magic crept over me. Ever since I was a boy I have needed this stimulus, this presence of the vision, of the face from within.

What was fascination, he wondered? There is a force behind it which is not an intellectual synthesis. He had never been able to learn, having to forget everything immediately, nor could he repeat himself—that would have been death.

But when fascination holds me in its grip I feel good, and equally forlorn when it fades.

Why did he not subscribe to formalism? He had always hated it because he could never believe in a substitute for life. Nothing could be done in cold blood. It made him uneasy. It was the same with love. He paused, then went on: he never lost touch with his visions altogether; they were as alive as he was, and as dependent on him as he on them. He could never be without them for more than three or four days, just as though they were guardian angels or spirits. That accounted for a superstitious fear that he would lose his vital power, just as formerly he had thought to lose his sexual power and so be bereft of life, of soul. He had to wait for inspiration and then work unceasingly. Sometimes he wrestled as long as thirty years with a single vision. If he could not complete it, then it remained enclosed within him and he could not proceed. It was a living inspiration impelled to form. A phenomenon appears. He never noticed the passage of time and would spend one or two years on a single figure. Then he would suddenly turn it right round on the same canvas like a piece of furniture, because it seemed too lifeless. It did not concern others, who did not see the vision, but he fed on his visions and the power he put into them came back a hundredfold. That is the intoxication of the visions: and the Goddess is one of them.

In 1912 Kokoschka gave a lecture in Vienna entitled *On the Nature of Visions*. He had just been reading it again and would still not alter a word. That evening, after the lecture, Berthold Viertel, the actor, had taken it away with him, declaring that he simply must borrow it; he wanted to study it in peace. Then he had lost it. Fortunately Kokoschka's memory was word-perfect and three days later he had written it out again. He had remembered it with his inner ear.[1]

Visions, keenness of hearing! That was the theme, the awareness of visions! That lecture was more important to him today than philosophy, humanism or present-day reality. The reason for man's seeming so dry now, so empty, was the failure of human sympathy. Man still complains, but is incapable of penetrating below the surface. A vision is a light which never left him; but in the background behind the light was the female principle, the significant, the reason for life. It reminded him of the scene when Faust descends to the mothers, and the passage where Hamlet addresses his uncle:

Hamlet : Farewell, dear mother.

Claudius : Thy loving father, Hamlet.

Hamlet : My mother: father and mother is man and wife, man and wife is one flesh, and so, my mother.

The female principle of life is more than an idea, it is a fact, a vital force. Woman is eternal. Life is like the earthworm. Parts die and rot and are replaced. But it is still the same organism—the essence of life, not a mechanical process. There will be an endless void, a long quietus; the worm will almost perish. But the sap will be preserved. In the sap lies the future which will fulfil the ancient myths.

He saw it all as physical fact, like a stone falling, or the stars in the sky. Why spend time painting pictures? he wondered. And the answer—the only possible answer: because he could not tolerate life without his visions. He knew that in fifty years' time it would be of no consequence, that mankind would no longer create anything, nor be capable of seeing. The process was already far advanced . . . man's blindness was growing.

The silence which followed these words was broken by the air-raid sirens—first one, far off, then more and more until the air was filled with their sound. The Luftwaffe was making its last desperate attacks on London. The radar defence system of the vast city was out of action, and for six nights on end London endured an almost defenceless period like the Battle of Britain. I shall never forget his face at that moment. It was like an image. The features and muscles were drawn together like stone, but a radiance lay on them. The first bombs began to fall, breaking the silence, and Kokoschka sat still. What was he thinking? This time he was on the other side. The two great wars seemed one to him, a logical sequence. He had seen them from both sides, had seen the cultural and moral collapse with his own eyes, had lived through the deepening tragedy of man's mechanization. And over there somewhere—the source of the bombs—were his relatives, his brother and sister; Vienna, Prague and the cities that had watched him strive for his art, with men in power who had called him degenerate and probably destroyed all his work. There were perhaps bombers at this moment scattering death and destruction and burying the culture of Europe under a shroud of sorrow.

Only when a bomb exploded nearby in Hyde Park, shaking the foundations of the house and knocking off some tiles, did he turn towards the blacked-out window. Then he stood up. The Goddess stared at me over his shoulder with her mysterious, sphinx-like eyes. Her gaze penetrated my soul.*

After about two hours the 'All Clear' was heard and we went down into the street. It was as black as pitch. The traffic sounded muffled. One could hear footsteps but see no one, only the light of small torches creeping about like glow-worms. That night we did not talk about the war. We went up Park Lane. A cold wind was blowing across the park and now and then a distant flash lit up the sky. We went into No. 52, where Kokoschka lived, and up seven stories in the lift, then crossed a narrow bridge joining two blocks

---

* Kokoschka asked me if I would like to go down to the cellar. He never went down himself and his wife told me later he had a fear of shelters, believing he would get pneumonia and die. Up here there was a chance, but if his guests felt uncomfortable he always advised them to go.

together like a piece of loose scaffolding in the dark. Kokoschka gave a short whistle once we were on the bridge to warn his wife that he was coming. So the door was open when we arrived and Frau Olda—a tall, boyish figure—greeted us in a voice hoarse with anxiety. Supper was waiting in the small kitchen leading off the living-room, and afterwards we drank coffee and smoked. Kokoschka had met Olda in Prague in 1935 and they came to England as refugees three years later. We talked of old times, then Olda began to clear away, but Kokoschka wanted to help her. So while he went into the kitchen to help with the washing-up he gave me a manuscript to read which he took from a small desk beside the window. His gallant thoughtfulness towards his wife is typical of the man.

Of all the impressions that filled my mind at that moment the one I remember most clearly was my surprise at finding Kokoschka married. Really there was nothing extraordinary about it, but I had always imagined him alone, even though surrounded by women, and I had never really appreciated the infinite loneliness which must afflict an artist driven from country to country; forced to abandon the little house in the Liebhartstal near Vienna, with all his books, documents, many paintings, with the memories of events which had become sacred to him, and to renounce the only safe place in the world—that home to which he had always returned while his mother was alive. I could hear a friendly argument going on in the kitchen as Kokoschka tried to do more than his share: Now leave that, dear, let me do it. You must be tired, too . . .

Several books lay on the table: *The Web of Belief* by Peter Cheltschizki; the writings and sermons of Meister Eckhardt; Kokoschka: *Dramen und Bilder*, with an introduction by Paul Stefan, who had been known as the painter's shadow in Vienna. This last contains the finest material that has been written on the artist. The true value of this essay can only be properly understood when one realizes that it was written in 1913 and yet summarizes in a few pages the essential elements of the art and humanism of Kokoschka. I was delighted to find the book there, because it had become a great rarity in the chaos and destruction of the war. There were various objects on the chimneypiece—the artist's toys. A finely cast and decorated Japanese stirrup, a Japanese soldier's bronze mask from the days before the country was americanized; two finely wrought Jugoslav distaffs and a small Japanese dancer of wood and silk. Not all were man-made, however. There was a huge pine-cone, a red pumpkin, a few speckled beans in a Chinese bowl and some oval pebbles. On the opposite side of the room was a silk Japanese Kakimono with a design of a cock and hens above the upholstered blue sofa. Two watercolours done by Kokoschka during the last few years hung at either side: a red lobster, snapdragons and wildflowers.

I took up the typescript and began to read. It was entitled *Disarmament of Children*. It is a moving document of the period just before the last war.[2]

Even in deep despair, when he had given up European culture for lost, Kokoschka tried to rally himself: he had faith in youth. He believed that youth was the emblem of the future. But what kind of education does it receive today? Mere boys are torn from their mothers to be prepared for war instead of for a life of freedom and maturity. Even as a child he had always mistrusted adults, and in the first world war he knew himself to be a representative of the younger generation against the older. Now he was talking of the *bourgeoisie*. Adults were dead, their hearts were sterile and therefore everything would be destroyed. Did anyone today think still that he should hand the world on to the next generation, not simply as it was, but better and more beautiful?

How strange it seemed that the most revolutionary manifesto of all should have been written by a painter. A document that exposes the insatiable rich and grasping poor equally, that derides conscious aims and opens with the words: 'God is not one, but all are in God. Everything is divine . . .' and ends with the call 'Kyrie Eleison, Pan is risen, the Infant Jesus and all the spirits and fairies.' I quote from *On the Nature of Visions*, the foreword to *Orbis Pictus* which is imbued with the same spirit as *Disarmament of Children*.[3]

Thus was the third face of Kokoschka revealed to me. He saw himself as St George and made a painting of the pure knight, chosen to destroy the life-consuming dragon. In *Still-life with Tortoise and Hyacinth* he became a mystic touched by the secret of mortality. Like St Anthony he fought against temptation, and his poetic writing, like a cry in the night, like a spirit, is wrung from the confusion of his despair. Kokoschka's mystical works may be likened in spirit to those of Jakob Boehme, Meister Eckhardt, Suso, Tauler, and Angelus Silenius. His early visionary writing reads like that of a medieval mystic and his first play, *Murder Hope of Women*, is a mystery play, a myth in modern dress. Kokoschka is a thinker who like a peasant understands the secret of growth; he is the youth who talks with death, the devil on his right, an angel on the left. Of all the modern writers only Flaubert has been able to combine the mystic clairvoyance and current scepticism manifested in Kokoschka's early painting and writing. But the third Kokoschka—the samaritan—pours balm on the wounds of time. As a humanist and reformer, as the evangelist of reverence for life, he wears the gentle features of St Francis; he embraces the sun and the sorrow of man and beast in his universal love; and he speaks with the tongues of angels.

> *Dov'è la vera charità et sapientia, quivi no è paura nè ignorantia.*
> *Dov'è la povertà con letitia, non è cupidità, nè avarita.*
> *Dov'è il reposo et il ricordo de Dio, quivi non è sollicitudine nè vagabondità.*[4]

While searching for Guinevere—like the knights of the Round Table, Sir Gawain, Parsifal, and Tristan—he had perceived the vision of the Holy Grail, and the symbol of existence took shape in the theme of Mother and Child, the age-old Madonna-motif.[5] I read on:

Older far than Christian love, the gospel of mother-love should move woman to try to force a universal decision on the proper education of children. They should long ago have demanded a reasonable education for their children, because it is after all they, and not men, who bring children into the world. And even a state that refuses the rights of humanity to its sons, that swallows up its children like a Moloch, is denied the right to force motherhood on its women. Politicians should read Aristophanes' *Lysistrata*.

Socrates, who was responsible for the first reasonable approach to education, declared: 'Absolute integrity of mind is the only virtue in this life.'

Kokoschka always opposed the war. The question, he thought, was whether mankind would act in time to prevent another mass-murder and cultural collapse or whether awareness and humility would come too late. I read on for a long time about the cause of spiritual crisis, the destructive nature of work geared exclusively to production; of the shrinking of human ability wherever completely uncreative work was done; of the problem of the International school, which was to be a harmonious development providing the certainty of significant social activity; and of Amos Comenius, who during a lifelong pilgrimage sought support from all the potentates of Europe for his ideal of a school governed by an international commission; how he urged the Pope, the Emperor of Germany, politicians and scientists of the time, but all in vain.[6]

'There was not time for reasonable projects during the Thirty Years' War because a serious interpretation of the commandment "Thou shalt not kill" would have meant the end of the war. Ethics develop only from the positive philosophy which rejects all ideologies.'[7]

As Kokoschka came into the room I laid the manuscript on one side, saying nothing. For what could I say? None of his ideas had been able to prevent the catastrophe. The peoples of the world were caught in a desperate struggle and we ourselves were living in a city where even at this moment the dead and wounded were being pulled from the wreckage of falling buildings and saved from fires that threatened to destroy the whole city.

The artist seemed to read my thoughts: it will be worse, he said, far worse. But do not despair.

The war was still being fought, the end of the devastation still not in sight, yet Kokoschka saw another conflict in his imagination. Perhaps this war would just merge into another, who knows? Then he asked: Can you tell me of any movement in history that has been more destructive than the barbarian invasions? The answer is the Industrial Revolution. Now the past has to be erased, nothing must remain, and the whole of Europe has to be destroyed to wipe out the memory of times when things were different, when other people existed besides our uniform slave society. After the barbarian invasions a few hermits were left who still preserved fragments of Greek thought, and there remained also the Arabic philosophy from the old Umayyad kingdom and the culture of the Jews in Spain; but industrialization knows no mercy. However hard it is for us, we must face the truth.

I followed Kokoschka into the bedroom to look at a book he wanted to show me, and noticed a pen-and-ink drawing on the wall. It was a portrait of that same woman, mysteriously smiling and whispering her magic spell. The Goddess? I asked. Kokoschka nodded.

I looked more closely at the drawing. The expression of the face went beyond the individual, and yet there was a quality of portrayal, of Realism which made a deep impression on me. Dürer's head of a Slav peasant-woman—*Una vilana Twindisch*—gives me the same feeling, and the two have indeed much in common. So I said: Is the Goddess a real person then?

Yes.

At the most unpredictable moments she had appeared unexpectedly in his life, and then vanished again. She was a woman who left a strange impression on him, but he had not seen her now for a long time. She could not come. And his gesture mutely explained the difficulties. This drawing was done a long time ago.

It was late. As we said good-bye Kokoschka suggested, If there's another warning go to the shelter—the underground is best. You aren't used to it yet. I walked on through the dark, and suddenly I thought of what I had been told as a child about the guardian angel who goes hand in hand with every man on his journey through life. And the picture came into my mind of a small boy walking along a narrow path beside a precipice. A winged, white-clad angel flew along beside him, touching his hand. The angel had a gentle smiling face; but when I tried to imagine it in the darkness of wartime London it took on the features of Kokoschka's Goddess. One seemed to flow into the other. And then I knew that the Goddess was the artist's guardian angel watching over his house and family, that even if she were alive, with an address somewhere, to him she was more: a loved one and a vital bond between the artist and the riddle of creation. Yes, she sometimes embodied creation itself and then again sometimes the vibration of his senses when he was inspired; she was the visionary perception of the riddle. Kokoschka appeared to me to be among the few who are painfully aware of the indivisibility of life and who suffer from the analytical, scientific spirit as from the blows of a scourge. He was a true follower of Goethe: '*Nenn's Glück, Herz, Liebe, Gott! Gefühl ist alles.*'*

Kokoschka worked for a full two years on the portrait of the Goddess. Further symbols of the will to destruction were added to the earlier ones—a grave-digger and children's corpses. The mother fleeing with her child in the turbulent background now turned towards the Goddess for help. In vain. Mercy had been banished from her features; her face was furrowed and tortured with the haggard look of inexpressible suffering. The hand which formerly lay on her breast, playfully inviting, now pushed away a lamb come to drink at the spring of life. It was as if youth were trying to find strength and sweetness again, but the age denied them. The Goddess was now fleeing from the present—only half of her body was visible within the frame. Her left arm turned back into the picture, forming a diagonal with her forefinger almost touching the gaping mouth of the mule as if to focus the devil riding on it. The guilt was his. But the devil moved diagonally on a different plane leading back into the picture, so that the lines never met. Hence the structure of this painting represents a metaphysical idea, depicting two hostile and eternally opposing worlds. At the end of the war he destroyed the picture in despair. Later he used the vision of the Goddess in the tryptich, *Thermopylae.*

What conclusions are to be drawn from these musings? Can we discover in them the relationship of Kokoschka the humanist to the mystic, and of the mystic to the artist?

* Call it happiness, heart, love, God! Feeling is everything.

Despite the obviously negative content of the picture we must at least recognize through the fact of its existence and its turbulent style, that the Baroque artist has overwhelmed the humanist, just as the humanism of Breughel overcame the medievalism of Hierony-mus Bosch. But why? Because the widespread humanism which evolved out of the rationalism of the Renaissance was not strong, vital or sound enough to withstand the onset of the forces ranged against it during a period of industrial revolution. It is necessary to probe more deeply to establish the relationship between man and creation, and civilizations that did not try were doomed. This Kokoschka knew, for he had experi-enced it, but he also recognized the inherent danger: that mankind would use psycho-analysis as an excuse to withdraw from its human obligations, to confound itself. Between this Scylla and Charybdis winds a narrow way, followed by the mysticism of early man, by the myths and drama of the Greeks and by the Christian mystics of the Middle Ages. Kokoschka had set out on that path when he was still a young man.

THE MELANCHOLY OF THE WORLD

Kokoschka was easily upset at that period and the war overshadowed everything. Often his nerves seemed to be completely on edge—especially during the final stages of the war, which he saw as the slaughter of a whole generation. He feared for his work and grew bitter and unjust. But it was hatred of the universal suffering that made him unreasonable, not concern for himself. He was tormented by the thought of the others who still tried to excuse and justify the war, while he could do so no longer. I realized that he did not confine the front just to the battlefields, but laid the blame squarely on both sides; and he tried to take up a position that no government or party could adopt as its own, bringing with it a world at peace, a new Golden Age in which Paradise would be regained and Utopia eclipsed by reality.

Kokoschka appeared to have lost his sense of political reality and to have quite forgotten the ambiguous nature of man. He lived in a world of ideas incompatible with the slogans of both East and West. His eyes were often clouded with despair. Even painting, which could have braced and reinforced him, did not distract him from the problems of the day. I realized that he was wearing himself out and to make matters worse he was unable to sleep because the flying-bomb raids on London began soon after D-day and continued for months. The mechanical nature of the weapon was for him a worse feature than its destructive force, because it rendered the raids absolutely inhuman. Kokoschka seemed to burn with an inner fire like a prophet of old. Realizing that life everywhere was being destroyed and that the man of the future, despite, or perhaps because of, his restless mental activity and education, would thirst after wisdom in vain, I determined to keep a record of everything I might learn from him. It would never have been possible to remember without writing it down, though at first Kokoschka was suspicious and uneasy. I tried to distract his attention and in the end he forgot all about it. He would sometimes interrupt me to ask, smilingly, if it wasn't all rather boring, since these were not proper stories. On the other hand, he was just as likely to encourage me: You're quite right, write it all down; it will be like reading the notes made in the margin of a manuscript by a monk several hundred years ago; it will be a happy discovery.

Kokoschka used every opportunity to discuss his ideas on truth. On one occasion he fetched a bundle of papers out of a cupboard and knelt down on the floor beside them. First he came across the introductions to two exhibitions, but discarded them because they had nothing to do with the subject although they contained some political thoughts. He even intended to write a book on art embodying his social ideas and hoped that thus concealed they might be discovered and understood in fifty or a hundred years' time. He was not writing for the present.[1]

Do you like Swift? he asked me. There may be a few people left in this country who can still enjoy him, even if his writing does etch its way into the mind.

Young artists, Kokoschka told me, had been to see him and among them a soldier who was now living on the knowledge that he could come occasionally to show him his pencil drawings. He had been painting in the style of the Royal Academy. So Kokoschka advised him to practise drawing. Soon, said Kokoschka, he was producing fine work, a sunlit landscape, for instance, one of the most difficult subjects—vibration of light. He was humble and would be lucky. He did not think of his work as art, but painted because he had to; he was alive and human. The others in his platoon spent their evenings drinking and gambling or going to the cinema, but he passed the time drawing.

I used to wonder whether I would ever be able to weave a true picture of Kokoschka's attitude to life and to society. I realize now that I was striving after the impossible, for nothing was fixed in Kokoschka's mind, to be grasped and explained once and for all. If a question probed too deeply, as if into a wound, he would say at once that he preferred not to discuss the subject. Behind him stood a rival—the past. He did not want to think about that, what he really enjoyed was telling stories, which he never ended.

One day I asked him: If a young man comes to you and asks, 'Why is everything so difficult, unnatural, so confused and aimless? How has it become like this? What shall I do?' how would you answer him? Kokoschka did not reply at once. Then he began to talk of Dürer's *Melancholia*, and wondered whether the theme ever appeared before Dürer.

That was scarcely the answer I had expected but I took up the subject. Not in Dürer's interpretation, I replied. The fifteenth century certainly recognized the figure of melancholy, but only in the popular and primitive form as one of the human moods. Melancholy was thought to be an aversion from activity of any kind, related closely to laziness, and an ignoble characteristic.

The explanation of Dürer's drawing was not conclusive. I mentioned Panofsky-Saxl and Groddeck, but it was Wölfflin who seemed to me to come nearest to the truth in rejecting the despairing interpretation of Dürer's *Melencolia I* of 1514: that knowledge led to no final enlightenment, nor the intensive efforts of man towards domination of his dark presentiments; it was rather a mood of a penetrating disquiet.[2]

That's it, said Kokoschka, that's how I see it. But does Wölfflin give a reason for this malaise?

I could not remember exactly, but I promised to look it up and the next day I brought the book with me.

Wölfflin sees melancholy as a disease of the spirit, which cripples mankind, but also as one of the four Aristotelian humours. Aristotle held that the serious, creative nature was inclined to melancholy. The word therefore has a double meaning, defined by Wölfflin more closely by reference to the work of Marsilius Ficinus on the Threefold Life which runs: 'All great artists are also melancholy—*omnes ingeniosos, melancholices esse.*'

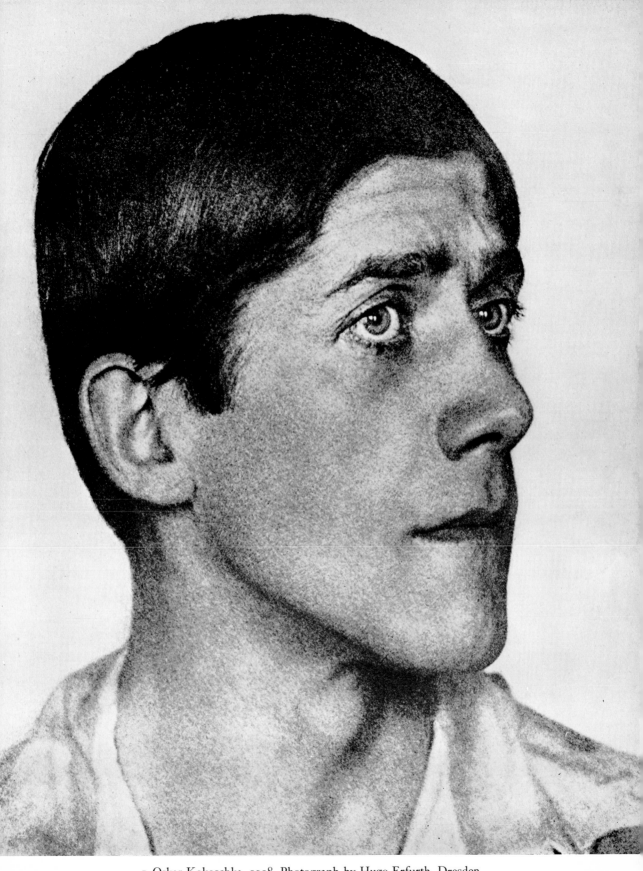

1 Oskar Kokoschka, 1918. Photograph by Hugo Erfurth, Dresden

2 The Artist's Father, 1918

3 Kokoschka's Birth-place in Pöchlarn

4 The Artist's Mother, 1917

5 Oskar Kokoschka as a volunteer, 1915

6 Still Life with Tortoise and Hyacinth, 1909
By Courtesy of the Österreichische Galerie, Vienna

7 Children Playing, 1909

Unfortunately that got us nowhere; Kokoschka felt it led us far from the problem he was considering. Then he developed the view that a new interpretation of the Dürer engraving can be drawn from the tragic reality of our time. Kokoschka conceives the artist as a man whose profession it is to observe and to see. Dürer saw everything clearly, even though contemporary literary thought was far behind. Man's condition had been one of melancholy since the Renaissance, because he cut himself off from life by his intellect, sinking ever deeper into materialist estrangement.

He returned to the problem of the young people who came to him for advice: If they had been only ordinary English, German, Czech or French soldiers he would prefer to tell them to destroy; everything must be destroyed. But these young men had faces and hands and eyes, each one a small miracle of life, and he could never bring himself to answer like that. So he sat down with them and, as always, wove a magic spell.

Kokoschka had been born with second sight, like his mother and grandmother before him. Once his mother was visiting relations and when they were having their coffee she suddenly put down her cup, saying: I must go home. Something has happened to the boy. Oskar's brother, Bohuslav, had cut his leg with an axe. She took the bus, but it was an hour before she got there. He was lying in a sea of blood, and would almost certainly have bled to death. Neither of them saw anything unusual in her sudden appearance. Even Kokoschka never questioned it—his mother had felt the axe. He, too, had this gift, but formerly it used to be even stronger. He and his mother were one, for was he not born of her womb? What part did time have to play? A hundred or two hundred years. What is it? What is the meaning of 'I', and 'You'—there is no difference. Then he went on: The sickness of our times is like leprosy. It has to be scraped away. Sometimes throbbing flesh remains, but one cannot tell whether it will become sound or remain diseased. It doesn't matter. The white man's culture is lost anyway.

And what will the future bring? I asked.

He did not know and it did not concern him, for he was not to blame. Then I suggested that there might be a primitive culture which still retained what he missed in our civilization.

Primitive, he cried angrily! What could be more primitive than the times in which we are living? One presses a button, one moves; press the button again and the movement stops. Ever since the English conquered the Spaniards and learned how to rule, things had got steadily worse. Kokoschka hated both Newton and Darwin: The world is in the hands of the scientists now; what they want is a static, orderly place controlled by everlasting laws. But laws like that do not exist. Life is intangible.

He had always lived empirically in this way: A flash of lightning; you put your hand in the water and caught a wriggling fish. Then it was dark again. Man is not an independent entity, but a vibration in the universe. Everybody releases electrical discharges from their personality. It comes about through contact, and sometimes from far away, depending on the sensitivity of the individual.

He experienced it like that. It is a dissolution of the spirit, of the nerves, of the seed, and very debilitating. That was why he so often felt exhausted and had to gather new strength. There were too many discharges.

As the fortunes of the war began to favour the Allies, the belief in democracy, humanism, freedom and a new life worthy of man began to spread but Kokoschka saw beyond. Everything here would be destroyed, he thought. Rescue would come from the East; the spirit of the Far East lives on. Does anyone realize that we have thousands of years of good will behind us? What have we done with the time?

I found it impossible to understand how he could paint at all. Since he had been here, he said, he had painted pictures only to warn people—political allegories—and other subjects only occasionally, when he could forget. Thus, Kokoschka, as one of the last Europeans, confessed his fear that the European mind was dead.[3] Valéry sensed it too, when he wrote, just before his death: 'L'Europe est finie.' It drove Stefan Zweig to suicide. In 1932 Stefan Zweig was still hopeful and expressed his belief in the European mind.[4]

'What is the spirit that forged the peoples of Europe and their ancient cultures into a creative society? The idea of Europe stems from the Roman Empire, which was so far-reaching and so deeply embedded that its collapse caused the moral and intellectual desert of the Dark Ages. Contact between the nations was lost, roads disappeared, cities were laid waste and with them the common Latin language, because the Roman administration no longer held the tribes together. Art, science, architecture, and painting failed overnight, like springs after an earthquake. The age was sunk in darkness so profound that not even history was recorded, whereas, four hundred years before, Tacitus, Livy, Caesar and Pliny had written their histories of the world,' and Herodotus, father of history, had towered above them all.

The task of reunification fell to the Catholic Church. Zweig seems to have been unwilling to recognize this unity. And yet the unification of Europe by the Romans was by no means complete, for after the defeat of Varus, Arminius cut his people off from the civilizing influence of Roman law and ideas, just as his ravaging descendants had today. As a humanist Zweig laid great stress on the linguistic links—on Latin 'which arose like the Phoenix from the flame'. 'The Christian monks took the common language, with the message it carried, down into the catacombs when they ran before the destructive fury of the barbarian invasions but the ideal of Catholic union was shattered by the development of national churches. Europe enjoyed another period of unity during the time of the Renaissance. A student at that time could study in Bologna, Prague, Oxford, or Paris, where he would learn the language of rhetoric, logic, and everyday intercourse common to all scholars of Europe. Erasmus of Rotterdam, Giordano Bruno, Spinoza, Bacon, Leibnitz and Descartes were all citizens of one and the same state—the republic of scholars—although separated by thousands of miles and many weeks of travelling. Yet the poets, thinkers and artists were closer than today, for all our aeroplanes, railways, and cars.' And later Baroque built an intellectual bridge extending from India to Mexico, but the nationalism that developed from the Age of Reason destroyed this last bastion of humanity. Goethe wrote: 'National literature is a thing of the past, the time of world literature is come.' Nevertheless a hundred years later Romain Rolland was to declare in *Jean Christophe*: 'Europe does not possess a book, not a poem, not a prayer, not even an act of faith common to every nation: it is an outrage which the artists of our time should rectify. There is not a single man who thinks and writes for all.'

And finally we hear Kokoschka's voice crying out in the wilderness of the second world war:

> All of us who had faith in man have run aground ... individual destiny no longer counts; I have to disguise myself as an intellectual to assert my humanity and am supposed to confess my allegiance to a particular party by propaganda, otherwise they say I am a monster. The will to destruction is everywhere. And because I am out of harmony and not at peace with myself, I cannot paint. Thirty-five years ago, when I could still believe, things were different. Can it now be otherwise? Time is running out.'[5]

For Kokoschka the tragedy of Europe had become the tragedy of European culture, and ultimately of man himself. I doubt whether he recognized the tragic situation of mankind as such or understood the sense of tragedy as defined by Unamuno. Despite everything, he had too much faith in himself for that. What disturbed him so much was the cultural collapse, but he had been aware of that since his youth.

In my mind I see Rembrandt in his studio. *The Night Watch* waits on the easel for the visit of the Burghers of Amsterdam. So Kokoschka stands in his studio before a much smaller painting called WHAT WE ARE FIGHTING FOR. No one had seen it; few even knew of its existence. This allegory of the hypocritical idealization of war had remained unnoticed in the 1943 London exhibition *Fight for Freedom*, organized by the Artists' International Association. His back half-turned towards me, he gives me time to consider it in peace. Grouped in a semicircle round the foreground and near to the middle axis of the picture a church dignitary in a mitre is blessing the troops (only their marching feet can be seen through a hole in the ruined wall; in the background they are fighting, escaping, yielding, dying), while with the other hand he drops a coin into the Red Cross box. Beside him is a general in an indeterminate uniform, then portraits of Schacht and the swastika, and Montague Norman, with a rickshaw between them carrying the head of international cartels in a wig and gas-mask and holding a parasol. The rickshaw is drawn by a coloured man. It is Gandhi wearing the knowing smile repeated on the Houdon bust of Voltaire in the foreground and on the base of which the word 'Candide' is inscribed. To the left is a strange machine. Two human arms; one, with a chain, gives the Nazi salute, the other conjures a blue rabbit out of the air. The arms wind themselves round a globe stuck all over with red flags; they represent the battlefields. It is just as if the devil had thrown them at random on the map of the world. The machine is being stoked with human bones and cartridges stream out from the other side. In the distance, far beyond the battle scenes, there is a single positive figure, a peasant ploughing. Over this gruesome landscape hovers, not the Holy Ghost, but a bomber. The largest figure lies in the foreground—a starving mother. She clutches a bone in one hand

and in the other a dead child who holds a rat as a substitute for a toy. Behind the woman stands a half-naked man with raised arms, the figure of the Jew crucified and branded with the letters P.J. The scene shows the backcloth of world history and this is the latest *Ecce Homo*. It is a portrait of mankind with its benefactors in Voltaire's 'best of all possible worlds'. The oils are applied transparently like water-colour and the sweet smell of corruption heightens the macabre impression. The foreground with its mother-and-child motif is painted a shrill yellow like a death knell.

I looked at Kokoschka. At first he said nothing. Only his bearing told me that this picture had caused him to be misunderstood and attacked. It had been dubbed 'unpainterly' and was seen as the degeneration of his creative power. No one had understood that it was not meant to be like an Impressionist summer landscape, or a still-life with sunflowers. Even its authenticity had been denied. He defended himself to me: the picture had long fermented in his mind. How could he go on painting flowers and ignoring the horror of what was going on around him? Pictures which could be used for the education of children he had already painted: a portrait of Masaryk with Comenius and Prague, and a representation of the *Wiener Kinderhilfe*, in which he had represented the social services of the city of Vienna. Children's games were depicted in it.

Breughel understood such subjects and Kokoschka had learned much from him. Then he asked: has materialism justified the endless sacrifices made in its name? That—and he pointed to the picture—is the result, the real result of all these efforts. Do you see the pattern on the bishop's mitre? Look closely and you will see a well-known Coat of Arms. On the rickshaw here are the pound and dollar symbols, and a bat. Schacht was included, not because he was a German, but as an economics expert. He could as easily be an American; Montague Norman, in agreement with him, is a wily nordic Mephistopheles. The third figure is hidden behind a gas-mask, symbol of the faceless one, far removed from the wrong he has done, the scene of his crimes—the Imperialist, wearing a wig, personification of tradition. Look at the fat hand of the bishop, that is the Church, preferring alms to justice. The general, this old idiot here, is the militarist who gives the order to shoot. Instead of stuffing all these people together after the war into a waxworks show, they are allowed to go on as before. The world is like a roulette wheel. Whoever wins—the man giving the Nazi salute or the democratic trickster—the war machine still has to be fed, bones into one end, bullets from the other. War is a normal condition in our society; peace is the exception. Do you see the prisoners holding their arms above their heads? You must have seen similar slave scenes in Assyrian reliefs. Our progressive civilization looks like that. War is the white man's means of expression. Indians know no war. Since his ascendancy the white man has become decadent, because he was isolated from other peoples. In the days when politicians had neither the modern means of propaganda nor transport man lived in peace; he had faith and dreamed and created. He knew nothing of progress and lived in piety. The world was infinitely large, men were few and life was good. Progress was the cancer. And now it has spread over the whole world. Life is being overpowered. The coloured man in the painting is not following humbly behind in his proper place. Gandhi. Coloured people have quite different

fingers; don't you think him sweet despite his ugliness? And he is bigger than Voltaire.
That is why he has a halo round his head. His achievements were truly amazing, without
power, without money, without party ideology. He is the only man who was able to walk
unharmed on the battlefields. No one dared to touch him till a fanatic shot him. What are
miracles? They are certainly not explained by the magical beliefs of primitive man, but
can rather be recognized in Gandhi's approach to the brutalized masses and governments,
unarmed except with reason. They would gladly have seen him dead, but none dared
kill him. That man was stronger than politics. In this picture of the powers of destruction
Gandhi is the last representative of humanity. There are people who are still one with
nature—peasants who keep the feast days and give thanks for the harvest. Their lives
are ordered by the seasons, whereas those who carry a timepiece are running away from
life. They are acquisitive, do not know what they possess, have no time, but ever seize
and clutch at the empty air. They stand outside life as if it were not true or were about to
fail. So they must quickly snatch at something else. But even the peasants are no longer
country men; they have become speculators . . .

Kokoschka had no faith in the trinity—Roosevelt, Churchill and Stalin, nor in the
one devil—Hitler. The dead mother lies still with unsullied lips—he believed only in
innocence, the rest was cant.[6] He thought highly of Voltaire if only because of his stand
against witch-hunting. His mission was the same as that of Comenius; Zola's part in the
Dreyfus case was much less important. Do you know that it was Voltaire who founded
the musical-box industry in France?

At one time, Kokoschka explained, he used to buy old porcelain very cheaply in
England and give it to his friends, because he wanted to rescue the fine pieces from the
philistines. He thought it would be safer with them, as he was always travelling. If
an object pleased him he would sometimes tell the dealers that their pieces were valuable
and worth more, and for this he gained the reputation of being crazy. One poor and
uneducated boy called Toby had learned a great deal from him. He was a barrow-
boy, selling fruit in the streets. Then he bought a decrepit taxi and drove the artist all
over London in it, calling him Rabbi because he was able to answer all his questions, and
following Kokoschka's advice in everything. The artist loved the streets of London
where there were junk shops filled with objects from all the corners of the world, from
silks and carpets to furniture and *objets d'art*. Georgian silver could be found for its price
as scrap, so Kokoschka told Toby: If I had money I would buy it all to save it from being
melted down. Buy old silver and you will be rich!

When Kokoschka came again to London, as a refugee, Toby was a rich man
and offered to present the artist, who was impoverished once more and living in an
attic, with a racehorse from his stable as a thank-offering. He had bought furniture
and silver from bombed-out houses and instead of sending it away to be melted or broken
up, had shipped it in wagonloads to America. But when Toby wanted to send musical
boxes over to the States, Kokoschka protested; they contained too much of the spirit
of Europe.

The artist wanted to use the proceeds from WHAT WE ARE FIGHTING FOR to help

the Hungarian Jews, who were in fearful danger at that time. He had a two-edged aim.
He wanted to prove the hypocrisy of government circles which professed sympathy for
the persecuted, and this fund was to help transport the Jews to England or America.
Kokoschka was convinced that they would not be accepted anywhere in those countries
where freedom and justice were at stake. To him the Hungarian Jews were the most
intelligent types he had met. When he was a young man in Vienna, just beginning to
paint, it was they who discovered him when he was holding a small exhibition in a café.
He owed his first success to them.[7]

The fund never came to anything.[8] Kokoschka presented the picture to the director
of a museum who had been 'retired' after an exhibition of Early European Art in
Zürich which had proved too expensive.[9] It was the first exhibition of its kind to be held
after the war.

Kokoschka took the picture down from the easel, leaned it against the wall and
brought another. ALICE IN WONDERLAND, he said briefly, the Austrian *Anschluss*.

This is the most affecting of all his political allegories. Here is a deeper anxiety than
the *Anschluss*—the fear that Vienna might be bombed. In the right-hand corner behind
barbed wire stands a naked girl, the symbol of Austria. A fig-leaf represents the un-
speakable truth, the abominable condition of the world resulting from the administration
of the three figures wearing the mayoral hat, the bishop's mitre and the military cap.[10]
Their gestures are a satire on the three monkeys, 'See no evil, hear no evil, speak no
evil'. The city burns in the background; a mother running away with her child is shot
down, while a whole street and a building with classical pillars go up in flames. In the
left foreground mankind looks on in amazement: a tragic variation on the mother-and-
child motif. The child's face is hidden by a gas-mask, a Red Cross purse dangles from
the mother's arm. The three male figures take up about a third of the picture. Their
heads are composed in a diagonal and turned towards the nude girl. The central one
points reproachfully to the figure, taking offence at the nakedness of truth, not at the
devastation. Truth, however, points with her right hand to the onlookers: you, too.
Behind her a piece of Baroque sculpture can be seen, the Virgin with Jesus in her arms.
Both are decapitated. In the filth of the street, at the feet of truth, lies the INRI of the
Son of Man, while the words OUR TIMES are inscribed on a newspaper in the foreground. Perhaps the secret of this painting lies in the fact that the artist painted into it his
love of the beautiful city of his birth, as well as all his bitterness.

During his exile in England, Kokoschka was painfully aware, more so than most
people, of the glorious works of art lying concealed in Central Europe. Vienna had no
rival but Paris. Its musical and theatrical life was brilliant, its literary tradition alive and
vigorous. The Viennese charm, musicality and light-heartedness—themselves the fruit
of a vibrant racial mixture caused by the meeting of East and West—had formed an
oasis for the European spirit. Vienna used to lie like a smile on the serious face of
Europe. During the war it froze into a tortured rigid mask.

In 1940, in Paris, Stefan Zweig was discussing the old days in Vienna: it was his
birthplace, and one of the most outstanding cities of our European heritage. Vienna,

founded by the Romans and honoured by Marcus Aurelius had always remained faithful to her task—to create and defend the life of the mind. If Hermann Bahr had been writing about the Vienna of 1940 he would have described it in a period of decay as did Zweig, and his criticism of conditions in Vienna written at the turn of the century would have been of secondary importance.

Vienna had never been the capital city of a national state; it was the centre of an Empire which extended from Mexico to the coast of India. The aristocracy that bred the patrons of art was continually infused with new blood, and the *bourgeoisie* was subject to the same influences. The presence of so many foreign elements made the city of Vienna ideal soil for the development of a common intellectual civilization. Of course, this was not so easily achieved; but stimulus from outside was always accepted. The city's real genius was to mix opposing forces, forming a new harmony that created a fresh element in European culture. As a musical city Vienna was unrivalled. 'Like Florence, which gained fame and glory by patronizing the greatest creative figures over a period of a hundred years—Giotto, Cimabue, Donatello, Brunelleschi, Leonardo and Michelangelo —so Vienna's magic circle embraced nearly every composer and musician of importance in a single century of classical music: Metastasio, king of opera, settled opposite the Hofburg; Haydn lived in the same house; Gluck taught music to Maria Theresa's children and after Haydn came Mozart, Beethoven, Salieri and Schubert, Brahms and Bruckner, Johann Strauss, Lanner, Hugo Wolf and Gustav Mahler. In over a hundred and fifty years there was no break, and not a decade nor even a year passed when no immortal work was created in Vienna. No city was ever more blessed with musical genius than 18th and 19th century Vienna.'

Kokoschka would have added the names of Arnold Schönberg and Anton von Webern to Zweig's list of composers. Love of music was inherent in the Imperial family, and the nobility tried to match and outstrip the Emperor. Musicians encountered the same connoisseurship among the Viennese *bourgeoisie*. However, values other than music, theatre, and literature thundered forth like a reproof from the city, echoing down to us through the deafening clangour of the present: the Baroque and the idea of Catholicism.

Baroque is the art of spatial construction. Kokoschka, an undoubted Baroque artist, has always rejected painting in planes, a method that seems to him nothing more than the creation of patterns. The swelling forms of the Baroque, its illustration of space and broken line, define an art of movement. Kokoschka acknowledges no art that lacks movement in space, nor is a mechanical movement implied. The origins of Baroque and its deep roots in the life of the people, and the reasons for such a powerful change of style, reveal a drama of the intellect—the dissolution of the Renaissance. The Baroque appears as an irresistible power of nature of spiritual origin. It was the expression of a new humanity of which Michelangelo was the first exponent. Wölfflin summarized its essence: 'Michelangelo never depicted good fortune; that alone proves him to have been reaching out beyond the Renaissance.'[11]

Movement and expression are my professional disease, Kokoschka once said jokingly: can you imagine the mountains, as the sun rises? Everything is still, wrapped in mist;

then one mountain peak breaks through, and more beyond, until the light pours over the scene like a waterfall, bringing colour and sound swelling like a choir. Baroque was the herald of a spiritual world, its faith was implicit, and that produced a fourth dimension—the infinite. Spiritual perspective was painted into the cupolas of churches and palaces. Pantheism, humanity, and the unknown filled the mind.

Kokoschka said he would never be able to measure his debt to Maulbertsch, a giant in his day, who meant more to him than El Greco, for El Greco was a mannerist leading nowhere, whereas Maulbertsch was spontaneous, sprung from the intuition of the people.[12] He explained how he had met the last remaining Baroque artists in Europe before and after the first world war. In Italy, South Germany, Austria, France, and Spain, from Rapallo to Avignon, he had talked with decorators who could still paint flowers free-hand in traditional style, and who created allegorical and symbolic pictures that were full of understanding and feeling for form. In Rapallo he had discovered an ancient school of sculpture; it was nothing outstanding, but solid, honest craftsmanship, in the manner of the Baroque with a thorough comprehension of the three-dimensional approach, of movement and material. One of the carvers was called Tocci, but there were four or five others who were just as good. They had a tradition of craftsmanship which had been handed down from father to son.

Baroque is a universal style; it appears in the South American art of the Incas, of the Spanish Catholics, in India, in the subtle craft of China and on the coast of Africa, in Byzantine Russia and everywhere in Europe. The faith only failed in the Protestant countries. Protestantism is too rational—it does not recognize the Greek projection of the ego in space and time, but believes in individual revelation of an abstract divinity as a personal creed. Expressionism is also Baroque and has therefore been attacked as degenerate. The Baroque idea also unites opposing spiritual values, that meet like powerful underground streams. They reflect the ambivalent stirrings of man's soul and perhaps this is what fascinated Kokoschka in the style.

'Baroque excites with scourges, then organs blow followed by the melodious piping flute. Baroque rips open the gates of hell dancing like an enchanter above the abyss; threatens every kind of horror till we are made soft and quiescent. It deafens and intoxicates; its mundane face renders us divine. Even its gayest mien is deadly serious. The Baroque offers comfort to every man, strength to face life and death; it is a journey through poverty and fear to peace and desire.'

'That is Baroque. The greatest life-hater, recognizing its delirium, can overcome the senseless, unreal and empty pageant and then, for the first time, enjoy its inanity with an indescribable subtlety, with the breathless awe of the artist who knows that it is all a game, but is yet aware, like the Greeks of old, that this game is the whole of life. Such men are flung into life, snatch greedily at it and are jerked back . . . they learn to enjoy renunciation, to be richly ascetic, and to do evil with piety.'[13]

Baroque combines sensuality, joy and worldliness with rigid Christian asceticism and the blameless heritage of Greece. It explains the sensual glow in Kokoschka's painting after 1918 and his inquisitorial rendering of the human face before the outbreak of war.

8 Adolf Loos and his wife Claire, *c.* 1931

9 Adolf Loos, 1909

10 Dent du Midi, 1909

11 Professor Hans Tietze and his wife, 1909
By Courtesy of the Museum of Modern Art, New York

It explains his pure and childlike devotion to the simple manifestations of nature; his sense of the grand gesture and of fame; his hunger for love and friendship combined with his need for absolute freedom; the dominance of the humanist ideal in his political morality and his estimation of grandeur and material luxury in the dark womb of his mysticism. It demonstrates that the transcendental and the mythical in Kokoschka's philosophy could go hand in hand with his rebellion against political power. For, over the years, his catholicism has proved itself to be rebellion.

One day I came in just as he had taken up a book on churches built in the Churiguerra style of Mexico. Look, he said, everyone must pass by these stairs and carvings to reach the entrance, and they describe the lives of the saints and martyrs. See these immensely high spaces, the almost crazy richness of the decoration, the ornament, the painting, they are like primitive, beautiful forests. A bloodsucker, an oppressor of the Indians, finally gave up his money to build them. Jesuits, who could scarcely draw, constructed it all with the help of the primitive Indians. Time meant nothing to them. It took ten, twenty, perhaps fifty years before it was finished. And for whom was it done? For the wretched Indians, who came over the mountains to mass and stood breathless in astonishment. If only I could have such faith, he cried, pointing to a group of Indians. Look at them. No one has stood like that in Europe since the time of Mabuse.

He felt the Renaissance had spoiled everything. He condemned the Spaniards for robbing the simple people, and then for allowing the Jesuits to build churches. He condemned the Jesuits for misusing their power and yet these marvellous buildings were the outcome! But what happens today when the industrialist exploits a country? In Africa the natives are punished for stealing, first by losing a finger, then a hand, then the whole arm. It is immaterial whether it concerns rubber, oil, diamonds or gold. Think of the Congo. There were forty-five million negroes with a long tradition of civilization, but after the Belgian Congo bank had been in existence for ten years only eight million impoverished slaves remained. It was a question not of race, but of the loss of creative opportunity. The things which the negro could do had been eliminated, nature itself and with it life. By what right? Huge fortunes were made in the slave trade at a time when slaves were being converted to Christianity. Then, when industrialization made slavery unprofitable, freedom became the catchword. In 1860 the American Civil War broke out.

Thereafter a different formula was used: conscription of the negroes with a ten-year contract and everything neatly provided for by law. During the war there had been forced labour for everyone in the colonies from the age of fifteen to fifty-five. And the result? Look at modern architecture; it resembles cement prisons. Mexico, Moscow, Stockholm or New York, it is all the same. This—and he pointed to one of the Mexican churches in the book—the white man can no longer do. It is finished.

A mentality with a taste for statistics recognizes only a reality that can be explained mathematically. Such people not only cannot understand that everything made by man's hand is not just a machine, merely something mechanical or useful, but a living creation leading to humility before the miracle of life; they know nothing about it at all. In 1850, at the time of the Restoration in France—hardly a memorable period—there were fifteen hundred different kinds of tea-rose in cultivation in France. And it takes time to develop a rose. That was not slavery but a labour of creative love.

Kokoschka had seen some very old shrub roses in Tunisia, their curving petals containing all the scent of the Arabian Nights. He always gave his friends flowers, orchids or roses. The hybrid rose, Maréchal Ney, was a fine flower that he admired and the man who tended the Wallenstein garden in Prague grew some. When Kokoschka went to Paris after the first world war he tried to find one, but was told they were not to be had—'Ce n'est pas une rose commerciale'.

The Japanese understand that flowers are an essential part of life, he continued: at the outbreak of war there were thirty thousand teachers in Tokyo schools teaching the art of flower arrangement. Without the Japanese and the negroes Post-Impressionist art would have come to nothing, nothing. Whence came the rhythm and melody of modern American dance music? From the Africans, the Jews and the South American natives. In Protestant countries share certificates had been substituted for pictures of saints. Where Baroque had been a unifying force, the industrial revolution divides. Civilization, despite its communications, still can forge no links, whereas the culture of the mind, though isolated and cut off, had forged a republic of learning.

Kokoschka believed the principles of the Catholic Church to be right. Of course, there had been evil popes and cardinals; that was inevitable. But the integrity of the individual, the unification of mankind was surely worth striving for? He had left the Catholic Church. He wanted to be clever and to set things right, which he was not equipped to do. Later he joined the Church again, influenced by a nun who had nursed him in the first war . . . but what had always attracted him to the Catholic Church was its ideal of the unity of man. The Protestants had made their churches national. There were, he thought, two extremes—either to be Catholic in the true sense, or completely egoist: the perfect Catholic unity or absolute selfishness. We have relapsed into egoism, while the coloured races still retain their closeness to creation.

Kokoschka took a very lively interest in the efforts of the Pope to end the confusion. He once admitted that Christianity bored him, but that he loved Catholicism. He considered the Pope had been right to save his wonderful city: he prevaricated and evaded with the result that the papacy is now the only power in the world with an ethical tradition going back two thousand years. That is worth remembering as a contrast to the spiritual collapse of Europe. Those two thousand years of watching, that unbelievably long unbroken sequence of experience, is not to be denied. The popes continually learned and made mistakes—that is human. The perfect, infallible man would be intolerable.

The Baroque idea and Catholicism were synthesized in Kokoschka's mind, and their fundamental characters are, of course, identical. But he interpreted Baroque not so much as a definite artistic style as a style of life, a spiritual condition.

The Baroque era expressed in architectonic symbols the interrelation between man's soul and his divinity. The new understanding of the cosmic position of man, inspired by the first astronomical discoveries of Copernicus, put an end to the priestly and feudal attachment to the soil that had made men vassals.

Baroque art, the product of the closely combined work of builder, sculptor, painter and musician, was such a finite expression of universal humanism that its aesthetic elements spread across the world and awakened local artistic tradition within a very short period, and it was only in this age—the Baroque—that a truly international art was first born.

The Germans composed music for Baroque churches, and the Czechs built the organs. Italian plasterers, Austrian painters, Spanish-Jewish embroiderers and goldsmiths, Saxon builders, French weavers and Tirolese wood-carvers all did their utmost to make the House of God also the house of man.

This essay by Kokoschka, from which I have quoted only extracts, ends with an appreciation of the Tirolese master, Mathias Bernard Braun, who worked in Bohemia under the patronage of Duke Franz Anton Sporck, a piece of good fortune that enabled him to realize his artistic ambitions. The following passage seems to me a sad commentary on Kokoschka's involuntary *incognito* in England at that time: *Here was the true aristocrat offering an unknown foreigner the chance to produce one of the most significant pieces of Baroque art in Bohemia. It is a flight of stepped terraces looking on to a broad landscape and adorned with giant allegorical statues. They lead to a forest of uneven stone blocks arranged as a temple to the Virgin. In the centre there is a mausoleum enclosing the tomb of the Duke who sleeps for ever here in the midst of his own creation.*

The vision in stone of Mathias Braun stands at Kuks today, a monument to a spiritual world very different from our political society riddled with class and national prejudices. It sets an unattainable goal for our time.[14]

When Singapore fell Kokoschka saw it as the Fall of the British Empire. He painted a quite small picture depicting that dramatic action, and called it LORELEY. During the war he often heard people saying 'What does it mean?'* Very few people recognized Queen Victoria in the astonished features of the old woman in this picture. Her head, wearing the crown, is turned angrily away from the fearful happening, and a green frog is sitting on her right hand. Kokoschka chose this as a symbol for Ireland—the Emerald Isle where, it is said, there have been no snakes since the time of Saint Patrick; the frog, therefore, is the only available reptile. The green tree-frog, a fresh-water creature, refuses to jump into the maw of the salt-water monster swallowing a drowning sailor.

Bosch and Breughel painted similar monsters in their representations of hell; in *Die tolle Grete*, but most vividly in the seascape now hanging in the Kunsthistorisches Museum in Vienna, which Kokoschka greatly admired. He once said to me, when discussing Breughel's painting: There are junks in the midst of a storm—it is frightful. Hiroshige is the only other artist who would have imagined it like that. It is only a sketch, but it contains the passion of Rubens, the soundness and the power of Rembrandt. And it is contemporary, like Renoir's last paintings after he became crippled.

There is a storm over Kokoschka's picture, too. Lightning flashes, a ship is sinking; both white and coloured men drown as they snatch at the lifebelts, and Neptune's

---

* The German *Lied Loreley* starts with the words: 'Ich weiss nicht was soll es bedeuten'— I do not know what it may mean. . . .

trident hangs over the scene, symbol of mastery of the sea. Far away in a lake of cold blue and light green there is a lighthouse, but it is out of reach.

In this picture Kokoschka painted something which he saw as an established historical fact, but he also tried to define his position towards English politics, a position which was general on the Continent. His attitude to art in England can be deduced from the fact that, during all the years he spent there, he never held an exhibition, whereas at the first opportunity after the war important retrospective exhibitions were arranged in Europe: 1947 in Basel, Zürich and Amsterdam; 1948 at the Venice Biennale; while in 1948 and 1949 a large exhibition was sent to tour the U.S.A. It was only in 1962 that a representative exhibition was held in London, four years after those of Munich and Vienna.

Tell your friends abroad, he once wrote to me, that I am not here in the position of every other refugee from the Nazis. You can tell them why I came to England. It was to study at its roots the fatal disease of our civilization. There is another power behind the fearful mask that we recognize as the Nazi evil, he went on: The man with the gun is not more guilty than the gun-runner. Now that Germany is defeated I turn against him. I found my *métier* in Germany and a world which suited me. Vienna was no good, it was wasted time. We knew that the Austrian monarchy was condemned. The English do not yet realize what is happening to their Empire; it resembles Austria before the first world war. They are already fighting, and for the first time for foreign interests.

He said he remained in England to find out if he was right. What he had only suspected in the first war he now knew for certain. He could have gone to America and become famous, even the Nazis wooed him but he repudiated them. Instead he came to England, sick and without money, carrying a half-finished picture under his arm.[15] Olda came with him, not knowing at all what to expect. . . .

After Munich, Kokoschka realized that Prague was a trap. He was persuaded to leave, bringing only what he could carry, in the last plane for England. Although his name must have been known at least to museum directors and art connoisseurs, Kokoschka was lonely and unknown in England. He had to begin again from the beginning. He could work only slowly and under great mental strain. His first portrait commissions were of Michael and Posy Croft.[16] At the end of July 1939 the Kokoschkas left London for Polperro, a village in Cornwall, where they met the German sculptor, Uli Nimptsch, who was later interned but released through the intervention of the Countess of Drogheda at Kokoschka's instigation.[17] In July 1940 Kokoschka was forced to leave Polperro because the whole of the South Coast was a defence area and foreigners were excluded. Thus he was in London during the worst of the bombing. He was sick and discouraged when he got back to London; but, as so often before, friends were there to help him, and he has recorded similar occasions in his book, *A Sea Ringed with Visions*.[11] Chatin Sarachi, former Albanian Consul-General in Vienna and later *Chargé d'Affaires* in London, was informed by Kathleen, Countess of Drogheda, that the Viennese painter with the strange name had arrived in London. She had heard it by chance from Dr Lothar, the former Editor-in-Chief of the *Frankfurter Zeitung*, whom she had met at a cocktail party. She did not know Kokoschka's address, but traced him through Scotland Yard, and the same day Sarachi went to see Kokoschka in his hotel. He found him in bed and soon realized that the painter was not only ill but also in financial difficulty. The war would go on for years; he would not be able to paint; his work in Germany was destroyed; his life was finished—so ran the gist of the conversation. Something had to be done quickly, and the most important thing was to get the artist out of the depressing hotel atmosphere. Sarachi had friends in Hampstead, who had a comfortable home with an empty studio which they were willing to let. The studio was offered to the Kokoschkas and they moved in.[19] The Countess of Drogheda got in touch with the well-known Hungarian doctor and relative of Lothar, János Plesch. He knew Kokoschka from the old days in Germany and took him under his care.[20] Kokoschka was still suffering from the effects of a bayonet wound in the chest and a head wound which he had received on the Russian front in the first war, but injections soon relieved these disturbances.

At his first visit Sarachi observed that Kokoschka's few belongings included a wobbly old easel, a battered box of paints containing a few squeezed-out colours and some worn brushes. Kokoschka was attached to his old painting things, nevertheless Sarachi, moved by the famous artist's poverty, went out and bought fresh colours, brushes, and canvases. In wartime England it was necessary to have a permit to paint landscapes and such pictures had to be submitted to a special committee; Kokoschka was bored by the red-tape and decided to confine his work to water-colours and pastels. Sarachi remembers having seen two paintings done in Polperro in the artist's Hampstead studio.[21]

He was concerned about the artist, whom he knew to be unknown in England, and introduced him to Sir Edward Beddington-Behrens, who was of great assistance. Years earlier, when in London for the first time in 1928, Kokoschka had exhibited thirty-four oils at the Leicester Galleries, not one of which was sold, although among them were some now famous paintings.[22]

Although desperately worried about the war and his relatives in Prague and Vienna, the artist worked unceasingly. When the bombing made the studio in Hampstead uninhabitable, the Kokoschkas moved into a block of flats in Finchley Road called Mandeville Court.[23]

One day Kokoschka showed me a picture redolent of his bitterness. The theme was hospitality, and it was called THE CRAB. It shows the harbour of Polperro in a storm. A ship is struggling with the waves; it is a symbol of political unrest. In the harbour, protected by jagged cliffs, a man swims to the shore. A giant crab is waiting to fall upon him as he struggles out of the sea. Kokoschka explained that a crab like that was an extraordinary creature. Its horrible jointed legs and monstrous jaws were a contrivance of the devil. What could be more apt than to use it as a symbol for disaster? The picture is composed of three elements: the Polperro scene, depicted so often both in oils and water-colour; the small figure of the swimmer, which, although it is subjugated to the composition as a whole, nevertheless provides its focal point; and finally the crab, so common on any shore, but here enlarged to giant proportions to support its allegorical intention. The destiny of the hunted man becomes a parable of the times. How could the artist forget the suicides committed in the first confusion in the airports and harbours of England by men who thought they had reached safety, but who were turned away? He once said that everyone was playing the same game, but in different roles. What is Nazism? he kept on asking. Is it a party card or an attitude of mind? Political ways of thinking are, however, universal. Hypocrisy has become a malignant disease in the free world. Fascists are strong, brutal men, who want power regardless of means. The smell of corruption creeps over Europe.

Sometimes he was overcome by a horror of mankind. He was never afraid, he said, of individuals, but of large crowds. And he was afraid, too, that democracy would turn out to be a superstition. Unadulterated nationalism is identical with Fascism, he thought. The end of the story is simply the atom bomb which is leading us towards another war. The first atomic bomb cost £500 million. With that amount of money the whole of Europe could have been saved. But no, it had to be spent vying with one another. Solon, asked to define the best type of government, answered: 'The one that causes the least injustice to the humblest member of the community.'—a far cry from the mathematical idea of the greatest good for the greatest number that so well suits our Darwinian economist's society. Part of the tragedy is that Schönberg is teaching in a girls' school in America and Bartok has come near to starvation there. In this country steps are just being taken to increase the birth-rate, like Stalin, Mussolini or Hitler. That's the way the economists think, when there are a hundred million people starving in Europe!

He rejected every nation's claim to a monopoly of democracy and found it absolutely un-believable that three men should decide the fate of the world and that we should be told nothing, except what they have eaten for lunch, while the bombing and killing goes on as before. Heads of governments plan the future together, but the only thing left for ordinary people is the hope of paradise beyond space and time. But do not forget crimes recoil like a boomerang.

Kokoschka often complained during those days of the effort he had to make in England to replace his milieu and former intellectual background, before he was able even to think: The people here have become Quakers and what kind of attitude is that? In England there is too little of the Middle Ages; in Europe too much. Cromwell had persecuted the faithful to death—that was why there was no underground movement in England; those who were discontented could stand on a box at Speakers' Corner. Bernard Shaw was the last *bourgeois* humorist; he keeps one eye on truth, the other on his enemies—hence the Fabians. It is amazing that Shakespeare ever happened in this country, for he openly speaks the truth. Take the beginning of *Henry V*: there you can see exactly how a cause had to be sought for a war. The rulers try hard to find a reason so that they can ask a blessing of the archbishop. But you cannot compare a twelfth-century war with that of today. Even Napoleon had a plan. But now there is nothing, nothing.

He was against all industrial societies, did not want to take sides. If he had to choose he would side with the children and found an international organization for war orphans. That would be a living memento. But the powers today would simply light another eternal flame for the Unknown Soldier and the hocus-pocus would go on as before. Our task, he said, is to try to understand now that everything is being destroyed. He would like to found and would probably be the only member of an underground movement of the conscience, he added wryly.

Kokoschka knew what responsibility he had as a European. There is, he said, an ancient mystic animus still alive in Europe. The Etruscan communities were not criminal people as the Romans described them, but isolated pockets remaining behind from an earlier archaic civilization. Among the Kabyl in the Atlas Mountains today, and the Celts until the Middle Ages, matriarchal societies were the rule; soothsayers, prophetesses, not priests, were their arbiters. The Romans were imperialist and patriarchal, like the English, and they suppressed these old influences. Some refugees managed to reach Spain. Afterwards came the Peasants' Revolt in North Italy. Saint Francis acted in the same spirit. The terrible crusade against the Albigensians in the South of France presents a sharp contrast with the luminous background of the French kingdom. They were suppressed and in exchange Europe got bigotry, witch-hunting, alchemy, and superstition. It was followed by the flight to Holland and the monastic movement and then it was the turn of England. The story of Piers Plowman is similar to that of *Ackermann of Bohemia*, who mourned the *unio catholica* in the picture of his dead wife.[24] The idea is always the same. Even Dante shows traces of it. Suddenly it reappears with the Waldenses in South Germany, Austria. They, too, were suppressed, but some escaped to Bohemia and were united with the Bohemian brothers. How different in character are the Bohemian brothers, and Jan Amos Comenius, their last bishop, from the nationalist followers of John Huss. They were brothers, educators, humanists. The first repercussion of these ideas can be found in Meister Eckhardt. You could make a map of the secret movement, and that is Europe—us, in fact. Europe's spirit was always hidden beneath the surface. In this war the whole heritage of learning will be destroyed. The leaven must descend into the catacombs once more. . . .

Kokoschka believed firmly in the ancient virtue in mankind that produces free individuals, thinkers, mystics, artists. The race remains fruitful, inexhaustible as Nature herself. This belief explains the composition of the allegory MARIANNE-MAQUIS. It describes the second front and the liberation of France. Marianne, symbol of the French people, sits balancing astride stools in the centre of the picture, spanning a spatial diagonal leading from the left foreground to the right background. A rat is running about, a shoe hurtles after it; there is a broken plate and a cat slinking along, while the Allied troops in battle-order sit around drinking coffee in this strangest of all bistros—the Café de Paris. The picture was painted in 1942, when the second front was expected daily but never seemed to materialize. Well-known emblems are represented—the victory sign of Churchill; the swastika; the star of the Soviets, the Hammer and Sickle—and famous military and political portraits are incorporated.

Kokoschka's political paintings are full of rats. In the picture called PRIVATE PROPERTY, painted in 1939, which the artist later gave to a Flood Distress Fund in

Holland, there are rats roaming around after food, just as Heine described them in his poem, *The Rats*:

> The seething rat heap
> Gnaws and eats and gnaws
> It stuffs and stuffs and never dreams
> That our soul is immortal.
>
> Hear, the vagabond rats
> Are coming closer.
> Their whistling screams grow
> Near—hundreds and thousands of them.

Kokoschka's dialectically slanted composition has all the riches of nature in the foreground; fish, sea-snails, and mussels arranged in a still-life, with a knitting, greedy, watchfull hag and the head of a cat behind, like a petty *bourgeois* copy of an Egyptian god. She is vulgar and overfed, more like public than private property, while in the background poverty leans heavily on a stick. The landscape resembles Cornwall. Its symbolism is universal, but abandons the moralizing sphere for the biological, where the powers of nature struggle against one another—cats, rats, and fish—as if rich and poor were two completely different races.

Kokoschka condemned and painted an allegory of the Munich fiasco as well as the Austrian *Anschluss*. In the background he placed Prague, the city he so loved, and in the foreground a table laid for a meal. The giant head of Mussolini like an Aunt Sally fills the foreground, and the ridiculous clown, Hitler, wearing a paper hat, is on the opposite side of the table, beneath which sits a lascivious cat with a medal on its collar representing France; on a pedestal, inscribed with the words *In pace Munich*, sits the British lion, its tail rolled up into the sign of the pound. As the guests sit down to table, where the 'Axes' are indicated by forks, two rats run across it, and when the roast bird—Czechoslovakia—is ready to be carved it flies away with the knife and fork stuck into its back and lays an egg. A mad land with everything upside down. Here again our thoughts turn to Breughel, to the *Tolle Grete*, in which the monstrous giant's head and gaping jaws represent the gates of hell, and to the *Fall of the Angels* in which a flying goose lays a white egg. Kokoschka's egg is red. The roast has flown—in its place is the egg. It broke on the plate and became an omelette. '*Tant de bruit pour une omelette*.' Actually he had wanted to paint white mice because of their giddiness, but then it would have become a revue not a picture. Finally he had abandoned it because it had a literary reference.[25]

There is no end to things, he once said: The urge to bring harmony into man's existence has always been the mark of sensitive, cultural periods, but nowadays the spirit is denied and the mind explained away by scientists as a mechanical function. No one believes in the spirit of man.

I knew that Kokoschka had grown weary by the bitter anguish of his wartime paintings.

III

MIR*

During the summer of 1944, when the flying-bomb raids were at their height, Kokoschka was advised by his friends to leave London and stay in the country for a while. He was unable to work and his nerves were visibly deteriorating. It was not that he bothered much about his own life, but the destruction depressed him and the name of every bombed city was like a knife turning in the wound. So he allowed himself to be persuaded to go to Scotland. I can still see him today, coming out into Park Lane with Olda, a cap pulled over the pale, greyish face, dark circles under his wide, blue eyes. A taxi was waiting. Everything seemed to happen to him without his co-operation, as if in his absence.

After some time in an hotel the Kokoschkas went to stay in a guest house in Ullapool, a fishing village near Inverness. A young Czech editor, his wife, a dancer, and I soon followed him.

The bleak landscape of Northern Scotland was reminiscent of Norway. Loch Broom lay peaceful in the spring sunshine and the contrast with the nightmare of London soon began to take effect. Kokoschka's creative spirit stirred. I realized then for the first time how much he needed contact with nature. His soul was refreshed and renewed like a tree in spring when the sap rises through its branches. He drew and drew, using coloured pencils, and spent every day looking for subjects to sketch. He seemed much younger than in London, more flexible and full of spiritual energy.

When he wanted to work he used to go out alone and had his special places where he would sit looking at nature. Sketch-pads and crayons were slung in a net bag, and his eyes forgot the devastation and sterility of existence now that they could rest once more on pretty girls, flowers, animals, and the sky. He was following a course, he said, smiling and pointing to his pastels; and after working all day he would be excited and happy in the evening. The yellow light in his room often burned late into the night. Kokoschka was writing his play, *Via Lucis des Amos Comenius*,[1] or he was reading.

The last time I had seen him in London he was reading James Burnham's *The Managerial Revolution*, and a book about Cromwell and Communism by Bernstein. Now his choice of books was quite different: *The Importance of Living*, by Lin Yutang, and the letters of Héloïse and Abélard.[2] But he was not trying to escape the war; that would have been impossible. He had not run away, he had come to do something that others could not do for him.

* MIR is the Slav expression for the prehistoric village community.

29

One day Kokoschka stopped in front of a rocky cliff on the road leading out of Ullapool. The rock-face was like a book, he said, and had asked his wife to study geology, because he was too impatient to start himself now, but one ought to know something about it. Then without a pause: Everything is deforested here, eaten away in the greed for money.

A sheep stood mournfully looking across a field and Kokoschka observed it for a long time. It reminded him of the carved wooden toys from the Erzgebirge mountains with those thin matchstick legs and the position of the eye. Just like that. A milkman came past in his cart. Kokoschka looked thoughtfully at the high-wheeled cart and said: That man still has a fine worthwhile job.

For some weeks the artist used always to set off in the same direction when he left the house. He went to see a horse which was grazing alone in a hilly landscape divided into small fields by grey stone walls. Sometimes I accompanied him part of the way. He had to pass by a mean little croft belonging to an old woman who was suspicious and silent at first, but who was gradually won over by the polite and smiling stranger. Her hairy face could often be seen peering after him out of the small cottage window. Even the dog was accustomed to his step and did not bother to lift his head, but wagged his tail in a desultory way. After a day or two she spoke to Kokoschka and thus he learned that she knew only Gaelic; he told her he did not know the language. Then you must learn it, so that we can talk, was her reply. One day when no one appeared he put a small packet of biscuits on the window-sill and when he was out of sight called out that he had brought something for her. Turning to me after a few minutes he said what a fearful world it was in which there was nothing left but to do such small things for people, especially children.

Loaded with herrings the trawlers came into the harbour and with them came the gulls, screaming and flapping overhead. The fishermen in black and yellow oilskins had strong, worn faces. Buyers stood on the gangways looking at sample baskets and trying to force the price down. On one side were the hard-working, honest fishermen and on the other the sly, tough merchants.

They are like two different tribes, whispered Kokoschka to me; he was fascinated by their long-drawn-out bargaining. Then he talked to one of the fishermen. This man told him he never read the newspapers, nor did he belong to any union or political party, otherwise he would have lost his independence. He said: We shall have to throw the catch back into the sea, because if we accept these low prices we can't earn enough to live on. We are fighting against Germany because we have been promised that there will be work for everyone after the war. Germans, English, French, it doesn't really matter. Humble people all understand one another.

Kokoschka was happy about the new friendships he made with men and animals and felt great sympathy for people struggling to make a living. He would point out the empty houses that lay scattered over the hillsides—all abandoned dwellings. The Scots had twice been forced to quit their homes, once because sheep-rearing was more profitable and finally because of the game reserves. A ship was waiting in the harbour and entire families left the district, leaving the houses to fall down and decay.

One day an old fisherman lent us a boat and Frau Olda and I rowed out to sea. I caught sight of the small figure of Kokoschka on the shore. There was something touching in his appearance and bearing. He had thrown his net bag over his shoulder and was walking down to sketch the herring fleet. I realized how free and simple the artist had remained despite temptation and fame.

A few days later we all went out in the boat. Kokoschka, who was never idle, was scarcely seated when he began to draw, the bag holding his crayons hanging round his neck. He sketched Olda as she rowed. There were porpoises in the bay. You never saw their heads, just smooth, shining bodies tumbling in the waves; near and far they seemed to dance around us. Kokoschka drew them, but only small sketches to remind him how they looked. He asked us if we enjoyed steering, pointing to the rudder, and when we got to the shore he laughed and shouted: Ullapool, all change! He was like a boy out on an adventure. The round boulders in the bay caught his attention and he stopped to sketch them eagerly, remarking that it would take a long time before he knew them as well as the horse. And when we tried to prevent his seeing the body of a dog washed ashore by the waves he begged us to let him see it as he would like to draw the gruesome object.

Occasionally I would go with him to see the horse. There was a little hut in the middle of the pasture where Kokoschka sheltered when it rained. We had to climb over several walls, but at last we came upon the animal. Kokoschka lowered his voice so as not to startle it. He had spent days here and thought he would be successful in perceiving the nature of the beast in the end. One's mind is quite distracted by the war; Kokoschka frowned and shook his head. I feel like a horse. It stares and bares its teeth like a battle charger. Look what short sturdy legs it has and how prettily it gallops! It has only two movements, forward, propelled by the hindquarters, and the braking effect of the fore-quarter. If you can draw it like that you can catch both form and movement. Form is function and if everything works, then form is right. By its incorporation in form movement attains its existence.

We came to a low wall and stopped: It always follows the same path, he whispered; it comes out of the hut in the corner and grazes slowly across the field. When the sun is hot it stands under that tree in the shade.

We had to stand quite still or we should lose its confidence. The horse was half wild and therefore beautiful. As it lifted its head to look at us Kokoschka said he should have brought sugar for it. Even the position of the animal as it stood to make water was tense and alive: Look how it rocks on its knees and how the thin fetlocks carry the heavy body.

He really enjoyed watching it and said softly: One is constantly forced into things one doesn't want to do, missing the important things. Time passes away on trivialities and we have only one life.

Kokoschka began to take out his crayons, so I turned and left him alone. I saw him again in the evening and he showed me some drawings. The horse was among them, the lines impressed deeply into the paper as if drawn with a knife. He was specially pleased with one of them, and thought it could not be improved. You could only do a horse like that once in a lifetime, he said, smiling; such success only came once. The Chinese had been doing it for a thousand years and Hokusai still had the trick of the ancients when it came to horses. Kokoschka always enjoyed looking at the Japanese artist's work, trying to catch its spirit.

The artist turned the leaves of his sketch-book filled with crayon drawings of sheep, rabbits, wild roses and raspberries: Plants have to be studied for a long time before you can understand the way they grow, he said.

Life had become simple and homely for him again.

Kokoschka prized our rowing-boat because it was the means of getting to a crescent-shaped bay which could only be reached on foot when the tide was out. It formed a kind of rocky amphitheatre where he liked to sit drawing in the afternoon. I was able to watch him working, to see how his crayons carefully followed the line of the cliffs, changing them into a coloured vision. He did not use a pencil. If the sun broke through the clouds his strokes grew more vigorous; its rays were like long arrows, the cliffs their target: Cliffs and rocks are as difficult to draw as the human face and need just as much study and observation. Look at that marvellous rock, there in the corner. It is yellowish quartz with a green tinge. It would be wonderful to have it at home to look at.

He was still thinking about rocks and cliffs later in the evening when he told us of the strange geological and archaeological discovery he had made in the garden of his parents' house near Vienna and how it had led him to discover traces of oil. This talk gave me an opportunity to penetrate into his mind more deeply, to realize his intuitive way of looking at every phenomenon; to see how he investigated scientific ideas, which seemed valuable to him as knowledge only in so far as they were endowed with the same principle as his knowledge about human physiognomy and movement, which enabled him to read a man's character.

Kokoschka was never interested in a subject for professional reasons alone. At one time he studied archaeology, but only in order to be able to understand associations and because it would help him to build a picture of life as a whole. As a boy he wanted to study chemistry, not so as to produce poison gases, but to learn to understand the secret interchange of the elements, their relationships, their sympathies and antipathies. He experienced nature in the manner of the early alchemists, who also used the expression *conjunctio* and *putrefactio*. And what could outmoded, incomprehensible formulae have to do with it—formulae that were difficult to remember and that seemed to him a mixture of scholasticism and mathematics? He had wanted to simplify the formulae and reduce them to pure and comprehensible mathematics, to write a chemical primer containing the secret of life. Fate prevented his going to the technical high school after leaving secondary school. There had been no scholarship available and because he was poor he had to abandon the idea of scientific studies. His drawing-master, however, felt that he would become a painter and arranged for him to have a bursary at the School of Arts and Crafts.

Whenever he came home from abroad Kokoschka used to dig in the garden of the house at Liebhartstal with his brother, Bohuslav. They would dig down several feet because they wanted to make a hill in the garden to increase the area of cultivation. Round the base of the hillock their spades hit against a limestone deposit in which they found ammonites and parts of other fossils, the shells of calcified oysters and some flints. These were finely worked, small and highly developed, like the work of diamond-cutters. They proved to be of the La-Tène period. Naturally he wondered how they came to be there. He was not surprised to find an oyster shell beside an arrow-head, for, next to the fishnet, the bow and arrow is one of man's first tools. But an ammonite—much more ancient, differently formed, more compact, looser in design, with the whorls turning in the opposite direction—surely that should have been found only in the ocean bed?

The appearance of the other shells was not surprising, because he knew that the sea formerly stretched as far as the Kahlenberg near Vienna. He had read a book at that time which propounded a theory, based on astronomical mathematics, that the moon must have altered its course at some not too distant time in the past. This ingenious theory was put forward by an astronomer and geologist called Hörbiger, who explained the appearance of the deserts and the disappearance of whole continents, the movement of seas and the origin of their salt content by it.[3] At the time, his calculations were accepted with some reservations, because it was the general opinion that many of these changes were the result of a collision between the earth and a large meteor, which originated in an explosion of a central sun, that was itself divided into our sun and moon. Hörbiger's theory also appeared to prove that the moon's path was altered at some time when mankind was far advanced.

The young artist, Kokoschka, was ready to accept this explanation which he brought into relationship with the myths about the sun and moon common to primitive cultures, the disappearance of Atlantis and the Flood. These myths could all be explained by the huge catastrophe postulated by the astronomer. The Bible too begins with the creation of the sun and the separation of land and water. Although Hörbiger's theory of the cosmic catastrophe supported the volcanic theory, repudiated by modern science, it still leaves us with the problem of what caused the original cataclysm in the sun.[4] Kokoschka, applying Hörbiger's theory to his ammonite, saw the whole catastrophe in the palm of his hand—the sudden disastrous flood, followed by an immediate dry period causing an immense drop in the waters, and with it the death of myriads of fish and other ocean dwellers. He saw the flint-makers' hutments on the shores of the lake after the flood and before the drought, which must have happened very suddenly, otherwise there would never have been so many stranded fish. It occurred to Kokoschka, however, that there must be oil deposits in the vast fish necropolis. He had seen the same kind of ammonite on his painting travels, and arrow-heads in Galilee and Lake Tiberias, in Syria and in the marshes of Tunis and Eritrea. Even in the middle of the desert in Tripoli, where one expects to see nothing but sand, he had found arrow-heads. There must be oil everywhere.

Suddenly Kokoschka changed the subject and began to discuss the history of culture. Apparently without forerunners the chariot was introduced by the Hyksos into Egypt.

Or should he rather speak of the appearance of the horse in Asia and the similar development which took place among the Celts. For the horse precedes the chariot and the next
step is bronze and metalwork. The Sumerians had no horses and it was only later in
their history that the wild ass and the horse of the desert were tamed. Bronze Age man
always had some kind of skill. If it was not something to do with boats, it was connected
directly with the horse and its appurtenances. They made small bronze chariots decorated
with reliefs, the sun always present in the design.

The horse is the historic signpost for the art of bronze, and the bronzesmiths inhabited
the geological belt where Kokoschka thought there was oil. And why? Because of the
tribal movements. People were driven from their settlements by mounted nomads
skilled in metalwork. They drove out the agricultural peoples, who had settled where
the retreating sea had left the earth fertile. At first they were only fishermen, but later
they learned to till the land. Herodotus recounts that the Scythians conquered the
Cymmerians (an offshoot of the Thracians on the Cymmerian Bosphorus) in this way;
the Israelites the Canaanites; while the Egyptians were driven out by the Hyksos and the
Sumerians by the Babylonians. Kokoschka went on: The oldest cultivated plant is the
soya bean, buckwheat the oldest cereal. Relics of these plants always indicate an ancient
settlement of the lakeside dwellers. The soya bean is the only climbing plant—as the
ammonite is the only fossil—to turn in an anti-heliotropic direction. The soya bean needs
as much space to grow as the circumference of a turning arm, but here we must digress
a little into the realm of philology. At that point a remarkable unity appears between
the linguistic, archaeological, geological and geographical elements. The Slav word *mir*
means peace, measure, the community, world-order, earth. The root of the word means
anything which turns clockwise, it means *to turn* in all early languages, whether Chal-
daean or Mesopotamian. *Ararat*, *Ra* and Lion in Arabic are all the same root.[5] But
what is the significance of this conception of turning? The women did the work on the
land, measuring the distance between the plants by a twist of the arm. Out of that simple
movement property, order, and a systematic society arose. Everything begins there, in
China, Egypt, or Mesopotamia. They were all sustained by the soya plant. *Mir*. Wherever
it was cultivated life was a co-operative affair run by women. The men either did no
work at all or they fought and robbed one another. It is incorrect, as T. G. Masaryk
tried to prove in *Russia and Europe*, that the word *mir* derives from closed male societies
dedicated to defence.[6] On the contrary, the word points to settled agricultural communities and means also proportion and, in music, harmony. And if we follow this line
of thought it leads us to the essential difference between civilization and culture. The
word civilization derives from Latin, *civis*, a citizen, the man, the warrior, and is part of
the conception of state. An ordered city life is also enjoyed by ants, bees, and termites.
But to cultivate means tilling the land, striving to some purpose; the hearth, breeding
and the rearing of the young. Culture is an individual thing, civilization a product of the
masses.

Then I understood why Kokoschka so disliked the expert and the specialist. He saw
them as the ogres of our time. Such people lose all sense of the whole and all knowledge

has to be arranged neatly in rows with no gaps. We should admire the dilettante, he said, being one himself. Enthusiasm makes them what they are.

He gave a lecture in Berlin on his experience and conclusions concerning the presence of organic petroleum. The question was taken up by the publishers, Ullstein. They introduced Kokoschka to Notman-Vögler, who owned an oil fleet and interests in the oilfields of Baku. Kokoschka wrote an article that was published in the *Börsenkurier* and later in a Czech periodical without disclosing the author's name. He was invited to a board meeting by Ullstein with Fitger, the explorer, and it was decided that they should travel to Persia together on an oil tanker plying between Holland and Baku, so that he could study the oil question seriously. Then they were to search over the regions in which Kokoschka thought oil might lie. He suggested that deposits would be spread over an immensely scattered area, but were probably rather shallow and not so rich as others. All this meant intensive study and new methods of exploration. Notman financed the whole operation. Then Kokoschka's father became ill—dying not long after—and that prevented his going. Later on the idea of the oil deposits had lost its attraction for him.[7] Just before the last war the Germans had started boring at El Qantara in the damp area between the three or four oases that Kokoschka himself had visited. The artist had discussed it even with Sven Hedin in Berlin. And now, when he recalled the story again in Ullapool, he was sadly afraid that the possibility of there being oil in Austria might have been one of the reasons for the *Anschluss*.

MARIA AND THE BULL

During those long summer evenings in Scotland the war seemed far away, and Kokoschka would often talk nostalgically and without distress of the past. I had the impression that he looked on his memory as a landowner who contemplates his treasures in the evening, seeing in his mind's eye the meadows, fields, and woods of his heritage, watching the cattle come home at sunset, sleek and well cared for. It is best to be a dreamer, he would say, interrupting his reflections; a man who does not know what life is really like . . . Even if he has nightmares he is at least preoccupied with his own ideas and not troubling himself with the future. The only difference between man and beast is that man is able to relate his vision to reality without prejudice to form a new and loftier whole. And the same difference causes the ultimate division of mankind, setting the artist apart. He is caught by momentary beauty, and experiences a sense of wonder. Reason is excluded, and the paths of insipidity and convention. Communion is the essence.

Kokoschka believed that every child is born in close contact with creation, but that education and social discipline stifle it; the destructive force of civilization gradually strangles the creative spirit until the child finally emerges as a conventional adult. Few people know the secret of spiritual continuity, only a very few artists.

Kokoschka has written down some of the experiences of his childhood; they were imaginative, rather than factual.[1] If one can break through the self-conscious framework and disentangle the facts from the stylistic peculiarities and attitudes in which the artist has cloaked them, the man himself, the artist, appears. Kokoschka does not reveal much from his early childhood, but it is of great importance.

He describes his first, incomprehensible, shattering encounter with death; his early erotic impressions and doubts; the city of Vienna and the suburbs where they lived, not far from Liebhartstal, where the artist later bought a house for his parents; the gardens on the Galitzinberg (now called the Wilhelminenberg) where he played with his brother and sister, Bohuslav and Berta; a place where great friendships were sealed and strange, secret things happened and whence there was a marvellous view over Vienna. Many years later Kokoschka painted this view of the city, partly as a *memento* and partly as a commission. It was born of the poetic memories of his childhood.

Kokoschka writes:

Vienna used to be much more rural. The outskirts, our childhood world, were a maze of

12 The Duchess of Rohan-Montesquieu, 1909–10

13 Auguste Forel, 1910

14 Knight, Death and Angel II, 1910

15 Oskar Kokoschka and Herwarth Walden in *Der Sturm*, 1916
By Courtesy of Mrs Nell Walden

16 Herwarth Walden, 1910
By Courtesy of the Fogg Art Museum, Harvard University

17 Double Portrait (Oskar Kokoschka and Alma Mahler), 1912

gardens. Fields and meadows were not far away; the vineyards, thickets, woods and small misty blue hills climbing towards the Rax faintly visible on the horizon.

We lived on the top storey; round the house ran a balcony where we could enjoy the pure air, which had been one of the reasons the family went there. We were quite small and had to stand on tiptoe to see over the top, but we were not allowed to lean out, like passengers in a train. Once when I was still very young I had to rescue my sister, who was a restless, fidgety child. She was a small, unreasonable person, who never reckoned with reality, but grabbed everything she saw with both hands. Fascinated by the coloured glass balls glittering in the sunlit courtyard, she lost her balance and fell, only just managing to hook her feet through the wooden balustrade, with its animal-headed pillars and relief design of interlocked snakes. I grabbed her by the skirt and hung on with all my might till my mother heard our yelling and came rushing out. My sister had always screamed like mad at the slightest thing just to cause a fright.

I remember, too, though not nearly so vividly, the life in our road. Drinking water, for instance, came into the house in barrels. I used to watch out for the van and was rewarded with a copper coin worth four kreutzer. Hot water for washing came in a big cart like a brewer's dray; once I saw a dog chasing a cat, with blood pouring from its nose. The red splashes went from the middle of the road to the wall of the house opposite. From where I stood I could not see our side, but at the time I did not realize that only half the street was visible. In fact, even now, no longer restricted by a balustrade, I still have to circle whatever it is that attracts my interest unless it is small and can be easily turned. Otherwise I only see the side facing me. And I suspect that is why we are forced to get behind material things in case they have no real existence. Perhaps this curiosity will kill me; because nothing is harder than to learn to understand oneself. An infant tries to grab its own big toe because it moves across his vision. And every morning of every day until we die we make something our own, altering our conception of space and proportion to contain our puny selves. Practical men who have not time for this kind of reflection are content with what other people tell them; romantics believe their mirrors; and lovers are irritable because their fallacies run wild, weaving a coat of many colours instead of truth, a carpet for the lewd and saintly dance of life.

I have often wondered about a strange event that I could never afterwards explain. My eyes were red with crying; a black coach was waiting in the street and I resolutely refused to take account of what was happening. I determined to keep my eyes on the wheels as they began to move. There came the pungent smell of lighted candles rising from the street in broad daylight and then the coach departed and dissappeared in a whirl of dust. But I had fixed my attention solely on the wheels. They were as big as the front door at first and diminished slowly into points that caught the sun, till they disappeared altogether. So I never realized that the fast-disappearing hearse bore the body of a boy not much bigger than I was. Whither was he bound? I, too, might have followed him, as brown hair followed my fair boyish curls, soon inevitably to become white, but instead I am the same person who wakes in the morning and goes to sleep at night. For ever?

Sometimes I would be drawn to watch a horrible scene in the street whenever a herd of oxen was driven into the city. The poor white-throated creatures, thirsty and tired, lowed and cried out for mercy. Driven from their pasture, they were blinded by the half-dark of the houses as they crowded upon one another, leaving the green of the suburbs for the high, shadowed walls of the city. The beasts, crushed against the walls, were forced up on each other's backs, while all the time the drovers ran alongside them cracking huge stockwhips to keep them moving. If they had not, it seemed from above, as if the horned procession would have arrived at the stockyards in a pyramid of bellowing, struggling flesh that threatened to reach my high window.

On summer evenings before the lamps were lit the windows were closed with muslin to keep out moths and insects. I remember looking at pictures in a book with a friend on the floor below. Since I could not read the captions I had enlivened the black-and-white illustrations with paints given to me at Christmas. This gave the pictures a perfume and taste like honey that comes back to me whenever I think of the Greek myths. That Greek city with its white temples and blue sky and the majestic mountains of honey-coloured marble seemed real to me. The Greek heroes were about to sacrifice a virgin and the high priest held a glittering dagger over her head; but a thunderbolt rent the earth, the ground opened and the blue bay, threaded all along its edge with white cities, shuddered beneath the lightning. I painted all the small, grey figures into the farthest background of the picture; some had children on their backs like our ancestors; and women were trying to save their few belongings wrapped in their tunics. War had devastated the whole landscape and bands of immense rats had emerged from their hiding-places into the daylight. And finally the archaic goddess appeared on a cloud, a crescent moon in her hair, to rescue my childhood friend from the altar and carry her off to safety—just as it was time for me to go to bed. My friend was called Lala and she was very pale. She wore a tartan dress and spoke a language that I could not understand.

The balcony was really our domain, and if you followed it round you could see the sun from almost every side, rising in the east in the morning and setting in the west when a cool evening breeze sprang up. Behind the house there was a large garden divided from the courtyard by a partition made of lanceolate arches of molten-glass panes and shining balls of red, blue, and green glass that glittered dramatically in the setting sun. But these hot colours were depressing in the heat of the day, because we were not allowed to go into the garden. The lure of the unknown garden became stronger in the autumn, beckoning with its broad, soft lawns and laden fruit trees. We were allowed into the courtyard only in the afternoon; but the garden kept its secrets behind the trellis, so nearly within our grasp. If only it were possible. The courtyard was plastered and bare, though it had a mysterious atmosphere. Our footsteps echoed round the well in the centre as if adults were walking there.

The well was built of worn red tiles and over it there was a beam holding a creaking winch from which a rope dangled through the square hole in the boards. The wood was rotten and both my sister and I had been forbidden to climb up or even to jump near the boards. But we used to snatch moments of delight when we lay full length on the wood and stuck our noses into the hole, greedily breathing in the musty smell rising from below, which contrasted with the sun-dried surface of the boards. The cracks were full of mites resembling small fish, and ants crept in and out of the hole. Their ceaseless movement; their sensitive antennae touching each other as they passed; the shimmering, transparent wings of the little waterflies, together with the mysterious noise of water dripping below, made an impression caused partly by watching and partly by listening. Sometimes a small piece of sand or lime-stone would dislodge itself from the wall unknown to the watcher above, who was aware of nothing till he heard it reach the water. They said a toad lived at the bottom of the well, but we never saw it. We used to try to stay awake on summer nights to hear it croak.

On just such a day our neighbour disappeared for ever. It was extraordinary; we had had to shut the front door leading on to the street because people said a steer had got loose; but, of course, the animal had nothing to do with the young woman's disappearance. I must have been the only witness to see it with my own eyes. Otherwise there was no one near, neither my parents, nor my sister, nor any of the other people who lived in the house; and certainly no bull.

It was to be expected that things could not go on as they were. The girl had taken a fancy to me; she loved me although I was already growing up. I was surprised when she kissed me tenderly on the cheek, crying softly. She used to give me sweets till I felt sick, but my mother was disturbed at such behaviour. I remember how she slid me gently off her knee when my mother came because she had been strictly forbidden to nurse me. When I was asked why I had gone into her apartment I only knew that a feeling far stronger than my wish to obey my mother had driven me to take refuge behind the girl's skirt and to slip through her door. She wanted to show me a plant on her window-sill, called Queen of the Night. This was growing, she said, in the skull of a child, although you could not see it, because it was covered with earth. Its flowers opened only in the evening, emanating a dangerous scent that made you feverish if you went to sleep, and that was the reason she kept the plant in her room. She said she hoped to die young.

Apart from me she was the only person in the courtyard. She was hooking the clothes line in zigzag fashion across the court and then she hung out her washing. Then, wanting to sprinkle the line with water—an old custom in Vienna to make the washing whiter—she picked up the empty watering-can and climbed on to the well-head. She stood straddling the well, but when she pulled on the rope with the bucket full the winch began to creak and she had to put the rope back on the pulley; as she did it she stood with all her weight on the well cover, laughing as it tilted and cracked. Then the blue sky grew suddenly dark and the depths yawned beneath the hole which had opened in the well.

It would have been impossible for me to look down the hole and I would rather have seen the bull, but there was always that stupid prohibition: Don't play in the street.

Everyone stood in the corridors and talked about it. The beast was supposed to have horns two yards across, to have gored small children and terrified even the adults. You could hear the shouts of the knacker's boys who had set off in pursuit. The corrida *faded away and I really don't know whether they caught the bull or not, and at last the door was opened again, but of course everything was over.*

I have kept my promise never to tell of the secret bond between myself and the girl who disappeared. The adults tried in every way they knew to find out, but their questions left me cold. All right then, she had gone, and would never come back.

I was too young to understand the reasons and when my mother knew we were within earshot she always told people that the steer had carried Maria off on its back so that she would never return. I never believed the explanation that the girl had died an unnatural death, because you hear so much gossip in an apartment house. That was certainly not what I saw. No.

These descriptions reveal the boy's eagerness to see below the surface, to discover the affinities that he could see from one side only, like the trail of blood leading from the middle of the street to the wall opposite. And tragedy echoes through it all: danger for his sister, the dog hunting the cat, the death of the boy and finally the riddle of Maria's disappearance into the well. What is the significance of the bull and the plant growing in a child's skull? Whence the rats and the huge, writhing snakes? The boy's curiosity, awakened by the savage life of the street and his passion for events, can be inferred from the poetic description of the unlikely happening at the well. It is accompanied by a creative urge driving the child to colour the black-and-white illustrations, till they have 'scent and taste'. At sixty the artist confessed that it was an essential part of his artistic perception. If a picture does not remind me of that taste then I am dissatisfied with it. The story embraces war, the garden of the rich neighbours, the humble grey plaster court and the child's obstinate determination to achieve truth and independence. I never accepted the adult's explanations! And finally the erotic symbolism that early touched him with its magic wand—the goddess, the mother of life.

The boy who had died in 1891 was Kokoschka's elder brother. The artist remembered how bitterly he had cried as he stood beside his mother at the graveside; how he grew older than his five years and saw things as they are. On the way home his mother bought him sweets, but he did not want to be comforted like a baby, he was grown-up and all-knowing. So he threw them away, though secretly, so as not to hurt her feelings.

This sensitive, highly strung child developed an almost hallucinatory fantasy in which truth and image are woven inextricably together. Both are true, both real, and he can scarcely distinguish between them. Fear and uncertainty and dreams surround him like a fairy forest. Caught in the web of his own problems and timidity, reality fades into the background and is displaced by the rich imagery of his inner mind. It is hardly remarkable that Kokoschka used to walk in his sleep when he was a boy. What trait is it, however, that defines the somnambulist in the popular mind? It is a nervous, hysterical condition during which short attacks occur, and is defined by Bricquet thus: 'The attacks are exact repetitions of disturbances, in which painfully vivid moral impressions are manifest.'[2] A psychological connexion between the moon and the psyche has been demonstrated in medicine. Modern depth-psychology follows in the footsteps of mythology, of geological and biological facts (moon, sea; moon woman) and of the romantic, poetic, and dreamlike experience of the moon's sphere. Kokoschka is inclined to believe in a cosmic influence on his nervous system, and is certain that it affects his art. He believes it to be the key to primary experience. On this path there is no harmony, nothing permanent, nothing final which can compare with the brilliance of the

Greek artistic ideal. The archetypal leads to the marrow, not just to the beautiful surface of life; vision realizes the essence, not the appearance, of ideal perfection.

After the strange disappearance of the girl in the well my parents arranged for us to play three times a week in a secluded corner of the park belonging to a Polish aristocrat. This garden was actually a hill crowned with a mausoleum, in front of which stood a marble Hercules. The hill was called Galitzinberg, after the princely family exiled to Vienna when Poland was divided by Alexander I. My memory of the park is confused by an illustration of an earlier palace of the Tsars of Zarskoje Selo which I cut out of a magazine some years later, but the reproduction never approached the glory of the original in my mind. Only in the theatre was I able to recapture the rich confusion of imagery: allegorical painted and carved figures seemed to live on the same footing as the castle's owner, along with the marble group, Cerberus, and exaggerated perspectives of childhood. This mise en scène, *where mankind is seen solely through the eyes of man, is the theatre's chief attraction for me. Palaces and parks were disappearing; land was being divided, hotel syndicates taking over the castles. Ex-servicemen lived in the ruins selling tickets and picture postcards to the public who wanted to visit them. However, the aristocratic world was still a fundamental part of the society in which the nineteenth-century Austrian lived.*

The imaginative writer Ferdinand Raimund always depicted his characters in this magic world; tragi-comical figures who wanted to climb higher and higher in the social ranks till they came up against the ghosts world. They were generally barons or at the very least a noble lord. The shabbier the present the more sleazy became the surroundings, and the pompously bowing, bourgeois *top-hats stupider. The classical theatre in Germany had suppressed folk drama since the days of Goethe and Schiller, but in Vienna it was still kept alive by the creations of Nestroy and Ferdinand Raimund. In the play called* The Waster, *the scapegoat of the old Viennese comedy, Punch, struts arm in arm with the parvenu nobility. He derives unchanging from the Italian Comedy, witty and talkative, like the* bourgeois *men and women, and steps out beneath the Corinthian pillars in marble halls that lead directly through aristocratic doors to heaven.*

The castle was probably only an ordinary wooden hut belonging to the park attendant, who kept a tobacconist's shop. My eyes saw his beard in an antique light, snow-white; he was translated into Hercules, the hero who chained the many-headed Cerberus. The tobacconist's bicycle leaned against the dog kennel. My sister put no trust in ancient myths, because she had the idea that I was making friends beyond her reach. I had to prove to her once that I was not boasting. But caution had become second nature with her. She had learned slyness and cunning to avoid my surveillance and endless teasing. Because I was older I had to take care of her; also she had to spend a lot of time in the fresh air because she was growing very quickly and was rather anaemic. So we used to play coach and horses. I fastened her to the reins and hit her with a switch so that she moved quickly. I clucked with my tongue and was very pleased with myself; 'Don't make such a row. Every driver uses his whip, it's a well-known fact. Anyone who howls is a rotten spoilsport.' My sister went on crying, so I winked and pointed at the tobacconist, whispering the unfailing formula: 'I spy something that you can't see.' With the immediate trust of a lost animal when it hears a familiar voice, she pricked up her ears. Now we both saw him. It was Hercules. Even I had not thought a moment before that the owner of the bicycle was really the legendary hero. I soon saw the laughter in her eyes again, for the fickle mind of a child is not long held, even by panic which paralyses those who trespass on forbidden ground. The child mocks at barriers. 'I know you, and I shan't believe it unless you ring the bell on the bike.' I would have preferred not to undergo this test, but then she would have told my mother that I had hit her. Whenever she laid down her conditions I was always compelled to try to get an advantage for myself out of this test of my courage. She knew my weakness and was well aware that I only sub- mitted because I was afraid of her mocking; for mockery gets under the skin and pierces one's armour. If I let her have her own way willingly, she thought she was able to break my will, but in fact she only bent it.

I had almost forgotten Hercules, for I was nearing the age of heroism, ready to face any danger, and then she could never mock me again. Never again. We peered through the twigs that concealed us from the eyes of the keeper. 'Don't pretend you aren't frightened,' she teased. 'You only have to stretch out your hand to the bell and ring it.' We made a bargain that this was the last time that she would provoke me, and shook hands on it. So I looked quickly round again: the customer was just leaving the tobacconist's and I jumped out of the shrubs and rang. But the dog on the chain was quicker. My sister fell over like a stone; just as she always did. The discovery that she could do this had often enabled her to get out of church when there was no other way for such a small person to avoid the press of adults. She was full of cunning. They all rushed to help her while the dog laid its teeth in me. 'Idiot, can't you see the notice that the dog bites? Now the baron is going again without paying for his cigars.' The keeper was furious. I heard my sister laughing. . . . I lay on the grass with a strange feeling of being the pawn in the game. The wind rustling in the trees brought solace and I thought the sky with the white doves would be the safest place to be. At first the gardener gave me some cherry brandy to get over the fright and then he allowed me to sit on his bike, because he liked children. Birds, butterflies, and flowers danced before my eyes and one by one were consumed in the everlasting light. The dove was the first bird to leave the ark, the olive branch in its bill; it had found it on Mount Ararat after the floods had receded. A long white beard hung in the sky above me, but I could not see properly—my eyelids were too heavy and I felt weak; thus through half-closed eyes, in the mysterious green light, I seemed to see the spirit of God. It is strange that God exists, I thought, for my heart was heavy. Although it is clear that the weaker sex willingly subjects itself to the stronger, nevertheless girls develop their intelligence with marvellous skill so as to gain one's respect. I shall marry my sister. The corners of the mouth twitched beneath the curly white beard and revealed the smile of God. The company of the Almighty was so inviting that I felt like asking why He remained alone in Eternity. Amen! Everything hummed gently in my ears. Like the park- keeper in his vegetable patch, God stood alone under the myriad stars. I supposed that angels, like girls with wings, sang and played harps in heaven, yet the Lord God was not married. Then I became weak again and was forced to close my eyes. 'Look at the kid—he is drunk,' said the park-keeper from a cloud of scented incense. 'That must have been the cherry brandy.' He held his cat, wearing a black collar, up in the air. 'I spoiled him, too, like my tom-cat, who got bread and milk every day. Useless creature. He has to fast today and will have to wear this black collar for a week because he pulled some feathers out of my dear little canary's tail, just as if it were an ordinary bird . . . he sings like an angel, my canary. But tomorrow the cat will get two white mice from me as atonement.' The keeper wandered off saying as he went that he hated white mice. They danced everywhere in front of his eyes. But I didn't like the smell of the schnaps and got up to wash my face at the Hercules fountain. . . .

There was a time when two girls used to come regularly to the park with their mother and she would sit reading while they played with us. Soon the elder girl and I had formed an unbreakable friendship. At five o'clock a tartan rug would be spread on the ground and tea taken in the English manner. I did not think much of the bitter brew, kept hot under a cosy so as to make sure you burned your tongue. I could never see the invitation as anything other than an effort to take part in a society game, the rules of which demanded that you behave as if to the manner born. During this tea party I forgot that I had to behave like an adult as my new friend enjoined me. She sat opposite me on the rug, dropping her gaze into her lap, like the ladies in Schiller's Taucher, *which we were just reading at school. 'Would you like more hot water?' they asked. 'After you,' was the answer demanded by convention, but I quickly withdrew my cup, so that the hot water was upset. The lady suggested to me: 'Please use the saucer, or my fine Japanese china will be broken.' At last we got up and left her to read her French book. I felt red-hot. I would never again be able to accept the invitation. My friend made excuses for the wet spot on her dress; but I could not. I did not want to play the gallant, however many crowns her mother had embroidered into her handkerchief.*

At home we always drank coffee and I was used to it. In the old days a native of Vienna who could not distinguish fifty different ways of preparing coffee could scarcely expect to be taken seriously on the reasons for the Austrian loss of personal liberty, or the loss of European freedom in general that led to the irreparable disruption of the balance of power. The truth is that in Vienna, even before the first war, a horrible brew of roast chicory was substituted for the magically potent eastern drink. The English are tea-drinkers—that is the reason, in Palmerston's words, why they make warlike alliances to counter imaginary dangers.

One can imagine the exciting atmosphere of the old Viennese coffee-house at the time (say) when Napoleon had his quarters at Schönbrunn, and again at a time when Bonaparte was writing his memoirs on St Helena thanks to the initiative of the Austrian militia and the faithless Marie Louise, and Alexander I sought to drive his vodka-inspired Cossacks ever deeper into Europe. The Tsar saw himself as the saviour of Europe. And all believers were to be caught in the universal net woven of the holy alliance founded on the mystic beliefs of the Muscovite saviour. Only the Pope, the Sultan and Metternich, creator of the theory of the European balance of power, stood aloof from this pact, because their intellect, sharpened by the coffee habit, dissented from such exaggerated ideas.

Coffee was introduced to Vienna by the Turks when they were defeated by Prince Eugen. The Turkish commander had to leave all his belongings behind in the Favoriten Palace, where he was quartered; it stood in the grounds where Schönbrunn was to be, and took its name from the fine view. He managed to evade capture by flight. Treasure and slaves stolen in Austria fell into Viennese hands and wild animals and camels appeared in the menagerie. But they did not know what to do with the coffee. However, by the intervention of his wife, a Turkish prisoner was allowed to open a coffee-house in Vienna—the first in Europe. Probably one coffee-house was adequate in Vienna at that time, just after the Ottomans' victorious and devastating advance had been checked. The threat to western Europe had decimated the population with famine and disease and many were taken prisoner.

However, artists of all nations then came to Vienna and there arose a new city, phoenix-like, from the ashes of the old. As the focal point of the Baroque and an intellectual centre Vienna took her place as the capital of an Empire on which the sun never set. The works of Haydn, Mozart, Beethoven, Schubert shone down upon the world like the rays of the sun, a world where people shuffled eternally between heaven and hell. But beauty and meaning must go hand in hand to complete the world, and the coffee-brewers must not be forgotten.

I learned that my friend's maternal grandfather was one of these bourgeois coffee-house owners. Her mother had married into the nobility; hence the von. *One of the daughters spent most of her time on a swing hung between the branches of a tall tree. Her sister, my friend, often had to use all her powers of persuasion to keep me away from the tree. She would angrily command the sylphide in the tree to adjust her skirts. My friend saw nothing, because she had short-sighted, tender eyes, shadowed with long, sweeping lashes. I relied on her greatly; she was trustworthy and very good-natured. I used to bring her all my essays to read.*

No one who has grown beyond the mysterious age of adolescence is ever again ruled so exclusively by the indolence, weakness of character, misunderstandings, vanity, inexperience and the fluctuations in health of puberty, that strain every nerve, eyes wide open, to reach the precipice to which this train of events inevitably leads. So in this description of my youth I have not tried to remember curious or strange events, now incapable of proof, that may have arisen solely out of childish innocence. A rudimentary event may only cause a splash or two in the still waters of time; a midge falls into a pond, the rings spread ever wider on the surface, and the insect is the cause of an all-embracing movement that stirs the deeps.

My friend suddenly darted away to look for a bottle of smelling-salts that her mother had mislaid. She was scarcely out of sight before her presence faded to a childhood memory, part of the past. The rolling stone gathers no moss; the naked fact revealed by the girl on the swing had made me abruptly awake to nature's contradictions. The dividing line between should and should not disintegrated, together with my innocence. The unpleasant part was the temptation to taste of the Tree of Knowledge. Yes. Me! Me! The girl was absolutely oblivious to my presence in the grass below the tree. My beating heart probably meant about as much to her as the devotion of her pet dog, when for once it was not scolded and banished for jumping up and spoiling her dress. A butterfly fluttered softly round her, alighting now and then on her skirt. Nothing betrayed to her the jumbled feelings that caused me to laugh and cry; it was like the sun and the wind scattering the blossom in April, or when you find the first violet hidden under a snowy leaf.

An essential part of the story was my friendship of the previous winter with a snow-clearer, just as the preparations were being made in our district for the carnival procession. I watched him day after day building the snow into high walls on either side of the icy streets. Everything was ready for the arrival of the procession of decorated floats which was preceded by a crowd of running carnival masquers: chimney sweeps and hunch-backs, bringing luck if you could touch them; soldiers in old-fashioned uniforms with red noses, bandoliers, and gaiters; a giant with rolling eyes; ghosts, blackamoors, magicians dressed as women carrying staffs in their hands or throwing coloured paper streamers. If one of the watchers was annoyed by being hit there was an immediate hue and cry and the whole band of fools fell on the sacrifice with crude jokes and lewd gestures, until the carts had passed by and the harlequins found new opportunities to attract the attention of the crowd.

The snow-clearer wore a hairy sack on his head, but not because he wanted to atone for his sins like the Jews. In those days the ash was still collected in sacks by the dustmen. It was wretched weather and so he had wrapped his head and legs in these sacks. In fact, he did not need to wrap up both legs, like his friends, because he had lost one in the war. I was flattered when the man with the wooden leg invited me one lunch-time when I was going home from school to come with him into the brandy shop belonging to Herr Borowitz. The snow-clearers used to gather every morning outside the inns to get the last dregs of beer from the near-empty barrels. Every man carried a rusty tin for this, tied round his middle with string. I was teased into ordering a kümmel for the man nicknamed the Aristocrat by his friends, and paying with my kreutzer owing to the school porter for tea. Yes, the young gentleman had to pay for the kümmel.

When spring came I was overjoyed one day to meet the Aristocrat near the park gate carrying a hurdy-gurdy. He wore his pensioner's coat and a shining medal on his chest given for bravery in the face of the enemy. He was very proud of the pensioner's imperial coat. He told me he had had to wait a long time for the hurdy-gurdy, making continual applications to the Ministry of War, because there were so many old soldiers who had lost eyes, arms, and legs in the last war. A hurdy-gurdy was the recognized indemnity for a private; long-service warrant officers were given posts as park- and garden-keepers, prison warders, overseers in the state brush and cigarette factories; as school porters, or doorkeepers in the ministries. Officers were rewarded with a tobacconist's and lottery kiosk. So my friend taught me something about my country's administration. But I wanted to know who had really been the enemy? Was it the Bosnians, carrying long knives between their teeth, which they used to cut from every decent Christian those parts which decency forbids one to mention? Had he been as unfortunate as that, I asked uncertainly? With a show of indignation he cast aside such a silly schoolboy's question and added that if such a thing were to happen a man's life was worthless to him. But he had only left a leg behind. Though he had been abandoned as dead on the battlefield, the next morning the medical corps had come galloping through the enemy lines to find him. Orders are orders and his name was on the hurdy-gurdy list. They abandoned his leg, he explained, since it was already cut off. Yes, those were the good old days, and he had had to wait twenty years for the hurdy-gurdy on which he now began to play the *only melody he possessed :* The song of Prinz Eugen, a noble Knight—

> He built a bridge
> He crossed, and
> Stormed the forts and city of Belgrade. . . .

At that time the so-called exact sciences were given precedence over the dead languages in which only philologists, philosophers, and apothecaries had any real interest. Like steel to the magnet I came to the science side at a time when the future of science was just beginning to open up. Progress brought this change of ideas. Excellent. Absolutely excellent. The study of science guaranteed a deeper insight into the nature of progress than classical studies. When I look back today and question my motive for so readily accepting the plan I realize that it was certainly the introduction of electric trams into our district to replace the horse tram. Schoolboys used to travel part of the way for nothing, hanging on behind the front coach out of sight of the conductor. But I had not reckoned with the speed of progress when I tried the new tram for the first time and I could not hold on ; nor could I jump off, as we had been wont to do. Soon I'd had enough, fell off and was taken home with a head wound.

The two great discoveries, printing and gunpowder, must have worried the history teachers when I was a boy. And as they had not much to say about the epoch which included these discoveries, the period was passed over in silence. As far as the discovery of printing was concerned it seemed to me a hellish invention, and only a means to increase the production of school books ; the other was even less to my taste. For, as my physics teacher used to say, I was not among the ranks of those who had discovered gunpowder. However brilliant the lecture from the desk on the subject of the laws of internal combustion I retained absolutely nothing except the attempt to understand the nature of things by experiment. Saltpetre, sulphur, soot, carbon, and vitriol could be had. I took it as a special turn of fate that my friend, the invalid of the former K & K gunners, had served in the Balkans where he was born. Loyalty to the branch in which he had served probably kept alive his interest in high explosive and also his friendship with some of his countrymen who called themselves anarchists. The boisterous nature of his Slav temperament should be excused a pensioned soldier, when a scientist such as Nobel could remain unperturbed by the potential effects of his discovery of dynamite. He was able to wash his hands of guilt by founding the Nobel peace prize. The pensioner saw no such abyss before him when he made the small bomb that I asked for.

The two daughters of the noble lady were the only people to share with me the secret of the explosive buried beneath the tree in the park. The pensioner had to miss the actual performance because he was not allowed in the park with his hurdy-gurdy. The task I had set myself was to blow up a huge ants' nest in the scientific way I had learned at school. My friend with the gentle eyes was sad about the fate of the ants, but her sister found them a nuisance as she swung in her hammock. My friend's remonstrances that my experiment would cost the lives of other creatures in no way lessened my desire to experiment, especially since, as I said, our relationship had begun to cool. Had she not been watching during the physics lesson, when a frog had been dissected? Women only grow war-like when they are in uniform. So I sent her away for some smelling-salts and prepared for her a Red Cross apron, so that she could represent the nursing service. You can see I had it all thought out. Everything was ready to light the torch according to the instructions in my primer. May my judges be those who, as adults, are freer to decide on their actions. I could have had no clear idea at the time of the beastly thing I proposed to do. I had decided to start the fuse with a burning-glass; but the embarrassed silence of the two girls when the sun went behind a cloud forced me to give up further attempts and to accelerate the catastrophe with the help of ordinary matches. Surprisingly enough it was the Red Cross sister who now pressed for execution, because she said the whole affair had already given her a headache. The younger sister up in the tree wanted to call out the time from the gold watch she had been given by her parents for her birthday. A short discussion with the 'nurse' convinced me that it would take an age before the lighted fuse crept along as far as the tree where the bomb was lying buried under the ant-heap. 'There might be an accident. We must wait and see what happens.' So I threw the lighted contents of the matchbox into the nest and leapt into safety. It was often the case that unexpected things happened when my personal courage was in question. With a thunderous crash a huge cloud arose and with it the city of the ants. It was gruesome but thrilling. Their wings and limbs scorched, the survivors fell to earth; they were like soldiers whose legs have been shot off, dragging the bloody stumps out of the firing line although the last line of retreat was closed. The maddened creatures dragged their eggs from fire to fire, almost like human mothers rescuing their children from disaster in wars of principle, the results of which have already been decided by a higher power. On this occasion the higher power stood indecisively on two legs realizing that the explosion had taken place at exactly five o'clock, the hour when the maid would bring the picnic basket. An unfavourable omen was that every attempt to approach the burning hole proved impossible. It was easy for the 'nurse' to cry over the fate of the ants, but my morale was disturbed for very different reasons. The floating cloud of smoke made the noble lady cough although she knew nothing of the explosion because she was deaf; but she soon smelled a rat and began to look round for the reason for all the smoke in the park. The bottle of smelling-salts had disappeared and she was beset by dizziness and palpitations.

When I realized my beastliness I felt ill. On only one other occasion did I think that anything might be worse, and that was during the war when I read of the destruction of Hiroshima. The name of the hero who had been responsible for the murder of thousands of mothers and children at a blow was passed from mouth to mouth and was hastily printed in extra editions throughout the world.

'We are lost', I whispered to my friend, 'but your mother does not yet know the worst.' Her mother stared at us and then asked where her other daughter was. Now that the smoke had cleared the girl could be seen lying motionless in the hammock. I was her murderer! Helped by the keeper, the woman did the only reasonable thing and resolutely lifted the unconscious girl to the ground. The rescue services were called and it was not long before she was given first aid and began to vomit. 'I am not her murderer,' I sobbed in such heart-broken fashion that I needed a towel to dry my tears, while the beloved got rid of the poison she had absorbed. In case this passage leaves the reader unconvinced, I must add that, in despair at

being banished from the Garden of Eden, I failed my final examinations in chemistry and physics.

From then on whenever I tried to get into the park I was confronted by the keeper standing like the archangel Gabriel with his sabre. The fairy palace in which I had dreamed away my childhood had distintegrated. The now forbidden park was surrounded by the enchanted hedge of innocence. They took me to a circus to cheer me up and there was a clown—poor pantaloon, only there to receive a thrashing he has not deserved—who had the idea of bringing his own garden gate into the ring, where he put it in place, opened the latch, went through and carefully shut it behind him with a huge key. He could just as easily have gone round or, better still, never have produced the obstacle that made him the laughing-stock of the whole audience. After that I felt less lonely. The clown made me realize that I had no need to be taken in by a silly gate when there were perfectly good ways of getting in at the back, where no one was watching. I had to see her again, if only from a distance.

The people living in the neighbourhood used the place to throw their rubbish. One day I climbed up the high fence, but my strength failed me just as I got to the top. I could not find a foothold, nor could I cling on with my hands because the boards were full of rusty nails. I have to admit that the longing to see my beloved that had previously lent me wings failed me now, and the sublimity of spirit worthy of such a high position had not taken its place. Instead I grew dizzy and fell back into space.

Loneliness forces every man to formulate his ideas of society, as did primitive man; and at last the realization that every social pattern is only a Utopian dream drives him back into solitude. This loneliness engulfs us in the emptiness that ends this story.

In my fright I had fallen into the council dung-heap. It was a real shambles swarming with every kind of insatiable creature. The liquid manure shot stinking up in the air and swarms of stinging flies arose from the body of a pig, long since dead and in an advanced state of decay. The doctor was called and I had to stay in bed a long time because my eyes were infected. The sun, that daily confers life and takes it away, seemed to burn on my wallpaper so that I could not bear to look at it. My mouth would not shut and a huge fly sat at the root of my tongue turning round and round laying its eggs in a circle. It cut into my throat like a red-hot poker. I could not move my tongue any more; it was too short and thick. The fever made me sweat, my heart seemed to pound against my ribs and I became suddenly delirious. The wall-paper was covered with green and red whirling suns. My brain seemed to flow away through my eyes, nose and ears like a foul, grey liquid and to evaporate in the room. I was lying under a thick oppressive cloud and there was no sound; then my dry skin began to tear and peel off in huge strips. Like strange white worms rolling themselves up in the sky, my sinews rose from the lumps of black and rotting flesh. Now my body had become a carcass thrown carelessly together, an empty basket made of ribs, its bones gradually falling to dust on the sheets. At last the countless whirling suns that pierced and burned my gaze turned once again into the familiar single, smiling sun that hurt no longer in its calm immobility. What was left of me resembled a photograph, or the echoing sound of the rosin when a bow is drawn across a pane of glass. But the process was much, much simpler than during the physics lesson, much simpler.

While she was nursing me my mother had concentrated on the picture of the Virgin with the pierced heart that the priest had placed on my breast when the doctor had given me up. And my eyes recovered because the priest had prayed for them. My mother gave me almond milk as a restorative; no kind of food or drink has ever tasted as good as it did in my childhood. Nothing could compare with the first cherries tied on a stick with their green leaves two by two.[3]

V

PARENTS

Kokoschka's mother was called Romana Loidl. Kokoschka believes that this unusual name—neither German nor Austrian in origin—is a combination of the words *Leut* and *El*, a place where people live. Near Ibbs in Upper Austria are the ruins of a castle beside the River Ibbs. There is a legend reminiscent of Hero and Leander whose heroine is the founder of the Loidl family. Every night a monk from Ireland used to swim the river to reach his beloved and she lit a lamp to guide him. Kokoschka's mother would laugh when she told this story, because the idea of celibacy was beyond her comprehension. So the monk gave up his orders and settled near Ibbs. Kokoschka concluded from this legend that he had Celtic blood in his veins and tried to find out more about the story: when the inhabitants of the Isle of Skye were being driven from their homes, those who could fled to the south, some to the Continent as missionaries. The Christian tradition in the Alps is pure Irish-Scottish, that is to say Celtic in origin.[1]

Kokoschka's mother was a good story-teller. She had a hard childhood. Living in the mountains a long way from the nearest school, she often had to stay all day and sometimes overnight as well in the winter, but she was never absent. Every year there was a prize-giving. At one of these she was called to the desk and the priest said to the class: here comes our best pupil, who will show you how well she knows her catechism. Romana repeated it without a mistake; but she was rewarded only with a religious picture, where-as the history book she was hoping for fell to the rich and lazy peasant's daughter, who lived comfortably not far from the school. That was her first great disappointment, although she was not an envious child. Kokoschka asserted that she was the most loyal, innocent person he had ever known.

Romana told strange tales of her own mother, who came of peasant stock from Styria and had the gift of second sight; but Romana never described it as a gift when she told the strange happenings, only shaking her head and adding 'extraordinary'. The grand-mother had many children and died young. One day when they were making hay in the mountains she suddenly grew tired, so she sat down for a while at noon under an apple tree. 'I feel strangely calm and everything is very beautiful,' she said, 'as if angels were singing. You know, Romana, next week I shall put on my wedding dress again.' (The wedding dress was preserved in a chest to be used at last as a shroud.) 'This time next week I shall die.' In the days that followed she felt unwell and went to bed. She asked to change her clothes; she wanted to say good-bye because she could hear the angels again. She died peacefully after the priest had been.

Kokoschka's mother had eleven or twelve brothers and sisters; he could remember a whole crowd of uncles and aunts. Their father was head keeper in one of the imperial forests and they lived absolutely alone in the middle of a dense forest in the high mountains. Because he had no men under him, Kokoschka's grandfather turned his own sons into keepers and assistants, and the bigger lads were always with him. They had to care for the plantations and were also responsible for the game. Their house was completely cut off in winter, and Hollenstein, the next village, was several hours away. The menfolk were often absent for several days. They carried their food with them and spent the night in forester's huts. Bands of gipsies lived in the district and people used to say they stole children. One day a whole crowd of them approached the house, whereupon the grandmother, who was pregnant at the time, called all her children inside, barred the door and picked up a gun. The gipsies threatened to set fire to the house, and the winter keep for the wild deer was already alight. Then she heard the call of her husband, who had returned with the boys in the nick of time. When they opened the door she dropped the gun, and within hours Kokoschka's mother was born.

In the little house where the Kokoschka family lived Oskar slept in a room upstairs, and whenever he plotted some mischief with his brother and then came down, his mother always knew. It went on like that for nearly forty years. Looking at the lithograph he had done of her, the artist thought it a good likeness; he had caught her character. The oil-painting was not so good, because she was ill when he painted it and he was afraid to look too closely for fear of what he might see. Kokoschka's father, Gustav, had died many years before and the boy, who lived with her through years of extreme poverty, became her confidant. Somehow she always provided a good meal for her family, even if it were only potato soup, and their clothes were meticulously washed and darned.

Romana was eighteen when she married Gustav, who was then over forty. It was a love match: she a child of the people, reared in the beliefs in trolls and gnomes; he a goldsmith and a man of dignity.

At one time the mother lived with her brother, the director of a large sawmill in Pöchlarn (this is the place called Bechelaren in the Nibelungenlied), close by the splendid Benedictine monastery of Melk. The night Oskar was born—1 March 1886—the mill was destroyed by fire, and mother and child were carried to safety on a wagon. Kokoschka believes that this incident was the cause of his tendency to panic, and that his mother's flight in childbirth is connected with his use of red in place of black in his paintings.

The international crisis in the 'eighties made Austria bankrupt. Kokoschka's father, a native of Prague, was forced to sell the family house in the Brenntegasse, and moved to Vienna, hoping to be able to continue working as a goldsmith. Things went from bad to worse; the days of craftsmanship were passing as mass production made everything cheaper. He even went to Paris to try to find work, but it was hopeless; in the end he only did repairs. Then he took a partner into the business, but the man deceived him and everything was lost, so Kokoschka's father took a job as book-keeper. He was usually laid off just before Christmas to save the bonus, and often after buying the Christmas tree there was nothing left for anything else. That is why Kokoschka has always hated

Christmas. He remembers one Christmas Eve very vividly; he must have been quite small, for his sister was only a baby and Bohuslav still unborn. His father came home laden with parcels, but without his old cane with the carved ivory handle; the mother looked questioningly at him, but said little; she realized that their valuable things were disappearing into pawn one after another. Kokoschka's father was cheated several times in his life. His Life Insurance was never paid and his partner stole his jewellery business for lack of a proper contract. He still spoke Czech though the boys did not. The chalice in the Cathedral of St. Veit had been made by his grandfather for his master piece, and it can be seen that his grandmother had been a beauty from Mánes' painting.[2] The Prague workshop was much esteemed and the Emperor Franz Josef used often to come in to buy a new snuff-box or to arrange for the setting of a fine stone and probably to see Kokoschka's beautiful grandmother. He would be invited to take coffee and the family used to tell how the Emperor handed his malacca cane and top-hat to Kokoschka's father when he was an apprentice and how they had to release the boy from his involuntary prison, because his whole head had been engulfed by the hat.

Kokoschka describes his father as a reserved and proud man, quite uncompromising and always battling against the world. That was one of the reasons he did not get on. His wife had a very heavy burden to bear and used to say gently: 'It is no use beating your head against the wall; it is the same for everyone.'

Kokoschka describes her as a good mother who thought always of her husband and children before herself. She had profound faith and saw life as a pair of scales: the one going up the other down. She had none of the tragic character of her husband, who was suicidally hard on himself. The boy, Oskar, had great respect for his father, from whom he learned to bear poverty proudly and not to betray his ideals, but there was a deeper understanding between him and his mother, who confided to him her small joys and anxieties.

The Kokoschkas had many relatives in Vienna. One of the artist's cousins was captain of the Palace Guard at Schönbrunn, and shot himself on account of a love affair with one of the ladies of the Court; an uncle had a music school in the Mariahilf district and was headmaster of the Theresianum; another uncle was Hofrat Glossy, director of the State Library—he had known Grillparzer as a boy and became an authority on Viennese cultural history. Kokoschka's father would have nothing to do with either of them, because he was poor.

Later, Kokoschka's father became ill and was advised to leave the centre of the city, so the artist bought a small house in Liebhartstal. By now Kokoschka was famous in Germany and had been elected to membership of the Prussian Academy of Science and Art. When he came home his father would ask: 'What splendid things have you been doing now?' and add jokingly, 'There's something in the paper about you again.' Fame meant nothing to him, he said in revenge against the world, but he enjoyed it vicariously for his son, at the same time warning Kokoschka never to think of money, fame or success lest they go to his head.

The old man had always been handsome; his hair was still brown and he had a long thick beard. The artist made a drawing of him, but was not satisfied with it, he once told

18 Entreating Woman (Bach-Cantata), 1914

19 Sketch for Fresco, 1914

20 The Tempest
By Courtesy of the Öffentliche Kunstsammlung, Basel

21 Knight Errant, 1915
By Courtesy of the Solomon R. Guggenheim Museum, New York

me, because he sensed that his father was close to death and he felt an inner resistance. But the old man was still very strong at seventy and could lift a chair from the floor with two fingers. He spoke several languages and was widely read. Even before Oskar could read, one of the first books his father gave him was Comenius's *Orbis Pictus* and also a shortened version of Homer's *Odyssey*. In the evenings he would read aloud from Schiller's dramas and from the works of Herder and Lessing. Later Kokoschka's library gave him great pleasure and he kept his art treasures in this room.

When Kokoschka had wanted to buy a house for him after his illness there was only one that was suitable: it had belonged to a Turk and it was therefore called the Little Turkish House. There was a marvellous green-tiled bathroom in it—at that time rather a rarity in Vienna. It would be fine, he thought, for his mother, as it was easy to keep clean. Kokoschka arrived from Berlin, and although he had made money there, as usual he had none left. He always needed more than he could earn, because he was very impulsive and could never look after money. So he had approached the dealer who handled his work, Paul Cassirer, a man of great integrity, and explained that he needed money. What for? To buy a house. That was too much for Cassirer, who replied that Kokoschka had no need of a house. The artist explained that it was for his father, but Cassirer would not lend him any. 'I don't want you to stagnate,' he said. 'I cannot have that on my conscience. Work harder.' Kokoschka replied that he worked as hard as he could and as much as it suited him. Cassirer was unmoved and threatened that they would have to part; Kokoschka accepted the implications of the threat, but told Cassirer he would never come back to him of his own accord.[3] So the artist got hold of the money by giving a promissory note and the house became his, though he had no idea how he was going to pay for it!

Kokoschka has always taken care of his family. When his sister married a naval officer[4] and the whole thing had to be financed—ceremony, wedding feast, and honeymoon—he managed, as if by magic, to get enough money for the actual event, but afterwards it was the usual story: how should he start again? Kokoschka remembers clearly how they stood, his father, brother, and himself, beside a wall, and his father asked: 'How much have you got?' He himself had a few coppers, but when Kokoschka turned out his pockets they were empty. However, he still had the top-hat and a return ticket to Berlin. Kokoschka has always behaved like a rich man of the world; money means nothing to him and he has always managed to get it from somewhere. Sometimes he even paid for his pupils to go to Italy and America. He rarely had any cash, but he was free, and he never borrowed. As a young man in Vienna he had had a crowd of adherents, no painters—he saw to that, and they used to sell his drawings in cafés for five crowns. They would put the money into his hat and spend it all drinking, smoking, and talking. For two years he never got home before six in the morning. He was always with his friends, never alone; there was no music, no women; he just did not want to go home to sleep. He never used to bother about food in those days, though he enjoyed eating goose-liver *pâté* in Piovatti's Jewish restaurant. At least it was something in the stomach, because they all drank an enormous amount. On one occasion when they had no money one of his friends spoke to an American and suggested that they should bet who could drink the most. Kokoschka had to win so that the American would pay. He could stand an incredible quantity of alcohol, but always felt ashamed when he met the people going to work on his way home. He would creep into the house, and his mother, who was waiting, gave him hot milk, telling him to drink it quickly before his father saw him. But she wept inwardly and told him he would kill himself, while his father would call out 'Where has the young devil been this time?' About noon the young artist used to slip quietly out of the house to go to the school of arts and crafts, where he was both pupil and drawing-master, and where he painted a great deal despite his lack of sleep. All his early portraits of Kraus, Loos, Altenberg, and Harta were done at that period.[5]

So much for Kokoschka's attitude to money. Generally it was taken away from him, he used to say, as soon as he got it; not because he did not know its value, just that he had no feeling for it and lived from hand to mouth. Fundamentally he despised it. In 1938 he arrived in England as a refugee with only ten pounds in his pocket, but he had been so used to struggles with poverty from early youth that it did not mean much to him. Just like his father, he was always short of money, even when he was over sixty, so that he could confidently declare in 1945: The time is ripe for money to be valued at its true worth. We are living through the last phases of the capitalist world. Money is like a bicycle, no use at all unless it is going.

Kokoschka admits that he has to remain at his easel whether he wants to or not. He cannot even stay in bed for a couple of days when he has influenza, but must get up and work, not because he wants to be always active nor because he is inspired, but because he simply has to paint; he believes this is the reason his work is so consistent. Life itself is never so real as when he is painting and he is always looking over his shoulder even when passionately stirred. His emotions are never so overwhelming as to make him lose his head entirely. He told me that if he felt like it he could influence anyone he liked, old or young, important or unimportant, child or foreigner. He could completely bewitch and hypnotize them. His only real dislike is the need to earn a living. He has often had a lot of money, of course, but it has always melted away because he takes no interest in it. His needs are modest: a few toys, something to delight the eye.

The young Kokoschka was one of the best-dressed men in Vienna, and in Berlin, too, he made an elegant impression. They used to say in Vienna that Kokoschka was such a shy boy that he did not dare to go into a coffee-house alone, and would often walk up and down outside until friends came and took him in with them; and he could not bring himself to say how much a portrait cost—preferring to walk out, leaving the picture and all the materials behind. That was what happened with Fritzi Massary, a woman who lived in a house built for her by Adolf Loos in Clarens. He simply walked out one evening and never went back. Loos asked: 'Didn't you like her?' But the answer 'Yes' was only to please Loos, who was very interested in women. It was just that Kokoschka had the greatest inhibitions about money. He describes it himself: *I seldom came to the point of signing these pictures, for in those days I was still shy of selling my work; when the decisive moment came I always sheered off. I preferred to abandon both picture and colour-box. But then came the problem of how to get more paints. There was no solving the riddle of how to keep going as a free-lance artist without starving. Many a time in winter did I press my nose against the frozen window of the Romanisches Café in the hope of learning how the celebrities inside there did it. . . . One, two, three, four, five, I counted on the fingers of my empty hand. What meaning there is in numbers! Raised to the tenth power, cubed, the square root found—only I didn't know how to turn the figures into money. It's money, not knowledge, that gives man power on earth!*[6]

That was in 1910. At the time of inflation, when he was a teacher in Dresden, he had to go to the office with a suitcase to collect his salary. But when he saw the official counting on his fingers in thousands, hundreds of thousands even, he suddenly felt a prick on his lip. It was quite swollen and he went away without taking his money. Ten years later in Italy he received an account from the bank in Dresden: he owed them a sum for bank charges. What irony! They had kept his money there all that time, brought it forward and calculated it; but in the end the charges alone remained as the inflationary value shrank.

In London during the war Kokoschka refused to exhibit his new water-colours. He explained to the gallery director that there was no reason for him to do so, because he did not need the advertisement and the gallery would be unlikely to get the prices he would expect. That is the other side of the coin. Prices for Kokoschka's work are very high indeed, and he once said to me that it was the only protection it had because people only understand investment. Often he would sell a work very dearly, and give the money to charity. He has always lived like that, like a pot without a base. In the beginning his wife protested, but now she is used to it.

When Kokoschka began to work in Vienna he was paid very little for a painting. Frau von Motesiczky relates how her friend Frau Dr Karpeles had a new painter recommended to her, a man in urgent need of money. So she commissioned him to do her portrait. Kokoschka went daily to her house; she found him a shy young man who worked silently and humbly for weeks on end at his easel. When the portrait was finished no one found it the least bit like her. Both the sitter and her husband decided it was quite incomprehensible and put it up in the attic at once with all the other unwanted junk. Several years later a man appeared who said he was an art dealer and was looking for contemporary paintings so that he could 'help the artists'. He acquired the painting for almost nothing. In January 1962, Frau Karpeles's daughter, Frau Neumann, came specially from America to see the portrait hanging in the Tate Gallery exhibition, the picture that is now one of the important pieces in an American collection.

Kokoschka was also short of money in Paris when he founded, with the music publisher Sliwinsky, a two-man association for the protection of consumptive barmaids. And when Dr Hugo Feigl invited him to come to Prague in 1933 he was living in great need in Paris. In 1936 he wrote to Dr W. R. Valentiner, Director of the Art Institute of Detroit: 'The newspapers, even in England, all had long eulogistic columns on my fiftieth birthday, so I am at a loss to understand how it is that I can apparently be the finest living painter (not, after all, difficult today) and yet have the greatest material worries. If I had been taught how to make armaments when I was a boy my life would probably have been less careworn and more restful. Why don't they buy my paintings? The dealers bargain shamelessly with me, wanting to make just as much profit as if I were already dead. They don't pay me enough to live on. So I shall have to die. Adieu, beautiful world and all you worthy Maecenases, for whom I wanted to paint so much.'[7] He also wrote from Polperro to Dr Valentiner about the sale of THE FOUNTAIN and the portrait of Masaryk: 'Although the French market still rules values and I can see therefore that there is little chance for me (that is, as long as I am alive), because I refuse to become a serial painter, who, like the French are forced to do, make share certificates for the Stock Exchange, I still hold that the Masaryk portrait should have some historical significance in the States. It has certainly not been diminished by recent events. I deduce that there must be a market for my work in America from the fact that the Nazis have sold a large number of my paintings from German museums not so long ago. I am the only one who cannot do it; pursued, shamed and penniless as I am, I cannot even get time to breathe. The weakest goes to the wall! Surely your rich men, if they only knew, would make a small sacrifice for European culture, while you are spared the misery that has once more overwhelmed Europe, by remembering the humblest sacrifice to nihilism, those who braved the most—the German artists'.[8] In the summer of 1947 he wrote from Sierre: 'I am the captain of a ship carrying all the aromatic spices of the East who reaches harbour only to be asked to exchange them for a mess of potage. Translated into pictorial terms it means that I do not know from week to week how I shall pay my hotel bill, and all the time I am painting splendid landscapes and other subjects—but I cannot sell them.'[9]

In the course of his long life Kokoschka has grown more cunning than money, but his art remains unharmed.

Both his father and his mother died in the artist's arms. The old man first, shortly after the first world war, and Romana ten years later of a broken heart.[10] When the father died the two brothers had to conceal his death from her. She knew the end was near and the doctor was called. Kokoschka's father lay dying for two days—it was so dreadful that the artist cannot bear to remember it. When it was all over he and his brother went with the hearse to the crematorium—his mother did not want to have anything to do with the funeral and afterwards she always talked as if her husband was still in his room. It seemed quite natural to her, because she never accepted his death. The old man's room was locked and never opened again in her lifetime.

The mother was like a child who could not understand what death meant. And none of the neighbours said anything, although one of them was a gravedigger. They understood. Nearby there was a famous wine parlour where everyone used to go, and they all agreed that Frau Kokoschka should not learn anything of what had happened. The subject was taboo.

In 1934 Kokoschka took part in an international schools congress in Budapest, where he spoke, as so often before, on the subject of Comenius. One day he was asked by one of the landowners whether he had relatives in Vienna, because there was going to be trouble on Friday afternoon about three o'clock. He hastened back to Vienna at once. It was at the beginning of the Dollfuss period when the modern workers' settlements in the city were bombarded and burned. Vienna had been very progressive and enterprising after the war. Dr Tandler, Finance Minister, put a tax on the Jockey Club and even on champagne and built the workers' houses with gardens and hospitals. Now it all lay in ruins and Dr Dollfuss made an ultimatum to the workers on the radio. He gave them an hour to give themselves up, otherwise the guns would be turned on them. And then the radio played the aria from *Rosenkavalier*, 'A Soldier's Life is Free'! Soon the houses began to burn in Favoriten and Ottakring. Ever since then Kokoschka has been unable to stand the radio and his mother was absolutely incapable of understanding how any government could shoot down its own people. That Austrians should kill Austrians completely broke her heart. Her optimistic attitude to life, to her homeland and to her children was fundamentally destroyed. They had a good view of Vienna from their little house, so she sat all the time on the balcony and watched, unable to sleep. She had a stroke while she was sitting there and for two weeks was very ill. So much for the Viennese heart of gold when even severely wounded men could be hanged, although they had been promised amnesty. On a hill opposite Kokoschka's house was a large castle owned by an archduke. He was called the Vegetable Duke and had been a prosperous landowner. The Socialists had confiscated the property and turned it into a children's home. You could see and hear the children playing there all the time, and Kokoschka's mother was happy watching them. Before that the castle had always been absolutely quiet and the Kokoschka family often saw the sentries marching up and down when they passed on their walks. The Vienna City Council wanted to honour the artist and commissioned a Viennese landscape for one of the chambers in the Town Hall, so Kokoschka painted a bird's-eye view of the castle seen from the house in Liebhartstal. It was like a Breughel—children playing in the foreground took up about a third of the canvas; the horizon lay far back, giving the artist room to develop a scene of intense activity and great depth, beyond which lay Vienna and the cathedral of St Stephen. The panorama stretched to the Danube and the Leitha Mountains. Kokoschka said it was his first picture with a political slant. The Dollfuss régime had been in power for only a very short time when the children were taken away and the castle became instead a seminary for priests. When Kokoschka saw it for the last time they were all carrying gas-masks; it was a horrible sight. His picture disappeared when Starhemberg occupied the town hall.[11]

His mother had been failing for a long time, Kokoschka told me, but she had no idea that she was dying. She lived in a dream and her life was like the theatre, a series of sad or happy endings. She was naturally very imaginative and never recognized the meanness of the world. The artist said she was the only person who really understood everything he did, far better than the connoisseurs, better even than Adolf Loos, whose perception was very acute. Sometimes she would say things that one could scarcely believe. Four of the best doctors were called in to see her, but it was of no avail. Then her sons planned a beautiful grave for her. They carried the body to Hollenstein—where she was born, a day's journey from Vienna. Her grave is there on a hill with a gothic spiral staircase leading up to it, but no cross—not from anti-religious sentiment but because it signifies death. Kokoschka's mother had always loved the procession at Corpus Christi when the little children walk on a carpet of flowers. She did not often go to church, though she, and sometimes even her husband, would pray in church if they were really in despair; but to go to a cemetery would be too much. So the boys took her body into the hills— to Mother Carey. No flowers were provided, because they die and are sad. Instead they constructed a copy of her house over the grave, small, with two pillars and her name engraved over the door: there she would feel at home and happy. Although she could not see it, her son knew she would have liked it, because from there one could see over the mountains and meadows she knew as a child, for she lies at the very top. The windows of the little house are always open. . . .

Kokoschka looked down after he had told me about it and I thought I detected a sadness in his face, or perhaps a fear that he had revealed a secret that words might harm and the world defile. Family feeling in its true sense—the link through his mother with his ancestors—means as much to Kokoschka as to the Chinese: They are a nation of families which often had as many as eighty thousand members. Like a beehive. They have learned and digested Western philosophy and yet still cling to their old traditions, so they must be right.[12] What use are all our philosophies? he asked. He had built a house for his mother . . . Immortality! Romana was alive in him and he was the same flesh and blood as his mother; he could not see it in any other way. He says that time has neither yesterday nor today and he never feels that he is growing old. It is like walking through a landscape, passing now a wood or a hill and now a valley. He was also bound to his mother by his clairvoyance.

Kokoschka painted KNIGHT ERRANT at the beginning of 1915, and it foretold how he lay wounded on the battlefield, suspended between heaven and earth. When he gave his lecture on the *Nature of Visions* he had drawn a poster showing the position of the wounds seven years before they were inflicted. There was another drawing, made on a fan—this time the artist was on horseback, fighting the Russians before the war had begun—that he gave to the woman who loved and hated him more intensely than most, and from whom he wrung his freedom like Jacob wrestling with the angel.

Adolf Loos used to enjoy telling the story of how Kokoschka painted a thickening of the wrist on one of his early portraits of a child with the hands of its parents. This feature was inexplicable until the man himself remembered that as a child, and long since forgotten, he had broken his wrist at that point. Loos is also said to have encouraged an elderly lady who spent much time with her seemingly innocent granddaughter with these words: Have your granddaughter painted by Kokoschka; he will reveal the most secret vices.[13]

Since the death of the artist's mother the little house in Liebhartstal has been occupied by Bohuslav and his family. For Kokoschka this house was a place where he could keep everything that belonged to him—everything, that is, that he had not cast off by the wayside to free himself of useless ballast. There was a cupboard in which some things of great sentimental value were kept, such as the spoon with which he was feeding his father when he died; a few important letters; an authentic marble head and an archaic marble figurine; a few books such as Dostoievsky's *The Gentle One* and Hamsun's *Pan*. During the war he used to feel wretched at the idea of their being sullied by 'dirty' hands. But his greatest worry was on account of his brother, Bohi, who is seven years younger than the artist. He was in a battleship throughout the first war and was at Cattaro during the mutiny. He did some painting, but his brother advised him not to exhibit and display his work at a time when art was becoming a commercial proposition. He wrote a long and very unusual book about the war. Kokoschka once said his diaries were like a ghostly dream. He never invented anything and was among those who declare that invention is unnecessary, that observation is sufficient. He could not find a publisher for his war story; Europe was not yet ready for this dry, spectral picture of life in times of trouble.

Bohuslav was a dreamer; instead of going to school he used to go to the woods. He would run out without a coat in the winter snow, quite alone, and of course fell ill. His whole life was an attempt to shake off his guardians: at school; during his violin lessons; at parties and meetings. And he used to annoy his brother by his behaviour. But he loved to write and would sit up all night at his desk instead of going to sleep. Sometimes he looked awful in the morning and he lived in constant terror that his brother, father, or mother would catch him. He was always on the run; but he was agile. It is a miracle that he survived the second war. Kokoschka worried greatly about him during the first two years after the *Anschluss*, because Bohuslav had stayed to look after the house. Only three days after the occupation of Vienna twelve Gestapo men came to look for Kokoschka. Rumours reached the artist in London that his brother had disappeared, but he was not able to correspond with him during the war lest he bring him into danger. Bohuslav would not give the Nazis Kokoschka's address, so he was punished by being forced to clean the latrines at a Nazi barracks. He survived, however, and for several years after the war Kokoschka sent him and his wife and son, Roman, food parcels. He says admiringly that Bohuslav has much more imagination than he has; a fantasy the scope of which embarrassed him. He, too, inherited second sight from Romana, and their sister is also gifted in this way. Kokoschka illustrated a collection of her poems and the head she made of him in clay is the best portrait that has ever been done of him.[14]

In the late autumn of 1947 Kokoschka left Switzerland for Vienna, where he saw his brother, the family, and the little Turkish house once more. He was acclaimed everywhere, sought and found friends again, especially among young people. They listened to him with rapt attention. It was said that his words acted upon the postwar indifference like a transfusion of new blood. Kokoschka himself wrote at the time: *I am always happy in Vienna when I see that youth, whose guide, mentor and friend I try to be, so hangs on my words. I wish that I could succeed in helping the young people to form a clear picture of the world that would encourage and enable them to live with dignity.*[15]

After he left Vienna, Kokoschka tried instantly to arrange for the provision of artificial limbs from America for the six thousand crippled refugees who had come to Vienna from the east.

THE FOOTHILLS OF ART

What, then, of the times, seen now in retrospect, that awaited Kokoschka—a young man gifted with a lively sense of experience, with a singing in his blood that told of the legendary sources of the life-miracle, with chaste heart, the desire for conquest, and the joy of discovery of a yet untried youth?

The Austro-Hungarian Empire was in decline. Its disintegration was slow but inevitable, although now and then it wore a buoyant mask amid the illusory charm of Viennese frivolity. Spiritual values were being attacked by the all-pervading corruption—morals, intellect, the Church, and the politico-economic structure. The thin glittering surface of fascinating uniforms, of Court balls and military bands, the splendid trappings of the Vienna State Opera, and the life of the cafés, could not hide the abyss yawning below. Love had been displaced by sexuality, religion by bigotry and power politics. Narrow prejudice overcame morals, while justice yielded to corruption. It was out of the poverty of the ill-governed masses, out of the misery of the proletariat developing from the onset of industrialization, that the multi-mouthed national hydra grew which ruined the Empire.

Kokoschka breathed the fatal poison of that decadent period with all the fervour of youth, but when his reaction came it was violent. Like a strong emetic, it wrung from him a cry of rage, and a frenzy of passionate disappointment struck him, breaking down the façade that veiled his inner eye. The smooth surface cracked and he saw what lay ahead—he was able to grasp the depth of the moral abyss caused by the poverty in which people lived, and he clung to myths and mysticism as the only hope of rescue from chaos and nihilism. He read ceaselessly, but hid behind a mask of *naïveté* and ignorance. He said he had never held a book in his hand, although his pocket would bulge with a copy of Homer, or the Bible, Dante, Shakespeare, Montaigne, Ariosto, Angelus Silesius, the Bhagavad-Gita, or whatever he happened to be reading at the moment.

He would often dissimulate if he thought it necessary. 'Embroidering', one might call it. When he arrived from the suburbs he was a young man, full of genius, or so at least he is described by the few who supported him from the beginning, rescuing him from despair when publicity was turned upon him as on a wild beast, in an attempt to crush him before he had a chance to develop.

Kokoschka had attended the *Realschule*, but it was not the true source of his education.[1]

When I was at school, he explained, I used to read books from the *Reclam* series under the desk, but unfortunately my education has many gaps, because the teachers used to interrupt. We never even heard of Byron at school. But why not, for he was a kind of genius—handsome, heroic, a poet and a seducer of women—we could have learned something about life from him. Instead we were always taught about Anastasius Grün. Who on earth was Anastasius Grün?[2]

It is obvious that, even as a boy, his many-sided character was not to be spoiled by conventional teaching, which collapsed in the attempt.

Sometimes he likened his mind to the deserts of Tibet, in which small temples of wisdom shine out. Knowing the most important things, he felt it his duty to convey his knowledge to humanity.

Although confused and tormented, he was a complete personality from the beginning, and as an artist he was true to himself. However clumsily and unconsciously at first, he resisted the 'arts and crafts' taste then reigning in Vienna which was influenced by *art nouveau*, the Vienna Secession, and the new tendencies of the Vienna workshops, held at the time to be the alpha and omega of modern art.[3]

Once, after the terrible experience of the second world war, he spoke of his feeling about his work. It was the time of the Basel Exhibition of 1947, when he was suffering from the fear that more than a third of his work had been destroyed by the war and the barbarities of the Nazis.

When the postwar painters were all still devouring Impressionism I alone remained myself. So every painting that has disappeared is a wound in my side. After his return from Switzerland in 1947 he told me that on the opening day in Basel, after the Exhibition was closed, he stayed behind, alone with his pictures. Thus he was able to find out the man he was and is.

Even before the first war Gustav Klimt's decorative art was despised by reactionary circles in Vienna. His exhibitions were the subject of such violent attack that, in the end, he withdrew from public life altogether. Speaking of Klimt Hermann Bahr said: 'Klimt's landscapes, like Stifter, contain the eternal Austria' and, paying homage in a provincial way to the national art of Austria: 'We want to create an art of Austria; let us wrap our art in its beauty.'[4]

The first modern Austrian artist of European stature was developing slowly towards his ultimate calling. What Kokoschka owed him is revealed in Klimt's own words: 'The young follow their own path and will probably go far beyond me. That is as it should be, for no one taught me how or what to paint. Only one kind of teacher is any good, and that is the one who can liberate the true genius . . . perhaps that is what I have been able to do for Kokoschka.'[5]

Kokoschka began his studies at the School of Arts and Crafts in 1905. Chemistry was now put completely to one side. His art teacher at the *Realschule* knew two sisters named Fröhlich, friends of Grillparzer, who had founded a scholarship for promising artists. Kokoschka was awarded his scholarship through the influence of his teacher, and jumped at the chance, because he had no money and wanted to contribute something at home, where money was often scarce. So he decided to follow the four-year course at the School of Arts and Crafts, as a candidate for a teaching post, and meanwhile dreamed that one day he would be able to take up chemistry again. But it never came to that, because he was discovered. His questing personality and undisciplined, unclouded spirit soon made an impression on his surroundings. For instance, he introduced the five-minute life study which demanded rapid comprehension from the pupil and helped the model, who was able to change her position all the time. Later he worked as an assistant in the same school. As early as his second year he was asked—to give him a chance to earn some money—to give a course of instruction in the study of movement, although he was still a student at the institute. The time had passed when he was compelled to draw for hours on end from a motionless model—some bearded old man with a staff, life-size figures 'from life' as it was called. The young Kokoschka stood at the back of the room, so he always drew very small figures. When his teacher objected he answered simply that since that was how he saw the figure he could not draw it any larger. Thus, he not only preserved his eye, but became a master pupil with a studio and models of his own without having served his full apprenticeship.[6]

He made innumerable angular studies of a small circus girl—one of his models of the period. These drawings later paid for his drinking bouts with his friends. Kokoschka was especially interested in the girl from the circus, because her limbs were so flexible.

It was only later, be told me, that he saw Hokusai's woodcuts and learned the Japanese approach to perspective. He was fascinated by the movements of the nude, because they were altogether different from those of the clothed body. A standing figure with staff and bathing-trunks was too boring, and to fill it out with light and shade was idiotic. He never did such ridiculous things, and that was why he chose the crafts. He wanted to make something real—a carpet, a book, or a poster, but at the Academy only 'art' was recognized, and that was conceived for a refined upper class.

He was studying William Morris at the time, and learned to admire him. The Vienna workshops and the School of Arts and Crafts had at least an intellectual link, and the pupils of the school were revitalized by the spirit of the Vienna Workshops.

Following the Morris example, Kokoschka wrote, printed, and bound a book. It was his first book, published the next year by the Vienna Workshops with the title *Die Träumenden Knaben*[7] (*Dreaming Youths*).

The scandal caused by the first *Kunstschau* in 1908 forced him to leave the school and to seek new sources of income. The cabaret called *Fledermaus*, run by the same people as the *Kunstschau*, could not support him. Here he recited, danced, and showed pictures with a magic lantern, calling his act *The Speckled Egg*.[8] To supplement his income he gave lectures in the technical school on bookbinding and lithography, following the example of William Morris.

The suggestion that Kokoschka was influenced by Japanese prints brings us to a problem that is often misinterpreted today. The search for originality by modern artists is fundamentally nothing more than an attempt to create a trade-mark, and leads in the end to a point where everything is ascribed to 'genius' and nothing to tradition—just as if there ever was an artist who could create works of art from within himself, like a spider weaving a web! Some writers on art, influenced understandably by art historians, swing to the opposite extreme, developing a pathological need to discover influences everywhere, even when there are none to be found, although they do not attempt to find traditional or intellectual links as for instance with the old masters. The detective instinct of these critics can be justified in writing of second-rate artists, because there is no personal element. It cannot be justified in discussing creative artists like Kokoschka, who have imprinted their stamp on an age. True greatness is *hors concours*.

Assuming, therefore, that Kokoschka could have seen Japanese prints, if only through a medium such as Klimt, before he did his drawings of the circus girl, nothing can alter the fact that Kokoschka possessed a powerful talent, a lively approach and a primary urge to draw that was wholly independent of artistic influence and springing directly from contact with reality. It is only necessary to compare his drawings with those of his contemporaries to see the difference, or to glance at his rough pencil sketches which were stolen from his studio during the war and coloured by a sad hand, to find the answer to the problem of talent and the art of imitation. It is true that ideas can emerge from stony ground, but they will never develop and come to maturity except in the rich soil of a personality who can endow them with life.

Kokoschka often had to defend himself against pedantic critics and pseudo-historical pronouncements that sought to diminish his genius and personality. Everything, almost without exception, that Kokoschka painted sprang from within; his was no dry intellectual desire to experiment, or to produce something artistic, and hence the impression made on him in his youth by the painter Anton Romako[9] and the Austrian rococo painter Anton Maulbertsch,[10] as well as his leaning towards Dürer, Altdorfer and Breughel and later the Baroque and classical forerunners, must be explained as a spiritual affinity. Sympathy and love alone can enrich such inner links.

The flowering of Kokoschka's colouring by contact with Impressionism, Expressionism, and the Fauves is not borrowing (what confusion with economic terms!), but a victory over the means of expression which had been his from earliest youth and to which he responded in the mute practice of everyday art.

The painter Faistauer wrote: 'Kokoschka is first and foremost a colourist. Although at first drawing seemed uppermost, and line appeared to be all-important, the colour is still there.[11] This is a perceptive judgement. It is only necessary to look at the TRANCE-PLAYER of 1908 to recognize the truth of this statement; or the STILL LIFE WITH TORTOISE AND HYACINTH (1909).

There are in the illustrations to Albert Ehrenstein's *Tubutsch* (1911) linear structures that have nothing to do with Cubism, but fulfil the artist's profound need to create a stable, spatial effect, because he felt quite insecure in his own surroundings—hence the posters for the *Kunstschau* (1905) and the drawings for *Sturm* in Berlin (1909 and 1910) that still slumber beneath a net of enchanted lines, and also reveal elements traceable to his intial contact with the primitive masks of the South Seas and New Mecklenburg. This was before the primitive had become fashionable under the influence of Gauguin, who inspired the taste for strong colour as well as primitive decoration which now blossomed to new life in the hands of Kokoschka, deepening to a full expression of modern intuitive experience. These drawings and posters reveal strange concentrations of energy, secret signs and hieroglyphs, focused on the sensitive nerve-endings, developing into an individual language of art to such a point that Rainer Maria Rilke declared that Kokoschka's eyes were X-rays able to see islands of experience. External influences and spiritual characteristics are not to be set down as in a ledger, and Ralph Waldo Emerson spoke truly when he said: 'A great man is like a huge magnet that attracts all art, science, and knowledge into its field. Nothing is left, everything is consumed; whatever does not reappear as power, does so as knowledge.'[12] It all depends on the creative power of the personality, which does not accumulate automatically.

Compare one of Kokoschka's early drawings with one of those by the art juggler of Paris in which a Toulouse-Lautrec type of head, shorn of all its original power, bleached and flattened into nothing—the portrait (say) of Yvette Guilbert of 1910—and one recognizes the presence of expressive formulas from the artist's soul. There is no sterile copying.

The painter Gustav Klimt and Carl Moll, president and director respectively of the School of Arts and Crafts; the painter Alfred Roller and the architect Josef Hoffman, the latter leader of the Vienna Workshops who designed the Exhibition building with its adjoining ice-rink; and Franz Čižek, with the participation of the youthful Kokoschka, combined to produce, with the first *Kunstschau*, a real impact at last on the artistic life of Austria.

'The situation of art in Vienna was such that there had been the beginnings of a successful revolution by the moderns. The most important names in the various fields were Josef Hoffman, Gustav Klimt, Hermann Bahr, and Gustav Mahler, although the latter had nothing to do with the movement apart from his opera sets. It was, in general, decorative in tendency, a natural consequence of the Ruskin-Morris movement in England that had greatly influenced Viennese ideas. The movement was increasingly emotional and anti-intellectual.

'The first revolution was succeeded by a second, more radical one, with Adolf Loos, Karl Kraus, and Arnold Schönberg at its head, and, later, Kokoschka also. He had been won over from the Vienna Workshops, but, being much younger, he did not fit into the circle very well, and was more of a protégé than an active member. That was also the Bohemian and night-club period, which was thought very revolutionary at the time.

'It was in this guise that Kokoschka made his first public appearance, hoping to "startle the old fogeys". It was probably essential at that time, and all part of the need to appear a little mad. Unfortunately, it also resulted in his not being taken seriously by those circles who were unsympathetic towards such behaviour.

'At the time of the first and second *Kunstschau* the disruption of the whole movement was well under way. The Secession had broken up. Till then Klimt had been the pope of painting in Vienna, and there was actually no one else of any importance. Stylization of art had been everybody's aim, but the faith was now destroyed because it happened that the French Impressionists were being exhibited in the city for the first time, although their movement was already part of the past. Vienna had really nothing to offer, except a decadent decorative style which was becoming ever more schematic. There seemed no possibility of innovation, because the Viennese artists could not overcome their fear of theories.'[13]

Kokoschka made a poster for the Exhibition, and his work was also represented by the drawings and lithographs done for his first book and by the hand-made book itself, by a clay sculpture of a girl,[14] several fans painted with dreamlike fabulous beasts (Kokoschka made about twenty of these for the Vienna Workshops, painted on swan-skin parchment and mounted in ivory and ebony), and four tempera sketches for large tapestries. The tapestries and fans—early works, now lost—as well as a plaster self-portrait now in the Boston Museum of Fine Arts, evoked amazement and dislike and were refused by the jury.

There were no galleries, Kokoschka told me, where new painters could exhibit. And at the School the only question was: who dares to show with us?

Kokoschka was inspired with ideas for wall-paintings, and shut himself in to work at a feverish pace. They were not simply outline sketches, but tempera paintings. They embodied his longing to see the unknown world, as well as his visions. He called them—intentionally—the *Dream Bearers*, and not, as they might have been wrongly named by the *littérateurs*, the *Enchanted Dreamers*.

Selection day came and, helped by a friend, Kokoschka arrived with his paintings. Three walls of the gallery were covered with pictures. The judges walked through all the rooms and came to the part where Kokoschka's work was hung. But the door was barred.[15] Kokoschka had forgotten that there was an opening and had fixed a large mural over it. No one could get in. Quick to seize the opportunity, he began to bargain with the judges, standing inside and shouting through the door that he would not let them in till they promised to accept his work unseen. They remained outside, solemn, in frock-coats and top-hats. Klimt was President, and Kokoschka called through the door: Herr Professor Klimt, I am glad to meet you. I am told that you have praised my work. There was a scuffling outside, and Klimt's voice could be heard trying to calm them: Let him alone; a foolhardy youth like him will be torn to pieces in any case. And when Klimt said that, he spoke from experience. Then Klimt replied: I give you my word; only let us in. Kokoschka watched him as he gazed at the walls, shaking his head and saying: Mad boy. But all the same! So Kokoschka, although he was so young, fought bravely for recognition. Klimt was the first to buy a drawing. Klimt's prediction had been right, for there hung the poster which produced so alarming an effect and upset the susceptibilities of the refined Viennese *bourgeoisie*.

Kokoschka had chosen a religious theme, as he was to do again, and infused it with a new life. It depicted a woman, red as a leech, with a dead-white Kokoschka on her knee—a new and brutally primitive *Pietà*. He had sent some startling works to the Exhibition—for instance, the clay head with open mouth and shaven skull, quite white, with a gruesome blue wash and decorated with veins over skull and neck as well as a network of nerves. Wherever he felt life throbbing beneath the skin he drew it. All the tender nerve-endings from which he suffered were painted. 'I wanted to see what was hurting me; then the pain would go.' He ascribes it to a certain inner toughness—a blaze of determination and will-power.[16] Adolf Loos bought the head; it was a symbolic purchase.[17]

Loos had come to the *Kunstschau* to mock, because he had a poor opinion of Josef Hoffman; instead, he discovered Kokoschka, and from then on would not let him out of his sight. The *Kunstschau* marked a turning-point for Loos, whose perceptive eye saw in Kokoschka the expression of a new era. The portrait head was his fetish. Loos took it away the next day and gave it to one of his former wives. Both the head and the poster imply the rebirth of Primitivism in Vienna, an expression of the spirit of the times which was independent of the west. Kokoschka became notorious overnight. He was a thorn in the flesh of the *bourgeoisie*, and the *Neue Freie Presse* persecuted him unmercifully. The result was that Kokoschka was dismissed from the School—a bitter blow which robbed him of his income.

In years to come *Der Stürmer* described his work in the same words—degenerate, decadent—as had the contemporary Press in Vienna, and repeated them again on the occasion of the defamatory exhibition in that city.

The effect of this violent Primitivism on the drawing-room aesthetic of the period is understandable; the paintings make a powerful impression, even today. The complacent Biedermeier monster tried to engulf this latest victim, but in vain. Kokoschka was saved by his sound instinct, by his horror of the smooth and artificial, and by his robust, rebellious nature.

Understandable, too, is Kokoschka's lack of reverence for Hugo von Hofmannsthal and Rainer Maria Rilke. Theirs was an Austrian art and much esteemed, but Kokoschka could only see it as decadent poetry. He did not hold it against them personally, but against the times it represented. He declared Rilke to be a Court poet in touch only with the nobility and, while not blaming him for that, he could not forgive him for playing the part of Tasso and doing it badly. How could Kokoschka bear to read the *Cornet* after experiences of war that still tore at his jangled nerves. To die crowned with roses was no longer possible; the Romantic period was over. And he hated the idea of presenting the Virgin as a lady in a poem; the Madonna was not an aristocrat. So he could not stomach Rilke, Hofmannsthal, or Werfel. He thought even Schnitzler (moving though he could be) no more than a *littérateur*. He was sorry that Rilke had died of a horrible sickness, alone in a tower. Only great suffering could have enabled him to write the *Duino Elegies* and the *Sonnets to Orpheus*.

Hofmannsthal he disliked for personal reasons besides. Once, before the war, he was at the theatre with Alma Mahler, and Hofmannsthal was in the next box. She played a rôle in Viennese society which displeased Kokoschka, and when she would have introduced the two men Kokoschka said loudly that he would prefer not to meet him. Much later they met again in Marseilles, staying in the same hotel. Hofmannsthal was carrying on a brilliant conversation with his companion at the next table. Kokoschka knew it was aimed at him, yet he got up inconspicuously and went away without so much as glancing at his neighbours.

His attitude towards Rilke and Hofmannsthal defines the quality that separated Kokoschka's art from the hypersensitive decadent *bourgeois* art in Austria and elsewhere. In the *Kunstschau* the drawings for *Dreaming Youths*, shown in a glass case in the centre of the *Salon*, caused the least animosity. They had originally been commissioned by the Vienna Workshops for a child's book or fairy story. The workshops also ordered a hunting calendar, for which Professor Löffler drew the decoration and Kokoschka the figures.[18]

Dreaming Youths was the confession of the budding eroticism of the growing boy. It was an adolescent work of great charm inspired by the artist's boyhood attachment for a seventeen-year-old Swedish girl called Lilith, who attended the school. She was blonde and handsome, connected in his mind with the Midnight Sun, and he loved the coral pink dress she used to wear. The book was intended to be a love letter, although it never reached the person to whom it was addressed. She appears also in many of the drawings for the *Sturm*; one of these the artist called: 'Anyone may comb the beautiful Lilith's hair'. He wanted to hurt her, because he had heard rumours which made him jealous. Her brother was a strong athletic person and Kokoschka used to enjoy wrestling with him, and although he was always beaten he came back for more, again and again. The rest were insipid youths. Lilith, who sometimes came into his studio at the school, had to model for him sleeping under a veil. She was the first woman to appear in Kokoschka's work; he always liked the company of women, seeking it at first instinctively and then quite consciously. He needed the presence of women; they were a profound source of temptation and purification, at once inspiring and dangerous. The most valuable side of his nature was unlocked in their company. Like Goethe, love for him meant *Glück ohne Ruh'* (happiness without peace) and he drained the cup to the last dregs.

It is astonishing to find so young an artist concerned with the burning problem of the war of the sexes. It was a problem which had exercised the preceding generation, finding bitter expression in the work of Felicien Rops and Edvard Munch, in the philosophy of Schopenhauer and Nietzsche, in the work of Strindberg, Ibsen, and Hamsun, and in the writings of Stanislav Przybyszewski and Otto Weininger.

The love between Lilith and Kokoschka suddenly died. Lilith had been the leech of the poster, sucking his blood till he lay, silver as death. That was also the first appearance in Kokoschka's work of the sun-moon myth. When he wrote the verses for her in *Dreaming Youths* everything seemed like a fairy story; and just as in dreams logical sequence is broken and thought and image change abruptly, so Kokoschka's language flourished like a tropical garden, flowering with new beauty, betraying his youthful, pulsating heart. The dreamlike figures of the illustrations, and the swinging branches surrounding them, scarcely veil the adolescent. The sweet melancholy, and the strong colours, recall scenes of wonder and awe, of gold, brocade, and precious stones from the medieval world.

The year 1909 saw a repetion of the *Kunstschau*. The exhibition of 1908 had been more a demonstration of the new taste in arts and crafts and the theatre in which the best talents of Vienna had participated, but the second show was a determined effort to open the door on the world at large. It was an international exhibition, bringing work by Munch, Van Gogh, Gauguin, Bonnard, Vuillard, Valloton, and Matisse. Germany was represented by Corinth and Liebermann, and Switzerland by Hodler. From Belgium came the work of Minne, as well as Toorop, Khnopff, and Ruyselberge—all Symbolists; and from England, Shannon, Gordon Craig, Bone and the Glasgow group, early Secessionists. Klimt was dominant in the Austrian section and aroused a storm of criticism with a picture of a pregnant woman. Kokoschka was represented once again by a poster, by the oil-painting of the actor Ernst Reinhold, called THE TRANCE-PLAYER, a *gesso*-covered clay head of Lilith, and, finally, an illustrated book, a sequel to *Dreaming Youths*, entitled *The White Slayer of Beasts*.[19]

From the beginning Kokoschka tried his hand in all branches of art. *The White Slayer* portrays the restless questing side of love. Cruelty, death, and love are the elements of this poetry in prose which seems to well like blood from his veins.

Literary critics were unwilling to accept Kokoschka's poetry as literature. Joyce was rejected also, and there is a close relationship between the two. In *Dreaming Youths*, however, Kokoschka more nearly resembles Rimbaud; Kokoschka's inebriated poetry is a spoken not written language. The original function of language—expression—emerges from the shape and structure of the sentences. Tone and melody are heard once more. That was Kokoschka's philosophy; life was a direct experience to be grasped, not just a shadowy phenomenon in print, overpowered by logic. It is essential to accept this standpoint to do justice to the artist's literary work. How deeply Kokoschka's convictions were rooted in his own character and the originality of his experiences may be seen from the fact that, thirty years later, he had given mankind up for lost, because they could only read, they could not see or hear, and only felt safe in the web of the written word.[20] Finally, he believed the crippling of vision to be the cause of the present spiritual crisis.

The sense of sight is an inner impulse, Kokoschka once said to me: The eye is like the hand. One impression is received, another ignored. The eye is more than an optical instrument and the sense of vision rests on an ancient experience, older, far, than speech. The language of the eye is not concerned merely with the exercise of the faculty of sight; it leans on a tradition of experience, its own world of the imagination. It is nobler than speech. The whole of mankind, even the cave-man, has developed around the vision of the eye. Man learned to see before he could speak. People of the south, and women, still possess a language of gesture, for they are conservative, even children speak with their hands. Since the Renaissance the thread of life has been broken; that is what is called Rationalism. The Dark Ages were still visionary, but with the advent of intellectual Classicism and Humanism the only admissible approach has been logical. Mass education by the State is an aspect of Rationalism.[21]

This viewpoint is also pleaded by Kokoschka in his philosophy of education; there he returns to Comenius, who, in contrast to purely theoretical instruction, taught the idea of visual education, and of the crafts, in his book, *Orbis Pictus*, which Kokoschka loved as a child.

22 The Friends, 1917–18

23 The Power of Music, 1919

24 Self Portrait, 1917
By Courtesy of the Von der Heydt-Museum der Stadt Wuppertal

Kokoschka was the cause of the scandalous sequel to the second *Kunstschau* because of a play. His new poster was to be seen everywhere in the city; a self-portrait in the style of the *Dream Bearers*, with blue outlines and a red shadow, a profile head with painful, open eyes, and a hand pointing to a bleeding wound in his breast. It roused the curiosity of the public. This was not Kokoschka's first essay in the theatre. In 1907 he had, for a wager, written a tragi-comedy called *Sphinx and Strawman, A Curiosity*. This, a puppet play, was produced in the *Fledermaus* cabaret (1911) and in the Dada Gallery at Zürich in 1917. The play relates the history of a man (Herr Firdusi, furnished with a giant, movable head, and a pig's bladder—the soul—on a string) who mourns the loss of his wife (Anima, the soul of woman).[22] She has gone off with an athletic giant who cannot see her properly because she has 'turned his head'. Firdusi loses her again later on to the 'wily serpent', 'the intellectual', Herr Kautschukmann. Only death, which appears on the stage in the likeness of a normal living man, implying that death alone is of any significance, can release him from his dilemma.[23]

The play is a dialogue, and the ideas are presented in nebulous and disjointed form, while double meanings weigh the balance on the side of comedy. Fragmentary ideas glitter, and the lure of the possible is felt through the play's perplexities. There were innovations in the technical handling of the sets also, often used later in theatres and revues. Kokoschka had insufficient actors to allow the appearance of ten mourning gentlemen in the last scene, so he used the simple expedient of painting them on to the backcloth. For faces he cut holes, and every now and then the head of the solitary member of the chorus appeared through one or other of them and spoke. *Sphinx and Strawman* is reminiscent of the Dadaist-Surrealist theatre current during and after the first world war. It was played again in Zürich on the 5th June 1966 on the occasion of the celebration of the artist's eightieth birthday. In 1917 Kokoschka rewrote and expanded the play and it appeared with the title of *Hiob*.[24]

Better known than *Sphinx and Strawman* was *Murder Hope of Women*, a drama produced by Kokoschka at the second *Kunstschau* with some of his friends from the Dramatic School—Forster, Ettlinger, Götz, and Reinhold, who were all to become famous. Ilona Ritscher, a passionate Croat girl, played the female lead, and Reinhold the male.

Kokoschka had an idea for the play, but no manuscript and no title. Undeterred, they approached Josef Hoffman and told him they wanted to act a play. Hoffman replied that they could do what they liked, as long as it cost nothing.

The students dug a ditch in the garden of the *Kunstschau* building; this was for the musicians, because there was no stage—they used boards and planks instead. In the middle of the set stood a big tower with a cage door. The floor leading to the door was black, so all the figures stood out in relief. Seats and musicians were borrowed from the café—in fact, everything came from there. Kokoschka had assembled his actors and musicians, but there was no play; nor any music, although he had whistled it through for them and given them their cues. Drums, pipes, clarinets, and a pair of cymbals made up the orchestra. Kokoschka wrote down the actors' lines and movements and there was only one rehearsal, which took place just before the first performance. The theme was woman holding man a prisoner in a cage, like a slave; man overcomes his bondage, frees himself, and kills her. The drama symbolizes deliverance from a sex nightmare. Both male and female appear with their attendants. She, at first, is the stronger, but he is victorious in the end. American, English, and Italian philologists all agree now that it derives from the sun-moon myth. One sees them both often in Kokoschka's pictures; they appear together, and are always speckled.[25] Kokoschka intuitively understood the young people and produced appropriate words for each one. It was a weird play, he said, thinking back.

The Croatian woman was absolutely white. She had a hoarse voice, blonde hair, a face like a lion, and a masculine chest. Later she, too, became a famous actress. Reinhold was red, his hair like flaming sulphur, and eyes as white and blue as stone. That was how Kokoschka painted him in THE TRANCE-PLAYER. The painting was later acquired by the Museum at Chemnitz, whose director was so enthusiastic about it that he took people especially to see it. It was hypnotic. Not that Kokoschka had wanted to hypnotize; it just happened that way.[26]

Imagine the scene! Dark night; attendants with torches on either side. Masklike faces, but not Grecian; they were more like the masks of circus clowns. Sinews and muscles on faces, arms, and ribs, as well as nerves and veins, were all painted in primitive colours, like the symbolic decoration at a tribal initiation ceremony. From a distance the effect was startling in the extreme.

Thus Kokoschka produced 'expressionist theatre' before Tairoff, although he did not set out to do it. He wrote and composed in the presence of the actors, explaining to them what he wanted, how he saw it. By listening to their voices he discovered the exact spoken rhythm for each character. The cadences of his poetry fell from the tongue; they stirred the heart and blood to mounting excitement.

The piece ought not to be read, for it would not have its effect. It has to be acted to show the leaden mob, the individual who liberates himself, the angry gestures. A hurtful word falls from the woman's lips, stressed by a movement. Now hear the drums beating, the notes of the flute. That was how it took shape, through the immediate performance of the actors. There was, however, no money to pay the musicians, and so the performance had to be put off. New posters were distributed offering to return the money to those who had already paid. Meanwhile Kokoschka's friends sold drawings to clients in coffee-houses, and after a week the play was put on. The whole atmosphere— the waiting and the posters (for the Viennese were only used to posters about shoe-polish or Odol)—ensured that there was a large audience on the night. For the most part they were an educated crowd who came for the fun of a row, for artistic scandals were common then in Vienna. Arnold Schönberg had been booed, but Wedekind's *Hidalla, or To Have and to Be* had them all fighting. Even private performances of *Earth Spirit* and *Pandora's Box* organized by Karl Kraus caused the most violent attacks.

There were a few courageous people in the audience, like Adolf Loos, who had brought Karl Kraus with him. On a slope behind the auditorium soldiers from a near-by barracks (a Bosnian regiment—primitive men in uniform) watched the performance, and when the man whom the woman had locked in the cage broke out and branded her, they rushed the barrier into the excited audience and tried to join in. Immediately hand-to-hand fighting broke out, and a real brawl started. The director of police—a friend of Karl Kraus—sent for his men, and Loos tried to bring some order into the tumult. He jumped up and began to talk: This man was a discovery; people should be grateful. But it availed nothing. The actors remained on the deserted scene, and Loos invited Kokoschka to drink his first whisky with him.

Murder Hope of Women is a mystery play,[27] only seven pages long, partly reminiscent of Wagner, but also of the legend of Gilgamesh. As in *The Burning Bush*, conversation alternates with archaic, Biblical language echoing like the *Minnelieder*, or a folksong:

Woman: The yellow disk of the sun flickers in my breath. My eye collects the exultation of the men; their stammering lust prowls round me like a beast.
Man: Stars and moon, Woman! Dreaming or awake, I saw a singing creature brightly shining.

Once, in the dark years of the war, Kokoschka told me he would read his plays to me one day, but not just then: it would make him feel too old. The time of his first theatrical ventures lay too far behind—when he was the object of every shattering event which today shows him the rift between reason and his visionary spirit and which inexorably led to the recognition that man is mortal, woman immortal.

That night Kokoschka walked through the city with Reinhold. Ernst Reinhold was a remarkably gifted Hungarian. Later he worked with Max Reinhardt, but never appeared on the stage, because he had a crippled hip. He had a spirit like Lubitsch, the speech of a Sonnenthal, and an absolutely phenomenal memory. Once, in the Burgtheater, he had given a performance of Shakespeare in which he played all the parts himself in English. He could say it backwards just as easily.

They walked together across the deserted Stefansplatz, under the speckled full moon, talking about the play. The full moon had always affected Kokoschka strangely ever since he was a child. Suddenly, as he was watching attentively, his shadow detached itself from the ground, and he called out: You there. Help me to get down, press on my legs. Can't you see that I am hanging in the air?

Kokoschka saw Reinhold's pale blue eyes, wide open and staring, and saw his own shadow—like a glistening fish slithering in a dark net—embrace the brilliant moonlit cobbles and then, slowly but certainly, begin to separate itself from his body.

It was a strange thing, Kokoschka said. It sounds incredible, like the story of Peter Schlemihl; but perhaps it can be explained by the whisky, following the excitement of the tumultuous evening.

He experienced a feeling, unpleasant rather than peculiar, which forced him to execute a swinging movement, beginning with his legs and going on up his whole body. The sensation cannot have lasted more than a few seconds. Unable to resist, he sank gently, in the end, into a horizontal position on his left side.

He saw Reinhold running away, shouting: You liar, you liar! He thought Reinhold was afraid. But he could still see clearly everything that was going on, although he found it difficult to believe that he was balanced in a horizontal position on air. That's impossible, he thought, quite against the laws of gravity. So he started to draw, tracing spider's webs as he had for *Tubutsch* to make a space and conscious surroundings for himself. Klee and Grosz got this idea from him. In this way his seizure was sublimated. It is painful to carry something within oneself and not to know exactly what it means, so he had constructed a net of lines for himself; not a geometrical affair with vanishing-points, nor yet the perspective common since the Renaissance, which he called 'one-eyed-man perspective'. Like the lens of a camera it had a restricted vision. One learned to draw like that at school, shutting one eye and measuring with a pencil. So what happens? A man with two eyes is transformed into a one-eyed monster. Kokoschka said he had been against this idea of perspective since his schooldays, because it seemed to him far too theoretical, giving an alien view of space. A child sees depth and distance with both eyes, and that is how it learns to understand them. Ostwald's theory of colour, which derived not from light itself but from mathematics, also seemed false to Kokoschka, who had constructed his own vision of space which had gradually broadened since his childhood into an apprehension of the world as a whole. The reason he appears in the centre of his pictures is therefore not vanity, but because the things he sees and paints are identified with him. Consequently he never believed in art theories. All his work was inspired by direct experience; none of it followed the modes of Paris or New York. He intensely disliked his work to be copied. His conception of spatial perspective had been hardly earned. He did not expect much of life, but something had to be done if you lost your balance completely and were unable to orientate. He suffered the same strange experience again when he was wounded in the head during the war. His sense of balance was upset for years because of an injury to his left ear.[28]

After the war Reinhold wanted to produce *The Burning Bush* in the Josefstadt Theater, but the police would not allow it. Kokoschka did not see him again for years, until they met by chance in London—he was always meeting acquaintances unexpectedly in foreign cities. At that time he was painting an unusual animal—a cross between a tiger and a lion —which had been given to the London zoo by a maharajah. The beast was fierce and wild. Kokoschka used to go to the zoo in the morning before the public were admitted. Although he hated the effort of getting up, he had to go before the animals were let out of their night cages. The keeper there was trusted so completely by the big cats that they would allow him to stroke them.

Kokoschka used to stand inside the barrier which kept the public from the bars of the cage, but at first he dared not do it with the tigon, although he wanted to be close, because he was short-sighted and the hissing cat excited him. The keeper used to wait for him to come before opening the cages, and allowed him to set up his easel inside the barrier. The first thing he heard was the sound of the beast's heavy breathing, and a pungent smell reached his nostrils. He told me that in the presence of unfettered power he would enjoy being torn to death. It had nothing to do with courage. He would be standing there waiting, his brushes in his hand, when it came thundering out of the darkness like an earthquake. It seemed immense, and Kokoschka, intense and alert, painted marvellously. He told me that he used to jump into freezing water as a young man to shock his system, and that kind of sensation was essential to him. He had to give it up, but sometimes he would hypnotize himself by staring for a long time into a light shining on water. In North Africa he took such heavy doses of amber that his heart beat like a drum.

Suddenly one day Reinhold appeared at the zoo when Kokoschka was painting. Since their last meeting in Vienna, Reinhold had gone to Munich, where he worked with Karl Eugen Neumann on a translation of the teachings of Buddha. When Neumann died he supported his widow for a long time, and helped to pay the cost of printing the translation, because it was not a popular work. Then he had been in a Tibetan monastery. He was travelling with a maharajah, he now explained, and was looking for authentic Sanskrit manuscripts.

Where are you staying? asked Kokoschka. At the Ritz. The Savoy had been Kokoschka's choice. Reinhold added: I arrived a few days ago with twenty suitcases. Kokoschka, laughing, said he had only six. But now they would go and eat at Abrahamson's Bar, where food was good and cheap. Looking at the tigon, Reinhold told Kokoschka: If that beast runs its claws down the length of the bars you are finished, along with your picture and easel. Kokoschka looked at the bars; they were indeed wide apart and he realized the danger. He went on painting, but outside the barrier, although it was not the same.

The relationship of the two men was always strained and slightly malevolent. The last time Kokoschka met him was also in London. Even in London he appeared eccentric, and his way of dressing and his behaviour always reminded Kokoschka of Hauff's story of the spurious Englishman who threw off his immaculate clothes one day to be revealed as a monster from the primeval forests. Reinhold's red hair had grown white in the interval, and he wore whiskers like those of an old English sailor. The two men went one morning to the famous Palm House at Kew; it was early, and they found it empty. They strolled up and down the alleys. Many of the trees were already so tall that you could see the glass cupola would soon have to be raised. Considering the Englishman's love of nature, and his extraordinary skill in raising plants and animals, it surprised Kokoschka that this famous botanical garden had such a neglected appearance, and the artificial, formal effect made him even more conscious of his isolation. But he was rewarded at last, and his curiosity aroused, by a Japanese miniature garden laid out on a table. It had streams and bridges in the foreground, leading from one pine-covered bank to the other, which rose in a rocky mound. Behind, in the distance, there were cliffs and shrubs, and the whole arrangement of artificial perspectives, paths, hills, and valleys completed the illusion of infinity, provided one was ready to be deceived. The English still measure the world in feet and inches, and judge the proportions of the universe only in relation to themselves, and climb up on this rope-ladder into space, like Baron Munchhausen on his own plait of hair.

Reinhold wondered why the place was so deserted, but Kokoschka's whole interest was bent on a miniature tunnel winding through the mountain. He wanted to see what there was beyond—to view the distant scene, another world. He wanted to be deceived.

Once your eye became accustomed to the dark you could feast your gaze on yet another landscape lying behind; there were alpine meadows gleaming in a ray of cleverly directed sunlight, and a waterfall that dripped slowly down into a soft damp valley, probably no bigger in reality than the kind of bird-bath you sometimes see hollowed from stones in churchyards. Here was all the freshness, the abundant foliage, which he had looked for in vain among the neglected giants of the Palm House. Kokoschka wanted to call his friend to show him his discovery, when he saw that he was sitting on a bench in keen and apparently frivolous conversation with an English nanny. The little girl in her charge, bored and forgotten, stood tracing patterns in the sand with her patent leather shoes. Then she lifted her arms above her head and spun round on her toes. The child was wearing a white and blue striped summer dress that stood out round her like the calyx of a flower (the flower, Queen of the Night, which used to open for a whole night once in the summer). The child looked at him with nut-brown shining eyes, and came trustingly to him with the poise possessed only by English children and asked what he was looking at. He had to lift her up a little so that she could see over the edge of the table and into the tunnel. He did it quite tenderly, for he could feel her ribs, with her heart beating like a little fish caught in a basket. He had once seen a play, though he could not remember where, in which by some trick the dancers on a darkened stage had seemed very small to the audience, no more than an inch or two high. Probably this picture, albeit unconsciously, was present in his mind when he lifted up the little girl. Why else should it reappear suddenly before his eyes?

He was not in the least surprised to see the valley, enchanting in its remoteness, peopled with figures which the child pointed out to him. Then, on the tiny Island of the Blessed stood the little girl herself, reminding him of a fairy ballet. But he had not even noticed that the child had slipped out of his arms until she called him with her cold, childish voice, apparently from the other side of the table. He glanced once more at the tiny charming figure in its white and blue dress, and ran round the table to the other side. The girl was not there, so he looked quickly through the tunnel again; nor there either. It must be hide-and-seek, a favourite game. Meanwhile, Reinhold, seeing him so indecisive, thought he wanted to leave, so he approached and looked at him with the same clear blue eyes as the last time in Vienna so many years before. Kokoschka could still hear his hoarse voice shouting 'Liar!' as he was running away from the Stefansplatz. But now, grown more cunning, he said with studied casualness: There seem to have been some visitors to the Palm House while I was looking at the Japanese landscape.

Of course, Reinhold answered as you would expect: I haven't seen anyone.

Kokoschka replied: Then you mean to say you didn't see a governess with a child? Today we have another of those electrically charged days, but in London!

They thought it better to go.

And the governess? You didn't kiss her really, you old woman-chaser? Perhaps it would be also wrong to say that he had seen the child, neglected by her governess, dancing for him alone in the tiny mountain landscape.

Let's go, he said roughly.[29]

Murder Hope of Women was dedicated to Adolf Loos, as *Dreaming Youths* had been to Gustav Klimt. Loos was Kokoschka's guardian angel throughout his early contests with the world, launching the boat of that rare genius into a sea which he knew would be lashed with passion, struggle, and poverty. And when there was shipwreck he always came to the rescue. It is not vouchsafed to many young artists, as it was to Kokoschka, to have the good fortune to be befriended by a man who believed in his powers before they were really mature, and who tried to shield him from the worst disasters. He advised, he led, he taught, he strengthened Kokoschka's self-confidence and gave him affection.

Kokoschka was not Loos's only fledgling: he also helped Schönberg and Peter Altenberg. He was a creative man, an *arbiter elegantiarum*—an innovator with a significant mind. Because she had consumption and he wanted to help her he married one of a group of English dancing girls—the Barison Sisters—and sent her at once to Switzerland. They came to Vienna to dance in the most elegant night-club of all, the *Casino de Paris*. And the others all married barons or bankers.

When Kokoschka lost his teaching post, Loos got him a commission from the host of the Griechenbeisl Inn, who collected pictures. He sent him to the best tailor in Vienna, whose shop he had built, to get his suits made. But, most important of all, he sent him abroad so that he could be unhampered and have wider opportunities of development. Speaking of Loos, Kokoschka says that he owes him everything. There in Vienna began a friendship which lasted for twenty years. Of course, Loos was very jealous, but he educated Kokoschka until he ran away.[30]

In 1924 they travelled together to Paris, where they had been offered the use of an empty house. They slept wrapped in blankets on bare boards—Loos, Kokoschka, and Sliwinsky—enjoying their absolute freedom. But not for long. Loos went home. Kokoschka could not stand it and moved to the Hôtel Foyot in the rue de Tournon, behind the Luxembourg Gardens.[31]

Loos gradually declined, both physically and mentally. He was suffering from an illness which destroyed many great men of the preceding generation. He quarrelled irreparably with Viennese society at that time, for reformers are never popular. He was accused of importuning children, and it was the three weeks spent under interrogation which drove him mad. He was acquitted; his kindness of heart, which led him to bring poor children to his home and give them a meal and a bath, had been misconstrued. Kokoschka saw him for the last time in Paris. His expression was like that of the mandrill Kokoschka had once painted in the zoo, and he was absolutely alone, isolated. He wanted Kokoschka to have dinner with him in the *Restaurant de Paris*, where lobster in red sauce was on the menu, but Kokoschka declined. Several days afterwards he visited Loos and found him in bed. He stared at Kokoschka for a long time and then said: Today we will eat together. Putting his hand under the horribly dirty sheet he drew out a huge lobster in tomato sauce. He sat up and swung it in the air.

Kokoschka saw the fever in his eyes, and his body through the torn, disarrayed pyjamas. That was the last time. The carpenter whom Loos had trained for many years, and who now worked for him if he ever had a commission, came to Paris to fetch him and to put him in a clinic in Vienna. He died there, never regaining his clarity of mind.

On the death of this strange man, a martyr to his art, Kokoschka gave a memorial speech.[32]

The commotion over the second *Kunstschau* made Kokoschka notorious. He was ferociously persecuted, by the *Neue Freie Presse* especially. Whatever form his subsequent work took, this paper attacked him viciously. Apparently it was not enough that he had been dismissed from the school, discharged from his teaching post, and driven away from the specialist courses. When he exhibited two years later in the Hagenbund[33], Franz Ferdinand, the Archduke, is reported to have stopped ostentatiously in front of his paintings and to have remarked: He ought to have every bone in his body broken. The manner of his treatment by the critics at the time gave rise to the expression 'the affair of Kokoschka', and he attracted as much attention as had Munch in Berlin. There were only one or two critics who could see potential greatness in the work of the 'Talented Terror', among them Ludwig Hevesy and Richard Muther.[34]

The *Neue Freie Presse* was a power in Vienna at the time—*the* power in fact. *Die Zeit*, edited by Hermann Bahr, and Karl Kraus's *Die Fackel*, were the representatives of a small group of intellectuals. The first was champion of the moderns, of Arthur Schnitzler, Richard Beer-Hoffman, Peter Altenberg, and Hugo von Hofmannsthal (Werfel did not come to Vienna until later); Kraus was an unrelentingly moral critic and the scourge of the war faction. Public opinion, however, was dictated by the *Neue Freie Presse*.

The revolutionary young artists had their stronghold in the cafés, and Adolf Loos was a regular customer in the Café Museum, where Kokoschka made his first appearance. The waiter was a good friend and a perceptive critic. An officer showing off would be treated with contempt, and when Kokoschka kept his hat on Fritz knew that he could not afford to order anything more than a glass of water. Kokoschka was living at Hernals then. Before the first war the Café Museum was frequented by many long-haired artists, among others Else Lasker-Schüler, and Mopp (the painter, Max Oppenheimer), who was from Bohemia like Karl Kraus. He wore a black suit, a black shirt, and gold braid. His principal ambition was to pass as a homosexual, although the fashionable triumph was to have a relationship with a married woman or a widow. Among the young people who still had to make their names were Alban Berg, the composer, the architect Josef Frank, Paul Zinner (Elizabeth Bergner's husband), young Socialists, and all kinds of others. Franz Lehar was one of the regulars, as was also the psychologist, Alfred Adler.

The youthful intelligentsia had adopted a firm stand in opposition to the operetta. Hermann Bahr wrote: 'In Europe everyone knows that it is always Sunday in Vienna, that the roast is forever turning on the spit. And, further, that it is the Capua of the intellect—one lives in a world of half-poetry which is very dangerous for the real thing. They can recognize a few waltzes by Lanner and Strauss—*Life Is a Dance, Happy to*

Be Alive, or even *Cheerful in Sorrow*. Probably they also know a few Viennese songs like *Der Wiener geht net unter*. It is a well-known fact that Vienna has the finest cakes, the smartest cabs, and the most cheerful, friendly people. . . . But those who are condemned to live here cannot understand all this.'[35]

Opposite the Hofburg was a café called *Grünsteidl* where Hofmannsthal, Hermann Bahr, and Schnitzler used to meet. When Bahr entered the whole café rose, an honour shared only by Victor Adler, the leader of the Socialist party. The Central Café—it later became the resort of chess-players—was frequented by the two friends, Altenberg and Kraus.[36] It was on the second floor and Altenberg used to say: I can't live unless I can breathe the air of the Semmering. Alfred Polgar put forward a fanciful theory: The Café Central lies below the Viennese Latitude on the meridian of solitude. . . . In that blessed room even the most immature person is credited with some talent. This strange coffee-house fulfils a need of the restless searching man, something that I can only call the 'cosmic disquiet'. He describes the literary and political currents which swept through it, closing with Hamsun's variation on Dante: All who leave bear its mark.[37] But between two and six in the morning the whole of Vienna met in the Café de l'Europe in the Stefansplatz.

All those who now live scattered about the world, however much they used to scoff and criticize, look back on the café life with nostalgia. Even a determined café-hater like Bruno Walter mellows: 'You have only to go once or twice to the same café for the waiter to recognize you and bring your favourite coffee—there were innumerable different kinds—and the newspaper for which you had asked on your first visit. Letters and messages could be addressed to coffee-houses. Events of cultural or historic importance, serious political and scientific discussions, took place there of course, and they were a hive of intrigue and endless gossip. . . . I think it would not be wrong to say that the period after the turn of the century till the outbreak of the first war in Austria was a time when conversation was on a very high cultural level. . . . The period of fine letter-writing, of sensitive and spirited literary confession was over, but conversation flowered. . . . When I think of the satirist Karl Kraus and his circle, of which the poet Alfred Polgar was an outstanding member, and of the exceptional poet Peter Altenberg and his friends in the Café Central, I have to admit the part played by the Viennese coffee-house in the stimulation of conversational genius.'[38]

Vienna was the most reactionary city in Europe at the time. Radical youth called it the voluptuous city of the Phaiakes. Public life, consisting of the Emperor, the Church, the Academy of Art, and the Burgtheater, was absolutely reactionary. The *Künstlerhaus* was a social club, but it had nothing to do with art. So the whole city attacked the *Kunstschau*, and with it Klimt and all his followers. Gustav Mahler was ignored. The members of the Vienna Workshops, Berthold Löffler, Franz Čižek, Alfred Roller, Kolo Moser, Larisch, and all the rest of the art-revolution were completely isolated. They were supported by Werdorfer, the millionaire, and they managed to survive, but interest in art was limited to the opera and the theatre. The tone was set by people like Mildenburg, Mittenwurzer, Sonnenthal and Kainz, and, of course, the elegant Girardi. Max Reinhardt and his magnificent naturalistic theatre came later. Moissi was a weak echo of Kainz copied by every shoemaker's apprentice. The Viennese had a musical tradition; Haydn, Mozart, Schubert, Beethoven, Bruckner, and Hugo Wolf were living names. Radical musicians were organized in the Conrad Ansorge Association, but Schönberg was not accepted. Every new idea had to fight its way forward, inch by inch. That was the reason for Bahr's complaint when he compared his own time with the great, cultural Austrian past of Walther von der Vogelweide and the medieval Court 'that flowered like the Court of King Arthur'. 'The Viennese', he said, 'have never tolerated a great man—neither Beethoven, nor Schreyvogel, nor Hebbel, nor Fischhof, nor Bruckner, nor Hugo Wolf, nor Waldmüller, nor Klimt, nor Burchkhard, nor Mach, nor Mahler, not one.' That was written before Kokoschka's impact on Viennese public life, but his name could well be added to Bahr's list. Bahr went on to ask: 'What will become of Vienna? Anything at all? Is there any future for the city? Any possibilities? To understand the Viennese it is necessary to realize the circumstances of Beethoven's death and how Grillparzer lived.' Bahr speaks of the profound Viennese stagnation: 'Nothing happens here, absolutely nothing. The boldest ideas and actions come to nought; they sink into oblivion.'[40] Such was the background against which Kokoschka's début has to be seen. He had to assert himself to avoid the death of oblivion, and he conquered where others had been forced to yield. One thing is certain: people were afraid of him. They even took seriously the rumoured joke that he was a man-eater.

Kokoschka both loved and hated Vienna, and his love-hate towards the city abides. One of its many causes was that both Mopp and Schiele copied him. Viennese art dealers remained passive, although abroad the pulse-rate of art rose high. The Impressionists had succeeded in the Berlin Secession, Edvard Munch independently. In the German theatre Otto Brahm was master and was the founder of German Naturalism. Every scene was handled with absolute faithfulness to nature. The great actors, Ritter, Wassermann, and Else Lehmann vividly mirrored the *bourgeois* situation of the period in the plays of Ibsen, Strindberg, and Gerhart Hauptmann. Josef Jarno staked everything on promoting Strindberg and became bankrupt. Reinhardt provided the new tendencies of Stanislavsky in Vienna with fresh romantic inspiration because Naturalism was already beginning to flag. When Hauptmann was famous in Germany he was laughed out of Vienna. Richard Dehmel was also successful in Germany; in fact, everything seemed to develop more easily there. In Vienna attempts were made to prevent Sigmund Freud from becoming a professor and the idealism of the workers' movement was denounced as 'Jewish'. Modern Austrian literature was even accused of having been bought by the chosen Association of Commercial Travellers. The Jewish element in Vienna was very active and radical, but that was general on the Continent. Anti-Semitism in Vienna was the equivalent of anti-progress, because revolutionary forces were seen behind every attempt at reform. Kokoschka always supported the Jews, and at one time they were almost his only friends because of their international outlook. But he believes that they should not have lost course after the frightful fate which befell them.

The Jews are denying their own tradition, he cried. *He* should lead the Jews; not because he wanted to lead anyone, but because they need a leader. The fools! What are they doing now? They are the only people who have no state and no natural frontiers, the only world citizens. Why don't they unite as stateless people? In the midst of the sadistic madness which brought six million Jews to their deaths Kokoschka warned: The future will only believe in those who suffered till they were only bare bones and raw flesh, and in the children.

Apart from the decadent and nihilistic side of political and social life in Vienna, there were, besides those already mentioned, valuable personalities, although isolated like oases in a desert; for example, Dvořák, Wickhoff, and Riegl, all art historians; Dilthey, the philosopher and sociologist; Freud and Adler, the psychologists; the historian and playwright Egon Fridell, and the writer Robert Musil. The *Salon* of Frau Dr Eugenie Schwarzwald, who had just opened a progressive school for girls and who was very active socially, attracted a circle of people who were of equal calibre with their opposite numbers abroad. Dr Schwarzwald had befriended the persecuted Kokoschka and engaged him to teach in her school for girls. Kokoschka taught his new method of seeing.[41] But officials had made a note of his name, and they now took the opportunity to crush Kokoschka and the all-too-progressive school with one blow. Kokoschka was forbidden to teach in Austrian schools at all.

One wonders what Vienna can mean to a man who experienced so many disappointments there. He turned his back on the city again and again, but he always returned. When he celebrated his fiftieth birthday in 1936, an exile in Prague, his friends in Vienna arranged an exhibition for the artist who had been lost to the country of his birth. Professor Carl Moll wrote in the foreword to the catalogue: 'Come and see the flower-garland we have woven from the seedlings you cherished. We send greetings and acclaim your work. Won't you declare yourself for Austria, for our common homeland?'

But what did Vienna mean to him in those early years when Kokoschka was still very young? He learned practically nothing in school, and therefore turned to the *Naturhistorisches Museum*, where the ethnographical section especially made a deep impression on him, and stirred his savage art from its sleep. The great respect which the public had for the Italian School made Kokoschka feel that he scarcely dared venture into the *Kunsthistorisches Museum*. That was only for connoisseurs. He felt happier in the natural history museum, where a marvellous world lay spread out before his eyes. There was also the suburban theatre, which the young boy sometimes visited with his parents. He had never seen a large stage before he went to the School of Arts and Crafts. The suburban theatre was really political, though the public probably did not notice it. Grumbling, and ridicule of the police, played a big part in Viennese life. The extempore acting of the folk players loomed larger than the leading article in the *Neue Freie Presse*. 'Have you seen So-and-so as the Chief of Police? You will laugh yourself silly.' In Vienna the folk theatre was still active, derived from the *Commedia dell'Arte*—the Italian Comedy which had enjoyed widespread popularity in former years. The German classical tradition after Goethe and Schiller, did not favour such a trend.

Raimund was greatly admired in Vienna both as an actor and as a poet who produced his own plays. The pieces Kokoschka saw as a boy were the successors of Nestroy and the Swabian, Benerle. Kasper had a cheeky way with him which allowed him to probe freely beneath the surface like a jester. It was a tradition with wide political connotations and it did not break down till after the first world war. In Leopoldstadt there was a Jewish theatre from the east. *Hamlet* and *Macbeth* were produced there in incredible burlesque. Hamlet would enter with a little walking-stick, like Chaplin, with a ball, a hat and dragging a toy ship along on a string. He repeated Hamlet's lines and then began to sing. These men, Chassidim, used a syncopated rhythm, something like jazz, and Kokoschka's early dramatic pieces had something of the same character. They were partly sung, partly spoken.

Were the museums and theatres the only things which meant anything to Kokoschka in Vienna? By no means; the young artist was fascinated by all those eccentric characters who lived on the fringes of society—Loos, Kraus, Altenberg, Schönberg, Anton von Webern; he painted their portraits. And there were the women, too. At that time, although he may have imagined it, Kokoschka had not experienced the heat and ashes of a great passion, with all the suffering, the doubts and emptiness that the sinking fire of love leaves behind.

NATURE MORTE

After the second *Kunstschau*, Kokoschka finished a work which reflects, more than the other early paintings, the atmosphere of those years and the youthful melancholy which is the sign of the creative man. The problems of existence loom over the young artist; icy solitude engulfs him. Will he be granted the strength to hold on, and to grasp the secret of life and death?

A whole procession of young artists springs to mind. Amiel of the *Journal Intime*, the young Flaubert of *Novembre*, Gerard de Nerval revealed in *Amélie*, Gide of the *Cahier d'André Walter*, the Goethe of *Werther*, Thomas Mann of *Tonio Kröger*, the Rilke of *Frühe Gedichte*, Hölderlin, and Keats. And if one remembers the self-portrait of the young Dürer with the thistle in the Louvre, or Edvard Munch's *The Dance of Life*, or the verses written on the days when death was fulfilment of desire and not merely a sacrifice to time:

> I wept to think of the care
> And sorrows of my lot;
> Not even death lights up my life,
> I hang like a sea-gull over the restless ocean.[1]

—then one thinks of Kokoschka's painting STILL LIFE WITH TORTOISE AND HYACINTH which he created at the age of twenty-three.

It is the masterpiece of a young artist in which he relates the mysteries of life and death through the problematical forms of nature—a white mouse with a pink tail and feet; a tortoise; an indian-red tomato, and the carcass of a sheep lying with bleeding head, its flesh coloured yellow, blue, and pink. An all-too-perceptible sickly scent emanates from the gleaming white hyacinth, because flowers smell sweetest when they are dying; their scent lingers over graves. The middle of the picture holds a jug, a homely object, forming the still centre of the composition, as if the artist had been thankful to find this simple thing with no aura of mystery. Everything else is a symbol of death.[2] The paint is thinly applied, the background formed by dark, merging tones of greyish-blue and violet. Behind the hyacinth is an icy blue. The paint on the carcass has been rubbed in, scraped off, and painted over again in layers of glazes. The effect is like mother-of-pearl, imparting a noble lustre to the picture. The over-ripe fruit in the foreground provides the strongest note of colour, contrasting with the frigid blue of the aquarium and the pink-toned salamander.

Kokoschka painted symbolically from the first. He always looked for life's deepest springs and tried to make the cosmic undertones of the visible world echo through his works. Hence he was familiar, even as a youth, with ancient wisdom, and became a master long before he dreamed of mastery.

STILL LIFE WITH TORTOISE AND HYACINTH has become a classic, hanging beside masterpieces of earlier times, mutely accepting its place in the halls of tradition. It displays the seriousness, the spontaneous ability of the Old Masters. The young painter has the eye of a Rembrandt for the miracle of light, and a profound sense of the symbolic meaning of colour. He paints the dereliction, resignation and conflict of the soul. The objects are taken from reality, but each one is chosen to express a primary idea or emotion. They are symbols, in the sense that the Cross, the Dragon, or the Tree of Life are symbols. In his echoing symphonic colour scheme the *vox coeli* rings above the sound of the organ.

The young Edvard Munch had likewise sensed the secret link between death and art. Suddenly, as it were overnight, it was made clear to him. Therefore, in a series called *The Frieze of Life*, he set himself to fulfil the task of art—to fashion the relationship between man and creation, to reveal something more profound than the reflection of things seen, or the ideas of his time.

Traditional still life exemplifies simply man's self-abandonment to his surroundings, whereas this painting, influenced by the Christian ideas of seventeenth- and eighteenth-century European art, is a *Vanitas*, a *Memento Mori*, in which death and mortality are uppermost. The subjects are caught in a *danse macabre*.

STILL LIFE WITH TORTOISE AND HYACINTH, however, is not merely the expression of Kokoschka's youthful melancholy. Kokoschka accused Hofmannsthal of living solely in the past, whereas he instinctively related everything to the present, the only palpable reality. Because he did not want to run away he endured great pain. He once said that one can recognize the period of a picture as easily as the date of a fossil. Hence, the STILL LIFE describes an age. The *fin-de-siècle* atmosphere at the turn of the century had been representative of an earlier generation. Modern man in the industrial age found himself suddenly uprooted; everything in which he believed was being called in question by changing values. But alteration in standards was only one symptom of a fundamental change in the mind of man. The sciences were developing with breath-taking speed; technology was rapidly changing the structure of society; politicians persuaded themselves that they were approaching an earthly paradise in which machines would take over man's burdens, never expecting that they would overpower him, nor attempting to understand the problem of leisure. Meanwhile, artists and intellectuals were obsessed by the decay of the soul.

Schopenhauer was a pessimist. His pessimism did not arise from the fear of infecting a deeply disturbed society but from his mistrust of human nature. The Greeks were also pessimists, because they distrusted the conception of *moira*—the total annihilation implied by human destiny and death. The writer of Ecclesiastes is pessimistic because he doubts man's ability to penetrate the secret of life and death, and because he suffers from the emptiness and nihilism which is the end of all activity. The *Epic of Gilgamesh* is pessimistic because it recognizes the helplessness of man and the mournful face of death revealed from the underworld. Kokoschka's early wretchedness and desolation was the melancholy and lonely lot of the modern intellectual, but he was not capable at first of carrying this resignation further. It was only later, when he sought to lighten the darkness because some explanation for the capricious nature of life as manifested by the war was essential, that he tried to separate the guilt of mankind from the profound will to live. Desolation was everywhere. He sensed it and portrayed it, thereby himself becoming part of the corruption. He had, in fact, accelerated its course, but he drew new power from the hotbed of decay. Kokoschka is the symbol of a transitory period; he sees the future uncoloured by the rosy spectacles of progressive thought. Sometimes he sees it as a new start, because that was how he experienced it. He told me that the despair which used to grip him would have killed a weaker man, but he had recognized the overwhelming transformation taking place, and felt himself more in sympathy with the cave-dwellers than with men dominated by machines. He admitted to being unable to handle a telephone, and made faces into the instrument so that his listener would not be hurt when he spoke through it.

The life of a work of art is reckoned in centuries, and is therefore not to be compared with the span of a man's life. Even if it was originally inspired by decadence it may yet play the role of a disturber of deep slumber.

The idea of decadence has fundamentally changed in the last decade. Nietzsche defined it as the critic opposed to creative man, the Christian contrasted with the Greek. We used to say that Jens Peter Jacobsen, Hermann Bang, Hofmannsthal, Oscar Wilde, Hermann Hesse of *Demian* and *Peter Camenzind*, and Hamsun of the *Mysteries*, were all decadent. Their decadence was a somewhat romantic, nostalgic boredom with existence, a distant echo of Byron's sense of melancholy described by Leopardi as the 'noblest emotion of mankind, not to be satisfied by any of the world's phenomena and therefore the most important sign of man's greatness'. Kierkegaard took fear and trembling as significant signs. After agnosticism and scepticism had destroyed his inner confidence man began to look for the source of greatness in sickness, unhappiness, and lunacy. 'All the noblest minds are unbalanced; only untalented mediocrities enjoy their lives', wrote Dostoievsky in *The Idiot*. Ugliness is described as beautiful because beauty has lost its spirit. Despite the fact that ugliness exists only in the mind of man—is only a way of looking, in Flaubert's phrase—as a measure of value it is negative; the atmosphere is one of corruption—apocalyptic and self-destroying. From here it is only a step to the intensification of the negative side of life, in which negation becomes an end in itself, taking on the character of absolute immutability. This is a potential revolt against the quintessence of life to which Kokoschka—unlike Kafka, Heidegger, and Sartre—never subscribed.

Kokoschka never really despaired, neither in life nor in art. When he came to analyse the melancholy neurosis of war he realized that it concealed a far deeper spiritual tragedy. The perplexity of our generation appeared to him as a crisis of the soul, and as a mutation in man's capacity to respond even in the thought-process, itself the product of the scientific mind. Now, like a doctor, he understood that his youthful sufferings had been a form of mental sickness and unbalance. The STILL LIFE of 1909 and the early portraits point directly to Kokoschka's criticism of the rational and mechanistic attitude which he believes to be the cause of our spiritual poverty and intellectual decline. The real danger always lies in man's notion of the world. This brain-child, tied as it is to its own age, becomes a cancer in proportion as it is deprived of life's riches. Hence the medieval vision of Paradise with the accompanying contempt for this world was as great a pitfall as the warlike, economic, utilitarian, and technological ethos of the present.

Kokoschka is a mystic, independent of saints and scientists. The true mystic, he once said, is much more of a scientist than today's scientists. The mystic concerns himself with the proper use of the mind, whereas the scientist applies his knowledge to sterile economic interests only. It is an attitude of mind which has robbed modern science of its freedom. Kokoschka finds psychology materialistic, although Freud is accepted because he is not only a rationalist but has all the other qualities besides without being aware of them, possibly even against his own will. Freud's Hungarian following— the *Imago* people—are malicious and make him ill. Jung is better, because his position is nearer to that of art and he understands formative processes. Adler, again, is too calculating. Modern psychology in general can tell us nothing that is new to the poet and artist; its associative methods are mechanical. One has only to think, on the other hand, of the complicated and quite different mental processes which inspired the Greeks. Their art was the child of pure experience, not a contrivance of the mind. However, it must not be considered as a formula, a method valid for all art, but as an aid to understanding, a spiritual attitude which allows one to reach out beyond the limitations of time. It is either a lifelong process or a spontaneous emotion lasting only a second or two. Everything outside it is temporal and measurable. For him time is contemptible, he has no use for it.

Kokoschka himself has no sense of time's passing, thinking of it in a dimensional way. The past lies behind. Emotional reaction inspires his vision of space. The former crystallizes his spiritual field, while space limits his physical range. Dimensions and visionary responses impel him to cling to his roots, to be at one with the life-force, as it must have been in ancient times. Our time-space structure cannot be more than five hundred years old.

Kokoschka sees two extremes: the creative spirit of art, of religious and artistic thinking, and the rational spirit of modern man, which works to a plan of cause and effect according to mathematical laws. The technological approach is universal; modern art would be unthinkable without it, and it has even infiltrated into language. Bodmer worked on a theory of the uniformity of language, including Chinese.[3] Obviously three thousand years of history meant nothing to him. The character, he thought, must be simplified and everything reduced to the absolutely basic, with basic English as a world language. Only the rulers were to be taught real English; for the rest, the basic idiom would be adequate. It was a completely ruthless plan for the vulgarization of the intellect

25 Dresden—Augustus Bridge with Steamer II, 1923

26 Lac Leman III, 1924

27 Karl Kraus II, 1925

28 The Painter and His Model I, 1922–3

and the further mechanization of life. Artificial insemination will surely become general, too; it is already practised by upper-class women, and if we can have a blood bank why not a semen bank? Some scientists have suggested an ideal language consisting of mathematical signs.[4] The brain is ruined by statistics; it can absorb nothing else. They govern our life. We are ruled by ciphers. Modern man has had enough of ideologies, and so he takes refuge in symbolism, only to find that he has jumped from the frying-pan into the fire. The consequence is that by employing logic the principle of cause and effect is used to link reality with an idea—in other words a symbol. Nowadays everyone suffers from these deceptive relationships, and from the distortions between reality and the ideal. Words are no substitute for art. A word is a symbol for a thing; it has nothing to do with the nature of art. A metaphysician today is a shadow without justification. What is art? Everyone knows the word *vitamin*, but no one knows its nature. Relativity, radio, penicillin, neutron—such is our language in which words have nothing whatever to do with the nature of the thing they represent. Space is an example; words render it flat. It is analogous to the medieval attempt to square the circle, for we no longer know what space is.

One can adopt a philosophical, literary, psychoanalytical, or sociological position, but none of it is essential to a knowledge of art. Negro tribes knew the principle of plastic art, but they never defined it because art was a language of seeing; they communicated what they saw. More than anything else, the world is frightened of seeing; it is surprising that labourers have not been blinded, for it is through the sight that true revolution is born.

Kokoschka often returned to this subject.

Protestantism, he thought, had finally succeeded in rationalizing the divine, while life had lost all its meaning. The first book on the education of princes was written by Quintilian—a primer for soap-box orators, explaining how mankind is to be indoctrinated.[5] Logic enables society to function on the basis of theories, and it is the oldest trick in the world for ruling people. Behind logic stand the police.

Science is logical, but wherever visual language is uppermost—in the relationship between the sexes and in festivities—there is life. One can only rule by disarming, and man is disarmed where he is robbed of his vision.

Kokoschka suggested that Renaissance perspective made its appearance at the same time as the rich bankers, and it was all part of an intellectual attitude. If once you begin to think in units of normality, like bankers, engineers, and scientists, if you can talk of normal vision, normal length, normal weight, what is happening to reality? Man has two eyes, not one, and two hands. The left hand is only clumsy because we are accustomed to think so. In a two-handed operation it has a separate function, making different movements from the right hand. It would doubtless please employers if both hands were the same, and could function equally, then they would have two automatons instead of one. It is the same with the eyes; they do not see equally. Whether he himself was short- or long-sighted or astigmatic was of no interest; he would never go to an optician schooled in normal vision. Kokoschka, who had been moving his eyes rapidly while he spoke, now shut them suddenly. He said they hurt, because they did not like being discussed. Then he added: Why shouldn't the opticians make men one-eyed?—they need not see more than a camera.

Kokoschka recognizes in symbolism an essential feature of the modern mass movement. He does not conceive the idea in the poetic sense of a Mallarmé, but uses it as a touch-stone of the times. We are living through a condition of profound symbolism which has developed out of the mathematical methods applied to life today whereby the structure of society is neatly pigeon-holed. A man is a number. Unless he has the right forms to obtain a ration-book he is not allowed to eat. This spirit invades the whole of life today. It is even found in biochemistry, in kinetic processes. The basic pattern of the attitude is a pragmatic symbolism. One thing represents another; man simplifies, generalizes, uses, forgetting that he is no longer in touch with reality. Numerals are only a means for measuring continuous processes and for counting mechanically the passage of time. Although scientists say this measurement of time is a fiction, yet numbers are exclusively used for it, and for almost everything else, hence the false sociology and the false econo-mics constructed from pure statistics. Primitive symbolism has become everyday currency. Mathematicians have invented coding systems for certain processes using colour. Weavers, dyers and seamstresses no longer need to use their eyes; whoever holds the key can order the colour. The chemist does not need his eyes, nor does the man actually using the colour. Symbolism is full of grand words, but man is being stripped of his pictorial imagination. A hundred years ago it would not have mattered, but today it threatens our very existence. Life has need of form, image, phenomena—not symbols. Symbolism needs only ideologies; the wisdom of peoples requires sensual images, a continuous development of the perceptive faculties. It is subject to change because it is a living process, whereas symbolism is sterile and dead. Scientific research into heredity serves to develop those characteristics which are most useful to political rulers. Everything that could direct or enrich the narrow path is destroyed. Culture, rich and many-sided, will be forced to give way.

Kokoschka thought the artistic crisis was reached when art took flight into its ivory tower. William Morris saw what was happening and, forewarned of the danger, turned back to folk culture. But he was too late, and his efforts deteriorated into the arts and crafts movement. The interest in primitive cultures—Tahiti, Bali, and the masks of Africa such as were seen in the *salons*—was typical of an uprooted society. Folk art was already condemned when museums began to collect it. Adolf Loos was a voice crying in the wilderness, for at that time classicism was a representational style imitating a foreign culture of the past. A great deal was said and written about culture as it is today, although scarcely anyone knew what it meant. Imperial Rome was classical because the Greeks had already been defeated; they painted as slaves in Pompeii or Alexandria. There was this difference, however: those Greeks were still capable of creation, and works of art were fashioned in a living tradition—a human world. Our world is not human.

The names of those slaves are unknown, though names are everything in modern art. Art in nineteenth-century France was classical; women were painted in their *boudoirs* in a kind of brown sauce. *Bourgeois* society withdrew behind its *portières*, and its women were pale and fragile. No one dared to display his wealth for fear of revolution. They retreated into solitary confinement with the mentality of the prisoner. Art was a prisoner, too; snuffling round a keyhole, it could only turn back to the past, to the cabinet of wax figures. A life was reconstructed with archaeological faithfulness that was no longer practicable. Then came the schools relying on optical science, the scientific conquest of light—the law of complementary colours had just been discovered—with its notion that seeing was purely an effect of the functioning of the optic nerve. Impressionism and *Pointillism* never understood three-dimensional space.

When he was in Paris, Kokoschka realized that art was on a false scent, and that was why he left.

If Renoir, as an old man, paints his country servant-girls or some fruit, he is expressing an elemental desire. The ancient Greek stirs once more, for the living urge is stronger than modern industry, and it was the primeval force which created the art of the people. But the uprooted cannot consciously turn back. Gauguin had tried when he could stand Europe no longer. Afterwards he became a misused symbol. Society played with the idea of the simple life, but Gauguin had Tahiti in his soul.

Kokoschka said he had never been tempted to run away from civilization. Fifty years after the death of Gauguin there are no longer any primitive peoples left in the world. Tourist agencies have seen to it that technical civilization has spread everywhere. Elderly American tourists wearing grass skirts and with flower garlands round their necks drink Coca-Cola. Kokoschka saw no refuge in flight to foreign countries; he escaped into himself. When Franz Josef celebrated his seventieth birthday he saw the fifty peoples of the monarchy dancing in their national costumes on the Ringstrasse in Vienna. It was an overwhelming expression of *joie de vivre*, like a waving cornfield threaded with poppies and cornflowers. That was the last time. Since then the people neither laugh nor sing. They go to factories where they hear music from a juke-box to the rhythm of their work. Their costumes are preserved in museums. Munch had understood. Kokoschka believed in his work, realizing that Munch was grieving over the sorrows of the time.

Though Kokoschka and Munch were temperamentally different and lived in a very different fashion, there was a definite link between them. Kokoschka continues where the other leaves off. They agree on fundamental issues—in their knowledge of death, and in the mythical slant of their philosophy. This is true of Munch, both in youth and old age, and of Kokoschka except during the prolonged travels which followed his Dresden period, and after the second world war. They have a common ambivalent attitude towards women; Kokoschka more so when he was a young man, but Munch always. They stood on the brink of the abyss that engulfed van Gogh. Munch was healed by contact with nature, Kokoschka by Greece. The nightmare faded; in Kokoschka's case it developed into a polemic against the obsession of modern man with economics, whereas Munch still believed that science and the industrial worker had a future. Kokoschka, like Munch, practised lithography because of its possibilities for spontaneous communication, and both artists were exceptional as portraitists and draughtsmen. Yet it is here that Kokoschka shows himself less harmonious; he represents the next stage in cultural decay. The cyclical nature of art, where one picture is inspired by another forming an intellectual whole, was a dominant feature of the work of Munch and Kokoschka alike. (The VIEWS OF CITIES, *The Daughters of the Covenant*, the *Concert*, the *Bach Cantata*.) Kokoschka also penetrated deeply under the surface. Humanism is the mainspring of both artists, and it is principally through their efforts that art has regained the position it occupied in the ages of great painting. Munch replaced the social narrative Realism of his time by intrinsic content. Kokoschka again took up a firm position against formalism from the beginning. The life-blood of modern painting has been draining away since the time of Delacroix. In his *Dehumanization of the Arts* José Ortega y Gasset wrote: 'The moderns maintain that humanism in art is taboo, but what does this antipathy mean? Is it a nausea produced by mankind as a whole, by reality, by life?'[6] Apollinaire, speaking of the Cubists, said that they approached their subject with a knife, like a surgeon.[7] Kokoschka believes Surrealism to have developed from an anxiety dream or a lewd play, while the School of Paris, with its concentration on abstract assemblages and calligraphic ornament, is either pure aesthetics or anarchy. There is no such thing as *poésie pure* nor poetry for its own sake such as would have delighted the Abbé de Brémont;[8] it would be quite inhuman. Form without a response somewhere in the human heart does not exist, neither in space nor time, whatever Henri Focillan tried to prove.[9] He was but a faint echo of Platonic and Kantian ideas.

When Kokoschka was first confronted with Cubism—in 1910, when he was in Berlin—he said at once that to have to paint to a system or a theory was tedious; even if the *avant-garde* did it, such rebellious pride only won a Pyrrhic victory. In every fibre of his being Kokoschka felt the disappearance of the world of universal images which counteracted the synthetic spirit that is widespread today. Even the Impressionists, he thought, had a synthetic philosophy because the laws explaining optical processes are synthetic. Kokoschka believes that one should dive head first into life, not creep around. He doubted the validity of the doctrine of *en plein air* and *sur le sujet*. It means that one took a doll out into the open and painted it. If mankind is natural, what is natural about these paintings? Behind the pathos of Seurat Kokoschka could see tragedy, because the universality, the wholeness of life was lost. He himself would never be able to earn his living as a professional painter, because such empty uninspired work did not concern him. That was why he never achieved a slow and cumulative success, since he was dependent on something not under his control, and the reason he spent his life painting was that only thus was he surrounded by Being in real and tangible forms. He could find a palpable image in painting. The Expressionist reaction to Impressionism was an attempt to cleave to essential values, like a cry in the night: 'I cannot cope with the world around me. Give me back the old reality, or I shall die.'

Art dealers in France ignored Expressionism until it began to 'pay', after which it was copied there also. Refinement of taste was the Englishman's refuge. After mature consideration he retreated into the world of Botticelli. The pre-Raphaelites set the tone. They were rich upper-class painters, and the rich are always aesthetes. There was no response in America, because it is a country without tradition, except from the rich *bourgeoisie* to whom art-collecting is essentially *le bon ton*. 'We buy Rembrandts and the Flemish masters. Conscious of our status, our experts are sent to Europe to give the paintings the ever-increasing value worthy of our collections.' That is aesthetics, too.

The Expressionist's call became the rallying-cry of a whole generation with the vigour to mould their vision.

Kokoschka explained to me that he might grumble today where he had been wont to praise, but that these were mere words, depending on how he felt at the time. Nevertheless, some things he had always loved, others he could not even look at, and the School of Paris left him cold. At the *Kunstschau* of 1909 French painting had not attracted him, because it was too decorative. That year the Stadtpark had been replanted; it was warm early summer, and you could almost see the tulips growing. They had pleased him more than the paintings. Van Gogh was different. The sunflowers were miraculous, and it was understandable that he attracted the *bourgeoisie*, for they shunned the sun and their women used sunshades. He even attracted workers, who hardly ever saw the sun. Kokoschka realized that van Gogh was a sun-worshipper. In Vienna he was in love with Japanese prints. Rembrandt's etchings inspired Hokusai who was the first Asian to experiment with Western perspective. His inquiring mind discovered Europe, just as the West discovered Asia.

Kokoschka's philosophy explains his attitude to modern art. He has no use for abstraction whatsoever, and post-Impressionism also leaves him indifferent. Sometimes he has preferred Gauguin to van Gogh. Then *Noa Noa* seems more significant than a picture by the Dutchman which he much praised only because van Gogh was mad. Van Gogh's painting of the *Woman of Arles* leaves him unmoved, for it might have been Sharaku, but Japanese foreshortening he has always admired, and he is enthusiastic about the way in which they master it. He accepted Japanese art instinctively, even as a young man. He placed Seurat among the great artists of the nineteenth century—a painter with the vision of the ancient Greeks. Any side of contemporary art which can be claimed as a sentinel for Greek humanism finds favour in his eyes.

Kokoschka is prepared to accept anything in the art of former years except the High Renaissance, which he finds too academic. Hence the Hellenistic *Laocöon* means very little to him, and Roman art—except the portraits—and architecture he likewise spurns. On the other hand, he has been inspired by the art of the catacombs and of North Africa because it is primitive and autochthonous. He despises Pompeian art, and 'school' art of any kind or period. Late Gothic—that mixture of Gothic and Renaissance motifs—is also anathema.

Now and then Kokoschka would talk of individual artists, admitting that he could passionately dislike an artist and yet later recognize a quality in the same man that appealed to him. The one consideration: he must not leave him indifferent. I have heard him mocking Cranach's naked Protestant Fräuleins, but admiring the same artist's portrait of *Anne of Cleves* and the *Red Cardinal* because he found them genuine.

Once again we are confronted with the contrast between Gothic and Renaissance. In

London's National Gallery there is one picture which stirs him deeply—it is Roger van der Weyden's *Madonna* and it has a quite mysterious *horror vacui*. It is a mystical response to space in which every corner is filled, with no place for the eye to rest, and it is placed beneath a house which is as academic and empty as a Raphael. Kokoschka avoids discussing Raphael, and yet there is the portrait of Baldassare Castiglione, in his opinion one of the finest pictures in the world.

When I asked him why he drew these sharp dividing lines he replied that it was because the paintings which inspired him had an inner life. Modern art seemed to him too formal and too deliberate, hence he never had any sympathy with it.

Once he talked of Leonardo's colour, which he finds quite impersonal except in the portrait of the Lady with the Ermine, when Leonardo suddenly becomes Gothic. The white, the frozen white of the ermine, is poignant, expressive. He generally finds the colours of the Italians too sweet and syrupy in comparison with Grünewald's disquieting red, green, and blue.

When Kokoschka spoke like that he was thinking, he said, not so much of the painter, but of his effect on the mind. As a young man he had been deeply impressed by Dürer, especially the silver-point drawings and the *Nativity* in Munich. But the *Self-portrait* of 1500, in which you can count every hair in the beard, had frightened him. He felt that he wanted to go and see the *Apostles* every day, and the water-colours done on the Italian journey. What a magnificent mountain landscape! Suddenly the mathematical perspective of the Italians lost its hold; perspective had killed the originality of his vision. Elsheimer was one of Kokoschka's favourites among the old masters, but every year he had a new favourite, discovering a quality he had not seen before.[10]

Kokoschka's attitude to art is like other people's attitude to society. He is pleased if he gets to know someone new; it refreshes him because he needs human company. But works of art are the company which makes him really happy. He believes in the immortality of great works of art, in which every generation discovers something new.

It is remarkable that the language of literature grows pale, probably because words change their meaning. Kokoschka, therefore, always returned to his proven loves—the mystics during the war, and later the Greek tragedians, and Homer and Herodotus. The Greeks and the mystics were always intelligible to him, although some of the others were incomprehensible however hard he tried. He could understand some parts of Shakespeare only with great effort and by studying the period first. On the other hand, he saw himself mirrored in a Chinese poem of three thousand years ago in which time played no part. The simplicity of such poems shines like a sunbeam. Even Goethe contained many references which were beyond him, and he thought it was because words had lost their value. The language of painting and drawing is more stable. Language is comparable with money, with a coin which is worn. That was the reason why he liked authors who were never common currency—the *Heliand*, for instance. If that poem is to have its effect it must be read on a fine, clear day with a fine, clear conscience. Who cares where the poet lived? That he was inspired by the breath of life is all, for if the writers—the vehicle—become too important, literature itself fades. The Greek gods were great because they were human creations. They are like the great figures of the Bible who immortalize the face of humanity, the face seen by the ancients for the first time. The figures of the Bible are inexhaustible like a fruitful woman. Kokoschka painted many of them: Jacob, Leah, Rachel, Lot and his daughters, Saul, and David.

During the war Kokoschka was preoccupied with the works of Heinrich von Kleist. Hölderlin was a pure romantic, but Kleist traced and resolved human problems. Michael Kohlhaas, for example, represented a champion of justice in a period of the greatest injustice. Kokoschka regarded Kleist as the last great architect of words, whose dramas are a brilliant cascade. In *Amphitryon* Kleist handled the theme of man's liberty. He tossed it into the air, and it burst in a blaze of light like a comet. The nature of God is the aspiration of the mind.[11] In comparison with Kleist, Kokoschka thinks Molierè's handling of *Amphitryon* purely formal, and Giraudoux in his opinion turned the whole thing into a joke.

One day Kokoschka criticized the general acquiescence in the supremacy of French culture. Everything pointed to the fact that it was no longer valid. The French take even their scepticism seriously now, and probably they will soon start to believe in the Café du Dôme as well. Kokoschka likes Cocteau, and rates *Les Enfants Terribles* among the best of modern books. Proust, too, although the work, in his opinion, tails off. One thing Kokoschka said he could not understand was the theory that a man could only begin to write when he had nothing more to expect from life. For this reason he preferred Gide, but also because he was a European. Kokoschka believes him to be one of the few present-day thinkers, and yet he, too, is a voice crying in the wilderness. He finds it surprising that no single party has tried to destroy him. Kokoschka said: Now that the size of a bomb is the measure of a nation's genius, when might is right, it follows logically that a sword held over the head is the only argument of any importance in the war of ideas.

Céline's *Voyage au Bout de la Nuit*, typifying the despair of the learned, is very moving and more gloomy even than Zola's *L'Assommoir* and Huysmans' *A Rebours*. Ibsen forecast the development of modern man in *Peer Gynt* sixty years ago, describing a young man of courage and imagination who loses his soul and becomes a heartless exploiter. Modern man knows nothing of the soul. That was the reason why Kokoschka loved Cheltschický, who depicts the anarchic revolt of the individual against the superstition of the State. His valuable book, *Das Netz des wahren Glaubens*, was banned in the time of Beneš, and remains banned.[12] And Hamsun's *Pan* he cited as among the most beautiful pieces ever written. Yet such a man can be attacked for his political view, which is ridiculous—for what can it have to do with his greatness? He ranks among the very few. . . .

These fragments contain the gist of Kokoschka's ideas on art and literature. They are woven from conversations spread over more than twenty years. In recording them I have made no attempt to achieve finality, only to light in flashes the broad sweep of his mind and to silhouette the impetus of his inner driving force.

He once told me that art was his world where he loved to walk. He has only to see a small medieval painting to be happy over it for a whole year. He can keep looking at it over and over again without needing human companionship. Whatever the cannibalism of the world, life flows through the artist as sap through grass.

Kokoschka did other still-life paintings apart from the one with the sheep. There is a very early one with a pineapple. Another of fruit, in a broad style, is thought by Berthold Löffler, his teacher, to have been painted about 1907. The later painting with a cat, sheep, hare, and fish, and another with a *putto*, live rabbit, and a cat, have the same allegorical significance which determine their content and composition, as with the STILL LIFE of 1909. However, although these two are painted in a different style from the old-master realism of the STILL LIFE WITH TORTOISE AND HYACINTH, and are indeed Expressionist in the sense that the broad and rapid brushwork suggests the inner excitement of the artist, they must nevertheless be considered together. They display the artist's developing technique as well as the integrity of his personality: the cat in the centre, with its human expression (it has the features of a woman who played an important part in Kokoschka's life at the time—the same face appears in early paintings and drawings); the rabbit above; in the left-hand corner the small Baroque gnome, and in the distance, on the right, a figure representing Charon pushing a small boat off into the unknown. The painting contained the elements of a nightmare that had to be thrown off—the boat setting off into space, the gnome (a funny little lost earthling), a small magician escaping from certain sexual danger. The cat (the *femme fatale*), and the doomed rabbit, are the principal motifs of the painting.

Nature morte as an expressive form was thus broadened and revitalized by elements which belonged to both landscape painting and figure composition, as Kokoschka's later landscapes and free compositions are similarly often filled with the dynamic spirit of the STILL LIFE.

These paintings are the work of a man who is passionately moved and hence indifferent to his medium, be it still life, landscape, or figure composition. The frontiers retreat; apprehension of the supernatural is all—that supernatural quality described by Flaubert which always appears at the beginning and the end of the artistic life of a people. 'Two mysterious ghostly figures attend the cradle and the grave.'[13]

Kokoschka is the last painter who has occupied himself with the world of man. Modern painters may know more about the cosmos, but he thinks that mankind cannot be ignored in art, science, or politics as is the fashion today. Kokoschka closes a period of European culture which will one day be considered a byword for mythical universalism. Nothing in the art of the period was achieved without deep realization of the eternal. All that came afterwards was different.

VIII

NEW HORIZONS

During the winter of 1909 Adolf Loos took a decisive step for the young artist's career. They went to Switzerland, to a village near Montreux where Loos's wife Bessie had been living in a clinic for some time. Leysin housed some fashionable patients and Loos felt that Kokoschka could make a name for himself there and develop his skill as a portraitist. Kokoschka's mother was anxious about her son; the 'lad' had never been abroad and in Vienna he at least got something to eat. She tried to persuade Loos to give up the plan. Only she knew how uncontrollable her peculiarly gifted son could be—how he used to wander off after a military band, then hang about with no food, and come home hungry late at night. However, Loos persuaded her that he was a man of the world and would be going with the boy. So the expectant but anxious youth received a gold coin from his mother as a reserve and set off with a small suitcase and his box of paints.

Many artists have described the majestic effect of high mountains—Leonardo, Dürer, Hodler, and Corinth. Kokoschka, too, was overwhelmed by his first encounter. The narrow valley of Leysin, ringed by mighty glaciers and mountain peaks, was populated by few people, like insects among giants beneath a cold sky. Kokoschka's standards unconsciously changed; something far older and more significant than man was revealed to him. But he was not yet ready; finding the chief theme of his art in the inner life of man for many years to come. At last, in 1924, the nightmare through which the works of this first important period had been created ended, and in new-found freedom he discovered the beauty of the mountains and the lakes, and perceived human greatness in architecture worthy to rank with the first dramatic impression made by the mountains. It was a momentous event in his life, changing him into the finest landscape painter of his time. He was confronted with creation without human intervention, and it worked like a catalyst, breaking up the flow of ancient timeless intuition within the compass of a small space to create magnificent paintings, immortal work, and a cosmic symphony of permanent greatness. These paintings contrast vividly with the experience of those others of his generation, whose hearts Kokoschka laid bare in his early portraits of them.

He was deeply disturbed and horrified to perceive the deathly sickness that had overtaken modern man. He suddenly understood the Biedermeier period, and the tragedy of his father's life rooted in the happenings of the time. His father had been a pupil of Zauner, the Tyrolese sculptor of statuettes. His father's destiny was related to that of his contemporaries, and it was this recognition of a lost generation that made Kokoschka the greatest portrait painter of the age, and linked him with Dürer, who was also engrossed by the introspective portrait. To Kokoschka's response to the Alpine landscape was added another primary emotion—that of love. His suffering and savouring of the paradox, man and woman, two eternally attractive, eternally opposing forces, transformed him into a great mythical painter. Art's jealousy of life; sex and the creative spirit; maternity —Eve and Circe; Pandora and Demeter, the Sphinx; the *femme fatale* of Felicien Rops, Strindberg, Nietzsche, Munch, Weininger, and Wedekind; and the *leit-motif* of the goddess—Maria, Gretchen, Beatrice, Solveig. Another decisive experience was won by his conscious experience of the mystery of death (his body bleeding on the battlefield while his soul triumphed over the physical condition to which his insatiable thirst for knowledge had driven him); the insight gained by the need to unveil the mystery—the mystic trinity of birth, reproduction, and death—was the act of a man who denied his ego to become a witness of creation. Whatever the events of Kokoschka's life, however he paints, thinks, or writes, his inspiration is drawn from this threefold source and can only be understood by it.

Loos brought Kokoschka to the sanatorium in Leysin where his wife was being treated. He arranged that the young artist should stay there on *demi-pension*, which meant only one meal a day, but it was expensive, and Loos received very few architectural commissions at the time. Nor had Kokoschka a dinner-jacket, an essential adjunct to the evening meal. So the next day Loos left Kokoschka alone in the elegant foreign clinic filled with the smell of death.

His first Swiss painting was VUE SUR LA DENT DU MIDI, one of his important early landscapes. The artist's responses and method of configuration are illuminated by the circumstances of this picture: 'On the station in Vienna were large photographs of the Alps, the mountain-railway, huts, and snow. I had studied them carefully, but when I saw the Dent du Midi in reality I did not recognize it. There was an immense, profound space which was completely lost on the photograph. You never get that impression in a photograph; it belongs to man's vision. After Loos had left I became especially aware of it, for I was afraid to be alone. I looked out of the attic window to the ground. I can still see the scene today—the waiting sledges, with horses blowing steam from their nostrils. Loos turns and looks up, but I am too far away to see his expressive, penetrating gaze. Yet only a few minutes ago he was here in the room, and now I hear the crack of the whip and the sledge pulls away gradually becoming smaller and smaller. Its path snakes through the landscape; the sleigh-bells are almost out of earshot. At last it disappears in clouds of powdery glittering snow. But Loos stood clearer than ever before in my inner eye. What happens to a mental picture when the optical vision which excites it fades? The problem, that will remain always in my mind, of something simply vanishing, loomed between me and the Dent du Midi. I had to resolve the balance between the interior and the exterior world, to harmonize the reflective spirit with tangible reality. That is why I painted the picture, and in it the space has a spiritual significance. Baroque is similar. The painting is not a composition. It was a task which had to be done, and when I had finished it my anxiety diminished.'[1]

Kokoschka's response to Loos's departure produced the inner image which supersedes reality. It is the mark of the Expressionist artist. The excitement of the past, the ambivalent and tragic character of existence, arouses a world within him which becomes more real than reality. This lack of balance between vision and the visible, this unclassical element, is one of the most significant marks of Expressionism. But there is another, equally important—the artist's urge to crystallize his vision, because it concerns him closely, and because the vision, the dream, and the psyche are more important to him than objective reality. This is especially noticeable when reality is out of joint, or in the case of the unstable, emotional state of mind in an almost completely untried boy.

Kokoschka's winterlandscape may be compared with Dürer's *View of Trient* and the *Nürnberg from the West*, both *circa* 1496. Dürer was two years older than Kokoschka when he set out on his Venetian journey. 'His was a marvellous vision of Trient', writes Wölfflin in his study of the great artist. 'No other German painter could have been entrusted with this magnificent scene. The mass of the sky, the mountain-range, the river, the simplicity of detail, and his response to depth and space. Foreground and background call to each other, like a voice and its echo. . . . It is most clearly apparent in several landscapes done by Dürer from the Brenner Pass.'[2] His way of circling the focal point of the scene is also characteristic of Kokoschka.

Without technique, because he had not yet acquired it, Kokoschka created from his emotional inspiration and understanding, just as had been the case with the portraits, producing moving, prophetic, and revealing pictures which were both subtle and primitive.

Kokoschka's experience in Leysin was a kind of 'Magic Mountain'. He painted pretty little Bessie Loos, who presented him to the Duchess and the Count Montesquieu-Rohan, whose portraits he also painted. Everybody there suffered from tuberculosis. The Count was very effeminate. His yellow face above the high, stiff collar made him look like a waxwork. The portrait of the Count of Verona also dates from this period.

Bessie Loos was supposed to rest in her room, but at night she used to climb out of the window and go dancing in the village. She died when Kokoschka was living in Berlin.

Our young Candide left after he had completed his portraits, and went to stay at Clarens, near Vevey, with a friend of Loos. On the day he left it was freezing after a heavy snowfall. His sense of isolation was slightly relieved by the gold coin tied in the corner of his handkerchief, but when he pulled out the handkerchief the coin dropped, sinking at once into the snow. He hunted desperately for it, but the train was due at any minute. Everyone helped him, but they only succeeded in treading down the snow, and there was even less chance of finding it. He stood there penniless. One of the bystanders bought him a ticket, and he boarded the train.

Lack of experience brought me a lot of trouble, Kokoschka told me. The woman I was going to paint was a disciple of Rudolf Steiner, and I was uneasy from the moment of arrival. I was at the mercy of others because I always had to think of money. The house was surrounded by police, who were supposed to be protecting the mother and son from the father, who was threatening to kidnap the child. It had something to do with an inheritance, or his education, I forget exactly which. One thing, though, I remember clearly: the husband had been in prison for assaulting children and had only just been released.

Kokoschka had been taken down into a room like a candy-box. It was decorated with gold and silver—Steiner's symbolism of the sun and the moon. The woman gave him almost nothing but lentils to eat, because she thought they would excite the shy young man. Like Potiphar's wife, she forced herself on him, but what could he do? The portrait was begun, and if she came too close he could only defend himself with the Prussian blue with which he smeared his fingers. Things continued like this for a time, but suddenly he could stand it no longer. Slipping unseen to the post, he telegraphed to Loos for money. The cost of the telegraph, incidentally, Loos had to pay. Loos sent the money— and Bessie—to his rescue. For that alone Kokoschka was grateful to her, and never forgot. So he returned to Leysin, and the unfinished picture (Kokoschka left it behind) was sold by auction in 1963 by one of the woman's descendants.[3]

One day Kokoschka heard a noise in front of the sanatorium—doors banging and people running to and fro. He looked out of the window, and there stood the woman from Vevey in feather-hat, riding-habit, and carrying a whip. She wanted to punish him, and drag him back to finish the picture. The young painter was terrified and hid, while Bessie and the others managed to persuade the Amazon to go home.

During the stay in Clarens, 'one day in early Spring, when the sun was glistening on the snow and the glittering lake lay still as glass, I saw a little girl on the wall. She was about fifteen, and was lying enjoying the sun. She looked at me through her lashes long and strangely. A fig tree was nearby, and the whole scene was like a fairy-tale. So I asked her name. It was Virginia. It took me a long time to realize that anyone could be called Virginia. I shall never forget. Later in Berlin, during my hunger-euphoria in the editor's room of *Der Sturm*, she became my dream-child, the creation of my loins whom I sought to protect from all earthly ills.'[4]

Adolf Loos sent Kokoschka to Switzerland again in 1910. This journey was financed through the agency of Loos by Herr von Ficker, whose portrait Kokoschka was to paint on his return. But first he was to paint Auguste Forel. Loos had urged him: Paint this great scientist, and then his portrait will be there for posterity when you are both dead and gone. So Kokoschka went to the Rhône Valley, where Forel lived in a small village near Aigle. 'We only met in the evenings when his work was over. His first words on meeting were: You realize I shall not buy the picture? I replied: I am painting the picture for Herr Loos who has commissioned it. This caused a certain coolness between us which was in no way lessened by the fact that during the whole of my stay there— two or three weeks—we had no kind of social contact. Of course it was difficult, for I did not know much French. He was not in the least interested in painting—hardly uttered a word the whole time, and made no effort to help me at all. Only loyalty to Loos kept me working. Every evening Forel carefully weighed out nuts and apple peel, which he solemnly ate. At last he had finished, and sat down. Can you see all right? or Does it matter if I go to sleep? was all he ever said to me. And sometimes he did indeed nod off. Then I could really study the way he sat in his chair, and see how the wrinkles on his face increased and deepened. Suddenly he seemed ancient. Myriads of small wrinkles appeared, like the documents of a man's life, and I felt that I must record them all, decipher them like old parchment and hand them on to posterity. His face, and especially his hands, fascinated me. His fame meant nothing to me, but the task set by Loos filled my mind.'

Forel's old eyelids stirred slowly and a glassy white eye peered out as if from another world towards the young man whose presence seemed to puzzle him. 'The eye grew clearer. I searched it profoundly, for it was the eye of a seeker wont to see beyond the appearance of things. It was the window of a brain whose intelligence I was trying to portray. My biggest problem was how to reproduce the scholar's knowledge when I myself was so ignorant. How to depict it for posterity? I had never read any of his work, and therefore had no idea what his interests were. His wife, who was an old lady, and his daughter, were often present at the sittings, and they would talk while I painted. Their conversations repelled me. I gradually realized that these people were discussing family affairs before me, a stranger, and were gossiping about relations. "He has accepted the woman, then?" "Yes. The family is founded, but there were disagreements, violent quarrels." I went on painting with set face. I was the unwilling witness of secrets of family life that I did not want to know. Strange problems of marriage and procreation were unrolled before my eyes. It was only at the very end of my stay, when the picture was finished, that I realized that they had been discussing ants. All three were biologists working together on the life of the ant. The portrait was sold by Loos to the Folkwang Museum in Essen, and it was the first picture there to represent the younger generation. Another thing I realized at the end of my stay was that Forel had never heard of Loos. He was so absorbed in his work that he accepted an invitation from someone he did not even know.'[5]

On his return to Vienna, after his stay with the Forels, Kokoschka was more than ever aware of the unfavourable atmosphere of his native city. Nevertheless, he continued to paint, mostly portraits, but left the capital after two months with the intention of staying abroad for good, although he did return to Vienna in the spring of 1911.[6] The hostility there had become very bitter, and after the first world war Kokoschka made his home in Germany, thence travelling extensively all over Europe. Later, the political events which led to the second world war brought him back to Vienna for a slightly longer period.

A short stay in Munich, and an even briefer one in Vienna, preceded his journey to Berlin in 1910. The capital city was as significant for Kokoschka's career as it had been for Munch's. Berlin had been growing ever since the victorious war of 1870 and it was a focal point for the arts. Other cities in Germany might actively try to develop their own regional artistic characteristics, but it was every artist's ambition to have exhibited in Berlin; every playwright sought to have his work produced on its stage, and every composer dreamed of conducting his own music there.

Munch had fired the first shot in the battle against academic art with his *Frieze of*

Life, exhibited at the request of the Society of Berlin Artists. That was in 1892. Under protest the exhibition was closed almost as soon as it opened. After this Munch showed his paintings through dealers, but the younger generation, led by Liebermann, took the opportunity offered by the Munch affair to found the Berlin Secession with progressive members of the Society. It represented the victory of French Impressionism, but certainly not that of Expressionism in the manner of Munch. That was to come later, when an *avant garde* splinter-group broke away to found the New Secession.

The intellectual atmosphere in Berlin on Kokoschka's arrival was much the same as it had been in Munch's day. Dehmel then was only beginning, whereas now he was at the height of his productive power. In the field of drama Ibsen and Strindberg were matched by Hauptmann and Wedekind, Tolstoy and Wilde, and later also by Gorki. The magnets of intellectual life were Maximilian Harden's *Freie Bühne*, Herwarth Walden's *Sturm*, Peter Hille's bohemian life, Zille's social satire, the *Volksbühne* inspiring its audience with socialist ideas, Futurists, and members of the two artistic groups, the *Blaue Reiter* (founded in 1911 in Munich), and the *Brücke*, founded in 1905 in Dresden and moved to Berlin in 1908, and finally the Café Grössenwahn with its Berlin bohemians who were far more bohemian than those of Paris. Pathological eroticism, nudism, Buddhism, psychoanalysis, anarchy, and revolution filled their minds. They were vegetarians, apostles of the people, pacifists, pan-Europeans, and popular scientists. Berlin was a breeding-ground for international ideas. All the night-clubs seethed with German Oblomovs and Johann Nagels; there were Rimbauds of Elbflorenz, Verlaines from the banks of the Spree, Ssanins and Chichikovs. Bakunin's ideas were cleverly twisted to fit those of Marx and Engels. One could be a peasant with Till Eulenspiegel, decadent with Nils Lyhne, or an imitator of Gauguin's Primitivism in Tahiti. All this went on under the watchful eye of Prussian militarism, and the Junkers, those granite pillars of Prussia, allowed French Symbolism, the Russian religious-revolutionary novel, and the Scandinavian drama of social criticism freedom to develop so long as they avoided politics. This artistic freedom, limited as it was, was the difference between Berlin and Vienna.

That short-lived artistic flowering in Berlin is of special interest today after the outbreak of Satanism and the second world war. It is almost as though there were some connexion between these two phenomena—the feverish haste of that cultural period and aggressive nationalism. It is therefore necessary to seek an explanation from the years which had gone before. When the German writer, Conrad, encountered Zola in the 'seventies he realized the stagnant condition of German literature. No German writer had European significance. Conrad looked in vain for a 'problem of universal interest', and for a writer with an original mind or a subtle technique. Against Turgenev, Dostoievski, Tolstoy and Gorki, Björnson and Ibsen, Hamsun and Strindberg—against Balzac, Flaubert, Zola, Stendhal, and the Goncourts—Germany could counter only with Dahn, Heyse, Freytag, and Spielhagen. Even Fontane and Keller 'only seemed worthwhile because they represented an excellent type of solid German homely reading'. Naturalism ran its course, but it really did not alter anything. Germans looked across the frontiers for inspiration, and names like Conradi, Hart, Sudermann, Wassermann and Bölsche had very little to offer the world. Painters, such as Stuck in Munich and Slevogt in Berlin, were scarcely known in international circles. Hence, however much Berlin may have acted as a hot-bed for a Munch or a Kokoschka, it was nevertheless these two painters in addition to van Gogh, Gauguin, the Fauves, and the discovery of primitive art, who decisively influenced German Expressionism. Liebermann, Beckmann and Klee are inconceivable without the French School. There were no German painters of international standing at that time, and it was only much later that Klee, Beckmann, and the Bauhaus were recognized abroad.

There was no German novel to rank with *Le Rouge et le Noir*, *War and Peace*, *The Brothers Karamazov*, *Hunger*, and *Within a Budding Grove*; no German poet with the mastery of a Rimbaud or a Mallarmé; no German essayist worthy of comparison with Taine, Saint-Beuve, Léon Bloy, or Charles Péguy. German theatre had grown old and stale, and it was Antoine who first brought in a breath of fresh air with his *Théâtre Libre* in 1887. Shortly afterwards Maximilian Harden founded *Die Freie Bühne*, and Otto Brahm opened the way for the Realism of Ibsen. Socialist enthusiasm and mass culture went hand in hand with Naturalism.

The break originated from the West—Huysmans, Verlaine, Mallarmé, Rimbaud, Verhaeren, Maeterlinck. The only German of universal stature was Nietzsche—a giant of freedom and a poetic genius despite his mental breakdown. He confessed, even as early as 1874, to adhere to a religion—'if you can call it that'—dedicated to the 'rearing of genius', in absolute opposition to the levelling approach of the naturalists. Education is hope; all solace is in art. Beside him Peter Hille, Bruno Wille and others pale into insignificance. But what a devastating result Nietzsche's philosophy had on the political development of the Germans! What an effect the hierarchic, austere Stefan George had on their taste! In their fashion Liliencron, Morgenstern, Dehmel, and Mombert rang truer. But it was vouchsafed only to Nietzsche, (and later to Spengler, Jaspers, and Heidegger) to make an impression on the outside world and to spread beyond the national frontiers. France, which he loved, also loved and honoured him, especially Gide and Malraux. Of the writers, only Thomas Mann attained European status, though perhaps Martin Buber and Hermann Hesse should not be forgotten. Apart from Nietzsche the greatest influences on the developing ideas of the time were Marx, Freud, Einstein, and Jung. They were the offspring of German soil, and although they were really scientists they had immense influence on both art and letters.

Some indigenous talents vegetating in the Austro-Hungarian Empire were scarcely noticed in Germany—Hermann Bahr, Arthur Schnitzler, Rainer Maria Rilke, Franz Werfel, Franz Kafka and Robert Musil. Rilke and Kafka became famous in the end, and Werfel gained a reputation in America. Musil is, even now, only gradually becoming known.

Kokoschka played an active and enthusiastic part in the spate of new ideas fermenting in Berlin when he arrived. A strong Expressionist movement was developing in opposition to science and the logic of language. The idea of escape from civilization, manifestoes of all kinds, radical verses and apocalyptic youth were the order of the day. At the same time the Marxist doctrine of dialectical materialism spread like an epidemic. Even so, no real personality emerged from the sea of new names—no single true originator of any great spiritual movement.

The catastrophe of the first world war was only possible because the politically and economically ambitious German drew his intellectual stimulus from abroad, being himself incapable of any spontaneous generation of ideas. The culture of Berlin was not German. It was a thin veneer covering the abyss of Prussian militarism. Nor was it European, for its logical developments were strangled at birth by nationalistic, egotistical forces. The real position of the German intellectual was explained by Gerhardt Hauptmann's retreat before the threat of reprisals over *Die Weber* and his flight into Romanticism, rather than by the intellectual anarchy of the Café Grössenwahn. The Germans who were felt to be the most German were the Englishman, Houston Stewart Chamberlain, author of the *Foundations of the Nineteenth Century* (*Grundlagen des neunzehnten Jahrhunderts*), the Frenchman, Count Gobineau, prophet of racial hatred, and, of course, Richard Wagner and Julius Langbehn—all of them tendentious, unhistorical, and arrogant. Wagner displayed the same failing as Hauptmann and betrayed his original ideas.

A true sense of values cannot be grafted on to a people artificially. Ideas can be honestly professed and objectively appreciated, but unless they are to remain the artificial products of a big city they must have time to mature in the people, just as grass grows and corn ripens. The misfortune of Germany was that she lacked the power to overcome the demon preventing her from forging a link with the humanism of Goethe and Herder, and with the great religious-mystic tradition that had been cut so fatally by the Thirty Years War. Naturalism, militarism, and rationalism caused modern Germany voluntarily to contract out of current European cultural movements. Hence, although Kokoschka received encouragement and, later, recognition, and although he attracted a group of understanding people, as far as his German contemporaries were concerned he was always the giver. As an Austrian, Kokoschka was able to avoid the doctrinaire amorphism of German Expressionism. The Germans needed me, he once told me.

He was saner. He came from a country that was not yet so rational, where industry had not developed so rapidly. But after the war all that was changed also.

Paul Westheim recognized it clearly: 'Kokoschka's art is to the Expressionists what Cézanne was to his contemporaries—Manet, Renoir, Degas, and van Gogh. They admired his struggle, but their aims were quite different.'

The old German spirit lives on in Kokoschka; not only that of the mystics and painters such as Dürer, Grünewald and Altdorfer, but also of the great musicians, Bach, Haydn, and Beethoven, and of poets like Kleist and Dehmel. Herder's humanism is stronger in Kokoschka than in any German writer since Kleist. He has fought openly against the fundamental German failing of chauvinism, spurred by his anarchical freedom in art and life and by his defiant hatred of war and every kind of prejudice and tyranny. Only one German painter came anywhere near him, and that is Lovis Corinth.

29 The Artist Painting in Tunis, 1928

30 On the Way to Biskra, 1928

31 London. Large Thames View I, 1926
By Courtesy of the Albright-Knox Art Gallery, Buffalo

32 Venice. Santa Maria della Salute II, 1927

The psychological condition of the Germans during the period of the two world wars was historically the result of their political failure; their choice of Luther instead of the Anabaptist, Thomas Münzer; the failure to understand the advantages of Napoleonic ideas—already clearly seen by Goethe—which, during the Wars of Liberation, became a national weakness, and finally led to the philosophy of Metternich in place of the *Code Civile*, and the failure of the *bourgeois* and the workers to evolve their methods of political negotiation.

German Expressionism is a more or less chaotic and aformal art, whereas Kokoschka, in company with Ensor, Munch, and later with Rouault and Chagall, refused to abandon form altogether. This strong sense of form and composition controlled and modified his power of self-expression, and converted the subjective visions of his fantasy into striking interpretations of the events of the time.

The tendencies of art and literature in Berlin during the first decade of the century have their foundation in events common to Europe as a whole. They originated in conflicts, the impact of which is still felt today. Naturalism was the artistic expression of an age that was deeply concerned with natural science, and which tried to substitute sociology for metaphysics and biology and materialism for religion. As early as 1892 Wilhelm Dilthey, one of the pioneers of the new scientific spirit, said: 'Metaphysics is nonsense', and it was not long before metaphysics was defending itself against the tedious utilitarian outlook of science as expounded, for instance, by Wilhelm Ostwald. Then Dilthey developed his theory of type and conformation (*Struktur und Typenlehre*), and modern psychology broke away from the mechanical, empirical psychology of Wilhelm Wundt. It fell to Freud to explain that 'true knowledge is insight into the unconscious'. Adler and Jung thought the Freudian sexual libido limited psychology to a too narrowly materialistic field, the former stressing the will to power, returning thus to Schopenhauer, and the latter expanding psychology into the world of myth.[7] Jung saw the human soul in contact with a greater, supervening mind, an idea that had originated with Freud.[8] The danger was that submersion of the mind in the psychological and the mythical would evolve into a modern magic. Only philosophers of the calibre of Bergson could move in this field unaffected.[9]

Edmund Husserl, developing his methods of phenomenology, was in line with Bergson when he returned intuition to its former primacy. Husserl was not searching for data of 'existentia' but for the 'essentia' of being. He looked to philosophy for pure insight into the essence of being.[10]

The neo-Kantians, Hermann Cohen in Marburg, Paul Natorp, Ernst Cassirer, and the sociologist Georg Simmel, likewise took a determined stance against materialism and rationalism,[11] and as early as 1887 Ferdinand Tönnies in *Gemeinschaft und Gesellschaft* (*Community and Society*) had distinguished with nice perception between culture and civilization—the organic and mechanical sides of life. Hence our problems, and even our terminology, have already a respectable age! Spengler analysed them comprehensively.[12] Rudolf Eucken developed his thesis of world empathy[13], and Walther Rathenau, a Minister and humanist who wrote before the war, called forth all the forces of intuition in opposition to reason. 'We are here', he said, 'not for the sake of wealth, nor of power, nor of fortune, but only for the illumination of the divine through the soul of man.'[14] Bergson had the last word: 'If, as a philosopher, I want to be a metaphysician as well as a logician, I must try to analyse the mystery of reality.'[15] He inspired André Gide, Romain Rolland, Paul Claudel, and André Suarès, and Charles Péguy said of him: 'Bergson broke our chains.'[16]

It is surely significant that the first International Congress for Aesthetics and the Science of Art, held in 1913, took the theory of intuition as the central theme.[17] The same conversion took place in art-history, and battle was joined in the first decade of the century.

Alois Riegl, a Viennese, sees art-history not only materially and formally as the history of skill, but also of the will. 'The features of earlier periods which seem strange to us are not a failure of technique, but must be considered as evidence of a different will to create.'[18] And Max Dvořák proclaimed art-history to be the unalloyed history of the spirit, and fought with determination against the idea of natural science in the field of art.[19] Worringer, following Riegl, developed a theory that a work of art is an independent organism of equal value with nature, and intrinsically independent of her so long as nature is understood to mean the visible surface phenomena. Naturalism is the expression of immanence, style of the transcendental.[20]

There were two conflicting ideologies in the world. The one, arising from science and technology, of a materialist, socio-economic, industrial-political nature, the other springing from the philosophy of myth, irrational symbolism, and metaphysics. The conflict is still not decided, even though the scales appear to be weighted on the side of myth. This spiritual conflict is personified in Kokoschka's work and philosophy.

Kokoschka soon recovered from the first strangeness of Berlin, and then he realized how much he had to offer the city. He painted and drew nearly all the leaders of bohemian Berlin.

Looking back, he said Berlin had resembled Vienna when he arrived. Herwarth Walden had seemed more interested in trying to launch modern dance music. *Der Sturm* was an insignificant pamphlet, really for music-lovers. It was only later that under his influence it became an art magazine. In a way Kokoschka formed a school.[21] When Rudolf Blümner read *Murder Hope of Women* aloud to Herwarth Walden, the latter was inspired to publish it, using the *Sturm* presses, with Kokoschka's illustrations and his own music. In July 1910 it was reprinted in a smaller format for *Der Sturm*. Walden invited Kokoschka to become co-editor of the magazine. He was the chief artist of those years, contributing a drawing and a literary commentary every week. He also became the circus critic.[22] He was fascinated by the life of the circus and had a friend who owned chimpanzees which he kept in his flat. There was also a girl snake-charmer, who did her act with two huge boa-constrictors, wearing a spangled dress. The artist never missed an opportunity to go behind the scenes, but one day his illusions were shattered when he noticed sawdust leaking out of a hole in one of the snakes. It was stuffed! He made drawings of everyone; the pretty little roller-skater, a dumpy creature, on her rink, and even of Yvette Guilbert, who was stranded in Berlin at the time. In his capacity as editor of *Der Sturm* Kokoschka went to interview her, and he also made a drawing of Richard Dehmel, not as the result of an interview but because the poet had made such an impression on him. At the beginning *Sturm* was honest, but Kaiser, Sternheim, and Teller turned it into propaganda. Kokoschka found their generalizations senseless—the official, the peasant, the worker! Everything was controlled by the *literati*.

Kokoschka recalls a fat and jovial innkeeper who was very enthusiastic about *Der Sturm*; no one could understand the reason, but he was always handing out money for *Der Sturm*, and to Dehmel. Dehmel, wearing a long greasy overcoat, would recite poems in his beergarden. The *Zwei Menschen* is a fine poem. Kokoschka could read Dehmel's face, furrowed in deep lines. Dehmel had a long dark head with black eyes, and acted as though he were blind. Kokoschka was reminded of Homer, of the Greeks. This genius was confronted with the *petits bourgeois*, for there were many like the innkeeper. The German is always a little pompous; he puts on his top-hat in the morning and goes to his office looking like an undertaker. On Sundays he has to go to the forest to pick mushrooms. He listens to the birds singing and is transformed. It is then that he sits down to listen to the poems of a Richard Dehmel.

As Kokoschka recounted his experiences of these early days he explained that he could only believe the evidence of his eyes. But in these people intuition was a substitute for intelligence; they could sense things. They had grown accustomed to silly flags and symbols since Bismarck, but here was a man who spoke with his own voice and told of women, of love. Now there was something a man could understand! That was the last time Kokoschka heard a song of love in Germany. But in Vienna they still understand, for, fundamentally, it is the spirit of the Baroque. For instance before the war the Austrians pictured the Abyssinians like the Magi; their ambassadors still wore feathered anklets. But now, after two generations, people think of them only as slave traders.

The greatest of German moralists, in Kokoschka's opinion, is Herder. His study of the history of the mind and his humanism are of great significance, and one should be grateful for such achievements. The French, in Condorcet, presented the world with a mechanistic philosophy, whereas Herder revealed the character of a people. For instance, he awakened the Slavs to the fact that they were a people, not, of course, with the intention of making them chauvinistic, but it was important for the future and not to be forgotten. The future, if there is to be one, will be able to use such knowledge.

In 1910 Walden's *Sturm* appeared under the title of *Wochenschrift für Kultur und die Künste* (Journal of Art and Culture) and in the same year Kokoschka's *Murder Hope of Women* was printed. Walden himself wrote novels in dialogue form, and dramatic epigrams; he set poems by Dehmel, Arno Holz, Goethe, and parts of *Des Knaben Wunderhorn* to music, also composing for the piano and orchestra. Until 1919 he consistently extended his activities, founding a publishing firm, organizing regular *Sturm* receptions, and, after 1912, holding exhibitions in Berlin and in the *Reich*, as well as abroad. He even founded a *Sturm* school, later the *Sturm* High School, in Berlin and Holland. He ran the Berlin office himself, but the Dutch side was entrusted to Jacoba van Heemskerck. In 1918 or 1919 a theatre called *Sturm* was founded, and an annual of the same name.

The specific doctrine was always Expressionism. The idea had first been introduced by the French painter Auguste Hervé for a cycle of paintings, and de Vauxelles, critic of *Gil Blas*, defined its meaning for the French public. 'Expressionism is not a fashion,' expounded *Der Sturm*, 'it is an attitude to life, an attitude moreover of the senses, not of the mind.' The aim was to make the doctrine purely artistic, uncompromised by political, social, or moral aims, hence its absolute contrast to Franz Pfemfert's *Aktion*. These two, and the *Weisse Blätter*, were the leading *avant-garde* journals in Germany. 'Expressionism', *Sturm* continued, 'contains the spiritual stirring of the time which puts inner experience before external events.' The art of the present will be the prophet of manifest perception, it will move and disturb.[23]

All kinds of new forces were stirring, stretching, as it were, in their sleep.

Kurt Hiller declaimed before the Berlin students whom he had invited to visit the 'New Club': 'Our faith is that we are creative beings, powers, says Nietzsche. If a man lives with people who are in accord with his nature, then his productivity is quickened and brought to fruition, says Spinoza. We live at a time of too much work and too little learning, when people are stupidly industrious, says Oscar Wilde. And Goethe: Nowadays one's duty is not to remain silent or to give way; everyone must talk and make a great noise, not to overcome but just to preserve ourselves. What does life offer us if we do not take it seriously, says Wedekind. Beware, beware, says Hofmannsthal, strange times are upon us.'[22]

Many foreign artists apart from Kokoschka exhibited with and wrote for *Der Sturm*, often for the first time. The list is impressive: Ensor, Chagall, Feininger, Picasso, Delaunay, Léger, Ernst, Duchamp, Villon, Metzinger, Gleizes, Kandinsky, Picabia, Marcoussis, Boccioni, Carrá, Severini, Campendonck, Isaac Grünewald, Jawlensky, Filla, Kubin, and Archipenko. German artists included Klee, Macke, Marc, Meidner, Gabriele Münter, Baumeister, and Schwitters. Poets were Strindberg, Tzara, Altenberg, Apollinaire, Aragon, Arp, Benn, Kokoschka, Dehmel, Mombert, Eluard, Hoddis, Scheerbart, Else Lasker-Schüler, Ehrenstein, Schickele, Mynona, and Hille. Writers were Bang, Breton, Brod, Cendrars, Döblin, Karl Kraus and Langer. Theoreticians included Herwarth Walden, Rudolf Blümner, William Wauer, August Stramm, Lothar Schreyer, and Kurt Schwitters.

Kokoschka's stay in Berlin had begun after Walden had gone to Vienna where Loos, patron and 'owner' of Kokoschka, immediately set to work on him.

Kokoschka must go with him immediately to Berlin. He had only been there once or twice before the war.

As usual, Loos handed him the money. When he arrived in Berlin, Kokoschka felt tired and dirty, so he went to a barber, and this man talked so persuasively that he ended by selling Kokoschka cream and pomade till he had to part with all his money. Kokoschka left all his purchases in the next doorway, and departed quickly in case anyone should see. So there he was, penniless once more. Things like that were always happening to him.

Someone would telephone telling him to visit a certain person at all costs. He would get the names muddled and arrive at another house where he was not expected. *Der Sturm* was housed at the time in the Nollendorf Platz. The scrawny young Kokoschka shared a small room there with Blümner, the short-sighted actor, who was propagandist of *Der Sturm*. They were both very poor. They had only a table, a chair and a towel between them. It was at that time that he drew all the portraits so famous today; of Loos and Walden, Karl Kraus, Dehmel, Scheerbart, Blümner, Alfred Kerr, Hermann Essig, Adolf Knoblauch, Max Berg, Gertrud Eysold, Yvette Guilbert, Nell Walden, Claire Waldorff, and Mechthild Lichnowsky.[25]

Besides the illustrations to *Murder Hope of Women* there were other drawings such as *The Child Murderess*, all of which were produced on a very frugal diet. Kokoschka lived from hand to mouth on quantities of cheap biscuits and coffee. On Sundays Blümner accompanied him to Aschinger, where they spent the single mark given regularly to them by Walden on hot dogs. Bread was free. The room, rented by Walden, was at the back of the fourth floor. It was a terribly cold winter, and there was no heating, because it cost too much. Towards Christmas there was a heavy snowfall.

'With the school-master's runaway son we used to go to the brothels to try to get warm. The fat women there, real suburban types, lived like a family. We were allowed into the room where the guests were received because we were like children. My friend Kulke blew soap-bubbles, and the women gave him cigarettes. Sometimes they invited us to have supper with them. There would be eel, sweet dumplings and Berlin white sausage. On Christmas Eve we were quite alone in the Nollendorf Platz. Blümner had brought a paper fir tree; we wished each other a merry Christmas and lay down. We had bought ourselves a Christmas present too: a packet of the usual biscuits. We were frightfully cold, and tried to keep warm by wrapping ourselves in our blankets. Blümner lay on the bed, I on the divan. Then I told him about Virginia, the little girl I had met on that warm day in Switzerland, and how she had gazed at me with a long questioning look. In my half-waking dream she became my daughter. I told the story almost in a whisper, Blümner joined in, and the biting cold wove fantasies out of our hunger and despair. Then we fell to quarrelling as to whose daughter Virginia really was—mine or his. In the end we agreed—she would be *our* daughter. After that we invented a life around her, repeated every word she spoke, described her every dress. When she grew up she threw us over in favour of a lover. She owned a tortoise, and took it with her.'

'Suddenly the doorbell rang far below, and we at once connected it with Virginia. Why was she ringing on Christmas Eve? Something must have happened to her. Perhaps she had tuberculosis. If she spat blood one would be able to see the stain on the snow. Someone had to go down.'

'Kokoschka suddenly jumped up, and so did Blümner. Now they were mortal enemies, and each blamed the other for this misfortune. They were both very excited. The bell had rung suddenly, so the whole story must be true! Who will be the first to find the blood on the snow?'

'Formerly Blümner had been an instructor in the Cadet College; he still had a rifle and bayonet hanging on the wall. He tore it down and attacked me. There was a shot, and he thought he had killed me, but it was only the *concierge* shooting at a cat in the yard below.'[26]

It was a time of excitement and of hard work. In 1910 Kokoschka had held a one-man exhibition in the Folkwang Museum, then in Hagen, Westphalia, and the following year he exhibited at the Vienna Hagenbund. The second exhibition brought more disappointment. However, Paul Cassirer's Berlin Exhibition of 1910, Kokoschka's participation in the *Sonderbund* at Cologne in 1912, and in Walden's *Sturm* gallery in Berlin, as well as in the Berlin First Autumn Salon, placed him among the leaders of the *avant-garde*.

That was the period of the portraits in oils of Walden, Blümner, and Wauer, who became an artist later, although at the time he was still working in the Maggi factory; of Tilla Durieux, the actress wife of Paul Cassirer, who shot himself when she left him to live with the millionaire banker, Katzenellenbogen, on his island of Brioni; and the portraits of Scheerbart, Peter Baum, and Dr Hugo Caro, the latter a lonely barrister who ruined himself by taking the cases of poor people and finally committed suicide. All these portraits bear witness to the artist's developing style and his freer, surer hand. Impasto and strong spontaneous colours combed through with tense brush-strokes, contours pressed in with the handle of the brush, scratched in with a finger-nail: thus the portraits of the period reveal the impetuous, passionate and profound nature of their creator.

One person he did not want to paint was Else Lasker-Schüler, Walden's first wife, even though she had given him a laudatory review in *Der Sturm* and despite the fact that he also figured in the poems which she published under the name of the Prince of Thebes. Kokoschka remembers her as a strange person. She used to wear pointed shoes and long trousers—rather dirty, but they were all that, more or less—and a black velvet dress with a red belt. Walden had a tall stand-up collar and a very pale face. He would sometimes put on two pairs of spectacles at once, always wore uncleaned cream-coloured buttoned shoes, and trousers that were far too short. The young Kokoschka was anaemic, but he wore suits tailored by Ebenstein. His English suit was superb, and he wore a Panama hat. Thus attired they set out on a propaganda mission for *Der Sturm* into the Rhineland. Everyone carried a huge parcel of the journals under his arm, and the innkeeper had given them thirty marks. They pushed a copy of *Der Sturm* through every letter-box in every street. They were jeered at by children and chased by dogs. Kokoschka confessed to shame as well as elation, but he had supported the group because he felt that he had to bear the responsibility. He was convinced that this was true art, and that everything else was *bourgeois* and mediocre. That was how they spread the word in the Rhineland, and it did produce some subscriptions for *Der Sturm*. Success at last!

Munich at the time was absolutely neutral.

When Kokoschka could not endure life in Berlin any longer, he wrote a card to Loos and went home to Vienna. The two great cities, Berlin and Vienna, were two opposing poles of this important period in Kokoschka's life.

THE INNER IMAGE

Kokoschka's sense of the decadence of his time is nowhere more clearly revealed than in his portraits.

The man who confronts me is my problem, he once said. He tried to capture the hidden, the suppressed and the unspoken, the essential qualities of the face and hands of his subject. These early portraits are striking and mysterious in their similarity. This unity is the result of the artist's intense response, which grips him so fiercely that all material and technical difficulties are overcome as if in a trance.

The first portraits are painted in the combined techniques already described and which are reminiscent of the later Surrealists. Although Kokoschka only really developed his colour after the first world war, it nevertheless plays a definite role in his early work. It has a symbolic individual value. Every portrait is in a dominant colour characteristic of the sitter, as, for instance, the strong contrast of black and red in Herwarth Walden's portrait, the exciting yellow of Karl Kraus, the livid copper-oxide green of Meyrinck, and the pink and blue of the TRANCE PLAYER. Within the given scheme softer colours play their part; they are often linear rather than painterly; angular or sometimes flowing, expressive or ornamental lines.

In the Walden portrait this flowing line becomes intensified into hieroglyphs, a cipher of the mind which was one of Kokoschka's most important discoveries. Kokoschka drew right into the picture. He scratched, smoothed out, and glazed so as to heighten the effect of the outline. The brush-stroke often seems to penetrate the canvas. There is an interplay of styles, for, despite the sensitive drawing, and the resemblance and expression often quite typical of the model, these portraits still retain a rigid, almost iconographical element. The original and untainted primitiveness is recognizable in the will to express the primary and the essential as much as in the mastery of difficult techniques. Empty spaces seem to stretch beyond the frame, throwing the figure itself into relief. Here is a subtlety and morbidity which is particularly well expressed by the tense and nervous brush-strokes. A remarkable example of this mixture of styles is the painting of the child with the hands of its parents. It has the charm of a primitive folk painting—the expression of ancient wisdom on the face of the child, the elements of the composition arranged on a single frontal plane, the child, the hand of the father and of the mother. However, the manner of the composition is not primitive at all, but immensely skilful; there is something exceptionally subtle in the colouring and characterization of the two hands, in their almost symbolic genetic significance. The landscape, DENT DU MIDI, also displays these two styles: the naïve detail of the busy foreground attained by the sharpness of the drawing, with the broad misty atmosphere of the mountains behind, like crystal giants wreathed in a web of light. The path converges under the eye, crosses the painting from left to right to turn upwards in a right-angle. It can easily be seen that the artist has overcome this dichotomy in the landscape, TRE CROCI, done in the Dolomites, because the subject is very similar: the mountains in the background, the sun, the horse and cart moving along the road. The dual styles catch a strong sense of distance in the landscape and, in the portraits, attempt to go beyond the pulsing vitality of the subject to express the unchanging quality in the person and character of man.

In 1911 Kokoschka's portrait style was already beginning to change, and this was caused, as always with this artist, by personal experience. The marks of Kokoschka's life can be read in his developing style, as fossils reveal the history of the earth. The vibrations of his inner experience are recorded in every phase as those of the earth on a seismograph. His art and life are closely interwoven in a manner unusual in an artist. During 1911 the surface of his paintings is, as it were, enamelled, resembling mother-of-pearl. The colours are applied in small cells like a honeycomb, and the colour range is as soft as that of a Tanagra figure. They tell of the short period when Kokoschka was concerned with *la belle matière*, when he aimed at the beautiful, the perfect, the static picture, because he still had faith in the harmony of life's opposing forces, and because religious experience made his hope of transcendence, redemption, and immortality a reality.

In 1909 he was already painting in a manner recalling medieval stained glass. The theme was KNIGHT, DEATH, AND THE ANGEL, an idea that he repeated later on. He certainly saw himself as the knight who fought against life's transience for the sake of the blessing from above, just as Dürer had fought and all the Middle Ages before him. It was followed by the FLIGHT INTO EGYPT, the CRUCIFIXION, ST. VERONICA WITH THE SUDARIUM, the ANNUNCIATION, and the VISITATION.

An important woman now comes within the range of this promising young artist. The young master of psychological chiaroscuro whose strength lay in the display of contrasts—contrasts of soul, of times, of colour, and of form—was drawn by her into the web of legend. The Venetian scene and, even more, the double portrait painted at Christmas 1912 are in this style, and, of course, finally the portrait of the woman herself.[1]

An airy web hangs like a veil over the painting called the VISITATION. It strongly recalls Cézanne's struggles with the problem of depicting space in a two-dimensional plane. The drawings published in *Der Sturm* in 1910 are interesting for the study of Kokoschka's personal sense of space and of his methods of reproducing depth. These, and the illustrations to Albert Ehrenstein's *Tubutsch*, display diagonal woven lines, the sole purpose of which is the construction of space. The next step occurs in the portraits of KARL ETLINGER and EGON WELLESZ, in which a scaffold-like screen appears which is filled in with colours but not yet formed by the colour itself.

In the double portrait with Alma Mahler colour functions directly as a modeller of space; the hands now appear to be three-dimensional, and, in future, the artist sees space in terms of colour only. The compositions of the Dresden period, such as the POWER OF MUSIC (1918–19) and the landscapes of the Elbe, were experiments with the use of colour as an expression of distance, arising out of a project for a crematorium that Kokoschka was designing for the City Architect of Breslau. The work, which was never executed because the architect died, was to be a memorial for the hecatombs of the victims of the first world war.[2]

To return once more to the pearly paintings of 1911–12, it is interesting to compare them with the icon-like work of the mature Rouault, and especially with the Christs and Pierrots and Clowns done after 1937. These are outline drawings filled with colour, whereas the young Kokoschka modelled figures and landscapes with tone and colour alone.

Before the first world war Kokoschka had developed a broad impasto style exemplified in the portraits of the painter Carl Moll; of his friend, the poet, Albert Ehrenstein; the publisher, Dr Robert Freund; the innkeeper, Franz Hauer; the composer, Anton von Webern; the visionary, Princess Mechthild Lichnowsky; and the portrait of Dr Hermann Schwarzwald. This development is foreshadowed, even in 1910, by the portrait of Else Kupfer.

The portrait of Ehrenstein displays a freedom of expression that is enhanced by a frugal application of paint, and by a use of light and shade reminiscent of Tintoretto. The style, especially in the portrait of Hauer, is vigorous and determined, and similar to the late manner of van Gogh.

The war acted like a spur to the development of this style. The artist used broader brushes, the execution of the painting became bolder, more vehement, and the tone values were intensified. The colour attains a decorative, expressive validity and, in the Dresden series after 1917, an intensity which is magnified by the broad planes in which it is applied, sometimes straight from the tube as pure colour. At that period Kokoschka's style resembles tapestry, and he was, in fact, aiming at wall-decoration.[3]

In 1925 Kokoschka was already a master. The portrait of Leo Kestenberg, the composition of which makes such an overwhelming impression, is crammed with narrative and pictorial events. Kokoschka's portraits, like those of Rembrandt, Velasquez, Goya, and Munch, are characteristic of his time.

All portraits until the nineteenth century were a straightforward record of things seen—statistical, descriptive compositions in contrast with the spiritual energy engendered in more modern art. A new conception of expression takes root, and everything from the following period displays a strong spiritual element. The late Gothic Dürer must have been aware of the imminent changes, as witness the portrait of his mother done in the year of her death, but his art nevertheless remains an art of representation, whereas that of Grünewald is an art of expression. Kokoschka occasionally strives, as in his later portraits, to combine the two.

In the portrait of Leo Kestinberg the narrative in the background is directly connected with the person portrayed. In this case the woman seated at the piano is Grete, the sitter's wife. In the middle ground we see Leo Kestenberg conducting; the building represents the educational centre where he, in his official capacity, tried to bring music to the people. In the portrait of the Countess of Drogheda a greyhound and a Chinese figure appear. The figure symbolizes travel and art-collecting, while the greyhound denotes the noble blood of this 'last aristocrat', as Kokoschka used to call her. He painted her in a noble pose wearing magnificent clothes, as the woman with a part to play in society. The portrait strikes a melancholy note. There are no more aristocrats, he once said to me, as he looked at the work. She had a head something like a Fouquet. Formerly heads were like that, like old coins, of pure noble metal, quite different from the alloys of today.

Kokoschka worked on this painting for a number of years. This picture needs three more skins, he once declared after about eighty sittings. After a certain stage he was able to look at it coolly; sobriety returned. But even though he might go on working at such a painting for years he could finish it quite suddenly and for good. I watched Kokoschka developing the portrait of this woman week by week, saw the veil of tragedy drawn across the young features of the Countess, the sadness of the dispossessed who still behave as if they owned the world. A born actor, who loves to weave a story around his sitters, Kokoschka expressed this idea by a certain rigidity of his body, a mimicking expression on his face, and a slight backward tilting of the head. He moved through his studio as though he were dancing up a flight of stairs. He acted out the fatigue and decay of youth. All this can be seen in the finished portrait. This development from a carefree protected youth into the troubles of age, and into a period of impending doom, can be seen beneath the mask of time that has so changed the face.

The portrait of Lord Croft as a young man has the Lion of England and the bust of the man who brought the family the title in the background, and the secondary interest increases almost to a dialectic in the portrait of Masaryk. The portrait of the Soviet Ambassador, Maisky, painted in a fluid manner reminiscent of Turner and in a technique deriving from water-colour, reveals Lenin, the orator, in the background facing a globe on which only Asia is shown.

Kokoschka worked long and painstakingly on his portraits. 'Have you finished already?' one of his subjects asked while he was still drawing. 'I,' said Kokoschka wryly, 'never finish when I have once begun.'

That is typical of him. One day he had a boy staying with him who enjoyed drawing faces. Praising him, Kokoschka said: Don't forget that everyone, artists as well as the public, has forgotten what art really is. Art is not for museums, but just this—to see how a face looks. Guard your talent for searching a face. Once, when asked by Dr Plesch how he composed his portraits, Kokoschka answered: I imagine that my subject's head is in a frame which is just the size I intend to paint the picture. Then I paint the parts which stand out most and work my way back gradually, dealing with each level as it comes, and in this way I obtain plasticity and vitality in a portrait.[4]

Often twenty pictures or more are hidden below the final version, and despite violent protest his agent, Paul Cassirer, often had to take paintings away to save them from being overpainted, with the loss of the earlier composition. Although all these paintings have many 'skins', Kokoschka likes to describe them as pure stenography. Apart from revealing his determination to penetrate his subject with deeper insight, they plainly reflect his philosophy—that life is not just a quest, the road itself is momentous, calling for a high courage and repeated attempts that gradually drain the life-force away. The rhythm of life is like opposing electrical poles which arc if they are touched together. It is a rhythm of tension and release, where complete collapse is death—a nothingness that can only be overcome by work.

He once wrote of the primal fear of death and the spiritual means to overcome it: 'Mankind in the mass tries to suppress this fear by a herd instinct which bemuses the awakening senses like alcohol.'[5]

Kokoschka's portraits are revelations of the individual. They reflect the temper beneath the mask. This portraiture is undoubtedly realistic in comparison with the abstract art of today, but it is an expressive and dynamic Realism born of a psychological interpretation of the projection of the inner mind, not just a likeness of face and hands. This is the essential element of Kokoschka's attitude to portraits and bears no direct relation to the development of his technique.[3] Not only the fascination, the joy of creation, inspires him to bring a face to life, nor the knowledge that he is creating a masterpiece, but the probing of a soul, necessary to satisfy his conscience as an artist. It is almost impossible to explain, although Kokoschka thinks it has something to do with superstition and the inability to produce a painting in cold blood—the necessity for the subject to take possession of his mind while he is working. It enables him to direct a shaft into the soul of man, who is dissociated and lost. Anton Faistauer makes a pregnant criticism of Kokoschka's first portraits in speaking of his 'invasion' of man, his 'vivisection' of his surroundings.[7]

It is of interest to examine more closely Kokoschka's attitude *vis-à-vis* his patron Adolf Loos. The portrait reveals a determined idealist, a crusader who is denied. Here is a man who swims against the current, never changing course. The clasped hands, the features lit by an eery light, the serious mouth and thoughtful eye, all combine to build our impression. And the eyes express the warmth which was as characteristic of Loos as his energy and determination. It is especially apparent in the drawing done in 1916, and this drawing is so unforced and unaffected, like a letter to a friend, but at the same time so masterly that it seems more remarkable than either the painting, which conformed to a convention of style, or the decorative, stylized drawing published by *Der Sturm* in 1910.

The portrait of Bessie Loos was painted as a *pendant* to that of the artist's patron. It reveals the delicate consumptive young woman who died a year after the painting was finished. The portrait of the painter Harta, compared with the austerity of that of Adolf Loos, must be claimed as a piece of pure Baroque inspiration. The arm's gesture, the poise of the head, and the smile frozen, as it were, in metal, are caught in spellbound astonishment. The problem of presenting movement on a plane without distortion is spontaneously solved. The portrait of Harta is one of a series of portraits of artists, among them actors Ernst Reinhold and Karl Etlinger; the painter Carl Moll; the singer

Hjalmar Ennehjelm; the composers Schönberg and Anton von Webern; the poets Richard Dehmel, Rudolf Blümner, and Albert Ehrenstein; and the author von Dyrsztay. But those of Karl Kraus and Peter Altenberg are the most important.

Kokoschka especially admired Kraus's work on the spirit of language. 'Language', wrote Kraus, 'is the medium of the literary artist, but it is not his alone, whereas colour belongs exclusively to the painter. That is why men should be forbidden to speak. Sign language is perfectly adequate for the thoughts that they need to convey, for we are not allowed to cover ourselves with paint.'[8]

Even this waspish short quotation shows the difference between Kraus and Kokoschka. Kraus was a whip-lash, a prophet in the wilderness. Kokoschka had a much freer relationship with him than the others, but Kokoschka was an exception; he had not been forced to cram his head with facts and he was the only one who dared to admit that he had not read the latest edition of *Die Fackel*. Kraus had a huge following.

This fanatical, near-sadistic, deadly-tongued critic, this satirist brimming with idealism yet tortured by man's desperate predicament, Kokoschka painted in the character of the lecturer and his audience. He also saw and painted the features that were most often deeply hidden.

Sometimes Kraus's eyes shone with such goodness that one was completely disarmed, said Kokoschka.

This tension between opposing mental qualities forced Kokoschka to repeat the portrait until he felt that he had truly caught Kraus's face, though Kraus's attitude to the first version was probably partly responsible for his decision to try again. The second version is one of the few where Kokoschka had recourse to a theatrical method of expression in order to draw attention to something special—in this case the strangeness he always felt when in Kraus's company. Thus, the arms are stylized forming a rhythmic component of the picture, while in the air flutters a metallic gleaming blue butterfly— the species *Morpheus*, an allusion to the fact that Kraus wrote, like a monk, only at night—with which the ear of the lecturer appears to be nervously linked.

In the PORTRAIT OF A BOY done in 1908 the impression of stiff elegance in the child is also stressed by an unnatural position of the arms, whereas the position of the arms in the Altenberg portrait is absolutely different. Kokoschka was especially drawn towards Peter Altenberg, whose way of life was one of 'full blooded strangeness, mocking all attempts at convention'. He was completely bald at forty, wore *pince-nez* with a ribbon, and looked like a walrus. He possessed the eye of a Socrates, and resembled an ugly faun, dressed always in most peculiar clothes; a shaggy overcoat, clogs, and a green jacket. He was obsessively attached to Salzburg and sold wooden necklaces in the streets of Vienna. He lived all his life in the Graben Hotel and passed his sleepless nights in the café. In Vienna he cut the same stocky figure as did Verlaine in Paris. His literary work is probably the best expression of the Viennese spirit, with its mixture of wit, sentiment, and sensuality. His short descriptive pieces, quick and penetrating, will ensure him recognition as a master in his field. It is the product of a generous nature in harmony with God, women, and children. He was 'an ecstatic prophet of the human body, of womanly grace and charm'. He was a fanatic of nature, which, for him, was 'the holy symbol of blameless freedom and integrity'. He loved the 'unfettered heart; the free body; all the arts of variety; the manifest overthrowing of the tyranny of the law of gravity; the prostitutes and their friends, who were free of the futility of *bourgeois* hypocrisy; carefree children and the nakedness of beautiful men and women; the woods and meadows; in short, a life free from the demands and restrictions of convention, fashion, or fear, modelled on a pattern of nature'.[9]

In the Pilsner café, where Kokoschka painted him with a glass on the table, he was always the centre of *bourgeois* attention. He was adept at holding two conversations at once, replying to the little man who addressed him from another table while giving his friends a running commentary *sotto voce*. 'What extraordinary people! Every one a Shakespeare!' When one of the artists overstepped the bounds of hospitality, as Mopp once did, by offering his friends wine as well as dinner, Altenberg said in amazement: 'Max Oppenheimer gets better and better every day!' But things were not always so idyllic. Sometimes Altenberg could be roused to fury. They took advantage of his ever-lasting poverty by withholding money which he was expecting, so that he had to wait for it. 'So-and-so is sleeping with such-and-such a man', and then it would begin. There were things Altenberg could not stand. Growing red in the face he would puff and blow, and spread out his hands defensively, and that was how Kokoschka painted him. It was the dynamic energy of the man that inspired the painting. Kokoschka could not bear the ignorance of the others, who did not realize what forces their teasing unleashed. Kokoschka openly took Altenberg's part and protected him. He told the attackers about an octopus he had once seen in the aquarium at Naples, which the visitors were goading with a glass rod until its eyes began to grow red and its tentacles lashed wildly around. Then Altenberg cried: 'A couple of sausages for young Kokoschka', and, really over-reaching himself this time, 'and a packet of Favorit, too.' (Favorit was one of the better kinds of cigarette.) The others were speechless. It was probably the only time in his life that Altenberg was the host and not the guest, and from that day he took Kokoschka to his heart.

Kokoschka at that time regarded Schönberg as the foremost composer of the day, and painted him with a 'cello as he had often seen him, playing chamber music with his students and special friends at home. Kokoschka was of the opinion that neither Mahler nor Stravinsky could compete with Schönberg, but he later changed his mind to some extent, and he now sees Anton von Webern as the more important innovator in modern music. He was not enthusiastic about Mahler's symphonies; only the *Kindertotenlieder*, written by Mahler after the death of his own child, touched him at all. But to see and hear Mahler conducting was an unforgettable experience. Schönberg was a small, dynamically active personality.

Tubutsch, which Kokoschka illustrated, he thought revealed Ehrenstein at his most personal and poetic. It was strong stuff—comparable with Gogol and Calderón, or Valéry's *Monsieur Teste*—great writing, Kokoschka thought, but Ehrenstein was never able to repeat it; at that time he was being driven almost to suicide by the futility of existence and this was his testament. And so Kokoschka painted him as a prisoner of his surroundings. 'That is not allowed here!' The words of Tubutsch ring true. Kokoschka was very attached to Ehrenstein. He even put him in one of the *Tubutsch* illustrations—touching, helpless, contemplating suicide with a ridiculous little skeleton crouching on his shoulder.

Kokoschka had an inner link with all his sitters. If he found them uncongenial they always had some quality which disturbed and therefore excited him. In the portrait of Ludwig Ritter von Janikowsky he perceived the resignation of a man caught in the grip of a mental sickness; in the Count of Verona, the ghostly presence of tuberculosis feeding on its victim; the delicate orchid-like quality of the Duchesse de Rohan Montesquieu; the self-denying shell of Ernst Reinhold, who was always changing his 'image'; and the Berlin lawyer, Dr Caro, who was ruined by his unbounded love for mankind and pity for the poor. He saw the mortal sickness that ravaged the features of the actress, Else Kupfer, and perceived the meaning of loss of sight in the BLIND MOTHER AND HER CHILD. His understanding of the fate of the *bourgeoisie*, of their reserved and inborn shyness as exemplified in the face and hands of Frau Dr Karpeles, arouses both our participation and our admiration for his skill.

We are repeatedly confronted with unusual and very talented women in Kokoschka's portraits; for instance, the lithograph of Emmy Heim, the paintings of Ruth Landshoff and Hermine Körner, and the series of ten portraits done in 1920 of Camilla Swoboda, the Viennese art-historian's wife, which became famous under the name VARIATIONS ON A THEME (THE CONCERT).[10] There are the wonderfully perceptive representations of the actress Käthe Richter and of Corona, India, and Recha, the sensitive response to the grace and poetry of young womanhood. Kokoschka presents the delicate, innocent, virginal figure in the portraits like GIRL WITH A DOLL and GIRL WITH FLOWERS IN HER HAIR; or the Persephone-Psyche type in PAMELA, THE BEAUTIFUL ONE or MINONA, hesitating on the brink between cloistered solitude and the adventure of life— the pensive girl whom he painted and drew as POMONA during the war. Then there are the more robust portraits of Trudl. They are redolent of healthy vitality, of awakening sensuality and the apprehension of the future. They build a bridge between the innocence of the earlier portraits and the later group which portray the comeliness of mature and beautiful women with their enigma of divine inaccessibility, consummation and temptation. Alma Mahler, for instance, and WOMAN WITH A PARROT, the SLAVE GIRL, and the allegorical SOURCE. The *bourgeois*, jealous, quarrelsome, Junoesque type of woman never appealed to Kokoschka, who preferred the type of Minerva or Diana, although Cybele, the Mother Goddess, always stirred him. From time to time, however, the sensual Faustian lover sought solace in the lavish, orgiastic type of woman. For instance, there are paintings inspired by Old Testament figures: JACOB, RACHEL, AND LEAH, or LOT AND HIS DAUGHTERS, for which Njuta Kallin modelled in Dresden, and also the portraits of the dancer Elsa Temary, the paintings called the ALGERIAN GIRL WITH A BARREL, TWO RECLINING WOMEN, and GALATEA, and the sketches done in Dresden for the DAUGHTERS OF THE COVENANT (Esther, Deborah, Hager, Miriam, Naomi,

Ruth, and Hefa). The numerous portrait sketches of the Rumanian Frau Merson also belong in this category.

The portrait of Evelyn, mother of Sir Edward Beddington Behrens, was painted from a girlhood photograph and from her son's description. Kokoschka reconstructed her face, relying on the similarity between her son's features and those of the photograph. It was a remarkable creative feat. Kokoschka wrestled with the painting over a long period as he tried to lend visible form to a man's memory, to exchange the face of death for that of life, to turn back the years and see the man as a boy, so that he could paint him into the picture protected by the loving hands of his mother.[11]

Sir Edward explains why he asked Kokoschka to paint the portrait. He had learned of Kokoschka's perceptive remarks on seeing the photograph of his mother for the first time, although it was a face which was completely unknown to him. It proved to be a significant commission for the artist. As it slowly developed the Madonna motif was transformed into an allegory of the indestructibility and continuity of life. Kokoschka began by observing the son—the extension of his mother.

Sir Edward had an aunt on his mother's side to whom he was very devoted. Kokoschka was introduced to her, and soon discovered that *she* had the social traits of the mother whilst Sir Edward had the emotional characteristics. Kokoschka touched his patron where he was the most sensitive. They would often talk about his mother, and Kokoschka developed his ideas that she was not dead, but had only drunk of the waters of Lethe, that her power lived on in her son. Hence he painted the hand of the mother on the edge of the composition, as though reaching out from afar to protect her son and defending him with her arm. The painting is full of movement; the child on its mother's lap wriggles like a worm. One arm describes a movement of rejection, the other reaches out. The effect is dynamic and twofold. The woman's eyes have the expression of her son's as his thoughts turned towards her. The wrinkles in her face are as if sculptured, a landscape wherein the eye may wander. The child is holding a coloured glass ball in his hand, and this is the strongest note of colour in the painting. In the mid-ground is a boat, two figures in the net of forgetfulness, whilst in the left background hovers a vision with two small green figures bathed in the light of peace. In the foreground a green lamp is painted on a yellow ground. This is actually the only real object in the whole composition, and even that is a symbol of light, of life. Nevertheless, it remains substantial in material surroundings, whilst above it the mood changes completely into fantasy.

Once, as he stood in front of the unfinished picture, Kokoschka remarked that true art can never be without movement. The links between the separate components of a picture and its content fuse through movement and separate like natural objects. They are like the sun rising over a mountain landscape. The mist fades and the peaks appear, slowly at first, then taking shape gradually, one after the other. The artist described how he looked first for the structure of the figure and afterwards for that of the composition, and the rest, he added, is the spiritual movement which is expressed by circling and attacking the object with colour. That is the only way to render it visible.

Kokoschka paints in layers. When he begins he sees a basic pattern of dominant colours. Red is to him what black is to most other painters. In this portrait it is contrasted with a very pale blue. There should be something between the two, but it is missing here. Looking at the mother's face one realizes that the mouth is pale and colourless; only the child glows red in the reflected light of the glass ball. Everything else is blue and cold.

Kokoschka saw this painting as an allegory. The whole subject was visionary, and the artist had to bring the son's memories to life. It was not a question of beautifying—the son himself did that as he looked back. The picture had to contain the old idea of death as the gateway to the Elysian fields and to the light. The only reality is the oil-lamp—the light of earlier times. It is possible that a French painter would have handled the whole theme in the manner of the image of peace in the top corner, in a static unmoving way. The dead woman had spent her childhood in France and was French in her emotional outlook.

One hand was on the canvas for a whole year—it had been there from the very beginning, the artist told me. A painting like this had to mean something tomorrow and the next day, like a favourite book which one reads time and again. Besides, he had to encompass the whole story of a life in his vision.

In the summer of 1944 Kokoschka stayed with Professor Emil Korner's family in Scotland, where he met Minona McEwen, a Scottish girl who spoke Spanish, having been born in Bolivia. She had been educated in a convent. The artist was fascinated by her intelligence and her unusual personality. She was capable of profound under- standing and combined this quality with a childlike, wide-eyed awareness. Kokoschka often talked to her, and came to wonder how to defend this unusual child from the corruption of the times.

He did a series of pastel drawings, feeling his way towards an understanding of her mind. Finally he painted her portrait from memory as the Goddess of Plenty, her face pink and white like apple-blossom, and dressed in pale blue, surrounded by fruit—a bunch of sweet grapes and two oranges gleaming like the sun.

After he went back to London the artist kept up a correspondence with this girl for years in an attempt to preserve the innocence of her mind. He wanted to make her a visionary, he told me, smiling, like Mechthild. She was wont to confide in him, describing the impressions of a young creature at the mercy of the dark hours of the night. She told how she looked at the stars as she stood among the cypresses and was suddenly made aware of the inaccessible universe and of her own insignificance. She wondered then about the nature of man. Peoples and languages develop and are gone, centuries flower and die, and man is but sand on the shore. Kokoschka, replying to her, crystallized his own philosophy. Modern man destroys everything tangible, visible, and material. He has nothing but words in his head, believes in them alone, lives and dies for them. The only hope lies in music. Therefore he told Minona to study music because it meant harmony. In older times men saw the stars as symbolic of the cosmos, of order and ever- lasting harmony, not merely as a contrast with the insignificance of man. Every letter

33 Adele Astaire (Lady Cavendish), 1926

34 The Mandrill, 1926

35 Courmayeur et Les Dents des Géants, 1927
By Courtesy of the Phillips Collection, Washington

36 Chamonix—Mont Blanc, 1927

contained a moral tale, and this time it was the story of a donkey, a rabbit, and a voracious goat. An innocent young rabbit brought a carrot to the donkey because he did not know what it was, although it both looked and smelt good, and should be good to eat. The donkey, a pedantic fellow, looked at it and said: 'It is a carrot, I know, and therefore edible; it has vitamins and must be nourishing. But I don't know whether the vitamins are in the leaves or the root, so I will go to the University to find out. Meanwhile,' he told the rabbit, 'don't eat it, but wait.' Then the goat came along and swallowed it, leaves, root, and all.

Minona's portrait hung for a long time in a corner of Kokoschka's house. Her face shone down on him over the Chinese porcelain, and the artist often talked of her. He had found her uncompromising Scottish stubbornness, which had scarcely been softened at all by her Catholic education, completely puzzling. Yet when I looked at the pastel-drawing he cried aloud: Don't touch, it is sacred. And, absorbed in the picture, he would murmur to himself: She was wonderful, like a flower. I would like to gaze at her face for ever. Yes, that is painting.

But the burning question now is, Why paint at all? For the future, perhaps? They will only use it for fuel.

Kokoschka talked repeatedly about the portrait at that time. He thought that perhaps he had had a glimpse of heaven in that picture, but he had worked it over many times, like the others. He likened himself to the dyer who dips his cloth into the colour until the picture is finished at last.

All through his rich creative life Kokoschka has turned continually back to portraiture. In May 1945 he painted an Irish lady who was a great lover of horses and a bold rider. He found the poise of her neck and shoulders beautiful beyond belief. So he talked to her beguilingly in a way she had never known before, till she bloomed and became daily more beautiful.

What a lovely woman! he said, when the painting was finished. He had almost fallen in love with her, so he painted in a little angel bearing a leafy garland to adorn her.

At the same time Kokoschka had in his mind to do a portrait of the scientist, J. D. Bernal, somewhat in the style of the portrait of Forel. But now he was an artist wise in the ways of the world, and no longer the dreaming diffident youth relying on his eyes alone. He therefore studied Bernal's most important work, *The Social Function of Science*.[12] He could not understand how the author could write in such a way and at the same time be engaged in the production of huge bombs, only because he was a crystallographer. Nor was Kokoschka able to understand the scientist's 'social reasons' for taking an active part in the war.

The two men met, and Kokoschka said afterwards: He has an interesting, attractive face, but thinks only of the discovery of atom bombs. But now that the artist had at last decided to paint Bernal he wanted to find out what was going on in the man's head. After all, heads were like the Russian toy—just a wooden doll with another inside, and another, and another. Kokoschka had always believed himself to be an anarchist, but then it occurred to him that it is the anarchist who throws the bombs, and that he could never do.

The portrait, however, was never painted, because the scientist had to remain in a secret place doing war work.[13] Even so, Kokoschka was so disturbed by the appalling consequences of Rutherford's great discovery that he could not do other than express his fear for mankind in paint.

Thus, instead of the portrait, he painted an allegory, ATOMIC ENERGY UNCHAINED. A beautiful spring landscape with tall trees and children playing with a ball, the foreground in brilliant light. A clown—or a scientist, perhaps a physicist, at any rate he looks like a scholar—holds a key in one hand and a watering-can with which he is sprinkling a giant oak tree in the other. A dove sits in the branches, while another 'dove of peace' circles anxiously round. Flags of all nations flutter from the branches and everything is cheerful and bright. A notice is pinned to the trunk, and on it are portraits of famous statesmen, like negro idols. These are the men of Yalta. On the left is a cage belonging to a circus, while in the middle-ground a woman sits watching a playing child. She cries as though her heart would break. The axis of the composition passes through her face, thus increasing the tension. From the cage in the background a fearful monster emerges, and the woman knows that her child will be dead in a moment. The clown has forgotten to lock the menagerie.

A remarkable portrait was painted during the summer of 1947. At Sierre (Canton Valais) in Switzerland Kokoschka was introduced to Werner Reinhart, the director of a large firm, an immensely rich man and a patron of the arts. Rilke had been his guest in the small castle of Muzot, and the housekeeper who had been employed to look after the poet was still with the family. At the very first meeting Kokoschka realized that he was dealing with a tortuous mind—like a tin of sardines, he said, terribly difficult to open, and impossible without the key. The artist, realizing the delicacy of his task, laid down certain conditions. The sitter was to give as many sittings as might be required, and Kokoschka wanted to be at liberty to dispose of the painting as he liked so as to be able to paint freely, unhampered by other people. Thirdly, the painter was to be given somewhere to work in peace. He was living at the time in the Hotel Bellevue, originally a castle. There was an empty room there, but it was cluttered, they said, with old furniture. They all went up the stairs, and the innkeeper's wife opened the door. It was a sunny day, and the light threw a pattern of stripes from the closed shutters on to the floor. The woman stood in the doorway, behind her Kokoschka, and then Reinhart. 'Have you seen it?' she asked, frightened, stepping quickly back. Kokoschka found himself standing in the middle of the room looking at a portrait of a medieval landowner, the man who had built the castle. Finally he decided not to paint there, because he found the atmosphere disturbing. So Herr Reinhart sat for him in the shade of a group of beautiful chestnut trees in front of his house. After three weeks the painting was so far advanced that the sitter thought it was finished. Reinhart was growing impatient because he wanted to go to India on business, but Kokoschka knew that the vital spark was still lacking. Reinhart went away, and Kokoschka painted the Matterhorn. When he came back to the portrait it was late autumn, and almost all the leaves had fallen from the trees. Now Kokoschka had to finish the picture started in the summer, but inspiration dragged its feet. Reinhart lay on the chaise-longue, wrapped in blankets to the ears, with the giant trunk of the leafless tree behind. Kokoschka looked at the heavy forehead. Like neolithic man, he thought. And at that moment the man's body twisted slightly from the hips, his eyes still staring upwards. Kokoschka suddenly asked him:

Weren't you in London thirty years ago, didn't you tell me? Yes.

And did you go to the Keeper of Assyrian Antiquities in the British Museum and ask him for a life-size plaster cast? (Hesitantly) Yes.

Of the Assyrian lion with a spear in its chest?

(Reinhart was amazed) How could you know that? Unfortunately I could not get the cast, but I still keep a large photograph of it in my office.

Kokoschka was able to add a few swift strokes of the brush and the painting was finished. He remembered that the sitter seemed shy whenever he caught sight of it. Reinhart's portrait was only acquired by the family after his death, and it now hangs in the museum at Winterthur.

One autumn day in 1945 a timid boy came to visit Kokoschka. His parents had sent him to say good-bye because he was going to stay with relatives in America to start a new life there. As the artist looked at the boy I could see that he was moved, more than was betrayed by his half-joking remarks. Gradually he became more serious. He wanted to give the boy a keepsake for the journey. He had never been in America, he said, although he had once been given tickets for the journey, but had never set off.[14] His pictures, though, were there like children, making a name for themselves. So he said to the boy: You are fortunate to have such a chance while you are young. But don't forget that over there money is the only measure of success. Society is entirely based on money —at least that is what most immigrants believe. You may think that the fact that they all go round like horses in blinkers is a form of discipline and self-control in some people and poverty of education in others. Moreover, immigrants seem to import this streamlined attitude without knowing it. Try to educate yourself. Open your eyes and never rely on hearsay. Try to live so that when you are old you can say: 'I am not ready to die, there is too much to see and to learn.' At your age one feels immortal, but life passes like a flash. You must live your life. Enjoy yourself, do not spend all your time earning money. Your days are numbered. Then, he turned to me and added: What will the young people do without me?

He said that he was astonished when he was a little boy to realize that adults had been here longer than he had, and asked them the same question: How could you have got on without me?

Turning once more to the boy, the artist confessed that he had never lived for money. He could have been as rich as any of the fashionable painters, but he preferred to remain independent and free. When he donated the fee for his portrait of Maisky towards the hospital at Stalingrad he had only five pounds in his pocket.

This man—and here Kokoschka picked up a copy of his portrait of the Russian

Ambassador—was taciturn. One of Kokoschka's English friends had persuaded Maisky to have his portrait painted in order that the fee could be given to a fund for building a hospital among the ruins of Stalingrad for both German and Russian wounded. Maisky agreed to sit three times in his study at the Embassy, but Kokoschka demurred, saying that he was a painter and not a photographer and must be able to see into a man's soul in order to paint a discerning portrait. The Ambassador read *The Times* throughout the sitting, saying not a word. Kokoschka, however, once goaded him: Your Excellency, now I have read the back page of *The Times* from top to bottom, could you please turn over!

Look at this face, Kokoschka said to the boy: It is impenetrable, like a mask. He was the most powerful wartime Ambassador and highly esteemed in London. He even managed to survive the subsequent party purge.

Kokoschka moved over to the table and began to turn the pages of the American *Arts Magazine*, drawing the boy's attention to the reproduction of his early double portrait of Professor Dr Hans Tietze and his wife. Munch had painted similar double portraits, such as Christian Gierløff and his wife, and Mr and Mrs Nörregård.

Kokoschka handled the problem of two people in one picture several times, as for instance SPOSALIZIO—the newly-weds—painted in 1912. It shows a remarkable contrast with the Renaissance handling of the same theme. The gesture of trust, of protection and possession, by the man is depicted in heavy hands laid on the woman's shoulders, while she points devotedly to her wedding ring. In 1917 Kokoschka painted a pair of lovers in a landscape in the vigorous style of the Dresden period. The cat in the painting lends a symbolic note to the atmosphere created by the figures of Käthe Richter and Walther Hasenclever. In 1945 Kokoschka painted a picture of a faun and a woman, and in the light-hearted manner common to both Gothic and Baroque he added two figures in coitus in the background. Only very rarely, for instance in the double female nude of 1913, is the emotional content reduced to the benefit of formal problems. Like his early religious paintings, it is also painted in facets, whereas the relationship of the two women with the ducks, in the 1933 painting, is approached quite differently. Here the human note is uppermost: the relationship between two friends, one fair and one dark—the attraction, affection, and laziness of a summer's day. In the WOMAN WITH A SLAVE, painted in 1920, the eye is drawn to the bold portrait of a woman at the centre of the composition, whereas the other figures are more a product of colour arrangement than of emotional expression, like Manet's *Olympia*. On the other hand, the SLAVE GIRL presents a human emotional relationship that is much more dramatic. The contrast between the rigid unswerving figure in the background and the kneeling nude woman who fills the whole foreground and gazes voluptuously into space is startling. The picture is enveloped in the glorious red of the painter's poetic palette, and is one of the most splendid paintings from Kokoschka's rich Dresden period. At almost the same time Kokoschka painted a mother and child in which the decorative colour and serene planes are stressed, as in the GIRL WITH A DOLL, whereas the earlier painting of the BLIND MOTHER AND CHILD emphasizes tragedy. The latter painting is peculiarly sculptural, and apart from the SELF-PORTRAIT WITH RAISED BRUSH, to which it is closely related, is quite isolated in Kokoschka's *oeuvre*.

In 1931 Kokoschka was working in a compact plastic style that betrayed little of his usual tense sensitivity—for example, the double portrait presenting two aspects of the same girl, TRUDL AS AN AMAZON AND TRUDL MATERNAL. The suave painting of the two Arab girls marks Kokoschka's new-found joy in life and light in Africa, as does the painting, done in 1925, of an Arab girl suckling her baby with a young negress sitting beside her and a camel in the background.

CHILDREN PLAYING—Kokoschka handled the theme again in BROTHER AND SISTER—is one of the artist's most powerful compositions concerning the relationship between two people. It is very personal in its approach and contains less of his earlier subjection to the old masters than, for instance, the ANNUNCIATION of 1911. The head of Mary, with closed eyes and indrawn breath, and the movement of the hands so characteristic of the artist, reminds one of Dürer. This painting is undoubtedly a major work of the early period. St Elizabeth rising with loving outstretched arms from the waves, her bidding arms denied by the gentle gesture of Mary, is painted in the mature style of an old master, notwithstanding the artist's youth, whilst the clash of colour and the impact of the nude in such a connexion are quite new. Again, in the painting called THE VISITATION, the solitary nude gives a sense of shock. But the contemplative head supported by her hand draws the attention away from her nakedness. Figure and landscape are woven together as it were with rays of light, drawing the background forwards and joining the foreground with the distance. It is a dimensional composition. And, like a glistening jewel of yellow, pink, and green, an Austrian village shimmers at the foot of the mountain.

Kokoschka told the young man that he had painted the Tietzes at about the same age as the boy before him. Dr Tietze was Professor of Art History. The portrait had never been exhibited, or even photographed, because it was a symbol of their lifelong companionship. Then Hitler drove them out, and the Tietzes arrived penniless in America. They had to sell the picture and lived on the proceeds. In Vienna the artist's brother had collected the fee in ten-shilling instalments. So Kokoschka's signature, although at first people would not believe it, became of greater value than those of the Finance Ministers in every country he had visited during the preceding thirty years. Some refugees brought his pictures rolled up under their arm with them when they escaped from Europe. It was all the capital they had. Thus his attitude to things proved itself stronger than money.[15]

But, one may ask, why should Kokoschka recount all this to the young man? Usually, when one person talks to another, it is because he wants something. What then could he want from the boy? Only that his words should fall on fertile soil and grow to maturity. So he continued: What is the nature of modern man? He complains that life now is worse than that of his parents, and they declare that life was better for previous generations. Recently there was a World Youth Congress in England, and the whole discussion turned on how work was to be found for everyone. It never occurred to anyone to question how the world could be improved. No one gave a thought to future generations.

You, my son, are a Jew. Next to the Greeks the Jews have best understood how to write history, and they have bequeathed to us a wonderfully rich human tradition—David plays the harp to soothe Saul's sorrow; Jacob wrestles with the Angel; Ruth in the alien corn, Solomon, and Job—so many pictures and descriptions of human situations. That was hundreds of years ago! Rembrandt lived among the poorest people, probably the most insignificant Jews in Amsterdam, but his contact with them, and with a poor Rabbi in the city, caused the seed to flower again. The Blessing was renewed in his wonderful paintings. In the olden days man knew how to make the world beautiful. Now, both rich and poor only try to exploit it.

Kokoschka pointed to a poster hanging on the wall which one saw everywhere in the Underground at the time—Christ leaning down from the Cross to help children. The poster had no political or cognate significance, and simply bore the words: 'In memory of the children of Europe, who have to die of hunger and cold this Christmas because of the war.' Kokoschka said he had done it to try to rouse the conscience of the people.

The boy asked one question before he left: 'What do you feel about religion?'

Throwing out his arms Kokoschka said: 'I believe, I believe; but I am not superstitious, and I do not subscribe to any dogma.'

There had been an exhibition of medieval German art at Schaffhausen in 1947 which made a profound impression on Kokoschka because it expressed his metaphysical experience and described a world of the past when the children of God were blessed, a time when supernatural Grace was bestowed on man and on creation.[16] 'The education of the soul of a religious man was a knowledge, a *Summa summarum*, that was communicable and was handed on. The idea of complete absorption in abstract thought, in which logic, like a mathematical problem, undertakes to resolve the riddle of eternity, and in which the philosophy of enlightenment replaces monotheism by deductive analysis, would have been recognized in the Middle Ages as insane. Europe inherited from the ancient Greeks the risks inherent in reason, in the denial of destiny. Freedom is limited by the outer world, by external impressions on the soul, and by blind chance, though the man who sees is not blind to chance. Freedom does not mean absurdity. A sense of personal responsibility and reasonable behaviour in the circumstances of the phenomenal world ensures a measure of moderation. Freedom of will is therefore fundamental to man's development in a catholic world. Exaltation beyond the self leads not to death, but to fusion of the sensate world with the human spirit, and brings compassion for the sufferings of others and revolt against man's inadequacy before the mercy of God.'

In the same essay written after he had seen the exhibition Kokoschka discussed the struggles of the pious against the materialism of the Renaissance, of the man who knows that he will lose his immortal soul if he declines the cup of bitterness. Kokoschka reminds us therein of the *Heliand*, that early Christian poem whose visions encompass the mystic experience of the West. The poem's substance is the natural revelation of Christ in the human heart, in contrast to the abstract theology of the Catholic world of the period. Catholics believe that all spiritual hope stems from acceptance and belief in this innate revelation, and all sorrow and discord from its rejection. Kokoschka's essay, *The Portrait in Past and Present*,[17] also interprets his unshakeable belief in the sanctity of life and in mankind.

THE TORMENT OF THE HEART

Przybszewski, inspired by Felicien Rop's lithographs *La Vengeance d'une femme* (A Woman's Vengeance) wrote: 'This is the tragedy of man destroyed by woman; the woman is the Whore of Babylon, Mylitta, the Whore of the Apocalypse, Georges Sand and Nana in one; an overwhelming symbol of the unceasing and ruthless war between the sexes.' *The Cry*, the famous painting by Edvard Munch, he saw in the same light: 'This is a frighteningly cosmic work, the final scene of a bitter struggle between mind and sex, a battle won by sex.'

Kokoschka's poems written between 1907 and 1918 reveal a similar attitude.[1] Even as a very young man he feared instinctively the intermittent bewitchment and rejection, long before he met the woman who was for three years before 1914 to fill his life with a burning passion, with pain and disillusion, with renewed love and hate, and before he had experienced that breath-taking, rapturous descent into an ocean of sensuality from which he was saved only by the primitive fear that he would lose not only his identity but also his creative powers.

'Senseless lust clutches at fear, insatiable search in empty space. Labour without birth, dance of the sun, shifting planes, the end of those who praised me.' In *Murder Hope of Woman* (1908) the man cries, 'O, your unmerciful word', while the dying Firdusi of *Sphinx and Strawman* stammers out: 'The spirit is passion's outlet. If it were not so passion would overwhelm body and soul, ravishing both. I believe in the spirit of man. Anima. Amen.'

What is love, that it drives man and woman to destroy each other? The longing to be together.

'Universal, brooding fear; nature lies waiting . . . what a miraculous breed is man, creating fertile vessels from phantoms . . . I burn with love.'

Then the pain of separation:

'I am sick at heart, like a flower in the dark. Give me your hand, O loveless one. Let me sit beside you once again, and close my eyes and dream away the past. God, I am afraid and weak. I cling to Thee alone.'

And Man's despair:

'My power of love is wasted; absorbed by you, it burns only fitfully. Softly the light fades and as softly returns, and touches you strange and ghostly shadow of yourself' (*The Burning Bush*, 1911).

This is the biological tragedy, the cry of love's slave.

'Sleeper, awake! A white bird has flown into the room and pecked out my eyes. Awake, sleeper! A red fish swam by, gorged with my blood. Bar the door, sleeper! A werewolf has devoured my heart' (*The Burning Bush*).

Man is the creator, not woman. Many years were to pass before Kokoschka understood that these were his own words falling from the woman's lips, whereas she repeated parrot-wise his words blinded and fatally wounded as he was.

'Who is the god who steals my words so that I think he is teaching me?' (*Sphinx and Strawman*, 1907).

And before he escapes her at last:

> Now shall you kindle your own light
> As it were by my love;
> The light burns by your flesh alone.
> Weary of searching for your soul
> You gave yourself to me.
> Thus you found yourself.
> Now when I draw away
> Softly, like a veil,
> Will you lose yourself again?

Munch depicted the same experience in *Ashes*—the emptiness and disillusion following physical love, the ashes left by a violent fire that has been fanned by a fierce wind. It is the message of Schopenhauer, Nietzsche, Strindberg, Hamsun, Wedekind, and Weininger, the suicidal tendency of a time in despair at its failure to find harmony. Lifted from its context it is original sin and acquaintance with death, man's loss of innocence through eating the Fruit of the Tree of Knowledge which tells of eternal life. It is the magic potion which bound Tristan and Isolde in suffering until death released them, the veil of mystery covering Eros in the presence of Psyche the lifting of which sacrificed love and happiness.

About 1911 Kokoschka was stricken by a passion which threatened to derange him. The attraction of a mature woman for a young man, an experience described vividly by Flaubert in *November*, the magnetism and ambivalence of the sexes in Baudelaire's *Vampire* and Hamsun's *Victoria*, are also a revolt against society that can only end in despair and renunciation. The poor, struggling artist, Kokoschka, and the society woman were incompatible. At last came the painful liberation, forcing the artist into an even darker, unimaginable emotional condition, driving him on towards self-sought death in battle. In *Orpheus and Eurydice* he sublimated his pain:

> Alas, alas! Misfortune is my lot. Distress, be gone.

The mortal conflict is illumined in this drama for the last time, and then came the desperate desire to kill the woman by transposing her into a fetish which he destroyed.

Kokoschka's passion overwhelmed him like a violent awakening, totally unpremeditated; it was a soaring freedom, a burning, unquenchable thirst. He was no longer conscious; thought was impossible. He was a stirring of the blood, a wave in the gathering stream of life, as if a sun had exploded in his mind blinding with its light, all thought consumed in the flame.

Intoxication of the senses, breathless immolation and raging jealousy, it was yet a triumph. She was one of the most beautiful women in Vienna, daughter of an artist and widow of a famous man. Very gifted herself, she was the centre of social activity, a proud, mature, and enchanting woman. Kokoschka was already acknowledged to be a painter of repute. She opened the doors to life, and in so doing made him a man.

He stood trembling at the source as he had once gazed awe-stricken at the mighty folds of the Alps. Then he longed for a child which should combine the beauty of Helen and the genius of Faust. This woman and their love would henceforth fill his art and all his thought. But he recognized the danger, saw himself enchanted, and broke away in another and almost fatal adventure. Art, Love, and War.[2]

That the woman was a widow was important. It was thought very poetic at the time, but Kokoschka had also a childhood memory of the widow of his uncle Scheba. Alma Mahler was very beautiful and, to the onlooker, fatally like Lilith in the 1913 portrait, as well as in the pearly double portrait of 1912.

Crowned, as it were, with the laurel wreath of love, she is like a goddess; their hands unfolding like the petals of a flower. Kokoschka's gaze is that of a boy no longer, his wide-open eyes are suffused with inexpressible mystery and lit by an inner light. In the powerful painting of THE TEMPEST both are pictured on an ocean lashed into fury by their blood, in communion with the elements and the stars. The woman is beautiful, earthly, mature and confident in the fulfilment of love. The man is very different; his face is resigned, meditative, expressing the memory of past suffering. It describes the effort to free himself from his sensual desire and from the loyalty that drives him ever and again back to the warmth and affection of the woman. Thought and emotion tear him apart. He wrings his hands in his dire peril, and tries to soften the conflict, but it increases and overwhelms him. Emotional agitation drove Kokoschka to paint this parable. The turmoil of his mind inspired his brush.

The composition is enriched with a mystic blue and green, and a perilous atmosphere is obtained by means of a shoreless sea, surging white-capped waves, and the wan sickle of the moon. The drunken boat,[3] borne on the crest of the waves, is lit by an eerie light, a shell encircling its precious burden. It is the vision of a dream powerfully imagined. Kokoschka was always swept away on the tides of life. His experiences arose spontaneously; they were in no way procured or contrived. In THE TEMPEST ocean and sky are smoothly painted without horizons, whilst the dominant cold tones are veined with rose and purple like marble. The centre of happening is marked by violent impasto, whereas the sleeping woman's body is smooth and lustrous like enamel. THE TEMPEST is magnificent—a superb and monumental painting in the manner of Tintoretto whose work made a deep impression on Kokoschka at that time.[4]

A woman of the Strindberg type, she had almost destroyed him, he once told me, but he managed to break free. The pain was overshadowed by the imminence of war. Physical separation forced an end to his intolerable anguish whilst leaving him in a mental turmoil which produced a condition of great emotional strain.

His relationship with Alma Mahler had already begun to grow wearisome on their journeys to the Alps and to Italy together in 1913. But at the time when his mother perceived his danger he was still the lover, who had disavowed even her lest he be thought less a master than a slave. For months he never went home. Then his mother took it upon herself to write to the woman—to appeal to her mature sense. She had already seen one man die; surely she would not want to break the boy's heart? And what was more, she explained, her son had a great future (Loos had assured her), and if he did not fulfil all the expectations of the connoisseurs, then it would be Alma Mahler's fault. Finally, she threatened to shoot her if she did not release him by a certain date.

His mother had not said anything to him about it, Kokoschka went on, and on the appointed day she actually walked up and down in front of Alma Mahler's house and it certainly looked as though she had a gun in her purse. When the artist learned about it— the woman dared not leave the house—he went at once to see his mother. He was cruel and inconsiderate, she had eyes only for his wretchedness. He wanted to play the cavalier, but she saw how unhappy he was.

Where had she found the revolver? he asked. She used to smile roguishly behind her hand. If you only knew, she answered. She had put her hand into the purse so that it bulged, and the woman was frightened. His mother's warm laughter reconciled them. That happiness was different, he already knew. He had written a poem to free himself from his obsession with Alma Mahler. It was entitled Αλλος Μακαρ—*Allos Makar* (1913), an anagram of their combined names meaning, in Greek, Happiness is different.[5] In 1945 Kokoschka read the poem to me in London. He read it slowly, stressing the rhythms, with pauses followed by a stream of words. Grouped thus together, their meaning, which was often lost in reading, became clear. Thus, while I listened to the onomatopaeic beat of word-groups like *Erd-Spalte* and *Schäume-Räume*, I was able to follow the underlying thought:

'Everything that walks the earth, that rends the heavens, seeking its warmth from others, that you are not and cannot be.' Followed by the narcissistic outcry: 'Desire leads back unto itself.' At last, resignedly: 'Man is afraid of the others' gain. His power wastes away in the other.'

The *Burning Bush* of 1911, a dramatic dialogue of shifting form, impalpable as a shadow-play, also touched on the mysterious relationship between man and woman. The Lover abandons the woman, but not without suffering: 'I see a man weeping on the ground, his beard besmirched with dust.' Woman, the object of his desire, is by nature faithless. 'The just man knew her, the stranger put her to the test. The beast attacked and devoured the man and spewed him forth. The wounds were gaping when love was sweet, man and woman.'

Woman has two avenues of escape; as a mother:

'Woman, you who trampled the snake, your heart swells in the joy of motherhood.' And as a pure untouched virgin:

'I long to encircle my lover unseen, like the calyx of a rosebud.'

But her release is short-lived, and she falls once more to longing—

'My flesh is like a burning bush.'

The man's faith is shattered—

'Are you human, then O long-haired one?'

Then at last, he rouses himself above his own destiny, recognizing the primal force of man and woman—

'Woman is innocent, but a shivering restlessness inhabits the man.'

And so he renounces her—

'Go, Woman!'

She casts a stone against his breast, and he cries—

'See, my life is fading in sacrifice.'

She seems only then, when he is dying, to be truly released. Falling to the ground she calls—

'I, too, suffer.'

Then, out of her unquiet insatiable longing—

'Forsake me not.'

Kokoschka was The Fettered Columbus, the discoverer of a new land—woman. And she it was who chained him and tried to turn him into a beast, as Circe enchanted Odysseus. The stammering richly symbolic prose of *The Fettered Columbus* begins, as it were, in the middle of a sentence. A white bird—the soul—hops round in the light of the full moon.

'A woman stands in the face of the moon, waiting.'

The poet is attracted by her—

'From the moment when the bestial lust seized me I was sick.'

Love changed him so much that his 'face was altered, becoming the face of a sinister creature with glowing eyes, such as inhabits lonely caverns in the mountains . . . out of the depths of my passion only my boyhood days seemed happy.'

'How can I explain that all my inclination for the sunlight disappeared, how thoughts of dying filled my mind—and of killing. How I reproach her burning love! Her clumsy hands have torn my sides as though with thorns!'

A dream appeases the boy after he has driven off the white bird—

'Groups of girl-children, longing to be kissed, float before my eyes. Girls watch me, holding each other's hands, like bunches of mulberries they are falling from a stem.

It is dreamlike language, avoiding every clear-cut idea like a myth. Thoughts crowd in, forming images and dialogues with an inner coherence which echoes in the ear sadly, like a forgotten melody: The enmity between man and woman has existed since time immemorial—

'And I will put enmity between thee and the woman, and between thy seed and her seed. It shall bruise thy head, and thou shalt bruise his heel.' (I Moses 3:15)

Kokoschka—'After I had concealed my knife beneath the cushions, could you not have been saved, I ask myself?' A love dialogue ends despairingly: Will you have my eternal life? Years of tortured longing pass 'until I prowled round in wild madness, railing against this senseless power. What is this beast that can only seize good in dreams? Then came a soft voice through the mists of evening: A friend's gifts must not be questioned. You have attained the everlasting dream and will never wake again. Dreaming you will stumble upon tumultuous bliss. Try to cross the dark bridge, for death is the snare of youth.'

Death alone can reconcile the agony of longing—

'Moon Woman, now that my body is lost, may we stay together always? Virgin Moon, was it the last time we were together that you aroused such terrible longing?'

Thus the strange poem ends with a question.

Kokoschka also saw himself as Job, whose suffering in the drama of the same name still could not shake his faith in the Eternal. Adam enlightens him, saying: 'You have set your wife too high.'

Hiob (1917), beginning with Adam's sigh of despair, Would that the Lord had left my rib in peace, contains illustrations which include one of the artist's finest red-chalk drawings.*

Hiob presents the grotesque comedy of the cuckold. It is written in a style owing something to both the folk theatre and the Old Testament, with telling blows against the seducer of mind and body, the friend of the family, the intellectual Mr Rubberman. It contains his complaints against Anima, the woman.

(Adam: 'A woman has turned his head, and now she makes a fool of him)—finally she prophesies in the dark over the dead Job—and Anima, who settled the cross on Job's shoulders, is in truth Eve.

The first of the fourteen scenes of the drama pictured by the lithographs represents Job, the serving-girl, and the parrot before Anima's door, while she empties a chamber-pot over his head. In the second scene Job appears with bandaged head accompanied by the Rubberman, his doglike face below an elegantly shabby top hat. A powerful drawing. Then comes Job and the poodle, Job with his cuckold's horns and Anima as a *bourgeoise*, with the Rubberman kneeling before her. The third lithograph depicts Job holding a skull and naked girls. It is perhaps the most impressive of the series, and is followed by the recumbent girl and the hotspur; the witches' curse, a Walpurgis-night scene with two figures; a pair of seated lovers with Eros and snuffling hounds; then Job crawling on all-fours wearing cuckold's horns; the parrot and an exceptionally erotic scene in the middle ground; the entombment of Job by Adam, the gardener, and the top-hatted mutes in the cemetery; the woman preventing the man from screaming, and finally, the last scene, Anima-Eve with her foot on the head of Job, with the mourners in top hats in the background.

Kokoschka made twelve lithographs for *The Fettered Columbus* (1916). The title-page shows Alma Mahler in profile, tensely drawn and hatched through with seismographic horizontal lines symbolizing the passion of love. Another portrait of her completes the series. Her head is supported by her right hand while she contemplates the furious

* Seven of the illustrations are done in red chalk, the remainder in black.

powers she has unleashed and cannot control. In the other prints the restless desperate man stands behind the woman, who lies stretched on a couch before the peaceful flame of a lighted candle, while in the sky the waxing moon rises. Another print shows the man kneeling before the woman, who hands him the Fruit of the Tree of Knowledge. She has the face of Medusa, and the moon is waning. Then the man breaks the fetters of love; he is the new Columbus, and St George the Dragon-Killer strides by. The scene with the embracing couple depicts the tortures of jealousy, whilst the foreground shows the figure of the martyred youth. Finally, there is a grandiose composition depicting the meeting of man and woman in a rocky visionary landscape, where they are seen as two alien invincible powers of nature moving on planes that never meet, in directions which must inevitably fail to cross each other's paths. Thus the tragedy ends. In the *Pietà* from the same series the woman bends over the dying man, and in the penultimate print she steps triumphantly over his bier. Other prints are apocalyptic—a Dance of Death, open graves, and a Resurrection. The bursting pillar of fame symbolizes Gustav Mahler, while the crowing, flying cockerel is the symbol of the young artist. Then there is the moving self-portrait with a skeleton in the moonlit wilderness, the vampire woman, and finally the man-eating beast, symbolizing the erotic passion of the youth with raised arms.

All these lithographs are imagined in starkly dramatic settings. Both external and interior action are portrayed on the same sheet in an apocalyptic and Zarathustrian landscape with threatening skies and gloomy crags, with suns and moons surrounding the figures and throwing their spiritual condition into relief. *The Fettered Columbus* and the Bach Portfolio were finished at Semmering in 1914, just before the outbreak of the war. Kokoschka's nerves were strung tight by the threat of war to a point where he could depict his future wounds. The two works, *Hiob* and *The Fettered Columbus*, were the confession of all he knew about life.

The most significant graphic work of the pre-war period is the Bach Portfolio. It contains visions inspired by the Bach Cantata (opus 60), *O Ewigkeit du Donnerwort*.*[6]

The Bach Portfolio is the way of liberation. It is a dialogue between Fear and Hope, represented by a man and a woman. Their flesh is gradually consumed to the nerve-ends and the bone. That was Kokoschka's own interpretation. Fear and Hope are not, however, so portrayed that man can be cast as Hope and woman as Fear. Kokoschka regards them as a manifestation less of the two sexes—hence the suppression throughout of the primary sex symbol—than of mankind. They afford a medium through which visual cathartic situations can be developed that are expressed in the music by the alternation of the male and female voices. For Kokoschka the great enigma was man's encounter with death. Whether this work arose from a critical personal problem or from the fear of himself in sexuality, which would have caused death to appear to him in its medieval garb as a warning (it is clear that his whole world was in danger of being engulfed in eroticism), or whether by the disquieting foreknowledge of war (since war would appear to him as a release from the bondage of love), the artist undoubtedly succeeded in sublimating his personal experience in a universal and timeless creation. The Bach

*Original German version on p. 143.

Portfolio of Kokoschka is undoubtedly a Mysterium; but it is not purely erotic.[6] Kokoschka sees maternal aspects of life in which love, growth, and the mysteries are all embedded. Hence the woman is the womb of life and continuity. At the same time the artist has a primitive fear of woman. He instinctively understands the sublimation of sex in art, of the transformation of the seed into the spirit. Art and existence are two contradictory worlds closely linked nevertheless by the mediation of man, whose condition vacillates unceasingly between being, becoming, and fulfilment. Man encounters many forms of death in his lifetime, but the man who leaves no creative work behind him dies, whilst the woman is immortal as life itself. Hence the artist is like the woman. Kokoschka confesses that he belongs to the underworld—to the mothers. Such a man may die many deaths but be resurrected, and this idea is foreshadowed in *The Burning Bush* of 1911—'I believe in resurrection through me.'

The complete edition of the Bach Portfolio has on the cover a pen drawing of a woman with outstretched arms, standing on a globe on the sea-shore, the classic motif of Fortuna. It also contains a youthful self-portrait, a reflection in a mirror. One hand is clutched to his breast, symbolizing his suffering in the world, while the other holds a pencil and wrests creation from suffering. The Portfolio was dedicated to the Countess of Mensdorff Dietrichstein, and bore the date September 1916. *The Dedication*, a poem by Kokoschka, followed next, succeeded by the print, *Dragon over the Flame*. It depicts the flames of life with the menacing spirit of evil hanging overhead. In Christian myth the dragon, like the snake, is a seducer of Eve, the symbol of Satan and the devil. The Renaissance portrayed the dragon as the enemy of the good and of the Divine. Most civilizations imagined a similar legendary creature combining the features of different and dangerous animals and symbolizing the Beast. The dragon appears for the first time as an adversary, although in China and Japan it is a symbol of power and beneficence. It is the spirit of change, and therefore of life.[7] Kokoschka uses it in a modified Christian sense as a symbol of temptation, and later in the same series with an eagle as the symbol of Victory.

> *Fear* Eternity thou fearful word!
>   O sword that pierces my soul!
>   O intimation of death!
>   O Eternity, time without end!

This is followed by the lithograph, *Wanderer in the Storm*, portraying a man whose consciousness is suddenly shaken by a flash which lightens the heavens, and which he grasps like a pilgrim's staff: Eternity—fear—love—work.

> *Fear* O stony path to the last battle.
> *Hope* My solace awaits me,
>   The Saviour stands at my side to comfort me.
> *Fear* The fear of death, the last agony
>   Draws near, clutching at my heart
>   And paralysing my limbs.

This is followed by a print in which the woman guides the man. His hands crossed over his breast, he wears a melancholy and resigned expression. The woman's arms are raised as she points with the left hand to the distance, past a leafless tree and an owl flying through the night. Beyond stands a gravestone with a skull and crossbones on the path which the figures leave behind. In the Renaissance this was a symbol for Golgotha. According to an early Christian legend, the Cross was set above the skull and bones of Adam so that every man must pass through the Cross to Eternal Life. Thus it is written, 'The first man Adam became a living being; the last Adam became a life-giving spirit.' (I. Cor. 15:45.) Kokoschka used it to express the difficult choice between love and the opposing pull of the artist's calling. In Egyptian folk-lore the owl symbolizes death, night, coldness, and passivity. It is an attribute of Ra, the Sun-god, who daily sinks below the horizon to cross the Sea of Darkness. Christian myth associates the night-loving owl with Satan, the Prince of Darkness. A symbol of solitude, the bird is often depicted near the dwelling-place of hermits. Its oldest attribute, however, is wisdom, and therefore it sometimes appears with Saint Jerome. Metaphorically the owl is also used as an attribute of Christ (Luke I, 79). This explains the appearance of the owl in paintings of the Crucifixion. In ancient Greece the bird was an attribute of Pallas Athene, and signified wisdom.

Hope	Lord, I await Your coming
Fear	Fear and sorrow bind me,
	I know not whither to turn.
	My fearful heart draws back,
	My tongue is twisted with pain.

This is followed by *The Supplicant*. The drawing depicts a naked woman kneeling alone and in deep despair in a bleak landscape with a cloud-wracked moon overhead. A print of such power has not been done in Germany since Grünewald.

Hope	My body is a sacrifice to God,
	And though the fires of purgatory may burn
	They will purify my sacrifice.
Fear	But now my guilt and sin will pass before my eyes.
Hope	God will therefore not pronounce judgement.
	He sets an end to the trials and persecution
	So that men can suffer them.

The next drawing illustrates mountains and a craggy landscape with huge rocks, a tree-stump and the rising sun shining over a marshy heath. Artistic licence allowing the sun to burst forth in front of the mountain-range, as if it were a halo above the man's head, lends unusual force to this drawing. The man is naked, as is his companion. His right hand supports his head while the left performs an explanatory, weary gesture, serving to underline the sad expression of his eyes and mouth. The woman's

37 Oskar Kokoschka, *c.* 1931

38 The Marabout of Temacine, 1928

39 Arab Women, 1928

face is wretched. But the light above his head may irradiate the dreadful heath?

Fear	My last retreat fills me with fear.
Hope	The Saviour's hand will guide me.
Fear	My faith is fast falling.
Hope	Jesus will bear my burden.

The rift between the Christian transcendental creed of the Bach Cantata and the artist's confession becomes ever wider. The desperate man and woman climb ever higher into the mountains. In the next print they stand beside the trunk of a dead tree leaning against a crag. They are naked and without hope. The highest peak of the mountains, their destination, is still far away. The man stands behind the woman, comforting her with one hand and pointing upwards with the other. Can these be Fear and Hope? Nay, Fear, rather, and belief in himself, despite the pain of parting and the *danse macabre* of the coming war.

Fear	The yawning grave is abhorrent.
Hope	The grave is an abode of peace.
Fear	Death is detested and feared by man,
	It is the loss of all hope.
Holy Spirit	Blessèd are the dead.
Fear	Alas, alas what danger waits
	The soul that must tread the path of the dying.
	The terrors of hell make death to be feared
	For the soul may be already damned
	When death comes to claim it.

Man and Woman stepping over a Dead Body—The path winds upwards towards the mountain peak. The man walks strongly, his right hand held to his ear like a murmuring shell as if he were listening to a distant voice. With his left arm he pushes the woman aside, and she stands with folded hands, her feet on the ribs of a skeleton, gazing dispiritedly at her companion. The underlying sense of this print is autobiographical.

Holy Spirit	Blessèd are they who die in the Lord.
Fear	If I die in the Lord,
	Is blessedness then to be my lot?
	My body shall feed the worms,
	Yea, my limbs shall turn to dust
	For I am a child of death—
	It seems that in the grave I am gone forever.
Holy Spirit	Blessèd are they who die in the Lord
	From henceforth.

Now comes the drawing which echoes the words of the Holy Spirit, 'Blessèd are the Dead.' It is the exultation of the artist's spirit. An eagle soars above a broad and distant landscape, surveying it with a sharp eye. Huge clouds are piled up in the background.

Fear   Behold I shall be blessèd from henceforth.
Hope, come fill once more my heart!
Now may my body rest in peace without fear
And my spirit look forward to everlasting joy.

Now the ancient enmity between man and woman is stark and clear. The woman interred the man. She sits astride the stone coffin, the sickle moon above her head. In classical mythology the moon is the mother-goddess who is often depicted standing above or on a crescent moon, expressing the power of Eternity. In Kokoschka's drawing the woman's face is full of sorrow, not Strindberg's hatred. The real tragedy is destiny. The grave yawns; we see the face of the artist framed by his hands. His vision of the future is revealed as the sun rises over the far horizon.

Chorus
      So be it Lord, if it be Thy will
Take me to your bosom.
Jesus my Saviour comes; goodnight, O World!
I am going to the Heavenly Mansion,
Whither I travel in peace
Leaving my dreadful sorrow below.
So be it!

So be it. The artist has overcome doubt and temptation and held to his chosen path. He is saved from death, depicted in the last of the series, the *Pietà*. He will live to complete his work.[8]

Remember the face of the man in THE TEMPEST which lays bare his thought. He seems to search within his memory for the meaning of creation, but the woman comes between. It is a rift in the soul of mankind. Seeking expression and fulfilment, it is blinded by love. He was not born for such misuse, for he was a knight in gleaming armour, galloping in fantasy, grasping the reins, and an angel stood on the path pointing upwards, whilst behind lurked the shadowy figure of death like some huge insect or maggot of the earth. Kokoschka had painted this theme in 1909.[9] Now the same experience was repeated. He saw himself as the KNIGHT ERRANT slung between heaven and earth—between the ghastly smile of Death and the woman set in a storm-lashed landscape. The letters of despair, E S, hang flaming in the sky: 'Eloi, Eloi, lama sabachthani'—'My God, my God, why hast thou forsaken me?'

The painting is grey on grey; land and sea painted in a sinister and austere palette, with a touch of brown in the foreground where the shells are lying, deep blue and green symbols of beauty. The crouching female figure beyond is tinged with pink, and the masts of the boats are barely suggested. Death is a wasp, menacing and burdensome, on the left of the two huge letters. In this painting Kokoschka predicted the nearly fatal wound he was to receive during the war. The picture was painted before he volunteered for service.[10] In composition and feeling KNIGHT ERRANT is directly linked with THE TEMPEST, in which the man's expression is one of resignation to his fate, of self-immolation in Heaven and Hell, an evocation of Death and Eternity. It portrays the will to experience good and evil, to sound the depths and scale the heights. The more Kokoschka drank of the fountain of life the greater was his thirst, and no experience was to be denied him. Years later he was to paint THE FOUNTAIN,[11] an allegorical picture which testifies to the enchantment by the woman, in the divine nature of which he believed, but which threatened to bind his spirit.

'THE FOUNTAIN is a large composition which I started in Dresden and subsequently exhibited in varying states in Tokyo, Paris, Rome and Vienna after 1922', runs a letter written to Dr Valentiner from Polperro in 1939.

'Sometimes we talked about God', Minona McEwen wrote to me, describing her meeting with Kokoschka, 'and he told me he did not believe in God but in the Mother Goddess, a great and beautiful spirit, benevolent and loving, not the harsh God who makes a note of good deeds like a banker that the payer may claim his percentage later.'[12]

Kokoschka remained a restless wanderer who forsook the inviting courts of beauty and love to follow his quest like a will-o-the-wisp across the world. He seldom heard life's magic voice telling him that he was one of the elect—that the gods only caused him to stumble and fall so that he would find himself again and be inspired to complete the work for which he was chosen. Nevertheless, even in the years of black despair when he was overwhelmed and stunned by the callous and senseless destruction of the war, he heard that voice. Then he would take his brushes and paint, charmed by its magic.

In the north of Scotland one day he heard a rock-dove calling. The call of the bird was the only reality in the fairy forest, which he composed and later called CAPRICCIO. The dove forms the centre of the composition. One can almost hear her cooing, but her expression is very like a death's head. She is the spatial as well as the narrative focus around which this poetic painting is constructed. The water falls coolly through the green, and its path crosses the gaze of a rabbit towards the dove. A girl is pointing with outstretched arm towards a goat, whilst her gaze encompasses both rock-dove and onlooker. A man is barefoot in the warm summer day, and is wearing a hat; in his hand a wooden cockerel, a symbol of watchfulness and caution and also of the Passion—the bird of dawning whose cry fell heavy on the ears of Peter: 'Verily, verily, I say unto you, before the cock crows thou shalt deny me thrice.'

And then there is the goat whose movements wild and shy are composed and confined around its astonished eye. In Kokoschka's imaginative world the goat plays an important part. It is the embodiment of fruitfulness and the nourisher of our Mediterranean culture, of Greek and Biblical ancestry. The painting is a symphony of blue, green, violet, yellow, and orange in which the relationships are pictorial and emotional. If you look at the painting for a long time, allowing the eye to rest on the enchanted forest suddenly it becomes clear. The goat is not a symbol, nor the rabbit, nor the dove, nor the girl in her blue dress, nor the half-naked man in the straw hat. They are real, because life is real and just as mysterious. Life seems to whisper, the rabbit is. But what is a rabbit? And why does the death's head entice us with sweet notes while the stream flows gently by? And why is the man carving a block of wood and painting it to make it look like a cockerel? In the first version there were no figures in the picture, only a cottage on the left, and a pillar and a lion on the right—a lion creeping round a pillar. 'Where is the end of all being?'[13] the dreaming youth had asked. There is no more need to ask. The grown man finds fulfilment in the experience of being, his renewal and happiness. It is the philosophy contained in the expression of the man in THE TEMPEST. This was not the last time that Kokoschka was to paint his way out of an agonizing situation concerning a woman, although no other so nearly destroyed him. For the sake of his art he forswore the happiness which could have been his, choosing instead creative unrest, resignation, and poverty. He had not been born so that he could experience happiness, but to bear witness to creation. The real-life fairy-tale which follows may help to clarify our understanding of the artist's attitude to woman.

He was in Istanbul, Kokoschka told me one day, and was painting the Bosphorus, when he received a telegram from Switzerland to say that a certain young woman had just arrived at a friend's house. To him she seemed a supernatural person. Every three or four years she would appear, talk with him for a little while, and then leave. She exerted a magic influence over him all his life. On this occasion he dropped everything and went straight to the airport, taking the first plane. It was bound for Italy. Below lay the Aegean with the golden islands of the Odyssey in the calm blue sea. He arrived in Venice, rushed to the station, and caught a train to Geneva, then another out into the country, where he arrived exhausted in the middle of the night. It was late summer. He had failed to find a car for the last stage of the journey and had done it on foot. This part of the journey seemed longer by far than the hundreds of miles from Istanbul to the Swiss border. He sent in his card, and after a few minutes she came out to greet him. He saw her face in the moonlight, and she talked softly to him as though it were only yesterday that they had met. They walked together in the garden for about a quarter of an hour, and he listened to her reasoned well-bred words, answering in the same tone. Then she took her leave, and he went away without having set foot in the house. This conversation had completely transformed him.

A few years later he suddenly left Paris to go to Annecy because he had heard a rumour that she intended to spend her summer holidays there. There was a catch in his voice as he told me, but I did not look up because I realized that there were some things he preferred not to discuss. After a pause he went on. Shortly before dinner on the day he arrived there was a stupendous thunderstorm. The earth seemed to shudder, the lake was lashed into huge waves, and the whole landscape appeared purple in the eerie light. They had been dancing together, when she suddenly decided that she would like to swim. The hotel grounds ran down to the lake and he waited for her at a prearranged spot. The moon rose. One of the guests came to see the effect of moonlight and lightning on the lake, and he stood just in the place where Kokoschka's friend would have to come out of the water. The artist could not bear the idea that this young Englishman, who had been dining with his family at the next table, should see her there. He would see only a girl who had been swimming in a thunderstorm and would probably think it eccentric. How could he realize that this massive storm was part of her presence, that she was only come to this corner of France and Switzerland so that she could rise, like Venus, from the foam, and that the whole atmosphere was therefore subject to other laws than those of Newton, which were doubtless all the young man could understand? Kokoschka could not allow such a sacred moment to be profaned. The man went on standing there in his evening shoes while Kokoschka vainly pointed towards the swimmer and the hotel. The man did not move, and Kokoschka was forced to a desperate decision. He stamped on his foot. The young man's face crumpled in pain. He turned on his heel and went back to the hotel, not hearing the stammered excuses.

The storm continued unabated on the following day, and Kokoschka saw visions. The moon rose again in the evening, and they walked along an avenue of trees lined with marble statues. One pedestal was empty and he placed the girl on it. He pleaded with her in urgent whispers beneath the shadow of the trees, and she declared herself ready to bind her life with his. When he heard these words he took fright, and could only say that he was unworthy of her, that he mistrusted himself profoundly, and that he was full of doubt and the meanest of men. All night he lay awake, and in the morning was in a state of mental collapse. He could think of no escape.[14] So he went to Geneva and telegraphed Paul Cassirer to meet him there, and then he tore up the very advantageous contract they had made.[15] Cassirer looked at him in amazement, repeating again and again, 'Are you mad? Have you any money?' Kokoschka had settled the hotel bill with his last note, and returned to Annecy completely without support. Then he was able to tell that strangely beautiful woman that he was penniless and did not know where he would sleep that night. He said he was worthless, everything else was illusion, and now she must realize how unreliable he was. Every word cost him dear, but she stood before him, smiling strangely. He left Annecy and went back to Paris, where he was so hungry that he even stole bread. He told me that he had often seen this woman since, and she was always near him. Once she appeared in Prague, again in Vienna, in Italy, and in England, and that time in Switzerland. She calls him and he must come.[16]

Hesitating, I asked: 'The Goddess?' Kokoschka nodded.

That winter his hunger and misery were increased by the bitter cold. The water froze in the studio. Kokoschka owned a mat, a folding bed, and an empty barrel which served as a chair. Ill with double pneumonia, it seemed as if he were fated himself to illustrate the knight floating between love and death. Love and death were never so closely mingled in his life as at that time.

The only person who came to see him was a Bulgarian painter with an immense beard, called Papazoff. He was a real peasant. He wore coloured puttees and always had a supply of onions, cucumbers, and tomatoes. His pictures were like fireworks suspended in a dark sky. It was not painting, but a kind of magic. He was a genuine abstract painter, who never succeeded and was thoroughly exploited in Paris. Sizing up the situation, he went away and returned with rum, coffee, cigarettes, and aspirin. Kokoschka still remembers the marvellous smell of the rum. Papazoff came and went like a guardian angel. While the artist lay ill in his studio the woman came to Paris and said that he should escort her to the Italian restaurant for dinner. He knew that he would be well enough, and that he would have the money somehow, although at the moment he could not lay hands on a *sou* in the studio. Papazoff came, and took a bundle of water-colours which he sold to the art collector, Rolf de Maré, the founder of the Swedish ballet in Paris. He came back with several hundred francs.

Kokoschka kept a small piece of wood in memory of that time. It is no ordinary piece of wood, for it was part of one of the steps in his studio-house on to which her hot tears fell. He cut it out as a keepsake.

As soon as he was well Kokoschka started to work again and took up his philosophical discussions with Tihany, his deaf and almost dumb friend. Tihany was also a painter much influenced by Kokoschka, but he painted in an abstract style. He was well versed in philosophy and hence, like Loos, was an educator as well as a friend. He was brilliantly clever, kind, and compassionate, and had a true political judgement. Although he knew four languages he could only speak with the greatest of difficulty, and only his friends could understand him. Despite this handicap he was greatly loved, and no one who ever met him could forget him. Kokoschka spent nearly all his time with him.

The decisive role played by women in Kokoschka's life made him very susceptible. He needed women, and he owed much to them as he had reason to fear them. The female side of life was always present, especially when he was painting. How strange, then, it seems to us, that a depth-psychological study of his handwriting should reveal an insoluble and therefore more fertile conflict, the implications of which must be resolved in the artist's subconscious mind. It reads: 'His interpretation of the world is spiritual and manly. His conscious and admittedly heroic aim is to break away from the mothers—the female principle, to overcome and even to kill them should the fear of being consumed by them become unbearable.'[17] It is doubtful whether a human being can ever entirely rid himself of such a conflict. The male and female principles are antagonistic, not capable of reconciliation; they are counterpoised. Tension is life as slackness is death. Therefore, tension and slackness, life and death, are antitheses which cannot be replaced by an ideal unity.

It is relevant while writing of the graphic works *The Fettered Columbus*, *Hiob*, the Portfolio of the *Bach Cantata* and *The Passion*, to examine Kokoschka's position as a graphic artist more closely.

'Drawing', wrote Henri Focillon, 'can catch the transitory and the eternal with an economy and force which exceeds even the rich possibilities of colour. It needs but pen and ink, and a few apparently aimless touches of wash, to express with astonishing clarity forms and pictures which are constantly passing through the artist's mind—a kind of living example of the thought process . . . always profound, quintessential, and full of life.'[18]

Kokoschka's drawing and graphic work is remarkable,[19] it is, however, of particular interest to examine its significance within the framework of his whole *oeuvre*. Kokoschka is undoubtedly a great draughtsman, hence a large and fascinating field of research lies waiting for the art historian of the future.

As a precise medium of expression the linear element has an important part to play in the art of a subjective Expressionist and portrayer of human endeavour. It is strongly emphasized in Kokoschka's early portraits and he never really suppressed it, although as he matured he extended the use of colour to express the furthest extremes of emotional tension.

That Kokoschka set a great deal of value on his drawings and graphic work can be learned from a letter written to Ernest Rathenau dated 9 November 1933. It runs: 'I pride myself that over such a long period, almost thirty years, my drawings have testified to my character. They are proof that I have neither gone astray nor denied myself. Nor have I borrowed experience. Since the whole of my work and even a selection from my earliest attempts manifest certain values which elsewhere have required the efforts of a whole generation (and, moreover, in a generally favourable age) to achieve, I believe I have discovered the long-sought style, and therefore I believe that my sacrifices have not been worthless, nor deprivations, of which I had a greater share than any other leading artist, in vain.'[20]

It would be true to say that Kokoschka began his career as a graphic artist in 1905, and whilst it can be seen that, in painting, his first mature compositions such as STILL LIFE WITH PINEAPPLE or portraits such as FATHER HIRSH were not completed before 1907, his first characteristic drawings—nearly all nudes of children—date from 1906.

The stylistic changes in Kokoschka's graphic work correspond to changes in his painting for the simple reason that they both develop out of the artist's personal reaction to life and the world around him. Much of his graphic work contains an autobiographical element—*The Fettered Columbus*, *Hiob*, *Orpheus and Eurydice*, *Ann Eliza Reed*, the *Bach Cantata*, and the *Chinese Wall*—whilst his powerful imagination is deeply stirred by myth and ancient legend, such as the sun and the moon in the drawings for *Murder Hope of Women*, repeated on the pictorial frame to the tapestry *Amor und Psyche* in the Festspielhaus in Salzburg. One might almost describe his Berlin period as a tattoo style. With his early portraits he became known as the artist with the X-ray eyes capable of penetrating beneath the human mask and unveiling the inner image—the subconscious mind—of his subject.

In his graphic work man dominates the scene. Though there are some landscape sketches from the period of his Italian journey, before 1914 and from the first world war, in general there are few landscapes. But there are many nature studies, coloured drawings made during the second war, in which the artist tried to keep in touch with nature despite the tragic circumstances created by man. In 1955 turning again to theatrical designing and costumes, he chose crayon as his medium once more.

Kokoschka employed several techniques in his graphic work. There are drawings in charcoal, pencil, pen and reed-pen combined with ink-wash or water-colour, red chalk, coloured chalks, and crayons. But he preferred lithography—black-and-white and coloured. He very rarely used the technique of etching. In all there were in 1918, four etchings for *Orpheus and Eurydice*; 1929, two illustrations for his brother Bohuslav's book, *Shut the Door, there's a Draught*; a few prints in 1931 and 1937; and, in 1949, an engraving of his wife, Olda, prepared for Masciotta's monograph on the artist.

The woodcut, a usual feature of the work of Edvard Munch, Ernst Ludwig Kirchner, and other German Expressionists, did not attract him at all. The technique was too slow for his spontaneous eruptive temperament.

His book illustrations are dictated by the demands of the theme. But Kokoschka often developed a theme of his own which arose from his inner experience. Every one of his drawings and graphic works is an independent artistic creation and ought only in very rare instances to be considered as a study for later paintings. Such as the *Wall-painting for a Crematorium*, 1914; the sketches for THE TEMPEST (1914); for the WOMAN IN BLUE (1919); LOVERS WITH A CAT (1917); TRUDL (1931); for the portrait of T. G. Masaryk (1936), or the triptych, THERMOPYLAE, of 1954.

The drawings done in 1908 which present profile and full-face simultaneously, a basic element of synthetic Cubism, and those of 1910 in Berlin foreshadowing certain automatic processes of the Surrealists, are proof that Kokoschka was, in many ways, a forerunner of styles other than Expressionism.

However, the ink drawings for Ehrenstein's *Tubutsch* (1911) demonstrate that he remained linked with tradition, despite his unremitting search for a personal and up-to-date style. Moreover, his art is a synthesis of this tradition. The traditional foundation here is old German art—Altdorfer, Dürer, and Grünewald—though its spirit is that of a twentieth-century artist, tense, highly strung, yet vital, and occasionally shot with humour; coloured with the tragic overtones of modern life; mixed with traces of the banal; illumined by irony, by the authority of an old master, and by a brilliantly inventive structural sense. The artist advanced along the path of fulfilment through his unceasing efforts to portray depth and dimension with a perspective distinct from that of the Renaissance. From the structural point of view the result was as revolutionary as that of Cubism. But it was a theory of space and Cubism peculiar to Kokoschka alone. This is the style he used for the *Tubutsch* illustrations, which reached its peak in the twelve lithographs of *The Fettered Columbus*. This Cubist element in Kokoschka's work served not as an end in itself but exclusively as a means of creating a new vision of space. His dynamic presentation and Expressionist distortions were all dictated by humanist, and in the case of *The Fettered Columbus*, autobiographical purposes. These distortions helped to form Kokoschka's later Baroque style. Baroque was essentially dynamic, emotional, and powerful, and hence Expressionist, in the same way that Romanesque art was Expressionist. Kokoschka did a poster for the *Kunstschau* in 1908 in which sun and moon appear simultaneously, implying the symbolism of man and woman (it is a *Pietà*), whereas his late posters—*La Passionaria* (1937); *Christ Rescuing the Children of Europe* (1945); or the *Child of Bethlehem* (1936)—are much closer to the Baroque tradition.

Before 1917 Kokoschka produced the eight lithographs intended as illustrations to Karl Kraus's book, *The Chinese Wall* (1913), and the lithograph portfolio called *The Passion*, as well as several chalk drawings, landscapes, and portraits. Stylistically the illustrations to *The Chinese Wall* resemble the *Bach Cantata*, while *The Passion* manifests certain Romantic-Baroque features. After the first world war Kokoschka's graphic production underwent a remarkable intensification and was subject to a new impetus, and the work done between 1917 and 1924, when his travels began, is very comprehensive. But during the actual journeys he rarely used graphic techniques.

By 1913 Kokoschka's drawing had radically changed. The angular character of his early work altered, and as his interest in Cubist spatial structure waned, the study of form, strongly dynamic in character, came to the fore impelled by a powerful urge which he wrested from his painting rather than from any other source. This tendency is especially noticeable in the lithographs to the *Bach Cantata* (1914), in which the distortions of the drawings are at one with the spirit of the whole. No longer exaggerated, they represent the tangible element of artistic expression in which small and large shapes, detail and whole, are in harmony. In these compositions, mature graphic style took shape.

Large portrait heads as that of Käthe Richter (1917), the Artist's Mother (1917); Hasenclever (1918); Max Reinhardt (1919); Hermine-Körner (1920); Maria Orska (1922); and the heads in the series THE DAUGHTERS OF THE COVENANT (1920–22), are further examples of this development. The fourteen lithographs to *Hiob* (1917), five engravings for his play, *Orpheus and Eurydice* (1918)—even as late as 1956 Kokoschka was making new designs with coloured chalk for the sets of this drama—the illustrations to Dirsztay's books *Praise to the Noble Mind* (1917) and *The Inescapable One* (1923),* and some figure-compositions in ink-wash from the year 1919, must also be mentioned in this connection. The development reaches its highest point in the portrait series entitled CONCERT, VARIATIONS ON A THEME (1920), where the soul of the sitter is miraculously laid bare by changes in the expression.

'Kokoschka's interest in plastic art was centred on man himself. The theme in these variations was no longer the changing light of the Impressionists, nor the physical appearance of the Realists and the Renaissance, but the spirit of man. It was a return to the antique and the Middle Ages. But Kokoschka the Expressionist had first to discover the significance of the theme for his contemporaries.' (Dvořák.) In so doing he succeeded in an artistic achievement which perhaps only future generations will be able to assess.

At this point Kokoschka's late style, his work after the second world war, begins to emerge. There are no more violent changes. He could not penetrate human understanding more deeply, nor exploit the power of expression further. In their place is a growing harmony and a moderation of contrasts.

The second great period in his graphic production begins about 1930. It is recognizable from its personal character, by his emphatic acceptance of life in the wake of the first world war and the years of decadence, discernible, moreover, in the acceptance of woman, of the eternal female element in the continuity of life. This is the period of the illustrations for Albert Ehrenstein's book, *Mein Lied* (My Song) of 1913, and the large drawings of nudes and female portraits in red chalk (1931–2), which are among the artist's best work. It is the work of a man who is vigorous and alive, whose spirit has

* *Lob des hohen Verstandes* and *Der Unentrinnbare.*

found peace after a storm, but who is still full of curiosity. The time was short-lived. The second world war was approaching, and with it the years of unrest, of need, and of moral wretchedness. There is a stylistic link between Kokoschka's middle and late periods in the series of red-chalk drawings which he made of his wife, Olda, and published as a portfolio in Salzburg. It contains ten portraits done between 1935 and 1938, and a lithograph of 1956.[21]

The nature studies in crayon made during the war, in Polperro (1939), in Fort William (1942 and 1944), in Ullapool (1945) and during his stay in London from 1940 to 1946, are persuasive examples of meditative intimacy with creation. Line is transformed directly into colour, and the spirit is reminiscent of Dürer's studies of nature. However, the style is not one of detailed Realism, as was so often the case with the Old Masters, but a dynamic, swift summary of natural forms, of flowers, berries, fruits, clouds, water, and rocks, as well as animals and birds, and also nudes, portraits, and human figures. It is but a step from here to the sketches for his later theatrical sets and costumes, the same shorthand notes, with the accent on form and structure which we have come to accept from Kokoschka, although in that case their form is dictated by theatrical demands and they are more illustrative of his imaginative interpretation of the action than Expressionist.

After 1948 Kokoschka still produced lithographs, though fewer than formerly. *The Magic Form* is a self-portrait in the guise of an enchanter, a satire on abstract art. In 1952 he had produced *Leda* and the illustrations for his own story, *Ann Eliza Reed* (ten lithographs and a drawing for the title-page), apart from some drawings of nudes, two of which were designed for James Plaut's book. There are the coloured lithographs of a greyhound; *The Fox and the Grapes* (1952); *Two Girls with a Dove*; *Amor and Psyche*; a self-portrait (1956), and the portraits of Gitta Welz (1953), Ernest Rathenau, Michael Tippet, Ezra Pound, the author of this book, and others.

In the summers of 1953 and 1954 Kokoschka produced a series of large drawings of nudes, and in 1953 the eight sketches for *Thermopylae*. Five lithographs were inspired in 1955 by Werner Egks's opera, *Irish Legend*. In 1956 he made sketches for Weber's opera *Oberon*.

Kokoschka's development in the 'sixties is characterized by an increase in his graphic work. Almost without a break between 1961 and 1964 he produced the twenty lithographs of the *Apulian Journey*, and the two portfolios of twenty-five prints entitled *Hellas—A Greek Journey*, and the seventeen illustrations for *King Lear*. The Apulian series are serene and sympathetic observations, whereas the studies of Greece are more of a testimony to a spiritual heritage. The marbles appear to breathe, as though the artist had touched them with magic. Shortly afterwards Kokoschka began a new series, the *Homecoming of Odysseus*. He seemed to be hypnotized by the immortal epic, reading it in Fitzgerald's new translation over and over again. He completed forty-four lithographs in the end, illustrating the whole story. At present he is working on the forty drawings to illustrate the story of King Saul and David. A painting with the same title was produced in 1966. It took up the theme on which he embarked in his Dresden period. But whereas the Dresden picture (since destroyed) laid the emphasis on the sorrow of King Saul and the rather wily state of mind of the young David, the later painting stressed the anger of Saul at the onset of old age, an anger shared by the artist at the time of his approaching eightieth anniversary.

The style of these late works remains the same as in the earlier lithographs and coloured chalk drawings. All bear the mark of the great man. They reflect Kokoschka's personal response to life, although their intensity is modified according to the subject and the artist's mood—a distinctive feature of Expressionism which is the outcome of the artist's response to reality. In Kokoschka's own words: 'The knowledge that comes from personal experience has an inner force. That experience which releases man from the bondage of transient existence brings a moment of eternal truth comparable to an act of birth. It is the expression of this inner truth which is socially valuable.'

Furcht:	O Ewigkeit, du Donnerwort,
	O Schwert, das durch die Seele bohrt,
	O Anfang sonder Ende!
	O Ewigkeit, Zeit ohne Zeit,

Furcht:	O schwerer Gang zum letzten Kampf und Streite!
Hoffnung:	Mein Beistand ist schon da,
	Mein Heiland steht mir ja
	Mit Trost zur Seite!
Furcht:	Die Todesangst, der letzte Schmerz
	Ereilt und überfällt mein Herz
	Und martert diese Glieder.

Hoffnung:	Herr ich warte auf dein Heil,
	Ich warte auf dein Heil,
	Dein Heil, Herr ich warte auf dein Heil.

Furcht:	Ich weiss vor grosser Traurigkeit
	Nicht, wo ich mich hinwende;
	Mein ganz erschrocknes Herz erbebt,
	Dass mir die Zung am Gaumen klebt.

Hoffnung:	Ich lege diesen Leib vor Gott zum Opfer nieder.
	Ist gleich der Trübsal Feuer heiss,
	Genung, es reinigt mich zu Gottes Preis.

Furcht:	Doch, nun wird sich der Sünden grosse Schuld
	vor mein Gesichte stellen!

Hoffnung:	Gott wird deswegen doch kein Todesurteil fällen.
	Er gibt ein Ende den Versuchungsplagen,
	Dass man sie kann ertragen.

Furcht:	Mein letztes Lager will mich schrecken,
Hoffnung:	Mich wird des Heilands Hand bedecken,
Furcht:	Des Glaubens Schwachheit sinket fast.
Hoffnung:	Mein Jesus trägt mit mir die Last.
Furcht:	Das offne Grab sieht greulich aus.
Hoffnung:	Es wird mir doch ein Friedenshaus.
Furcht:	Der Tod bleibt doch der menschlichen Natur verhasst.
	Und reisset fast
	Die Hoffnung ganz zu Boden.
Heiliger Geist:	Selig sind die Toten.
Furcht:	Ach! aber ach! wieviel Gefahr
	Stellt sich der Seele dar,
	Den Sterbeweg zu gehen!
	Vielleicht wird ihr der Höllenrachen
	Den Tod erschrecklich machen.
	Wenn er sie zu verschlingen sucht;
	Vielleicht ist sie bereits verflucht
	Zum ewigen Verderben.
Heiliger Geist:	Selig sind die Toten, die in dem Herren sterben.
Furcht:	Wenn ich im Herren sterbe,
	Ist dann die Seligkeit mein Teil und Erbe?
	Der Leib wird ja der Würmer Speise!
	Ja, werden meine Glieder
	Zu Staub und Erde wieder—
	Da ich ein Kind des Todes heisse—,
	So schein ich ja im Grabe zu verderben.
Heiliger Geist:	'Selig sind sie Toten, die in dem Herren sterben,
	Von nun an.'
Furcht:	Wohlan! Soll ich von nun an selig sein:
	Soll stelle dich, o Hoffnung, wieder ein!
	Mein Leib mag ohne Furcht im Schlafe ruhn,
	Der Geist kann einen Blick in jene Ferne tun.
Choral:	Es ist genung: Herr, wenn es dir gefällt
	So spanne micht doch aus,
	Mein Jesus kommt: nun gute Nacht, o Welt!
	Ich fahr' ins Himmelshaus,
	Ich fahre sicher hin mit Frieden.
	Mein grosser Jammer bleibt darnieden.
	Es ist genung.

Johann Sebastian Bach: Sämtliche Kantatentexte unter Mitbenutzung von Rudolf Wustmanns Ausgabe der Bachschen Kirchen Kantatentexte. Herausgegeben von Werner Neumann. Breitkopf und Härtel, Leipzig 1956.

KNIGHT, DEATH AND THE ANGEL

The first world war engulfed not only the Austro-Hungarian Empire but the whole world of Kokoschka's youth. For him 'Austria' conjured up so many different peoples—Vienna, the processions of the Feast of Corpus Christi! He remembered how he and his sister, she in white, he in blue, with candles and lilies in their hands, walked on a carpet of flowers. The whole city glistened. The sun was brilliant. They came to the High Altar without understanding the miracle which took place. The Priest, the Archbishop, the Emperor with his guard, said Kokoschka—if you sweep all that away nothing is left but a shell. It all disappeared with the war.

The Good Soldier Schweik said of the Austrian Army: 'Those uniforms with gold buttons, the horses, the marching men—you mean to say that you sent something as beautiful as that to war?' No one yet realized what war could be, and the flower-bedecked soldiers marched off to music just as though it was an ordinary parade. It was the last medieval war. Kokoschka wore red trousers, a light blue jacket, a golden helmet, and tall white thigh-boots. They even shaved before battle to be a smart target for the enemy. The Russians already wore field-grey and were equipped with spades, but when the Austrian dragoons at last got grey uniforms—they called them their stable kit—and spades, they did not know what to do with them, and complained that they did not know how to dig. But they learned from bitter experience the meaning of Schweik's words: 'Don't shoot, there are men over there.'

Kokoschka volunteered for the army and thought he would like to join the dragoons. Loos pulled strings to get him into one of the crack regiments, because it was by no means easy to choose a regiment. Loos, however, arranged it, and he even had a card printed with a picture of Kokoschka wearing his dragoon uniform, which could be bought in Vienna, as if he were a *prima donna* or a court actor.[1] Loos worked it all out. Kokoschka could not join the infantry; he would never be able to bear it. The artillery was unthinkable, because he was hopeless with mechanical things; moreover, he loathed the idea of mechanical killings. If he had to go to war, then, he wanted hand-to-hand fighting. Then at least one out of two would have a chance of escape. Kokoschka could never grasp the idea of killing men he had never seen, although, he once told me, he would be able to murder some people he knew without a qualm. His mother bought him a horse called Minneloh with the money made by the sale of THE KNIGHT ERRANT, and the horse dealer must have been very impressed by her, because the animal was a good one.

The young Kokoschka stayed with the first patrol because this was the only way he could hide his ignorance of military science. He did not even know how to read a map or how to draw one, but that was his way of 'malingering'. So it came about that he rode with his Brigadier into Lemberg and Kowel. He remembers how they came to a small town on a hill overlooking the River Bug occupied by the Jews and found Ludendorff's manifesto translated into Yiddish and nailed to the doors of the houses. It was bitterly cold. Kokoschka fell in love with a beautiful Jewess and helped her to carry water from the river. However, she preferred a Swedish cavalry officer, a woman-chaser, who captivated all the girls. So Kokoschka left her, telling her to carry her own water.

Kokoschka affirms that he died in Lutek. It was indeed an experience which might well have cost him his life, for the circumstances were dangerous, and his curiosity made him wonder what it would be like to die.

He was crossing the Bug, leaning well back on his horse so that it would not know he was there, and leading other horses by the bridles. As he came to the bank a group of Cossacks appeared trailing their lances, and riding small ponies so that their feet were almost on the ground. They attacked, crying fiercely: 'Stoj! Stoj!' He laid spurs to his horse and galloped like the wind. He was a good enough rider when in danger, but otherwise not at all. As a boy he had been thrown from a horse and had damaged his kneecap. But he rode well with the Cossacks after him. His horse was of bloodstock, and when urged to a gallop had a habit of turning its head, showing the white of its eye, and biting. He was hoping that the animal would not choose this moment to bite, when he was shot in the head and fell. As usual when anything dramatic happened to him, it was moonlight. He regained consciousness to see a Russian bending over him with a white mask-like face and dull eyes like stones. He drove his bayonet into Kokoschka's chest. It seemed to take hours, although he wasted no time. The Russians may at first have carried him off and then concluded that he was beyond help and decided to give him the *coup de grâce*. Kokoschka had never shot anyone, and although he had his finger on the trigger of his revolver he did not pull it. The Russian was a huge man, but Kokoschka did not shoot. He believed he was doing something important, but Kokoschka thought it senseless and debasing to shoot—it was night, if he pulled the trigger the man would collapse —Crazy!

'What tremendous courage!' I exclaimed as he described the scene. He denied it: Not at all; I was always very nervous but very inquisitive. It was terrible when the Russian bayonet pierced my tunic and the steel bit into my flesh, but my terror gave way before a strange sense of desire, as though it were a woman.

So he rolled on to the blade and saved his life, for the bayonet missed his heart. Kokoschka describes it as the most profound experience of his life and concludes that an intelligent person can experience death as a form of sensuality provided that it is not caused by cancer or some long-drawn-out illness.

Then his blood flowed, it seemed, out of every part of him, even his eyes, so that his throat and heart appeared to ebb away. Years later, in Dresden, Kokoschka heard a fat singer in the part of Donna Anna. He was deeply moved by her rendering of the aria,

O crudele, O grausam, and especially by her almost supernatural rendering of the staccato. Kokoschka had always had delicate lungs, and as a boy one lung had been affected. The war wound on top of that caused adhesions of the lung and he had always spat blood a little. When he heard the voice singing he had a haemorrhage followed by a feeling of release and thought that Mozart must have experienced similar sensations, otherwise he could not have composed the music. Later, he learned that Mozart had actually died of a disease of the lungs. At the time Kokoschka felt compelled to go on listening to the opera. Frau Gela, his mistress, kept a lace handkerchief in which she had caught some drops of blood.[2]

Kokoschka's eyes twinkled and he said to me: Women are strange. Then he described how he once opened a vein in Dresden. The house where he was living was icy cold and damp. He had rheumatism, was starving, and was afflicted with nervous trouble, but he didn't want a doctor. He had a beautiful Chinese bowl with a *sang-de-boeuf* glaze, blood red, and it made him think of Petronius. Two of his women friends were there with him, and he took a sharp knife and slit a blood-vessel in his arm. The blood welled out—a marvellous red. The girls stood there holding his hands and the bowl between them. But he had forgotten to prepare a bandage and fainted from loss of blood. They bound the cut and fell to abusing each other. The bowl full of blood stood in the middle of the room while one girl attacked the other with a red-hot poker. When he regained consciousness he smiled gently at them and peace was restored.

He lay helpless in the Russian woods with his right arm and leg paralysed and eyes squinting. As his consciousness ebbed slowly away he saw the sun and moon together in the sky and had an impression of floating on air, like the painting THE KNIGHT ERRANT which he had done at the beginning of the war and like the vision of the sun and moon in his play, *Dreaming Youths*, shining as if on another plane.

Then the Austrians came back over the battlefield and he was once more in the hands of his friends.

After the war Kokoschka kept exclusively to the company of women, nor would he shake the hand of any man whom he knew to have taken part in the war, because, he argued, these men had all committed murder. Normally, they would have been hanged. He described his own entry into the war as a kind of sacrifice. For a long time after his injury he suffered from persecution mania and agoraphobia. His sense of balance was so deranged that he could only walk in circles and he had to set off in the opposite direction to arrive at his intended goal. He could not stand straight, but always leaned to one side. This tendency already disclosed itself when he walked across the moonlit Stefansplatz in Vienna with Rheinhold after the performance of his play *Murder Hope of Women*, but now his wound was the physical reason for its renewal.

He was taken in the end to Vienna, where he was received into a military hospital in which nearly all the nurses were daughters of the nobility. He was looked after by an angelic young aristocrat of eighteen and they became great friends. He dedicated the introductory poem of his *Bach Cantata* to her. Her family's estates were in a forest not far from Vienna where there were wild boars, and although he was not in the least afraid of these animals the trees reminded him of the fighting in the forest in Russia when he had seen more than one hundred and fifty men die at one time. His nurse understood his state of mind, so every day she led him in a donkey-cart into the woods, talking softly to him all the time. 'Do not be afraid. . . . Do not be afraid.' Her patience was in-exhaustible, and in the end he was able to go alone into the forest. He wrote his essay *On the Nature of Visions* during this period, and it was conceived as homage to her.[3]

When he was still in Russia, in the hospital at Wladimir Smolensk, Kokoschka worked on his play, *Orpheus and Eurydice*. As his right hand was paralysed, he had to memorize the words. Because of the seriousness of his wounds he had been placed in an isolated ward, since the ambulance men had supposed him to be a high-ranking officer. The epaulettes and the yellow stripes indicative of rank on his collar were so soaked with blood that they had mistaken them for gold. When he was at last brought back behind the Austrian lines he was conveyed in a rickety farm-cart beneath lowering skies across the Polish plain. Then the words fused into a play, linking him by invisible threads to his former life. The war would have seemed to him like a frightful dream but for his wounds. His old emotional disquiet stirred into wakefulness, for as he lay on the battlefield staring at the sun and the moon the war between the sexes had appeared once more to him like cosmic powers, the companions of death into whose stony eyes he had stared. He was Orpheus descended into the underworld; Odysseus pursued; he was Gilgamesh who searched to the ends of the earth to learn the laws of the underworld and overcome his fear of death. Could he bring Eurydice back from the shadows once he had killed her image within himself? Could he who believed in his own resurrection also raise others from the dead, and in all their former glory? But as he composed his new play he gradually threw off his chains:

> The arid song of the Earth
> Is all our little lives embrace.
> Eternal bliss is not so—
> This love, this longing,
>   Must be hate—[4]

Years later he succeeded in breaking loose in an altogether uncanny way, and this chapter of his life is to some extent pathological. Unnerved by his personal experiences, and by the war, he came very close to insanity. Kokoschka manifested certain emotional features dominant in the mentally sick which also appear in the beliefs of primitive peoples at an early phase in their development. In his determination that this woman should have no further part in his life, that no woman should ever hold him in bondage, and from the desire to rid himself for ever of her image, he substituted a fetish for reality. This was a life-size doll exactly like her in every detail. He wanted to fill the gap left by her absence without running into the danger of being once more at her mercy. His first words when he arrived back in Vienna were connected with her. Ignoring the anxiety suffered by his mother, who had feared that her son was dead, he asked heartlessly: Where are the

40 Self Portrait with Cap, 1932

41 Prague. View from the Schönborn Gardens, 1935

42 Thomas G. Masaryk, 1935–6
By Courtesy of the Carnegie Institute, Pittsburgh

beads? The woman had given him this chain and it was the only thing of hers he possessed. He had remembered it even as he lay on the battlefield struggling with death. Now he had to know where it was. He did not even notice that his mother's hair had grown white in this short time. She was terribly confused and could only stammer that she had hidden the chain somewhere, but could not remember where. Then, as she searched vainly round, her trembling hands knocked down a flower-pot full of dry earth. It broke when it fell to the ground, revealing the necklace among the earth and shards.[5]

When Kokoschka told me this he took his head in his hands at the remembrance of his heartlessness towards his mother.

The doll was made, but before it was finished he suffered overwhelming agonies. The letters that he wrote to the girl who undertook the work are so full of gruesome detail that they are more like a clinical history than the confessions of an artist, although this was the title under which they were eventually published.[6] This correspondence, which lasted from 22 July 1918 to 6 April 1919—that is, a full nine months, the time it takes to bear a child—may perhaps help to clarify the mental background which earned Kokoschka the nickname of The Madman among women like Karin Michaelis. The letters were accompanied by large working drawings to which they referred.

This episode took place in Dresden, the city he had visited several times from Berlin and his home after 1917 until 1924, when he set off on his wide travels. Friends were invited to give the doll a worthy reception; a cab ordered for a drive through the park, and a chambermaid was even engaged to look after her. Then he saw the doll lying in its huge box for what it really was—a horrible apparition, the very realism of which precluded all doubt that the whole episode was the work of a madman. Kokoschka, who was suffering from dread of any contact with the world, had tried to substitute the past for the hostile reality of the present, and so superimpose a false presence in an attempt to obliterate the emptiness of the past. By substituting the doll for the strong-willed capricious personality of his beloved he had hoped to re-shape his life and be able to work with untrammelled mind. Such was his dream. But faced with the uncanny horror of the doll, whose weird appearance was exaggerated by the fact that they had all been drinking freely, the sick artist and his friends took it out and buried it in the garden. Someone must have been watching, for the police began to make inquiries as to whether there had not been murder done. So Kokoschka secretly disinterred the doll, washed off the earth, and painted its portrait as the WOMAN IN BLUE.[7] He even thought of building a mechanical contraption inside it which would sing *O crudele, O grausam* from *Don Giovanni*. I learned in Dresden that Kokoschka used to take two seats at the opera, one for himself and the other for the doll. When it was at last beheaded and destroyed the powerful emotions which had engendered it seem finally to have been laid to rest. Thus the fires of his passion died down, though they blaze fiercely still in her memoirs.[8] The artist had painted the story of his love on six fans which he had given her before he went to war.[9]

In the autumn of 1917 Kokoschka was sent to Stockholm to see a specialist because he was still suffering from disturbance of his balance. The doctor was an Austrian Nobel

Prize winner, Professor Baranyi, living at Upsala. Despite his depressed state Kokoschka had to undergo a painful treatment in a mental hospital. With weights in either hand he was seated on a fast-rotating stool. The result was to produce an artificial cerebral spasm. The official situation was that he was unfit for military service, but could be pronounced fit for civilian service, and because he was an example of the kind of case claiming total disability pension the tests had to go on, despite the torment caused by the treatment. It almost killed him. When at last he was sent back to military headquarters he succeeded in getting a job as a war correspondent.

He told me once that he had only twice wept before other men, the first time because he was powerless to stop the senseless torture which was endangering his brain, which Baranyi dare not denounce because of his oath of service. The second time was when the Nazis marched into Austria. Then he went on his knees and pleaded with influential Czech politicians in Prague to do something, telling them to make the excuse that the next sacrifice would be Bohemia. They should send the army, which was well armed, for there would be no need to shoot, only to threaten. Nothing was done; at that time every nation treasured the idea that these things were the internal affairs of the countries concerned, although it was clear for all to see that international disaster was imminent.

There was talk in Stockholm of peace, and in the new atmosphere the German Ambassador arranged a private performance of the *Burning Bush* in Kokoschka's honour. One day the artist met three Indians walking in the winter street and they looked completely lost. They reminded him of the Three Kings and he spoke to them. They replied to his questions that they were there because of Henry Ford's Peace Ship which was expected to arrive in the harbour.

Whenever he was up Kokoschka was able to paint in Stockholm and he did a view of the harbour from the Mosebacke. As always, he chose a high viewpoint so as to obtain a panorama and be able to immerse himself in the scene more than would have been possible from a lower position. Also he painted portraits of the astronomer Svante Arrhenius, and of the writer Selma Lagerlöf.[10]

At the banquet after the performance of the *Burning Bush* he sat beside the Countess Karin F. She was dazzlingly beautiful and he was captivated. She had given him a silver box containing flowers as a homage to his poetry. She was pro-German, while her mother, who never spoke anything but French, supported the Allied cause. Every day, they went in a white ship to visit the islands of the Archipelago, a paradise to Kokoschka, and every day he sent her a bunch of red roses. He loved her, he told me, passionately, like every other woman he had ever loved. He used to go every day to the main square in the city to look at the exchange rate which was posted on a notice-board. The Austrian crown was falling, and his officer's pay was not large. Roses grew daily more expensive and he was compelled to live on herrings and coffee, the cheapest food. Frau Karin's husband was mortally sick and died while Kokoschka was there. He liked her small daughter too, so his beautiful friend tried to persuade him to stay in Sweden. The war, she said, was lost in any case. Kokoschka saw his danger and had to extricate himself. How could he possibly desert and abandon his Emperor? He was a lieutenant in one of the finest regiments. Dressed in his gold helmet and red and blue uniform, he had once been guard-commander at Schönbrunn when the Emperor had come to one of the windows. So he had to shout—how did it go again?—'Present . . . arms!' in his loudest voice. No, no—he could not betray all that. Kokoschka chuckled to himself as he recounted the conversation to me.

Still suffering from his wound, he left Stockholm, where he had to choose between love and honour, duty and seduction, with the exchange rate as a distress signal, herrings for his diet, and red roses as a symbol of the susceptibility of his heart to feminine beauty.[11]

Kokoschka suffered the consequences of his head wound for many years. In 1926 he was in London, and went to Lock's in St James's to buy a bowler hat. He was looking for the reinforced kind used for hunting, hoping that the weight would have a good effect on his insecure sense of balance. The salesman looked at him and said: You shall have one. Kokoschka told me it was more difficult to get a hat from him than to cash a bad cheque at a bank. No one knows anything about hats any more, the man went on. They haven't the strength to wear hats of this kind. Hats are still tough, but men are not.

Kokoschka was not very happy as he sat in the Swedish train which was taking him nearer to the front and to certain death with every mile. But a miracle occurred to alter the path of destiny. On Dresden station he was called from the train by a strange-looking man—Dr Fritz Neuberger. It was like the strange appearance of Albert Kollmann in the life of Munch. This man said he had been commissioned by Albert Ehrenstein[12] to find Kokoschka, an officer of the dragoons, and get him off the train. After a few days, however, Kokoschka continued to Austria and thence to the front on the Isonzo, where he was shell-shocked while serving with Hungarian troops in a trench. Invalided out at last, he was taken to a military hospital in Dresden, and this short stay made him decide to settle there after the war. The man who impressed him most was Fritz Neuberger. He seemed to know everything about the result of the war and the armistice, and to have access to all camps, so he had no difficulty in getting information. He had the ear of Ludendorff, as well as of leading industrial and revolutionary circles. He was an intellectual clearly suffering the last stages of consumption and he died soon after the armistice. He accommodated Kokoschka in the Dresden military sanatorium and then in the *Weisser Hirsch*. He had gathered round him there, in a small unpretentious inn, a group of artists brought together by the war, whose discussions on almost every subject were enthusiastic and frequent: Ivan von Lücken, an admirer of Tolstoy; 'God the Father', Dr Neuberger; a young actor from Prague, Ernst Deutsch, and a writer, Walter Hasenclever; as well as Paul Kornfeld, a poet, and Käthe Richter, who was an actress in the Albert Theatre in Dresden. All these became Kokoschka's close friends and he painted group portraits of them in which their reactions to the gradual collapse of the mighty war machine and the revolutionary upheaval which was destroying both Austria and Germany are revealed. The first is called THE EXILES, and its sitters are pictured as outcasts. Käthe Richter and Dr Neuberger are in the foreground, and behind, looking over his shoulder and a little to one side (as was his habit), the latest arrival—

himself. The landscape is bleak, autumnal. The other portrait—THE FRIENDS—depicts
them grouped round a table with Walter Hasenclever in profile, his head resting thoughtfully on his right hand, his left arm on the table. Behind him to the right is the half-
concealed head of Ivan von Lücken, with Neuberger full face, resting on his left arm.
The foreground shows Kokoschka, back view, and on his left Käthe Richter in profile
holding a glass, whilst behind them framed in the door an inquisitive servant-girl
carrying a carafe of red wine tries to overhear snatches of conversation.

On the table stand a bowl of fruit, a glass, and an ash-tray. The vigorous, broad
calligraphy of the brush-strokes and the rich tones—blue for Neuberger's suit, green for
Hasenclever, and Käthe Richter's purple dress, with pink, yellow, and ochre touches
and the Baroque light magnifying the dramatic effect as though they were conspirators
plotting in the vaults, create a vital painting of close-knit friendship in time of trouble.

Its original title was *The Gamblers;* as Hans Tietze explains in his article, *Oskar
Kokoschkas neue Werke.** Kokoschka had written to Tietze as follows: 'These are my
friends playing cards. Their passions are stripped naked, and they are immersed in a
mystic colour which binds them all together as light binds an object to its reflection in
a mirror, lifting them thus to a point—part real, part reflected—which transcends both.[12]

At first Kokoschka took an active part in political events. He was not on the side of the
reactionaries but published lithographs and pamphlets against the senseless killing. It is
relevant here to recall his appeal to the people of Dresden, suggesting that the leader of
every party ought to wrestle in Homeric fashion in the arena of the Sarasaini circus. It
nearly caused his death. In the last months of the war Dresden had become a refuge for
radical politicians although, of course, the city had never lost its splendid cultural traditions. The Florence of the Elbe was now about to regain its former position as the foremost
artistic and intellectual city of Germany, the position it had held in the seventeenth and
eighteenth centuries when magnificent buildings such as the Frauenkirche, the Brühlsche-
Terrasse, the Italian village and the Zwinger had made Dresden one of the finest cities
of the world. Its unrivalled art collections drew many foreigners, even in Goethe's
time, and the city's magnificent position athwart the Elbe added to its attraction. Now,
once again strong new currents of intellectual activity were stirring. The Deutsche
Werkstätte and the Weimar (soon to become the Dessau) Bauhaus made their contribution to the new artistic movement of the democratic Republic. The finest German books
of the period were published by Jakob Hegner (in nearby Hellerau) whilst Jacques
Dalcroze, Mary Wigman, and Palucca, the inspired inventors of Expressionist dance,
had their studios in Dresden and attracted pupils from far and wide (Rudolf von
Laban worked elsewhere).

During this period of renaissance the Students Council invited Kokoschka, the
least amenable of men, to shake the cobwebs out of the Dresden Academy of Art in
1919 by accepting a professorship. The Academy won prestige from the appointment
which assured it of a leading position. Kokoschka's students described him as an outstanding teacher who, by liberating their power and understanding, set them on the road

* 'Oskar Kokoschka's New Works', in: *Die bildenden Künste*, Vienna, 1919.

to personal experience. He was both friend and preceptor. He stayed only a few years, time enough for the weaving of a legend which was strengthened when he suddenly left his post and abandoned the city. The result of his urgent need for independence and freedom was the emergence of the greatest painter of cities and landscapes of our time.

At the Academy he followed the methods which had already gained a name for him in Vienna by introducing the five-minute nude in action. One day a member of his class was about to throw a paper ball for the model to catch—the students were expected to draw her in movement—when someone made a crude joke. Kokoschka turned on him furiously: What on earth are you thinking of? Don't you realize that you have a nude woman in front of you? To another student, a pupil of the academic Naturalist, Richard Müller, conscientiously drawing in every hair, he said, vigorously rubbing the whole thing out: How can you be so unscrupulous? By perception Kokoschka understood the eye's response and the throb of the heart interpreted in a drawing.

Friedrich Karl Gotsch and Hans Meyboden were his two master pupils. But it was absolutely necessary for him to get away from people whose work was a failure. There were some student tragedies, enormous jealousy among the women, and abrupt departures. Kokoschka waited impatiently for the arrival of two students from Scandinavia— Musse Krake from Copenhagen and Miss Reisse from Finland. Gotsch relates: 'Kokoschka was always on the look out for something unusual, and he was very excited in anticipation of the arrival of these two girls. There was no way of convincing him that the two Scandinavians were very shy and simply did not understand him. They used to cry when he criticized them. Then he felt like crying himself. For him there was adventure and mystery in the game.[13]

In 1963 I asked Hans Meyboden to write down his memories of Kokoschka. In November 1919 Meyboden, a boy of eighteen, stood nervously in the Dresden Academy on the Brühlsche-Terrasse outside Kokoschka's studio, whither Professor Czeschka* had advised him to go.

'The interview seemed like a dream. How was I to reply when Kokoschka asked me why I had come? For, of course, it was fate that had brought me. I plucked up courage to ask why he had accepted me as a pupil. He replied that he had seen a watercolour I had done of Hildesheim, and that if I persevered I would succeed in the end. Then he did something which he later always prevented if ever we came into his studio when a half-finished canvas stood on his easel. He led me down a short staircase into his work-room and stood before an unfinished picture, THE POWER OF MUSIC. He could not possibly have had any idea of the impression the picture made on me. I was deeply moved and inspired, although it was with a sense of foreboding that I heard the words of the oracle. I had stepped unprepared into the painting's magic circle and was led far away, into a distant land. Kokoschka had vouchsafed me a glimpse into the sanctuary— his sanctuary. The woman with the trumpet, with the flowering mallow in her hand, was my guiding light henceforth.'

* Professor Carl Otto Czeschka had been Kokoschka's favourite teacher in the Kunstge-werbeschule in Vienna from 1905 to 1907.

'Since that day I have never lowered my sights, and my memory of the dark November morning and the style of Kokoschka's painting has fused into an indivisible whole. That was 1919. . . .'

'Kokoschka left the Hotel Weber and moved into one of the pavilions in the *Grosse Garten* where he occupied two simple rooms. On one visit he showed me some of his treasures—a white Japanese *No* mask in a box covered with black velvet, the patina and impenetrable expression of which reminded me of the woman's yellow face in THE POWER OF MUSIC. Near the bed hung a reproduction of a Van Eyck in the Zwinger collection (it was the small altar triptych by Jan Van Eyck in the Dresden Art Gallery). An African white wooden mask stood on a high cupboard. He told us that was how he wanted to look when he became old. As our perception grew we saw ourselves diminished. Kokoschka was once talking with another well-known painter about the Van Eyck, and he said one must stand patiently before such a painting, waiting, like a subject before his king, till it spoke. He tried to convince him of the mystery of the painting and its concept of space. He told us one day that his favourite painting was the large diagonal composition called THE PAINTER.*

Victor Wallerstein, the Berlin art dealer, stood almost speechless looking at one of Kokoschka's drawings: How does he do it? When he was working on THE PAINTER, Kokoschka decorated his easel at intervals with little coloured windmills. These acted in some way like a compass to him, but their connexion with the picture was incomprehensible to me.

'I shall never forget the paper masks in his studio during the winter of 1919/20. Their presence in Kokoschka's house and their relevance to his vision made them especially significant, and there I could sense the relationship with his paintings. At one time Kokoschka was working on a self-portrait with the tower of the *Hofkirche* soaring upwards in a blue sky. I was fortunate to be able to follow the painting through several phases. When I saw it a second time the church steeple had vanished and had been replaced by a woman. Later, another woman appeared on the opposite side. One evening Kokoschka called me into his studio to show me a picture in which a woman was sitting upright with a second, kneeling figure. I realized that this was the canvas with the self-portrait: LOT AND HIS DAUGHTERS, 1922/23. When the artist saw my astonishment he remarked: But I always knew that it would have to have a perpendicular feature like that.'

Another episode concerned the painting SAUL AND DAVID.† As the result of political riots in the Post Office Square a stray bullet penetrated the canvas of Rubens' *Bathsheba*. Kokoschka was very nervous and strung up in those days. He had always looked for a reconciliation with the rebels whereby, like David playing on the harp before the angry Saul, he could at least soothe his own unrest. When the picture of Saul and David was in its initial stages he said: 'Thus far Kandinsky'.

'If Kokoschka wanted to describe the peculiarities of the face of a man he knew well he

---

*THE PAINTER AND HIS MODEL, I, 1922/3.
†SAUL AND DAVID (FRAGMENT), 1921.

would twist his own face about till he thought he looked like him. Then all we had to do was to read off the features.'

'In the evening the Academy porter Fritsche used to wash the master's brushes. Just to look at them loaded with fresh colour made me believe that I could learn the secret of their magic. I have Fritsche to thank—the porter used to collect torn water-colours out of Kokoschka's wastepaper basket and repair them for his 'collection'—for sometimes allowing me to go secretly into Kokoschka's studio in the evening on my way home. I stood and gazed with fast-beating heart enraptured by the stolen moments. Thank you, Fritsche! But, alas, our surreptitious looking never really escaped the artist's attention because our pictures betrayed us. That explains his inscription in the Paul Westheim biography which he presented to me: "My dear Meyboden, remember that life is much too short to allow time to wander off the path. There is only time enough to learn to know oneself. That is all I can teach you. In friendly and anxious appreciation, OK." '

When Meyboden's father asked for advice about his son's future Kokoschka tried not to paint too rosy a picture.

'Your esteemed letter puts me in a difficult position because I cannot dismiss your parental anxiety by the simple method of reporting unfavourably on your son's progress so far. Nor can I allay your fears about his chosen career, for I believe that the material and spiritual dangers will increase the more deeply he immerses himself in his vocation. You will understand that, for the artist, progress is not an end in itself. Art is an occupation which can only be rewarded by inner satisfaction, and the dictates of his conscience provide the only measure of an artist's worth. It is therefore impossible for the school to give any pupil a formal recommendation. But even if your son is prepared, like many others before him (myself included), to face a life of deprivation, struggling against material things and himself, a life threatened by constant insecurity, there is still no guarantee that he will not finally be destroyed by this craze. But who am I to discourage a man who feels that he has been chosen, before thousands of others, to find the Holy Grail? No. As a true teacher I shall encourage anyone who dares to face life, lest the Divine image be robbed of its priests, and life of the spirit of antiquity. The pupil who approaches with awe will be warmly received. Yours very sincerely, OK. Dresden, 31 October, 1920.'[14]

Gitta, daughter of Victor Wallerstein,[15] the Berlin art dealer and art-historian, a friend of Kokoschka, adds some of her memories to those of his former pupils.

'Of all the people I have met he was the most remarkable and unusual. His exceptional poise, all the glittering facets of his personality, his playfulness, his laughter, and his way of seeing and understanding things most ordinary people would overlook, all left a unique impression.'

'I was sixteen and a half at the time and had left school rather young to study ballet with the Berlin State Opera, but I was not a vivacious or buoyant child. Oskar Kokoschka took me out to lunch at the Esplanade one day, and walking home we fell to talking about journeys and foreign countries, and he pressed me to learn as many foreign languages as possible. I don't know why, but the future suddenly seemed frightening and confusing, and as I stumbled along the tears started to roll down my cheeks. Kokoschka must have seen this out of the corner of his eye, and after a few moments he said: "You know, Gitta, you must not be afraid of life." He had realized that I was not crying because I was lazy, nor because I would or could not learn. He knew that I was afraid.'

'In 1921 Kokoschka was nothing more to me than the friend of my parents, an artist who wanted to paint me, whom I liked very much, for I was only a ten-year-old lady—and that only in company. A terribly shy child, I remember the day my father brought me to the sitting in Dresden and went away leaving his daughter in panic-stricken terror. I could scarcely understand Kokoschka's Viennese dialect and my mind was filled with imaginary terrors—what if you don't understand when the Herr Professor speaks to you? But how I actually addressed him when it came to the point I no longer remember —probably not at all if it could be avoided. It was not as bad as I had expected. I sat silent on a chair, Kokoschka talked, and I could understand almost everything. He talked about the war, and how he had been wounded and had a bayonet through his chest, and he told me he was often in pain. I can see his tall figure now silhouetted against the broad slanting window of the studio, his fair hair falling across his eyes to be pushed back with the hand that held the brushes, an especially beautiful hand with finely tapered fingers. His eyes were blue and shining, and his whole person seemed to have an aura of its own. He never wore a painter's smock, but always a close-fitting leather jacket with woollen sleeves so as to keep his wound warm. In my imagination I connected the leather jacket and the story of the lance with a tale told by Walter Scott.'

'During the eleven days in which I sat for him I scarcely ever had to sit down, but could run about as I liked and play with Gerda Müller the actress, who came to the studio every day. I could practise my first ballet exercises round the giant coke-oven, for I had just begun my training, and he waited patiently until he caught me, or whatever he wanted from me, in the right light. Sometimes he held the tubes of colour up to my dress or my hair and asked me solemnly whether they matched. He was usually punctual for the appointment, but sometimes we had to wait—once more than an hour, though I have forgotten why. Anyway, he often made people wait for a long time for all kinds of real or imaginary reasons, so I must have been an exception. Not that I was of such importance to be sure, but because he had first known me as a child, whereas all the other men and women of his acquaintance were already adult, so he never lost his protective feeling that I was a young small creature which had not yet learned to walk by itself. Our friendship remained on this level until our last meeting in 1936, when I was certainly quite grown up. That was the reason he always looked after me (he expected everyone else to look after him) and overcame many social prejudices on my behalf. He even sat with my mother and me through a whole performance of *Turandot* in a box belonging to the Superintendent Tietjen, strolled with us in the foyer during the interval—he, for whom all crowds and public appearances were a nightmare—and all for the sake of a sixteen-year-old girl. Here I am touching on what I believe to be the fundamental difference between my friendship for Kokoschka and that of nearly all the other women he knew, because there was never any question of anything more than a friendly relationship between us. Once,

43 Olda, 1936

44 Oskar Kokoschka, London, 1945. In front of 'Alice in Wonderland'

45 Marianne—Maquis, 1942

46 Portrait of a 'Degenerate Artist', 1937. Detail

47 Minona, 1944–5

48 Pamela, 1959

for a brief moment, he tried to persuade himself that it was not so, but only because he happened to be rather lonely. He enjoyed pretending. He was a real actor. He suffered, grew jealous, was wretched, defiant, protective, tyrannical and spoilt by turns. He thought to amuse the other person by losing his head, but it was partly to goad his friends to fury, or just to be a protagonist. But, as I said, he was never emotionally involved with me; he was always free to come and go, and needed no jealous fear. I was never waiting to catch him. I needed nothing from him. Since I was still half-child the other female members of his circle tolerated me. Apart from Gerda Müller, I met Niuta Kallin* in 1926, Frau Rosenstein, Elza Temary (a Hungarian film star whom he painted at that period)† in his studio at Paul Cassirer's gallery in Berlin. I remember also a visit by Dorothy Thompson.'

'That winter in Berlin saw the portraits of Leo Kestenberg and Fritz Wolf completed. I used to go almost every afternoon to the studio, because Kokoschka had started on a second portrait. It was about three-quarters finished when he had to break off to do more pressing things (more lucrative subjects such as landscapes). Unlike the first portrait, I took a real interest in the second, and it held great promise, but it was never finished, and was probably painted over later. We often lunched in his usual haunt, the Esplanade, where he enjoyed introducing me to the different hors-d'oeuvre. He used to eat boiled beef on the bone almost every day. Sometimes he would take me to a cake-shop and order dozens of cream cakes. I could never eat many, but that was his idea of what a child would like; but often, scarcely two hours later, he would send a breath-taking bouquet of flowers, usually orchids, accompanied by a card with an irresistible message. That made me far happier than cream cakes.'

'He used to become fascinated by some special aspect of his friends—a particular movement, feature, or facial expression. He used to see a face as it had been, and a fold or wrinkle could move him to tears. While he was working he was a lover towards his subject—both men and women, he was in love with his vision, not necessarily with the reality. Tender, charming, enraptured. He would say an occasional word, or sing or hum to himself undefined snatches of melody. In my case he was fascinated by a small blue vein which stands out unusually clearly under one eye, as well as by some lines at the corner of my mouth, and my long legs. He nicknamed me Anaconda, the giant snake, partly because of my long shin-bones and partly because of the play he used to act when we were together, in which he despaired over the reptilian faithlessness which allowed me to take an interest in other men instead of devoting myself exclusively to him.'

'I saw him only sporadically in Berlin during the winter of 1926/27 and 1930. He was usually away, but we used to write to one another. When he was in Cairo—I think it must have been in 1928—I remember writing to him: "I would like to call you *Du* now; perhaps it will make you happy since you are so alone and far away!" He was

---

* Niuta Kallin, a Russian. She was his model for India and Recha in two portrait drawings. She also appears in the paintings JACOB, RACHEL AND LEAH, LOT AND HIS DAUGHTERS, and PAINTER AND HIS MODEL I.

† ELZA TEMARY, 1926/27.

almost certainly not alone, but he wrote a letter at once in which he seemed touched and overwhelmed as though something miraculous had occurred—and up to a certain point it was true.'

'In July 1930 he invited me to join him in the Italian village of Anticoli where he had been staying for some weeks. In the meantime I had been promoted to solo ballerina in the Berlin State Opera. I was twenty, and therefore could be considered quite grown up. Apart from a visit by Signora Sarvatti, who had personal access to Mussolini, whose portrait Kokoschka was considering, we saw no one besides the peasants who lived in the village.'

'Kokoschka worked in the morning, went for a walk, lunched, and took a siesta. Then he set to work once more, went for another walk, and had supper afterwards, joining in whatever activities were going on in the village in the summer evening. He was not producing a great deal, but working on the picture of a girl, with one of the Italian village girls as a model. We often used to climb a hill nearby to watch the peasants harvesting and still using traditional methods with oxen treading out the corn. Suddenly, in the brief space of four days, he painted the marvellous landscape, ANTICOLI, HARVEST IN THE SABINE MOUNTAINS. All day he sat there in the burning heat with easel and colours, sharing the wine of the peasants, and, in the evening, leaving the canvas in a nearby sheep-hut. He might have painted more landscapes in Italy, but suddenly something went wrong and he decided to leave. The change in him was remarkable. He lost his facility to get on with the local people. He became reserved and irritable and, strangely, seemed to lose his ability to speak Italian. As if he had forgotten every word he knew he left all the arrangements for the packing of the harvest scene, and for our departure, to me. We travelled together as far as Rome, where after two days I left him and returned to Berlin.'

'In 1934 I received a letter from him, though I do not remember where from.* Since the last time we met I had left Berlin and was living in Zurich. In December of that year I travelled to Prague, where Kokoschka had settled, and there I spent the four weeks of my Christmas holiday. I was a member of Trudi Schoop's ballet then, and had spent six years travelling in all the free countries. We spent nearly every day of my holiday together. We used to meet at his hotel and then go to an excellent delicatessen on the Graben, where he ordered innumerable sandwiches. If he had no appointment in the afternoon we went for a walk, through the interesting parts of Prague—the Old Quarter, the Jewish cemetery, the old Synagogue—and we discovered all kinds of restaurants. Later on he worked, mostly on landscapes, I think, and several times he attempted to make a drawing of me, as well as a water-colour portrait, but they were not successful.† In the late afternoon, about five or six o'clock, his friend Edith Sachsel would join us and we went out to eat. He could not have seen many other people—at least not fre-

---

* Vienna, Budapest, or Prague (Ed.).

† There are, however, three fine water-colours from the Dresden period in existence, MÄDCHEN MIT BLAUER KAPPE (Girl with blue cap), a full-face bust, and a half-length in profile and a half-length three-quarter profile.

quently, otherwise I would remember them. He seemed to be in poor health with a chronic infection just then, and we tried to look after him, and he used to get a devilish enjoyment out of keeping his "slaves" busy. In appearance he was much the same as in Italy in 1930, though perhaps a little more fine drawn. But he had less money than at any time since I had first met him. He was risking everything in an attempt to get into contact with the influential people, and particularly the Czech Minister of Culture. Oskar Kokoschka was a man to whom *largesse* and free spending came naturally. It suited his temperament. But he also had a mother and a younger brother to look after in Vienna. What their relationship really was I never knew—his actions spoke only of loving care, but they all had very strong temperaments and other factors must have been present.'*

'After those four weeks I saw Kokoschka for only two very brief visits in the summers of 1935 and 1936, in Prague. That was the period of the Masaryk portrait and of many revolutionary ideas concerning the sufferings and well-being of mankind. Kokoschka was feeling very hemmed-in in Prague. I have never known him to stay for so long in one place. Of course the world was changing, and he no longer had the means to make a clean sweep and go. It was dreadful to watch him pacing his cage like a wild beast, whereas I, through my work and good fortune, was able to move about freely.'[16]

Gradually he began to fret at his enforced stay in Dresden and at the continued presence of his friends, who pursued him like ghosts from which he could never escape. He was already restless when his position as Director of the Academy was at the point of confirmation, because he feared that he would settle and become too comfortable there. For he was, in fact, very happy in Dresden. So he tried to press the administration too far by demanding the magnificent Baroque mansion in the Grosse Garten for his own occupation, secretly hoping that they would refuse and that he would then have an excuse to withdraw. But his request was granted. Everything was done to please him. He lived there in solitude, tired and withdrawn from society. He instructed his maid that she was to turn all comers away with the excuse: The *Herr Rittmeister* is resting and thinking.

Kokoschka called the maid Roserl, as though she were a Viennese, but her real name was Hulda, and she was, in fact, the servant of the Gallery Director, Dr Hans Posse, but he sometimes lent her to Kokoschka. The Posse family lived in the other house in the garden. The maid was a young fair girl whose head had been completely turned, and Kokoschka originally took her on to look after the big doll. He was living in a twilight world, scarcely able to distinguish the real from the unreal. Strange things were always occurring and there were many 'episodes' in Dresden. When the divine Roserl, as he called her, entered the room she began to play a part immediately. Elsewhere she was the prosaic Hulda, but as soon as she crossed his threshold she was transformed. A white frilly apron, a magnificent broom, and her costume seemed so perfectly theatrical that

* Kokoschka's sister, Berta Patočková, whom Gitta Wallerstein does not mention, was living at the time in Prague with her husband, a General in the Czech Army. He had formerly been an admiral in the Austro-Hungarian Navy.

she became bemused. She would talk about Keyserling, how he had published a new book, because she heard so many intellectual conversations at the Posses' that she imagined herself part of that world. So Tagore had been arrested in the Market Place? That was certainly interesting, but what was he like? She imagined him with cloak and long hair, with onions, beetroot, and peas to eat—everything, in fact, that was unobtainable at the time. He had long yellow teeth and the police arrested him because he was walking around the city in his nightshirt, without stockings. He is a philosopher and therefore had no pockets. . . . Frau Köpenick, Dr Posse's housekeeper, would call out 'Hulda!' and then Roserl would throw off whatever role she happened to be playing and leave. But she always came back. Once Kokoschka was lying down, so she came in very quietly. She knew he was not asleep, but it did not matter; she acted out the part of trying to avoid waking him all the same. She was wearing black stockings and had fine legs, which she very well knew, so she deliberately played the part of temptress. Climbing on to a stool, she tried to reach a high shelf. After a brief struggle with her conscience she opened the cupboard, where there was a piece of chocolate, horrible postwar stuff, but she could not resist it. As she put it into her mouth the key of the cupboard dropped to the ground. The artist pretended to wake up, though he had been watching the whole performance. She lost her balance and nearly fell. She was full of imagination, a naïve country girl with blue eyes. 'Hulda!' came the voice from below.[17]

Political excitement and violence increased. Pacifism, Communism, and a general anti-*bourgeois* attitude came to the fore, and the kind of work associated with Otto Dix, who was beginning to paint pimps and prostitutes, aroused great admiration. It did not impress Kokoschka. He had seen deeply into men's souls, and his only comment was that it seemed to him too 'sweet', typically Biedermeier. Everybody addressed each other as 'man', and 'no more war' was the order of the day. In fact, despite the daily episodes and shootings, which Kokoschka condemned, he remained almost unmoved by events. It seemed in those days as though his past life were unfolding before him. It was something he already knew, but which no longer concerned him. Everyday events paled in comparison. In Dresden he lived the life of a rich man.

He really only felt at ease with women, and once an extraordinarily bizarre thing happened. He invited twelve women whom he had loved at one time or another to a performance of *Don Giovanni* (he once confessed that his net spread very wide). He sat in the box with the reigning queen, who was a very talented artist.[18] Each one of the twelve believed that he was there on her account, and they were all invited to his house after the opera. It was a winter's night, and they were just leaving the theatre when a fine carriage pulled up beside them. A man got out and handed a lady to Kokoschka, who then drove home with her and Frau Gela. It was reminiscent of the *Tales of Hoffman*. In the candle-lit room the servant passed noiselessly round the table, wearing white gloves. Kokoschka explained that he was a horrible puritan individual, and was always lecturing and quoting the Bible, and in order to express the full weight of his contempt he held the plates with his thumb in the soup. That supper, *à la Don Giovanni*, exactly symbolizes the dreamlike atmosphere of the Dresden years. The astonishing thing is that Kokoschka ever found time to do any work; nevertheless it was during this period that his art began to unfold in a new way and to become broader in scope. Like Rembrandt he was inspired by Biblical themes—SAUL AND DAVID: JACOB, RACHEL AND LEAH. He also painted a self-portrait with two of his friends with Dresden Neustadt, the view from his window, in the background. It was entitled LOT AND HIS DAUGHTERS.

JACOB, RACHEL AND LEAH has a fundamentally erotic atmosphere as, for example, MOTHER WITH A CHILD IN HER ARMS, which has the terrifying story of Frau Gela, retold in *A Sea Ringed with Visions*, as its subject. The abnormality which had reached its climax in the affair of the doll reappears as a significant element of the unfinished self-portrait of 1922. The artist in his smock works with outthrust head, his studio window with a background of Dresden Neustadt visible, and a mask, like those described by Hans Meyboden, on the left.

The colour in the paintings of 1922 and 1923 is vigorously applied with broad strokes and primary tones, and this marks the end of the phase characterized by the violent and impasto application of the paint—THE OUTCASTS; SELF-PORTRAIT, 1917; LOVERS WITH A CAT; ORPHEUS AND EURYDICE; THE FRIENDS; and KATJA. A more calculated effect of distance is attained (these works were conceived in that sense), the colour is intensive, and form is huge and monumental. THE PAGANS, and the portraits of CARL GEORG HEISE and HANS MARDERSTEIG, were also conceived in this broad and powerful style. These two men were editors with Kokoschka of the art-review, *Genius*. But the colour does not reach its climax till the POWER OF MUSIC and the many VIEWS OF DRESDEN—the magnificent variations on the Elbe bridges with the river and the new city in the background.

Apart from the Old Testament figures painted in these new strong colours there are also WOMAN IN BLUE, PAINTER AND HIS MODEL I and II, and the portraits of GITTA WALLERSTEIN. Also, WOMAN WITH A SLAVE, CHILD WITH FLOWERS AND A CAT, MOTHER AND CHILD EMBRACING, GIRL WITH DOLL, PAINTER WITH DOLL (this was the life-size doll of the Dresden period), MOTHER WITH A CHILD IN HER ARMS, SELF-PORTRAIT WITH FOLDED ARMS, GIRL WITH FLOWERS, and THE PERSIAN, but most important of all were the luminous and vigorous paintings called SUMMER I and the SLAVE-GIRL, which are the finest examples of this period.

The lithographs to the PASSION were also done during those years, and we can recognize Kokoschka's own features in the long sad face of Jesus—it was an *Ecce Homo*, portraying the sufferings of mankind repeated again in different forms. Another drawing shows his friends Dr Neuberger and Käthe Richter in the *Flight into Egypt*—Flight, the Garden of Gethsemane, Crucifixion—all universal, recurring situations in the history of humanity. Kokoschka also drew some large portrait heads for lithographs in Dresden, as, for instance, Walther Hasenclever, Fritz Neuberger, the two heads of Corona, and an absolute masterpiece—the portrait of Käthe Richter. He tried to form an impenetrable ring of women round him as a protection against the outside world, and so he painted a record of them all in the portfolio—*The Daughters of the Covenant*. It was the covenant of a man who had known the passions of love, death, and resurrection, and whose lot it was, like Sir Galahad, to seek the Holy Grail to find the answer to the ultimate problems —the meaning of art and life.

It was also at this time that Kokoschka began to co-operate with the German stage in the production of his plays. The very first performance of *Hiob* was given on 3 July 1917, though, of course, it had appeared ten years before in Vienna in its original version and under its former title of *Sphinx and Strawman*. *The Burning Bush* was also performed. Kokoschka produced both at the Albert Theatre in Dresden and the Kammerspieltheater in Berlin. There was a theatrical scandal, and Reinhardt was afraid that the audience would break down the safety curtain. The police had to hold back the people in the street outside. Käthe Richter and Ernst Deutsch played the chief parts, and as a gesture of friendship *The Burning Bush* was dedicated to Käthe Richter and *Hiob* to the man of suffering—Dr Neuberger.

Sphinx and Strawman and *Murder Hope of Women* were both written in 1907, and thus Kokoschka can be seen to be the real creator of the experimental or 'ecstatic theatre'.[19] Several years before the appearance of the first German Expressionist plays, he had exerted a very wide influence in the Expressionist and Dadaist theatres, and on Expressionism in general.[20] Additionally he evolved many new ideas in his productions which were later taken up and widely applied. And, of course, there were the scandals. For example, Reinhardt's productions in the Deutsche Theatre in Berlin in May 1919, one of the effects of which was to ensure that Kokoschka's name would be firmly linked with the modern German theatre. It is only now, at last, that literary historians are becoming aware of his importance, for his contemporaries were scarcely in a position to pass an objective judgement, and Wilhelm Fränger in Heidelberg, alone, raised his voice in defence against the bitter attacks of the *Frankfurter Zeitung*. Even today Karl Otten puts the beginning of German Expressionist drama at 1910 instead of 1907–8,[21] yet Ludwig Rubiner's introduction to *Der Dramatische Wille* certainly applies to Kokoschka's first plays: 'The nightmare experience of our generation has given birth to a dramatic language of destiny and will. The drama is the spiritual expression of our time. People today read plays as they formerly read stories, like a straightforward book.'[22]

The fact that neither Kokoschka's Expressionist prose nor his first lyrical dramas are included in German anthologies can only be ascribed to the blindness of many literary critics. *Dreaming Youths* (1907) and *The White Slayer of Beasts* (about 1908) were undoubtedly outriders.[23] Albert Ehrenstein had a more lucid vision when he wrote his essay on Kokoschka in the 'twenties.[24]

In that field, however, where artist and poet must be judged together, Kokoschka's powerful figure comes into his own. This became clear in the important exhibition— *Expressionism, Literature and Art, 1910–1923*, which was held in the Schiller National-museum in 1960.[25] Today we have experienced Existentialist and mythological Symbolist drama carried to the furthest extremes in the theatre of Jean Paul Sartre, Jean Genet, Eugène Ionesco, Samuel Beckett, or the neo-classicists Jean Cocteau, Jean Anouilh, and Jean Giraudoux, forerunners of the 'Angry Young Men' typified by John Osborne, and it has become perfectly clear that Kokoschka opened the door to the new drama many years earlier.[26]

On 11 April 1920 *Murder Hope of Women* and *Hiob* were produced by Heinrich George in the New Theatre, Frankfurt-am-Main, arranged by Zingler's *Kunstkabinett*. In the same year on 23 July the *Burning Bush* appeared on the initiative of a journal called *Die Gemeinschaft* (Community) in Heidelberg. *Dreaming Youths* was recited as a curtain-raiser before the performance. In 1921 Paul Hindemith's musical setting of *Murder Hope of Women* had its first performance in the Landestheater, Stuttgart, and was repeated on 26 March 1922 at the State Opera House in Frankfurt. On 2 February 1921 *Orpheus and Eurydice*, Kokoschka's more easily comprehended play, had its first performance in Heinrich George's production at the State Theatre at Frankfurt-am-Main; Gerda Müller and Heinrich George played the title roles. It was 27 November 1926 before Ernst Křenek's opera with the same title was first performed at the State Theatre in Kassel. A new production of *Orpheus and Eurydice* was given after the second world war on 3 December 1950 at the Arts Theatre of Frankfurt University, and on 23 June 1951 another new production at the Neue Bühne in Hamburg. The third act of the drama *Comenius* was performed in the Avant-Garde Theatre in Berlin in 1959. The same play was performed in the Kunsthaus in Zurich on 5 June 1966 to celebrate the artist's eightieth anniversary.

Of all the artists whom Kokoschka knew in Dresden, Lovis Corinth was certainly the most outstanding. Hans Posse arranged that they should meet. Corinth, since his stroke, was displaying a significant liberation in his work, as a result of which both his landscapes and his portraits closely resemble Kokoschka's style, as Paul Westheim remarked in *Kunstblatt*. Corinth had a head like a bull—so Kokoschka thought—with protruding eyes. They used to sit drinking together in an inn, and Corinth would clutch a glass in his trembling hands, muttering to himself: 'Mother-breast, mother-breast.' Mary Wigman, the Expressionist dancer, also lived in Dresden. There was something in her nature of the female he had portrayed in *Murder Hope of Women*. She was like an animal-tamer with her pupils; she lashed the girls into a wild and primitive state by her dominating character, only to quiet and control them in the end. She was able to slacken or increase emotional and physical tension by her over-riding will.

The success of his two Berlin Exhibitions—the *Landscapes* (1925) and *Man and Animals* (1927)—brought Kokoschka recognition at last as the leading artist of Germany and Central Europe.[27] At the same time he was often short of money in Dresden. Once he was offered a bundle of marvellous Japanese paper for two hundred marks. He had it sent to his studio without having the slightest idea how he would pay. As he sat in the garden wondering what to do a stinking sewage cart passed by. It was drawn by oxen, and there were several others behind. Drowsily he said to himself, if there were seven everything would turn out well . . . and started to count—one, two, three . . . six, seven . . . Then he heard the sound of a horse behind him and was wondering how this could be, for there were no longer any horses since the war, when two warm hands were laid across his eyes: Who is it? he asked in astonishment. A woman's voice replied. She said she knew his paintings and wanted to meet him. She was attractive, so he asked for her name and where she lived so that he could visit her, apologizing for not being able himself to invite her, and explaining that he was quite out of money. In Dresden he used to send his women friends orchids because Rothe, the flower shop, grew the finest orchids in the world, and he had credit there. She must have orchids, too, to be on the same footing. But she refused to tell him her name. Then, he said, he would call her Morpheus. He was not to know, either, where she lived, but she would send for him when it grew dark. He allowed his eyes to be bandaged and was drawn by her horses up a steep hillside. On arrival he found himself in a large old mansion containing an important collection of Morpheus moths.

But in the afternoon, just after they had met, he went to the Academy where Paul Cassirer was waiting for him. Immediately he asked: Have you any money? Cassirer responded: 'How much? Would four hundred marks be enough?' Three hundred would do, Kokoschka replied. Then he would be able to pay for the paper and still have some left for orchids. Such things often happened to him.

At that time Cassirer said that he had come, even though he was much the older, to make up their quarrel in Vienna. Cassirer put his prices higher, and every painting cost more than the last. Kokoschka asked him if he thought it was sensible to quarrel about a house, because when he was determined about something he would not give up and he had needed the house for his father, who was ill. This second (actually third) contract was so favourable that it allowed him to undertake journeys to Bloney (near Vevey), Italy, Vienna, and Paris, but he broke it afterwards in Genoa. He felt that it was endangering his art, and he did not want to be driven into serial painting. He was afraid of becoming a 'Paris' painter.[28]

The most important picture of the Dresden period is, without doubt, THE POWER OF MUSIC, in which his sense of colour, vigorous composition and brilliant brushwork are more accomplished than in any earlier painting. This picture occupies the same position among the artist's compositions as Leo Kestenberg among the portraits. Apart from the romantic story of its inspiration it is important because it reveals the artist at the height of his power. A delicate lightness and vibrant vitality invade the work, all the more striking when one realizes that it was originally entitled *Strength and Weakness* and that it depicts the theme of hostility between man and woman for the last time. A Dionysiac classicism inspires it, a song from a bursting heart, a thirst for life already fore-shadowed in THE PAGANS—an uninhibited love-scene—and in SUMMER, with the woman reclining against a luxurious landscape.

Kokoschka's POWER OF MUSIC and Munch's *Dance of Life* were both exhibited in the Brussels Exhibition of 1958, in company with representative works of other schools and the varied styles of the abstractionists. It was a unique opportunity to examine again the claims made by Expressionism to be a genuine and significant artistic style of our era. One day he said to me:

You must at all costs go to Vienna to see my retrospective exhibition, for in our non-figurative day, when chimpanzee art can be seen alongside the products of the action painters in the Institute of Contemporary Arts, this is the last exhibition which is really imbued with the genius of the West. Perhaps Europe's artistic mission has now been fulfilled, and by that I mean ended, for one thing is certain, no grass will grow in a future technical world.

And speaking of THE POWER OF MUSIC: 'Both titles were mine—THE POWER OF MUSIC and STRENGTH AND WEAKNESS. The last referred to the colours; red, yellow, vivid orange and cold blues—weakening, feminine colours. THE POWER OF MUSIC was inspired by the subject, because the shrill trumpet-call is yellow in impasto on the canvas, which almost shudders with the strident luminous colour glowing like stained-glass (something that Rouault never achieved, and van Gogh seems dull and grey in contrast) like a living creature that is stirred to action. This is what is really meant by 'action-painting', and there is scarcely another example in the whole history of art with the exception of the Grünewald at Colmar, Dürer's *Apostles* in Munich, and Titian's *Pietà* in the Academy at Venice. In any case, this painting is the sum of all my experiments in Dresden to try and produce the sense of heat and cold from colour. You should really see the original. I had an opportunity to see it again recently after thirty years and I was speechless before it, especially as I had been studying a huge van Gogh exhibition in New York which was fresh in my mind. The colours in THE POWER OF MUSIC are such as a pseudo-philosopher and romantic talker like Kandinsky only dreams of but never develops beyond the test-tube stage. But that is quite enough for the abstract *sputniks!*'

We realize that Kokoschka sees himself as a symbol against the background of history, as did Goethe in the last century.

THE POWER OF MUSIC is one of the greatest paintings of the first half of the twentieth century. Colour is the key—colour which is like the revelation of an inner force, a surging vitality and an ecstatic *joie de vivre*. The painter's reinvigorated senses, his new-found faith in life and love, his rediscovery of beauty, suddenly free his power of expression, fettered till then by the horror of war, with the concerted vigour of strong colours. The background is a polyphony of blue and mauve composed of islets of spontaneous colour. The tones are like the beat of a big orchestra when suddenly the trumpets sound —here the yellow and orange-red of the figures. Unity and balance are ensured by the flower in the female figure's hand, a mauve mallow which seems to grow out of the relationship between the two colour groups. Hence the flower is also a symbol of desire. The different tones of green also help to soften the harsh contrasts. This abundance of colour goes a long way towards explaining the musical title. Colour is not the only element of the painting, however, although it is certainly dominant.

After analysing the first impression governed by the predominance of colour, further consideration leads one to the conclusion that Kokoschka's artistic aim was to intensify the effect of colour by the co-ordination of differing tones—the only way to achieve the contrapuntal qualities of a composition. This was in contrast to the German Expressionists and the influential *Fauves*, whose avowed aim was to enhance the effect of colour as design by enclosing and flattening it.

Kokoschka sees this painting as the realization of his Baroque heritage: THE POWER

OF MUSIC was the first of a series of compositions in which I was able to express in my own way what I had so admired when I was young in the Baroque murals of Maulbertsch. The difference between Kokoschka and the German Expressionsists is in the latter's use of primitive means to produce a permanent *fortissimo* compared with Kokoschka's subtle refinement in the use of strong colours and tonal values.

In this work colour is related to a strict, even traditional discipline in composition. The picture's dynamism in the colour-range and in the theme itself is developed in a strict diagonal, following the head of the female figure to the foot of the boy. Each figure occupies almost exactly half of the canvas, the flower is more or less in the middle, and because of the intensity of colour, the boy seems stronger and bigger than the woman, thus enhancing the whole dramatic character. The horizontal axis links the boy's left eye to the woman's right shoulder, and both figures are subject, within their own half of the painting, to the diagonal composition; the woman's left eye, her outstretched arm and head, follow one diagonal line, with the boy's body and the wrist of his right hand as another. These two diagonals form the traditional inverted triangle of the Renaissance. Structural austerity is used expressly to underline the fact that the passionate colour of the painting has been tamed and bridled by form, once again in contrast to the methods of Nolde and Schmidt-Rotluff, but in accord with Edvard Munch.

After discussing the musical affinities of the colour and the strict discipline of the composition (which is itself an important characteristic of music), we may turn to the problem of colour symbolism. Colours here are only symbolic in so far as they express a human mood or emotion, in the same way as van Gogh's painting of the *Café in Arles* (1888). Intellectually the painting describes the war between the sexes (the contrast between cold and warm colours) and the horror of the young man at his first encounter with mature womanhood. The youth holds his hands to his ears to shut out the sound of the trumpet and seems ready to jump out of the frame with fright. This is another example of Kokoschka's developing the interest around the edges of the composition, an artistic device whereby the onlooker is drawn into the action.

The painting may have another and deeper meaning. When one considers that the artist came to this theme from personal experience (and the similarity of the woman here represented to those of the autobiographical paintings such as PAINTER AND HIS MODEL I, JACOB, RACHEL AND LEAH, and LOT AND HIS DAUGHTERS, is close) it seems very probable that the painting expresses not only the artist's fear of temptation and the dissipation of his power of love which he wants to devote to his work alone (an echo of THE TEMPEST), but also the powerful and self-advocating feminity which awakens sensual desire. The original title stresses the triumph of the female principle, and this is also symbolized in the strong colours. The animal breaking in from the background increases the symbolic effect of the painting and at the same time provides relief from the intense blaze of colour.

The colour, then, is only a device, a door which opens the way to far greater treasures. It is in absolute contrast to the work of lyrical abstractionists such as Mannessier or Bazaine, for it produces a more profound experience than abstract colour and pattern in isolation. Kokoschka is of the opinion that colour alone is not enough to create a picture. He uses it to create an image which not only stirs our intuition but also satisfies our senses.[29]

It is no accident that colour has a connexion with music. The liberation and musicality of colour is probably the most significant event of modern painting, for joy in colour is primordial—a breath of Dionysius. The physical analogies between colour and tone are a question of science rather than art and may not be pursued here. The personal experience of the artist is our sole concern.

From his childhood and his schooldays Kokoschka took an exceptional interest in music. The rhythm of his life and the dreamlike, anti-logical, dynamically unbounded nature of his character all signify a close relationship with music. He was once chosen to sing a solo, *Gloria in excelsis* (with the great *fresco* by Maulbertsch in the dome of the Piaristen church overhead), but before he reached the high *Deo* his voice suddenly broke and he swooned. That was the last time he sang in church. Afterwards he was supposed to learn the violin, but he did not get very far, more on account of the expense than any other reason. His uncle was professor of music in the Theresianum in Vienna, so he was able to have some lessons free, but his memories are exclusively of the hours he spent waiting in the music teacher's house so as to be able to take the place of any pupil who might not turn up.[30]

The portfolio of the *Bach Cantata* is proof of the way music inspired him. Once, Professor Kestenberg played through the whole of the St Matthew Passion to him, and Kokoschka made fifty drawings inspired by the music. Mozart's *O crudele* had, as I have already mentioned, a profound physiological effect on him. The music mesmerized him; he lived in a dream, enthralled by the woman singing the part of Donna Anna. He kept a record of her aria for twenty years, like a piece of wedding cake. Strangely enough he took no interest in Ottavio, and did not even know the music of his part. In Vienna in 1920 the art-historian Karl Swoboda played a great deal of music to him—Monteverdi, Gluck, Haydn, Mozart, and Handel, and Beethoven's opus 113. Swoboda's wife, Camilla, who was very musical, sat listening, and thus he drew her. Watching how her face changed under the impression of the music he saw her in his mind as a young girl through all the easy stages of life until she suddenly faded and died. It was a strange experience, and he put it all into the drawings. Swoboda was assistant to Max Dvořák, who made trenchant comments on this series, which was called *Variations on a Theme*. Kokoschka was happy to be so well understood. Dvořák apprehended the spiritual changes not as impressions but as a true transformation of the mind. He spoke of the 'inexhaustible and continuous flow of the life of the soul', citing the words of Delacroix: 'Facts do not count, for they are ephemeral. Ideas about things abide, because their essence is ideas.' We can understand Kokoschka's surprise and sorrow when he learned, in 1947 on a visit to Prague, that Swoboda's wife had died at Auschwitz, for Kokoschka had a clear insight into her destiny. He has told me that he is sometimes frightened at the percipience of his inner eye. It had been thus with the 'goddess' too.*

* The 'goddess' died suddenly in the autumn of 1963 of an illness which he seems to have foreseen many years earlier.

Kokoschka is quite capable of falling asleep at a concert, when R . . . plays Rachmaninoff. And once he slept right through Verdi's *Requiem* with Toscanini conducting. However, he told me that he had heard a Mozart quintet played in Hampstead by refugees who were real music-lovers, and that it had been a wonderful experience.* Kokoschka declared that he did not hear music with his head but with his spine. No sooner did the music touch his spine than he felt like weeping.

An artist with this temperament is certain to find inspiration for his work in the concert hall. All the same, Kokoschka never thinks deliberately of his work when he is listening to music, although the impressions gather in his mind. He told me that when he followed the sequence of musical development from late Mozart to Beethoven's last works he could see the changes in life itself. Just as the schism of the Reformation is perceptible in Grünewald, so Beethoven pictured an empty heaven. The deaf Beethoven withdrew from that bleak unpeopled world to shut himself away for ever in isolation. Kokoschka could hear it, and see it too, although that does not mean that it had anything to do with visionary imagination—it simply came from his spine. He knew nothing of the theory of music and could scarcely remember a motif, but music can be recognized like a landscape. It was apprehended on the plane of sensibility, the core of emotion, that lies behind perception, and which itself has nothing to do with seeing and hearing, because it is, in a sense, behind their frontiers. And music has always produced the same reaction in him, like a man in the presence of his beloved.

Once, in Vienna, he told me, he had attended a series of concerts of Austrian music, beginning with early Haydn and continuing to Schönberg's last work. He had been a great friend of Schönberg's, and the composer often used to play to him. He remembers how he once explained to Schönberg the principle behind the story of the trumpets of Jericho. That series in Vienna made him realize that the 'landscape' remained unaltered from Haydn to Schönberg, whereas Brahms was quite different—the difference between day and night.

Formerly he had never been able to tolerate Brahms, he explained. He found him unattractive, like Dostoievsky, whose works, apart from *The Gentle One* he had never read. It was far too analytical. But he was able to understand Brahms now, since he had become so pessimistic after the collapse of the monarchy. He was suddenly vouchsafed a glimpse into another world of sentiment, a world of musical sensibility that had been closed to him before. The period from Haydn to Schönberg seemed to him Baroque, to which Brahms is hostile. Schönberg, to be sure, had invented a new way of writing music, but Haydn was just as atonal before the collapse of the old régime. In those days the whole world went to pieces—the moral, religious world that suddenly ceased and was lost. It was not necessary, Kokoschka thought, to know that Newton's laws had been discovered, for it was apparent in music. Neither Beethoven nor Schönberg wanted to quit the old world, but Brahms was different. In the music of Bach the Baroque man is lost in melancholy puritanism, but he has still not abandoned

* 1945, in the home of the painter and restorer, Sebastian Isepp, who was very musical and held regular concerts of chamber music in London.

Baroque architecture although he no longer sees it; the arched vaults still stand and the flights of stone stairs mount ever upwards. The music of Bach seemed to Kokoschka to personify man's relationship with architecture, and hence ultimately with mankind itself. Reformation man limps round in small rooms with no feeling of community left; people squat together in *bourgeois* houses and offices, while society has no home. The Baroque church had formerly been the expression of the life of the community, a plastic solid form. Bach had need of it but, because the community was no more, the only way to express the Baroque world of architecture, the universe, was in his music. In Germany alone was such a conception possible. Kokoschka found Handel too superficial and pompous, he told me. He composed royal programme music, and accompaniments for banquets, sleigh-rides and funerals. To him Handel's music describes nothing more than eating and drinking, with no conception of the deeper sensibilities of mankind. Haydn he found quite different. In his music you can hear how warmly the spring rain falls on the earth, how the wind beats against the walls, how humbly the composer listens to the fearful thunderstorm. In Bach, too, one can hear the sighing and tribulation, the agony of the dying Christ, the thirst after truth, the weight of destiny. . . . Kokoschka can hardly bear to listen to five bars of Handel. Even Bach could compose light-heartedly for a special occasion—for instance, the popular Brandenburg Concertos—one has to laugh. Yet a cheerful country dance by Mozart could move him easily to tears. The peasant is lumpish, and the violin artful—he could see it all in his mind's eye. Impressions on the ear were transformed into form, an inner form that debates long whether it will become vision or music.

That was Kokoschka's experience with Leo Kestenberg. The dumpy man sat before him. He was not a virtuoso, but it was important to him to bring the ideas in the music clearly to the fore. Although it was a man who sat at the piano playing rather crudely—Kokoschka suddenly saw a woman with fine hands clearly as if he had drawn her before. She might have been standing before him, but the short fat man was still sitting there vigorously playing the piano. Kokoschka painted her into the portrait.

Professor Leo Kestenberg, who worked in Paul Cassirer's publishing firm, was also the editor of the journal *Der Bildermann*. A pupil of Busoni's, he supported the idea of *The Education of Humanity through Music*. First consultant in the Prussian Ministry for Science, Art and Popular Education, he was appointed chancellor in the Prussian Ministry of Culture. He first met Kokoschka in 1916 in connexion with *Der Sturm*, and commissioned from him the lithographic series of the St Matthew Passion to be published in *Der Bildermann*. He also used to visit Kokoschka in the *Weisser Hirsch* sanatorium in Dresden when he was recovering after the war, and they became lifelong friends. Kestenberg was the intermediary in the advantageous contract with Paul Cassirer. Before the outbreak of the second world war they met again in Prague as refugees.

Kestenberg wrote of his portrait:

'In 1926 Kokoschka invited me one day to sit for him. I was happy and enthusiastic, and he started at once. He asked me to come regularly but not before the late evening.

However, that suited me perfectly because I was occupied at the Ministry all day. He began to paint with a certain playful hesitation, and I realized gradually that four or five pictures had been started, each one of which he had painted over. He used to call me jokingly "The Prefect" during these late sittings, which often lasted far into the night. But one night an immense surge of creation overtook him, as if he were guided by the hand of God. From then on he finished the painting with steady rhythmic strokes of the brush. The portrait is larger than life, and Kokoschka's favourite trick of inserting whole stories into his portraits also influenced mine. There I am sitting, with tight fists and an energetically determined expression, in the centre of the picture. Not an inch is left on the canvas without movement and life, and my wife is sitting playing the piano in the background. A symbol of my connection with the labour movement is a workman bearing a heavy load, and on the side—almost a *pendant*—the corner of the *Volksbühne* building. It is certainly a portrait of me, but also of my character and my soul in the most sublime sense.'

'Kokoschka, or Ko as he used to call himself, most generously made me a present of the picture and it is my most treasured possession. It is really a gallery piece, and has been exhibited on numerous occasions, but it needs a big room to achieve its proper effect. At an exhibition in the Berlin Academy of Arts it was hung quite alone on one of the main walls with correct lighting and position.[31]

Kokoschka's enjoyment of music was increased when he left London for the Lake of Geneva in 1953. There at Villeneuve he found that he had the composer and conductor, Furtwängler, as a neighbour, living at Clarens, near Vevey. They became friends, but alas, only for a short time. In 1955 Furtwängler arranged that Kokoschka should design the setting and costumes for *The Magic Flute*, which he was to conduct at the Salzburg Festival. Kokoschka also painted a portrait of the 'cellist, Pablo Casals, in Switzerland the year before. Wilhelm Kempff, the pianist, is an annual and very welcome guest both in Kokoschka's house and with Frau Furtwängler. It is natural, therefore, that Kokoschka's autobiography on records is interspersed with references to favourite pieces of music, for instance, Beethoven's String Quartet in A minor, opus 132; Gluck's *Orpheus and Eurydice*; Anton von Webern's Variations for Piano, No. 1; Wagner's overture to *Tristan und Isolde*; (Kokoschka also loves *The Death of Siegfried*); Beethoven's third *Leonora* overture, and the overture to *Egmont*, all of which he often plays for his own enjoyment.[32]

XII

ORBIS PICTUS

Kokoschka left Dresden suddenly one night without warning anyone of his plans. His departure marks the beginning of an important new phase in which his abundance and technical mastery brought him to the fore in Europe within a very few years. By 1930 he had emerged as one of the greatest painters in the world. A new stage began; like Edvard Munch, he turned his back on his negative early period, which was characterized by revolt, dissent and anarchy, and was determined by the neuroses of the pre-war period, the atmosphere of war, death, political decadence, and the destructive power of love, and, instead, moved towards a positive, life-affirming future. It was like a shrill cry coming after the nervous torment, a sudden outbreak of vitality which swept the past away like a storm.

He needed freedom to develop, and as soon as he sensed that growing success and his assured position were threatening his liberty he snatched it back. He possessed powers, far beyond the imagination of smaller talents, capable of undermining his very existence when directed against himself, but which now drove him to powerful action. A splendid butterfly emerged from the larva, setting its wings to the wind and dancing in the sunshine.

The world lay glittering and fresh at his feet; he was born anew and longed to feast his eyes, to live his life to the full. He was overwhelmed by the spirit of Dionysius, by violent thirst and longing. His was not Hölderlin's noble resignation and retreat into idealistic pride, sorrow, and melancholy, but the Nietzschean assertion of sensual power and cruelty. This was no whimsical idyll. Kokoschka saw idealists as dissatisfied people always wanting to change things. For him the transitory nature of things was an integral part of the power of production and destruction, a recurring death and creation. 'The land flows with milk, wine and honey, and the air is full of the scent of the incense of Syria', so sang the enraptured Bacchantes of Euripides.

Kokoschka had never before been so near to happiness, and he dedicated himself without reserve to the manifold beauties of the earth. The dark shadows were gone, the nightmare flown. Kokoschka hurled himself into this new adventure and was inspired to create a powerful symphony to show mankind that life was good. Like Comenius, he wanted to present them with an *Orbis Pictus*. He longed to sing of the world's riches, the foreign lands and exotic vegetation, distant tribes and tropical days and nights. He longed to embrace the whole world in his jubilation, to paint with mirrored awe the Garden of Eden which finds in the breath its mystery and in the eye its master. The cities of the world, nestling like precious stones on the mountainside, beside sea-coasts and along river-banks, the creative spirit of man and the deeds in which the history of the world is mirrored, would fill his canvases. These paintings echo like Herder's *Voices of the People*—they are a recognition of the world's unity. Wherever he stumbled upon the spirit of creation he sought to communicate it to his fellow men; he tried to encourage friendship and to increase love and understanding where others sowed only discord and disunity. Wherever he travelled he found friends and understanding—in Egypt, Italy, Turkey, or Spain. He was drawn by the beauty of women, lost his heart and lived his life to the full.

Even his later writing still mirrors the romantic glow of those days in *The Sea Ringed with Visions (Spur im Treibsand)*: 'In Jerusalem I heard tell of the beautiful Jewish girls on the island of Djerba (Tunisia), which is the Island of Odysseus, the legendary home of the goddess Calypso.' And so he determined to find the Queen of Beauty in that distant community, 'Hara-Svira, founded by the Jews before their exile to Babylon. They were not ghettoes like those in Tunis, Algiers, or Morocco. The young Jewesses were worthy descendants of their graceful Biblical ancestors.' Kokoschka convinced himself of its truth in an impetuous adventure so as to fulfil his vow to find and paint the most beautiful Jewish girl. 'I laughed and cried when I saw the lovely girl sitting in an alcove . . .' Many similar occasions were incomparably described by Kokoschka in his *Letters from a Traveller in an Imaginary World*. The first is dated Stockholm, Winter, 1917; the second, Dresden, Spring, 1919; the third, Dresden, 1920; the fourth, Aigues-Mortes, September 1924; the fifth from Jericho, 1929; the sixth, from which the above quotation is derived, from Djerba, 1929; and the seventh from Ireland, 1945. In addition there is a collection of strange events brought together under the title of *Easter in Cyprus*.[1]

The paintings created by Kokoschka tell of the happiness and freedom of those years spent ranging through the world. The inspiration of Beethoven's Ninth Symphony —the brotherhood of man, a golden age of world peace and of creative activity—is woven also into the intellectual origin of Kokoschka's large landscapes and portraits of cities.

The power which had previously been directed into the metaphysical and transcendental Kokoschka now extended to embrace the whole world. His art sprang from a genius described by Thomas Mann as 'civilized magic': 'This modern creative intellect recognizing the basic tenets of the epoch into which he was born, and, lacking all traces of snobbishness and futile reversion to the primitive, becomes a seer even as he looks. He is an initiate, despite his undeniable breeding and latter-day taste; an able dreamer, a master of precise fantasy, by whose magic spirit becomes nature and reality is interpreted to the spirit.'[2]

What ecstasy of movement and sense of space is there! What concord of colour and form! How the action is crowded within the frame, the canvas bursting with life! A cry of jubilation, the worship of the life-giving sun! It is Spinoza's confession, *Deus sive natura*. For the first time in Kokoschka's work the Baroque is life-affirming; the divine

49 Kathleen, Countess of Drogheda, 1944–7

50 The Artist and the Author, 1962

51 In the Artist's Studio

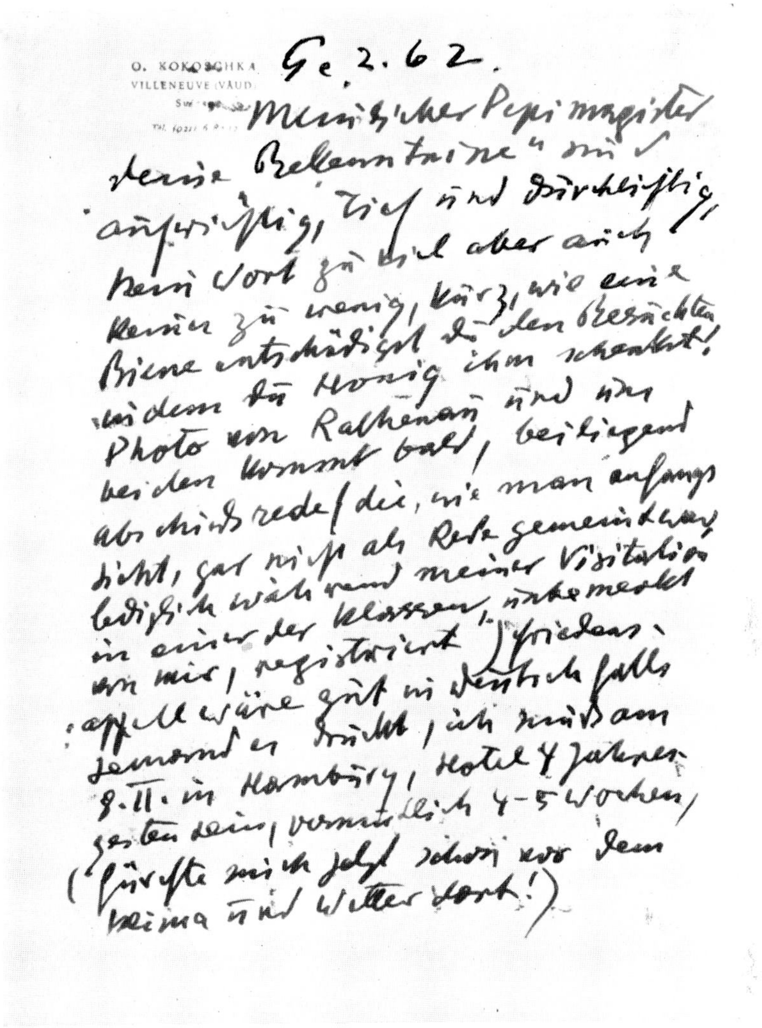

Ge. 2. 62.

O. KOKOSCHKA
VILLENEUVE (VAUD)
Switzerland

Mein lieber Pepi magister
deine Bekenntnisse u. die
aufrichtig, tief und durchsichtig,
kein Wort zu viel aber auch
keines zu wenig, kurz, wie eine
Biene entschädigt, die den Besuchten
indem sie Honig ihm schenkt!
Photo von Rathenau und der
beiden kommt bald, beiliegend
abschiedsrede (die, wie man anfangs
dichtet, gar nicht als Rede gemeint war,
lediglich während meiner Visitation
in einer der Klassen, unbemerkt
von mir, registriert) Frieden i
appell wäre gut in Deutsch falls
jemand es druckt, ich muss am
8.II. in Hamburg, Hotel 4 Jahres-
zeiten sein, vermutlich 4–5 Wochen,
(fürchte mich jetzt schon vor dem
Klima und Wetter dort!)

52 Kokoschka's Handwriting

53 The Goddess, 1939

54 Florence, View from the Magnelli Tower, 1948

55 View of Hamburg Harbour, 1951
By Courtesy of the Museum of Modern Art, New York

is inherent in the objects themselves, not hidden somewhere behind. The artist is here both pantheist and Greek; he perceives the divine in the earthly, and for the first time, after so many years of torment, he sees through the eyes of the Mediterranean peoples who have never lost the tradition of Greek antiquity. His world is the sky above Lyons, its light pouring down on the gulls circling restlessly above the river; the glow of colour in a Toledo street; a prospect of the Thames with its bridges striding far into the distance as they fling their arms to the banks; the hot desert of Egypt embalming one of the eternal aspects of civilization; the bleak Scottish hills, or the parched crags of Palestine— it is an art of painting which would have delighted Nietzsche's classical eye, for it is the seed of his sowing. Kokoschka's painting is a victory over reality and the means of representation. Diderot's *Essai sur la Peinture*[3] called for an art like this—'*Touche-moi, étonne-moi, déchire-moi, fais-moi trésaillir, pleurer, frémir . . .*' (Touch me, astonish me, destroy me, cause me to shiver, to cry, to tremble . . .) But the world of fantasy which had formerly offered an infinite extension of the poetical now seemed to him but a narrow field. Life and its richness lay waiting; he had only to reach out his hand. Art blinded him, he felt dizzy, like a man on a cliff. One can feel it in his paintings—the sense of vertigo, the ecstasy and the insatiability of his eyes.

One day, when the patina of time has done its work and all who knew the mind of modern man are dead, an historian may try to read the history of our time—the Dark Ages, as it were, an epoch of brilliant technical invention and scientific progress, matched by a fatal dehumanization in which, here and there, a saint, an artist, a sage, stands out in splendid isolation. When all those men whose names fill the columns of the Press have long since been absorbed into that amorphous mass, the basic element of life and origin of all the misfortunes which we call history, then will Kokoschka claim his place—great, modest, natural—beside Grünewald, Rembrandt, Breughel, Goya, Hokusai, and Munch. Men will stand in awe before his paintings, as we today before the tapestry, the *Apocalypse of Angers*. They will be rapt and astonished and they will realize that this was a life which was fertile and great.

Kokoschka's first landscape, and particularly the views of the DENT DU MIDI and TRE CROCI, stand alone in his production. Stylistically they express the different stages of the artist's development. If the HUNGARIAN LANDSCAPE (1908)[4] may be said to be an impersonal, experimental painting, even more than any of the portraits, then the DENT DU MIDI (1909) must be accepted as a *pendant* to STILL LIFE WITH TORTOISE AND HYACINTH and the portrait of AUGUSTE FOREL (1910), while the rich colour and entirely non-linear quality of TRE CROCI (1913) can be compared with the portrait of CARL MOLL (1913–14). STORM OVER NAPLES (1913) reveals the same Baroque effect of light—the sun breaking through the clouds—to be seen in the later views of cities, and the ALPINE LANDSCAPE NEAR MÜRREN displays the fascination that high mountains and the unlimited space of the alpine peaks held for Kokoschka. The SAXON LAND- SCAPE (1916–17), post-Impressionist as it is, is an isolated instance whereas THE HUNT (1918), achieves an effect of tapestry, foreshadowing the rather coquettish, elegantly decorative RICHMOND TERRACE (1926). THE LAKE OF ANNECY I (1927) is also very difficult to classify in Kokoschka's work because of its almost Chinese mono-chromatic simplicity. It is as if he were playing on an unfamiliar scale. The HARBOUR SCENE IN STOCKHOLM (1917) first displays the characteristics of the city series which reached its climax between 1924 and 1930. The fifteen views of Prague, painted between 1934 and 1937, hold a special position in Kokoschka's *oeuvre*. The artist painted the city of his forefathers more often than any other. The Prague views are not so compact in colour as those of Dresden. They combine the sense of distance of the London views with the light atmospheric character of the pictures painted in Italy, Spain and Africa, as if the painter had somehow compounded north and south, cold and warm, something indeed of the character of this historic city which Alexander von Humboldt reckoned among the seven finest cities of the world. Kokoschka contrived a synthesis (especially in PRAGUE FROM THE VILLA KRAMÁŘ, PRAGUE FROM THE GARDEN OF SCHÖNBORN, MOLDAU HARBOUR, I and II; VIEW FROM THE MOLDAU JETTY (I–IV) between his early linear detailed style and the colourful style of his maturity which signifies an astonishing intensification of his means of expression. Two paintings of Mährisch-Ostrau were the outcome of the artist's visit to Professor Emil Korner and his wife. Kokoschka also became a frequent guest later, after they had emigrated and come to live in the house of Elrig in Scotland (1942–5). At Mährisch-Ostrau, Kokoschka did a portrait-drawing of Frau Else Korner, and subsequently a water-colour of their elder daughter, Eve.

He did not paint very many landscapes during his stay in England—two in Cornwall, POLPERRO I and II (1939); SCOTTISH COAST (1942); SCOTTISH LANDSCAPE WITH SHEEP (1944); and LANDSCAPE AT ULLAPOOL (1944). It was only later that he painted several new London views.

After leaving Dresden, Kokoschka and his Russian friend went first to Switzerland, to the solitude of Lake Geneva. He stayed five months at Bloney, near Vevey, where he painted several views of the lake. Then followed a short trip to Italy, resulting in paint-ings of Florence and Venice, then a stay of two months in Vienna when his father died. There he painted the self-portrait, PAINTER AND HIS MODEL II, which includes the self-portrait from the Viennese poster of 1912 with his hand pointing towards his heart and the Russian woman in the background. This painting binds past and present to-gether, while the strong flat colours of the composition and the primitive expression of the man create a new stylistic synthesis. I remember in 1962 he was looking at some photographs of himself. One he liked very much. In it he was seated on the steps of his garden with gardening tools, an apron, and sandals. He looked robust and challenging—like a tribal chief, he said happily.

The portraits of Arnold Schönberg and Hermann Schwarzwald III (a friend and partisan from his early Vienna days) were also painted during this period, as well as the landscapes of Vienna and the Liebhartstal in which the surroundings of his own home are clad in all their summer glory.

From Vienna he travelled with Adolf Loos to Paris, where he painted the splendid PLACE DE L'OPÉRA, also a strange painting with sculptures on the roof of the Opéra and a portrait of Nancy Cunard. In the same year we find him at Bordeaux and on the beach at Biarritz. Then, after another brief stay in Vienna, where he remained long enough to paint the second portrait of Karl Kraus, he lingered in Provence on the way to the French Riviera.

Walking through the huge retrospective exhibition at the Tate Gallery on 3 November 1962, Kokoschka stopped before a painting of the Bordeaux theatre. Discussing the problem of space, he said: there was pure colour, such as he was using in Dresden, but not Impressionist, nor was it just atmospheric space. A painter like Boudin had no sense of space. But look here, he said, pointing to the street shooting back into the picture, it is like an express train tearing away into the distance.

To Paris once more. Afterwards Avignon, venerable seat of the Popes, Vernet-les-pins, Monte Carlo, Aigues-Mortes, and Marseilles were all painted in turn. In Marseilles he had arrived at the gateway to Africa, the magnet for all French artists—Delacroix, Flaubert, Matisse, Gide—Black Africa and the inspiring monuments to a brilliant past. Kokoschka, however, went first to Spain and Portugal passing through Madrid, Toledo, and Lisbon. The street scene done in Lisbon is somewhat isolated as to style, theme, and format, as is the later picture of the London slums which offers a macabre comparison with the sunny, colourful scene in Portugal.

In that year Kokoschka went to England for the first time. London as a city made a deep impression on him. The journeys undertaken in 1924 and 1925 to France, Spain, Portugal, and England were financed by an agreement with Paul Cassirer and Jakob Goldschmidt ('Jaköble', whom Kokoschka painted in 1925) and Moritz Gutmann, the art dealer. The further journeys, and especially those in Africa, were made exclusively under the aegis of Paul Cassirer. A short sojourn in Amsterdam was one of these. Dr J. H. F. Lütjens, seven years younger than Kokoschka, who was in Cassirer's employ and later became a director of the firm in Amsterdam, was at that time commissioned to travel with the artist on his journeys. He describes their first encounter: 'I met Oskar Kokoschka for the first time in Amsterdam where he stayed for a very short time, scarcely more than a week I think, making four small paintings—AMSTERDAM, NIEUWE MARKT; KLOVENIERSBURGVAL; the AMSTEL RIVER, and MONTALBAANSTOREN. He did not show me the painting of the Amstel river, but I accompanied him to the scenes at the Nieuwe Markt and Montalbaanstoren. One evening we went to Edam in a taxi. Although it was raining slightly he asked to have the roof open so that we could stand and see the landscape. He was very impressed by the wide plain, especially when we came to the Zuider Zee. He said he thought he would be old before he could paint a scene like that.'[5]

In 1925 Kokoschka stayed for a short time in Berlin, where he painted the portrait of the author, Ernst Blass, and the BRANDENBURG GATE.

In 1926 he returned to London. This was the year of the magnificent compositions LONDON LARGE THAMES VIEW I and WATERLOO BRIDGE, which count among his most significant townscapes. Seen from above, as are most of his land- and townscapes, the effect of space and light is more splendidly dramatic than in any of the Old Masters.

The secret lies not only in its Baroque energy, its freshness and vigorous colour, but also in the construction. The painting has two focal points and exhibits the perspective and simultaneous juxtaposition of lines and surfaces, and combined with the *chiaroscuro* it produces a strong effect of vitality. On the same visit Kokoschka painted the cliffs at Dover and the aesthetic atmosphere of Richmond.

Dr Lütjens writes: 'When Kokoschka was painting these English pictures—DOVER, FLOWERS IN A VASE, ADELE ASTAIRE (now Lady Cavendish), MANDRILL, TIGON, DEER, and RICHMOND TERRACE, he was living in an elegant small house near Park Lane. He used to go in the early morning to the Zoo in Regent's Park before it was open. He and the tigon understood each other and could almost talk together. He added an imaginary landscape. He would have liked to make a picture of the riders in the Row from a nearby residence but could not get permission. Instead, he painted RICHMOND TERRACE which he was able to do through the kindness of the owner of a private house.'

The year 1927 was important for the artist. He painted the marvellously serene picture of Lyons and the mountains, Courmayeur, Chamonix-Mont Blanc. 'He wanted to paint only the highest peaks, and the first time we stood on a glacier was a tremendous experience', Dr Lütjens remembers, laying his finger thus on a facet of Kokoschka's nature that gives the key to his psychology.

At last, in January 1928, he left for Tunis by way of Venice, and in 1929 set off for the eagerly awaited Bosphorus. In between he went back to the north, visiting Ireland and Scotland. He was attracted by contrasts, for, in the same year, he experienced the desert heat of Egypt, travelled to Istanbul and Jerusalem, and then in 1930 came back to Anticoli in Italy. Afterwards he went to Switzerland (Annecy) and Algeria. During 1926–7 in Berlin he did several important portraits and some more animal pictures. In Venice he painted the church of Santa Maria della Salute for the first time. After his return from Asia Minor Kokoschka went to Munich, where he painted a portrait of the famous Hungarian collector Marcel von Nemes—it is a jovial picture, full of dash and verve.

In 1932 he travelled to northern Italy—Genoa and the Ligurian coast, Santa Margherita and Rapallo, where he remained as the guest of the Consul Bob Gesinus Visser till the autumn of 1933. The painter Rudolf Levy was also living in Rapallo at the time. Those were difficult days for Kokoschka. The world crisis, started by the American crash of 1929, reduced him to poverty again. Since 1927 he had been renting Pascin's *Villa des Camélias* in Auteuil, near Paris, as a permanent *pied à terre*, but by 1933 he could no longer afford it. The gathering political storm left him for years without means of support. Paul Cassirer had committed suicide in 1926, and in 1931 the new directors of the firm, Dr Walther Feilchenfeldt and Dr Grete Ring, were no longer able to renew Kokoschka's contract. So the artist returned to Vienna to live in Liebhartstal. He wandered restlessly round Europe, painting in Paris, where, in March 1931, he exhibited at Georges Petit's Gallery, and in Vienna, executing a public commission in 1931, and at Nogent-sur-Marne. The last Paris journey of 1933 is like a sad echo of the crescendo of his life and work that had begun with his flight from Dresden. From Paris he returned to Vienna.

In 1934 his mother's death broke Kokoschka's last link with his home. He nevertheless stayed for a while in Liebhartstal, but it was not the same. While he was there the Nazis gained control in Germany. Now the star of Dionysius waned, and the song in his heart was silenced in the urgent drive for self-preservation and the bitter fight of a humanist for his rights. He travelled from this time only as an educationalist (to Budapest in 1934), or as a refugee, following in the steps of Comenius, the Master of the *Orbis Pictus*, who wrote in 1688: 'I led the life of a nomad with an ever-changing camp, never a home.'

The important views of cities which Kokoschka painted during the years between Dresden and Prague—those with the two focal points—are also the most important landscapes of this century. Only Munch and Corinth (the landscapes of the Walchen lake), the later van Gogh, and, much more rarely, Manet worked in the same spirit. The landscapes of the Impressionists are completely different, but Expressionists, such as Soutine, were greatly influenced by Kokoschka. The LAKE OF GENEVA (1924), TOWER BRIDGE (1925), MARSEILLES HARBOUR II and MADRID, PUERTA DEL SOL (1925), VENICE, SANTA MARIA DELLA SALUTE I (1927), MONT BLANC, THE COURMAYEUR AND LYON (1927), ISTANBUL (1929), PRAGUE FROM THE VILLA KRAMÁŘ (1934-5), THE MATTERHORN I (1947), FLORENCE FROM THE MAGNELLI TOWER (1948), VENICE, SANTA MARIA DELLA SALUTE IV (1951), DELPHI (1956), or the OPERA HOUSE, VIENNA (1956) are all visions of scenic beauty that could only be created by an artist who combines technical mastery with a deep sense of the traditional. Has any other artist since El Greco in his *Toledo* picture concentrated so much into a landscape as Kokoschka? 'This is no simple portrait of a landscape; it is the swift revelation of a mind inspired by the daemonic powers of nature to add her voice to the magnificent scene which, as it were, with a single stroke reveals the ephemeral nature of material things, unveiling their metaphysical being.' These words, written by Max Dvořák in his study of Mannerism and the works of El Greco[6] might well be a description of Kokoschka's finest paintings of cities. These are the paintings, not the early portraits, which show him at his greatest, for they all bear the stamp of genius. However deeply felt Kokoschka's humanitarianism, however thunderously the writer might declaim, forecasting like a seer the downfall of modern man, it is nevertheless in these landscapes that the great liberal master is to be found, offering the treasures of the kingdom which he has suffered and struggled to conquer. The battle is over, the last trumpet has sounded, and now behind the painting we discover the astonished eye of the artist, a child once more, responsive to the harmony between the world and the ego, between the idea and the means of presentation, the painter who rejoices in the perplexing richness of existence.

There are other landscapes—FLORENCE, THE BANKS OF THE ARNO (1924); BIARRITZ, SEASHORE; PARIS, THE LOUVRE AND THE TUILERIES GARDENS; AVIGNON, AIGUES-MORTES, TOLEDO and the paintings of Amsterdam (all 1925); DOVER CLIFFS, or LONDON (both 1928); the DOLCE BRIDGE (1929); or ANTICOLI

(1930); landscapes at Rapallo (1938), Polperro (1939), Pontresina (1952), and others which are more like sketches. They are full of life and movement, even with a certain dash, but they also exhibit a uniformity which precludes comparison with the first group. However, every experience in Kokoschka's life bore fruit, and the nervous brushwork of some of the Prague landscapes, which often manifest completely new characteristics, stems, in fact, from these.

To describe the extent of Kokoschka's experience during these years of excitement, daring, and vision is no easy task. Between 1924 and 1938, and even later, he returned continually to Paris. Yet he was never really at home there, for a deep sense of antagonism and discord had developed between him and the Paris art-trade. Only in Paris was it possible that a dealer to whom he owed money could actually shut him in the Grand Hotel to make him paint, shouting through the keyhole that Kokoschka had always wanted to paint Paris from there, so here was his opportunity to do it and get himself out of debt. Kokoschka was in Paris in 1933 when the Prague art dealer, Dr Hugo Feigl, sought him out to persuade him to come to Prague. 'My business took me to the gallery of my old friend Adolphe Basler, and in the course of conversation I happened to mentioned Kokoschka', wrote Dr Feigl.[7] "Kokoschka," said Basler, "is not getting on very well here and seems to be irritated by the Paris art world. If you would like to visit him he would certainly be very glad." With that, he already had the telephone in his hand to announce my coming. In less than an hour I was in Kokoschka's studio in the rue des Orchidées, or Chrysanthèmes, I cannot remember the name now, only the smell of a flower garden. It was an unusually roomy studio with bleak walls, entirely without furniture, and with a large picture leaning against one wall. I think it must have been THE HUNTER, with Kokoschka as a hunter encircled by women.* At the back of the room the artist himself was sitting to an English sculptress for a head and shoulders. He jumped up to greet me. When I suggested that he should come to Prague and paint some landscapes for me he nearly kissed me. "That has long been one of my dreams. My sister is there too and I would like to see her again." After the first meeting six or seven months passed and I began to feel that Kokoschka had forgotten the suggestion which seemed so fascinating to him in Paris. But one clear sunny autumn day he appeared with his friend in my shop in Prague, saying: "Here I am. I am going to make Prague my home for the next few years." The next day he had settled down to paint.'

Of all the painters whom Kokoschka met in Paris he liked Pascin the best. Pascin was a genuine bohemian. He was small and elegant, with improbably beautiful hands and fingers, who never stopped drawing, who appeared and disappeared without warning, and who was like a prince in Montmartre, surrounded by every race—Negroes, Creoles, Turks, and Greeks—who admired him and lived on him in whatever café happened to be his headquarters. Subsequently, after an unhappy love affair, he began to drink, and degenerated gradually until, in the end, he committed suicide.

We once sat for three whole days and nights without moving, drinking with Pascin and the Swedish painter Dardel, Kokoschka told me. Our beards grew, yet we were not

* Probably THE FOUNTAIN (author).

drunk. It was . . . But words failed him as he tried to describe their exalted mental state. He shook his head and rolled his eyes. When I told him that Dardel had died in 1943 he said: He was a tender plant, the eternal youth who could not grow old. Kokoschka had always felt, he said, that Dardel would not live to become old. He used to send the boy dark red roses. He was such an aristocrat! His wife was a very attractive person, too, and inspired the character of the heroine in Alain-Fournier's novel, *Le Grand Meaulnes.* Fournier was killed in the war. Dardel was so beautiful he—and Kokoschka loved one another greatly and kissed like Greek youths.

Kokoschka made an indelible impression on innumerable people. He attracted them because he needed them, and he left behind him a memory such as only a rare and unique person can inspire. It was as if he waved a magic wand and the world around him burst into flower, and people began to think in a way which would never have occurred to them before. He aroused sensations which normally they feared. His Dresden acquaintances had often acted in an extraordinary manner under his seductive and trance-like influence. 'I had never met Kokoschka before,' wrote Dr Feigl, 'but when I went into his studio and spoke to him it was like the meeting of old friends after a long parting. When I say that a true friendship developed between us over the years it might sound presumptuous, coming from an almost unknown and unimportant art dealer, if it were not that it so well defines his generous and deeply human personality.'

'To meet Kokoschka was to encounter genius', were Josef Adler's words as he looked back on the early days in Vienna. 'Most people used to shake their heads when he spoke because he would eliminate long trains of thought and grasp the heart of a subject—it was startling, subtle, illuminating. In the end it became the distinguishing feature of his style.'

'The moment I came into contact with the work of Kokoschka I was on enchanted ground', wrote Professor Leo Kestenberg. 'Then when I met him (I think it was in the year 1915) that impression was intensified, and it never suffered the slightest shadow, but was continually renewed throughout the years by his shining, generous, and warm nature. I seem to see the many people whom I met in his company—and there were many well-known names among them—as so many marionettes strung on wires which he manipulated to give them life.'

'His silences, as much as his often brief and incomprehensible comments, revealed a world of ideas to which his whole transcendental art bears witness.'[8]

'Munch and Kokoschka had the greatest influence on my development', confessed the Prague painter, Paul Bergner-Bergner,* to me once. 'I could always sense the human motive lying behind their work which was inspired by profound emotion and no mere artistic attitude. And surely nothing is more important than this today because it is the only means of escape from the dilemma within which mankind and art are imprisoned.'

Once in London (it must, I think, have been in 1945) I met Kokoschka at a cocktail party given by Sir Edward Beddington-Behrens. There were about twenty guests, and we looked at the paintings—mostly by Kokoschka—and drank and chatted. But it was not

* Paul Bergner-Bergner, who studied in Weimar and Dresden, became first a teacher and then director of the *Freie Akademie* at Mannheim after the second world war.

long before all the guests had gathered round Kokoschka like a bard of old. He sat there, somewhat taciturn at first, in that elegant and worldly atmosphere, dressed quite simply in a brown jacket with a blue aertex shirt and grey trousers—the natural magnet for everyone's attention. They each told a story about OK, as he was always called in England, and Anton Walbrook, the film star, who was among the guests, related how he had once been in Munich and madly in love. Kokoschka was interested in the same woman and threatened to shoot Walbrook if he caught sight of him. Walbrook accepted the challenge and strode out of his house, feeling like a Biblical hero and convinced that at any moment he would be shot by a bullet from his rival. Kokoschka, however, was no longer in Munich, having departed with the girl to the Rhineland!

Kokoschka quickly joined in the fun and described how he was once challenged to a duel in Berlin. He was a good shot, but so also was his opponent, and the affair would probably have ended in tragedy. It was a wild escapade connected with a woman but in the end it was settled quite unconventionally.

As they left the party Kokoschka said to Walbrook in Viennese dialect: 'Be a good fellow and come next week, then we can weep together.' It was a time when Vienna was being bombed and Kokoschka looked to another Viennese for comfort.

On one occasion Kokoschka was entertaining some English society people. Then I learned how charming he could be. He pulled out all the stops, mischievously wove political remarks with his theories of art and left his guests breathless at the spate of ideas, making them laugh and moving like quicksilver among them. He broke the ice of social convention and fascinated everyone, but he would interrupt his flow of talk suddenly: Who did he think he was, talking like that! And he swept away everything, like cleaning a slate. A portfolio lay on the table. It was the Bayeux Tapestry. He opened it and began to explain. Yes, indeed, that was a real revolution of movement. You could see the space—the white here, between the legs, no need to measure it; it is a revelation. And all his guests looked, like astonished children, at the illustrations which Kokoschka had placed on the floor.

It is relevant to wonder how much he had altered, if at all, since the early days in Vienna. Scarcely at all, it seems. 'As a young man', wrote Dr Eugenie Schwarzwald, 'he was very quiet. People standing at a distance might well have thought him deaf and dumb. But when he did make a remark it was extraordinary in its insight—often abstruse and disconcerting as well—so that even the dullest person could scarcely fail to grasp its meaning.'[9]

The artist told me one day that he fell in love with a woman in Egypt, the wife of a nobleman, who was as beautiful as a Greek statue. His mind was full of her image. He had a rival whom he hated for a long time, but it turned out that he was the wrong one because she was in love with Cocteau, although he was a homosexual. Kokoschka thought his rival was Maurois, and therefore he would not read his books. She was very rich, but died in Paris of narcotic poisoning. Kokoschka, too, had tried narcotics, especially amber, which he used to add in the form of a white powder to his coffee, because it produced such extraordinary effects. He experienced periods in his life, he told me, when

56 Galatea, 1953

57 Amor and Psyche, 1950–5

58 Duck Shooting, 1942–3

59 Sketch of Masks, 1963

he was, artistically speaking, asleep, and others when he was awake, but if he took amber the world was his. Kokoschka spent a whole day in the oppressive heat and dazzling light painting the pyramids—without the drug he would never have stood it. The Egyptian sun is deadly, although normally he likes to paint with the sun in his face.

He went to Palestine with Albert Ehrenstein. On the shores of Lake Tiberias were stone ruins, absolutely black stones and unendurable heat. The lake was almost invisible under the heat haze. People were living among the ruins in corrugated iron huts. Myriads of flies rose in a cloud, and when Kokoschka sought the reason he saw a camel standing on three legs; the other was broken open at the hip-bone—red, raw flesh. Women dressed in pastel colours, pink and green, sat on the ground. They were all pregnant, and a crowd of children swarmed about them and there were flowers in a fanfare of yellows and reds. It was like a glimpse of hell. The sky was dark purple and everything seemed black because the light was so strong. He had painted the sun before as a black speck, a contrast produced by the strong light.

On the Palestine border a man looked at their passports. He was 'a Viennese from Ottakring in disguise'. Kokoschka did not conceal his ideas about the Jews. What were they doing now? Tel Aviv was shooting upwards like a mushroom city—skyscrapers but no drains, and the place stank. Malaria was rife. The whole city had been built as a speculation in case the lake produced natron. Capitalism was the same here as everywhere else. X . . . speculates in Zionism, but the poor Jews building their kibbutz had to sleep with their weapons. The Arabs only stole from necessity without any sense of moral wrong. But that did not need guns. The Arabs had been incited to attack the Jews who came into the marches to plant eucalyptus which grows rapidly but needs a great deal of water. They used paraffin to destroy the mosquitos. When the eucalyptus at last took hold the settlers were dislodged. The Arabs admitted that they were paid to cause trouble. One of the artist's friends, Ben Gurion, later became Prime Minister, and he worked for reconciliation. That was a good man, but there were also others. In Jerusalem, Kokoschka added, they stayed with a Jew who went through all the motions of religion—he prayed, was orthodox, and evaded the law on the sly. Kokoschka was the 'goy' who had to light his cigarette for him on Saturday. (Could I please have a light?) Such people never realized that all this gets one nowhere. Of course, if an old man stands before the Wailing Wall, tearing his hair and beating his breast, it means the same to him as Mecca to a Moslem and it is sincere. But his host in Jerusalem had never done it before he came to Israel. Kokoschka said to the man from Ottakring: The Jews are playing cowboys and Indians; they are no better than all the others, although formerly they were. He said he liked the mystic qualities of the Galicians, the Chassidim, which they still retained, and Martin Buber, who had transmitted their imaginary world to the West, was a personal friend of his. The Spanish Jews liked to give themselves airs; they were the ones who emigrated to Holland and England.

In Tunis, Kokoschka saw some wonderful mosaics. Rich Romans, fearing revolution, had settled there and brought their books and art treasures in search of peace in Africa.

Their Greek slaves came with them, artists who had made classical replicas in Rome and Pompeii. However, if you consider Pompeian art, it is clear that any talented Austrian decorator of the Baroque period could do it once he had learned the method, for instance, in Salzburg. But there in Tunis the slumbering classical tradition was roused till it became almost Greek once more. The artists encountered negroes, Kabyls, Arabs, and Nature herself, not just a model. Then suddenly, after fifty years, they began to create the most marvellous things—splendid mosaics with simple motifs, flowers, fruit, and fish. But, Kokoschka said, American tourists walked over them with high heels and took small pieces away as souvenirs, while the French had not even bothered to have these beautiful things photographed. Kokoschka always gave the keepers a few francs and asked them to be sure to see that visitors wore felt slippers. You see, they don't even know what they are treading on, he said, trying to explain to the men, and they must not be allowed to break off any more *tesserae* for souvenirs.

Kokoschka loved his life in Africa and wished he had been born there. But he had always felt at home all over the world. You were free to wander anywhere in the old days, when only Russia and Turkey needed visas. You scarcely bothered about a passport, and wherever you were you could look about you, not caring about the morrow. You were free then, like a tramp, but it was gone now for ever. He said he really liked the negroes, Arabs, and Kabyls. Once he visited a region where the negroes lived in caves; many of them still spoke German, having taken part in the Occupation of the Rhine. That was a mistake. Marshal Lyautey was very brutal. Not long before, the ancient city civilization of the Kabyls had been discovered. They were a fine, proud race but he herded them together and cut them off from their water supplies in the name of 'pacification'. Kokoschka took part in meetings of the rebels; he had many friends in Syria, Tunis, and Morocco. It was incredible how the Arabs clung together.

The first chief whose portrait he painted was one of the Prophet's anointed, the Marabout of Temacin, with a skin like grey bronze, who lived in a palace near the Saharan city of Biskra. His family was said to be descended from the Prophet, and he occupied a very high position in the religious hierarchy. The combination of religion and worldly power is not confined to Europe, said Kokoschka. To the faithful he was the mighty Vizier of the True Faith, touched with the image of God. He could heal the sick and make the blind to see . . . Pilgrims came from far and wide to enter his presence.

Kokoschka had heard so much about the Sheikh that he wanted to paint him. Because, he told me, he had already had some experience of healers and miracle-workers. The last member of the Guild of Magicians he had known was a corporal in the French Army in a negro regiment in Damascus. This corporal came from a district of Senegal and had been drafted into the army in his capacity of state magician, because the Senegal negroes also demanded spiritual comfort after their fashion. The only difference between the medicine man and the monotheist officials of the army was that the black priests never rose beyond the rank of corporal, while their luckier one-god colleagues started as lieutenants. Of course, they could dedicate the flags, which the medicine man could not, although he represented infinitely more gods. Kokoschka thought that very unjust. His friend, the corporal-medicine man, had never dissembled his opinions to Kokoschka: Believe me, he said, they cannot do any better than I, and I can dance and eat fire as well. Or do you think they can really work magic?

The people all swore by the Sheikh's miracles. He is God's anointed, they said. The awe of the populace was enough to make the French administration very wary of the Sheikh. He had four splendid cars; was that not magic enough? A bank and a mosque were being built simultaneously in the city, the bank by modern methods. Cranes, tractors, and huge hammers were set to prove their superhuman power and the work was directed by three architects. But the mosque was built by eager human hands. Building materials were dragged to the site, and the construction was controlled by a half-blind Kabyl builder who had no blue-print, but kept everything in his head. Kokoschka made friends with this natural architect whose only instrument was a piece of measured cord. The dome of the mosque was to be supported by eight hundred pillars. The Kabyl went quietly round, measuring the distances with his rope and giving the devout and obedient Moorish masons their orders, using only the hand and the eye, palm tree trunks and clay, to form the dome ready to receive its coloured glass mosaic. A latter-day Michelangelo. Kokoschka watched in amazement as the master-builder rapidly completed the gleaming decoration of the cupola.

A missionary belonging to the Order of the White Fathers said he would introduce Kokoschka to the Sheikh, who often came to see how the mosque was progressing. One day the Kabyl master-builder said: The Marabout is coming today. The Sheikh appeared, driving in a powerful Mercedes, accompanied by several French officers. As the car drew near it grazed a restive horse. No harm was done, but a huge figure in a burnous arose from the back of the car and struck the chauffeur across the face. That is just like the Sheikh, said an awe-stricken Moslem to Kokoschka standing near by. The Sheikh went to look at the mosque. He was a handsome man with noble features. The missionary explained that Kokoschka would like to paint him. It is not possible, he replied, because my religion forbids it. But the priest had already foreseen this obstacle. Kokoschka had promised that he would not paint anything that threw a shadow —he would paint a portrait without a shadow. Good, said the Sheikh. You shall paint my portrait.

He invited Kokoschka to come to his Zaoura, an adobe palace, luxurious and magnificent, decorated in a mixture of European and Arab styles. Kokoschka noticed a small girl of about ten in the palace, the Sheikh's only child, whose eyes appeared to be infected. You must send the child to an oculist, he said to the Sheikh. It is not right to allow a child whom you love to suffer like that. Do you think so? replied the Sheikh, appalled. So the child was dispatched with numbers of relatives to Constantine, where an operation in an eye clinic saved her sight. The miracle-working Sheikh was very grateful to Kokoschka for pointing out that it could be done.

The Sheikh had a peculiar family. One of the men was a simpleton who carried about an ancient muzzle-loader—nor did he always shoot into the air. You had to be careful. While Kokoschka was working, people would come and watch and exchange opinions about the portrait. They reminded him of European aristocrats, who are also inclined to express some strange ideas about pictures and painting.

The Feast of Ramadan came round. The Sheikh, pale and drawn from the long fast, learned that the painting was finished. We shall have a feast to celebrate its completion. All the luxury and pomp of the Arab millionaire was paraded—Sèvres porcelain and golden vessels, just like the Arabian Nights. Kokoschka sat beside the Sheikh, who had spent a long time looking at the portrait, which pleased him very much. He understood it—proof to Kokoschka that this descendant of an ancient family was still a part of his people. They used to discuss philosophy together with the French monk, which made him realize that the old Arab doctrines were still alive just below the surface, and, still more, that Europe is lost because the roots of the old European civilization have dried up in the arid deserts of scepticism.

At the banquet Kokoschka said something to the Sheikh that he had long had in mind. He had a question to ask him. It was said that the Marabout was God's anointed and that the miracle of the 'Baraka' was still alive in him, that he could heal by the touch of his hand. But Kokoschka could not believe in it. That he was powerful was plain to see, and a powerful man has always had power over a crowd. But did he believe in 'Baraka' himself?

The Sheikh looked at him in astonishment. No, he quietly replied, I do not believe it. I sit in a cage and am quite alone. There is no magic in me, otherwise I would not always be longing for the impossible—to be an ordinary man.

Of course, the Sheikh could have avoided the question, but he replied, and Kokoschka felt a sense of relief, for truths which one has long known, coming from the mouths of men who live by their negation, are doubly to be valued. Kokoschka himself did not believe in divine right, only in youth that mocks at such ideas.[10]

Kokoschka has continued to devote much of his attention to youth in his later life. He believes that the future of the world is in their hands and that is why he attracts them. In the late summer of 1953, the year that he left London for his house at Villeneuve, he founded the International Summer School at Salzburg.* Every year hundreds of young people from many different countries gathered round Kokoschka in the 'School of Seeing', as he called it, not to become artists but to learn to become men who could see and think. He started a similar foundation in the autumn of 1955 at Sion, quite near his home. He was driven to develop a theory of education inspired by his own character which he had already tried in Dresden.[11] All the wisdom of his experience came spontaneously to his lips in a speech of farewell given to his pupils in 1961.

> I would like to say a few words to you before you leave, and this is our last day together. I have already visited the top classes and shall come to the others later because I do not want to miss any of my children. I have been so charmed with what I have seen today. One example is the work of the boy I call the Sailor—he has always interested me—and he is not the only one! There are, I know, at least ten or fifteen instances from whom I expected very little, because I thought them too unaccountable, lacking in self-discipline,

* Kokoschka taught there himself for the last time in 1963.

chafing like young colts. But suddenly, within the last few days, they have pulled themselves together and the achievement seems to me almost like a miracle.

You see, I have only words to explain to you what I would like, what I want. And the teachers working with me who are responsible for your education—your visual education—they too can only speak, they cannot show, because it would be wrong to paint for you to watch. That would only tempt you to imitate.

No, it is something else. I want each one of you to speak with his own voice, and a number of you—I do not know how many—do so already. Most of you have formed at least a vague idea of our aims. You have obscurely discerned the difference in our teaching from that of an ordinary school, and how different it is from what is called art or modern art today—and you are right, for it is completely dissimilar.

But I do not want you to go away and parade yourselves as artists before a public lacking all critical judgement, which has nothing to do with it anyway. I just want you to learn to open your eyes—as I have said a hundred times—so that in this short time you can learn a way of reproducing what has happened to you, and be able to express the fullness of your experience.

For it all stems from experience; that's the nigger in the woodpile, because most people today never experience anything. The world is too chaotic. We have no culture, nothing—neither culture nor inner peace. Peace in the world outside we cannot expect; it will never happen, since men are cannibals. But inner peace is within everyone's grasp, although its absence is due to the failure of the big institutions, and of State education above all. Education is individual, and we even have to be told that it exists, because generally you hear nothing about it at all. I think it is essential. Inner education brings an inner clarity in its train, a purity of vision and therefore of thought. The looking must always come first—because man senses, comprehends, and finally thinks.

Nowadays people do not think. They are all logicians with an aim in view—some small profit or an increase in salary—and the politicians who fumble with an H-bomb threatening the world are just the same—stupid, obtuse!

I am not concerned with your social life but only with your search for inner harmony and your ability to learn to think and to conduct yourselves like human beings. Sometimes a man has an experience and his eyes are opened. He is presented with an opportunity, struck by lightning as it were. It is—without introducing any theological notions—like a blessing from above which must be imparted to others so that one may master the sense of isolation and accept the social order. You will understand that to look upon one's fellow men as a means to an end—as cannon-fodder in war and, as now, just raw material, labour, for the nation—is a purely bureaucratic idea, a statistician's concept which leads only to crime. There never was so much crime before.

Encroachments by the police and cruelties are fast increasing. The world is nothing but barbed wire—but, no, let us forget the politicians. It is of no use to work ourselves up, for the individual can do nothing but try to keep his hands clean. It is especially true of young people, and that is why I am a teacher. I have always taught the young, and now—and this is my conclusion—education depends absolutely and only on learning to see, and, having seen, to understand. What is seen is intelligible only to the individual, and is for him a stroke of good fortune. It cannot be taught, or weighed out by an apothecary, nor bought in a white packet. No school can teach it; it can only be apprehended by an individual, a man who may be more experienced.

I have had a long life, and I am always alert for experiences which will open my eyes. You see, I know—indeed I realized when I was only eighteen—how short life is. We are like insects who live only for a day, but even if life lasted for a hundred years it goes past so terribly quickly that one must always be on the alert, because the man who has never lived is as good as useless, just a cypher on a statistical list. He is of no interest to me, for he has never lived like a human being.

This human happiness is what I want to give you—now and always. So if you have felt even an inkling of what I mean in the short month you have spent here, that is wonderful. But now you are morally bound to proclaim it throughout the countries whence you came —Iceland, Ceylon, Canada, Israel—I know not where. I charge every one of you, however feeble his strength, to spread his knowledge, not on the school's account, nor for my sake, for it has nothing more to do with me. The ability to waken other men is yours. It is a mission, and although we are not aware of them, there are many similar underground movements, intellectual and emotional stirrings, which may be the reason for the world's existence. If the world were left to politicians alone—men without imagination—we should long ago have gone under. Men are like sheep—millions, milliards of men running like sheep, like lambs, like grasshoppers, behind a leader who is, of course, a sterile creature with an illusion of power but without understanding.

Now you are part of that other stream, the stream of the mind, that is pledged to carry the torch. You have to see and to understand, do you realize?

But listen—or are you tired? [No, from the hall.] I was once—I must have a cigarette. No, no one else, but if I don't have a cigarette I shall get excited, and I want to avoid that, because excitement by itself means nothing. One must have a reason, and mine is that I must let you all go now, and I feel sad. . . . I am afraid to see such fledglings exposed to the dangers of this world-without-fantasy. Yes, that's it, a world without fantasy—and I know, for instance, what it is like in America. Americans are so kind and generous, but the noise, the neon lights, the propaganda—they make one cynical and desperate. How can the individual survive? Every country is the same, every continent. Even in Asia and Africa now you find this terrifying mindless equalization. It is all part of our technical age, in which man himself goes unrecognized in the rivalry of production, in a world of machines and robots with which he dreams of controlling the universe. . . . In *Faust* Goethe wrote a bitterly ironic poem. Faust, blind and old, cannot see the long coffin-shaped hole which the lemurs are digging to receive him. He thinks he has conquered the world, controlled the oceans and the cosmos. He is master of the universe. Yes, that is Faust, but no one has noticed it, no one has learned the lesson. The ending of Faust has been called optimistic, but surely nothing is more pessimistic than the sight of an old man, blind and careworn, watching, as he thinks, the turning of the sods for his gigantic project when it is nothing more than the digging of his own grave?

Of course it is wonderful to fly about in space but what is the result? Only that the individual becomes more impoverished than ever. Man was never so emotionally starved as he is today, despite the gadgets, the toys, and the technical tricks. But that is the nature of our mechanized civilization. Electric light is undoubtedly a boon, and it is probably pleasanter than lighting candles, but it is not indispensable. Yet we are trading our souls in exchange for electricity, or the atom-bomb, or some other stupidity.

In Mesopotamia I was once present at the opening of a tomb (the contents are in the

British Museum) in which men and young princesses lay slaughtered among the mules and the chariots—it was the grave of a priest-king.

The priest-king is now in Baghdad I believe, because that is where I saw the remainder of this excavation. I suddenly realized as I looked that he is holding a mirror in his hand. Judging from the skeleton and other things from the tomb he was a young man, and I wondered who put the mirror in his hand and why. Then I thought, the Queen must have given it to him, the Queen who would be buried at his side but who lived long after him, as he probably died very young. It could have happened that as she grew old she used to go to the tomb of her husband, the prince, and look in the mirror. But why? Perhaps she came to understand, for the first time in the history of the world, that man dies when he grows old—and so she descended into the rock to gaze in the mirror of the dead. She looked at the mirror, although she knew the King was dead. Then she became afraid. Would the spirit of the King pursue her, disturb her dreams, and cut short her life? And so she had come every day. I do not know; I only feel that it could have happened like that; that she breathed in the mirror to give the dead King life. And so it is with me. I speak as if in a mirror to bring you to life.

You are young, go now. Yes . . . Goodbye, then.[12]

Kokoschka's career and his position in the hierarchy of painters developed through several phases, first as an Austrian and a German, then as a European, and after the second world war as an artist of world fame; but there are four definite landmarks. The early portraits, still lifes, and dramas made Kokoschka notorious rather than famous in the Vienna of 1910. Nevertheless they made his name known, and his patron Adolf Loos prophesied that he would became a great painter. Ten years later Max Liebermann, the leading artist of Germany, hailed him as the 'Crown Prince' of German painting. The occasion was a banquet over which Liebermann presided when Kokoschka presented him with a bouquet of roses and called him the 'King' of German painting. The title 'Crown Prince' was Liebermann's charming response to this compliment. Kokoschka was the most celebrated and probably the best-paid artist in Europe in 1930, and his was undoubtedly the greatest name east of the Rhine. At his first exhibition in London in 1928 the high prices asked for his paintings made a considerable stir. The Leicester Galleries were asking £1,350 each for the paintings of CHAMONIX-MONT BLANC, VENICE, SANTA MARIA DELLA SALUTE, EL KANTARA, the portrait of the MARABOUT OF TEMACINE, and the MANDRILL, and £1,000 each for THE CAT (1926), and THE HUNT (1918). Not a single picture was sold. These were high prices at the time, more than would have been asked for Bonnard, Utrillo, Vuillard, Soutine, or Pascin. In 1929 the Hamburg Kunsthalle paid 15,000 marks for the painting of Tower Bridge.

The slump and inflation of 1929–31 reduced Kokoschka to poverty, and in 1933 he was literally starving in Paris. His financial recovery in Prague was overshadowed by world politics, and he had to endure financial stringency in England during the war. But after the end of the second world war things really began to improve. England, with her orientation towards Paris, recognized his stature only after the great retrospective exhibition held in the Tate Gallery in 1962, pronounced by Kokoschka to be the finest exhibition of his work ever mounted. In December 1961 the portrait of Herwarth

Walden (1910), which the artist had given to Walden and which was bought in January 1953 by an American for nearly £6,000, was withdrawn in London at £23,000 and sold privately the same year for a higher figure. In 1965 the Hamburg Kunsthalle paid 650,000 DM for a Dresden landscape (£55,000).

Only Paris still withholds the acclamation that Kokoschka's work really merits. But the activites of Dr Hugo Feigl and Curt Valentin in the United States, and the support given him by James S. Plaut, Director of the Institute of Contemporary Art in Boston, Dr W. R. Valentiner, Director of the Detroit Art Institute, and Richard S. Davis, Director of the Minneapolis Museum, has meant that Kokoschka quickly won over America through exhibitions, lectures, and the impact of his personality. In 1950 he attained world-wide recognition. Kokoschka, representative of Expressionism and, as he himself affirms, the last painter, has taken his place beside the modern French masters.

Kokoschka, who had been a member of the Prussian Academy of Science and Art until 1933 (he resigned in disgust when Max Liebermann was excluded), and whose pictures in public collections, four hundred and seventeen in all, were declared 'degenerate' by the Nazis in 1937 and either destroyed or sold abroad, was awarded the Stephan Lochner medal of the City of Cologne in 1951. Vienna, and Pöchlarn his birthplace, each gave him the freedom of the city. Pöchlarn, and later Salzburg, named streets after him. In 1952 Hamburg awarded him the Lichtwark prize. In 1956 the President of the West German Republic, Professor Theodor Heuss, presented him with the Order of Merit founded by Frederick the Great. In 1959 he was made Commander of the Order of the British Empire by Her Majesty Queen Elizabeth II, and Oxford University honoured him with an Honorary Doctorate. In 1960 he shared the humanist Erasmus prize, awarded in Copenhagen, with Chagall.

Similar circumstances and emotional reactions to those which occurred after the first world war inspired an abundant harvest of landscapes and paintings of cities after the end of the second. The realization of his longed-for freedom in the postwar world, and the richness of life, produced the magnificent mountain paintings of Switzerland in 1947. The pressure had been great. The dam burst its banks.

Sir Edward Beddington-Behrens, who owns THE MATTERHORN I (1947), arranged for Kokoschka to meet the mountain guide, Wilhelm Perren. Sir Edward describes in his autobiography how Perren helped to carry the painter's easel and materials to places known only to him, and stayed to watch Kokoschka painting their beloved mountains.

THE MATTERHORN is one of the mightiest mountain landscapes ever painted by Kokoschka. The magnificently wild scenery was accompanied by a tremendous upsurge of inward emotion. Kokoschka, lacking the last inspiration, had laid aside the portrait of Werner Reinhart, and was searching for another motif. Zermatt was for the tourists and the Gornergrat too panoramic. Disappointed, he went on climbing towards Sitten and, following the path, came upon an hotel standing quite alone—the Riffelalp. He looked round. If he could use the balcony on the third floor he would be able to paint. Fortunately a whole wing on that floor was empty, and he was able to rent it while the hotel was closed. Kokoschka went on to the balcony straight away and stayed there until the next day, just looking. It was absolutely wild, no trace of man to be seen. Below hung the precipice, and beyond that the ridge of the glacier without any foreground. The huge cliffs were like jagged moon-crags, as if a giant meteor had fallen there. Kokoschka lived on the balcony for nearly three weeks. Once he got dizzy and nearly fell. From the climb, he explained; he had been 'on' the mountain all the time. Men like Hodler could never paint such a scene because they wanted to be really on the mountain, Kokoschka said. The mountain guide climbs to the peak, but Kokoschka could feel the mountain pressing down on his own head. Thus the magnificent landscape was created—dramatic proof of the sixty-year-old artist's reserves of power.

Then followed the journeys to Italy, first Venice and Florence in 1948, and Rome the next year. In 1950 he went to Salzburg, to Hamburg in 1951, then back to the Engadine and Venice. Kokoschka painted Santa Maria della Salute, a church which he loved, for the fourth time in 1951. He went to Pontresina in 1951, then painted another series of London views. The VIEW OF THE DANUBE AT LINZ was painted in 1955, also the landscape at Villeneuve where he had settled; and other studies of the Lake of Geneva, VIENNA, THE STATE OPERA HOUSE, a view of Cologne and the interior of the cathedral were all done in 1956. His first Greek landscape, DELPHI, was painted in the same year. This opens the later phase of the artist's life and work in which his style is determined by the Grecian idea of beauty, by the myths and landscapes of Greece. And still he spoke, not with the voice of Apollo, but with the dynamic foreboding of Dionysius—

> As on the day that lent you to the earth
> The sun stood high above the whirling worlds,
> The course you entered then, defined the law
> By which for evermore you prospered and aspired.
> So shall you be: nor destiny evade
> Prophets and sybils told it long ago,
> No time, no power, ever can destroy
> The minted form that living thus unfolds.[13]

The great monumental works are all stamped with this character. In 1944 Kokoschka had talked of painting frescoes—'but where, and for whom?'—and it was not until 1950 that Count Antoine von Seilern commissioned the three-part ceiling painting, PROMETHEUS, for his London house. Kokoschka finished another monumental painting, a large triptych, THERMOPYLAE, after working on it for two years (1952–4). It was acquired by the University of Hamburg. In London in 1950 AMOR AND PSYCHE was begun originally as the left wing of the Prometheus saga. It was finished in 1955 and then used as a design for a tapestry woven in Vienna. Several examples, some with a pictorial border, were made at that time.

THESEUS AND ANTIOPE was another classical theme which occupied Kokoschka for many years, and Herodotus (the central figure of THERMOPYLAE) is depicted in a later painting gazing like a prophet into the distance, whereas in the triptych he is writing. Kokoschka wrote explanatory essays to both these great paintings:

THE PROMETHEUS SAGA

I have been asked to write a few words about my recently finished PROMETHEUS SAGA which was shown publicly for the first time this year in the Biennale. I am well aware of the danger that my interpretation will not be up-to-date, but my excuse for that will be that I was not painting the modern world demanded by fashion. I freely confess that in this painting, the largest at least in size that I have ever done, I have intentionally disregarded all the taboos of the international art world today. This painting was meant to reveal content and space, as every European living in the stream of history has a right to expect. I have preferred a concept of space to which I have consciously added a fourth dimension of movement, discovered in the Baroque period, and this to a certain point allows the onlooker to follow the events portrayed in the painting in temporal sequence. I am well aware that this will be blasphemy to abstract painters because the *Fauves* decreed, as a first principle, that pictorial imagination must be reduced to a two-dimensional plane, and this is undeniable so long as it is only a question of solving a problem of wall-decoration. However, if two-dimensional vision expresses the philosophy of the long-haired bearded youths who gather in the cities of the world to discuss modern problems of existence, and who prefer to discard their clothes along with their European traditions to be ready, in the guise of *sans culottes*, for the coming revolution that is supposed to outstrip even the 'Back to Nature' philosophy of Rousseau, then at my age I suppose I must be patient, for, so far, every generation has proved that the must in the barrel turns to clear wine in the end.

Even the danger, foreseen by many in the political field, that man will become nothing but an impersonal cipher, may yet be overcome. After long consideration I have consciously returned to the means of spiritual expression used in the days before Europe had begun to disregard its own cultural heritage, in the belief, without opening myself to a charge of imitation and plagiarism, that I am thus preserving the artistic tradition of Europe. I do not think that every generation has to begin at the beginning, but I believe that the liberal artist ought to leave theorizing to the dogmatician. I was an active participant in the First and a passive participant in the Second World War, and I came to the conclusion that the social task of the artist is to crystallize his vision and experience, to interpret in its widest sense the meaning of existence, because analysis, regulation, and the destruction of our personal lives has already gone too far. It has penetrated to the very soul of man, right to the psyche, and psychoanalysis of course is no help. In a proletarian society such as ours it is more than ever necessary to strengthen our links with the past lest we reach the point at which every individual in his intellectual arrogance makes it his business to push the engines of destruction to the limit, mistakenly assuming that the loose brick will fall on his neighbour's head. Even if he does not possess an alert social conscience, reason alone ought to convince the artist that incomprehensible, invented art is pointless, that unless it can transmit experience, the spark of life, it is valueless. Insight alone changes us from beasts into men. The life of an aesthete in his ivory tower is equally pointless; it is wasted, isolated, the life of a troglodyte. We should remember that ultimately the world does not exist for any single person; it is not turning for our benefit.

I realise how the young artist in Italy staggers under the burden of artistic tradition. Yet he has been guarding the heritage of Europe in his mind, in his temperament, in his features even, since the days of the ancient Greeks. They called the world on this side of

Greece, as far as they knew it, Europe, but it is a cultural not a geographical concept, and when this idea is in danger of being destroyed mankind is the loser. The coming generation is in the position of a son whose father has squandered his inheritance, but they have not fully understood the principle (for it comes only with maturity) that they too have a duty towards the future. It is an age-old concept, still alive in the great Games, that a runner must hand on the torch, till the last-comer places it on the altar at Olympus. The pious monks of the Middle Ages had to struggle in intellectual endeavour and spiritual need every hour of the day to keep faith with God, and to preserve the divine spark of their own souls. But since we began to sacrifice on the altar of reason our education would have us believe in second-hand experience, in arid doctrines, theories, and Utopias.

So it is especially to the youthful artists, the future guardians of Europe's spiritual heritage, that my Prometheus Saga is directed. I come from Vienna, frontier city of the Roman Empire. The historical function of the Roman Empire was to transform the Hellenic tradition into a European possession by communicating its wisdom to a widely-scattered human group. So I borrowed my symbol of intellectual arrogance from antiquity in the story of Prometheus, whose overweening nature drove him to steal the fire so that man could challenge the gods. But Prometheus is mortal, and is consigned by the Moira, which punishes the arrogant, to the realm of the mothers. Prometheus is a timeless symbol, and should therefore be distinguished from neo-classical allegories which are time-bound. Man recognizes in Prometheus the dangers of breaking the laws inherent in his own nature.

The more we dream of Utopias and over-estimate ourselves, the greater the danger of failure in a visual system that deliberately ignores reality. But as our existence is lacking any interpretation as a mystery, despite all analytical materialism, the struggle to represent visual experience expands far beyond the sphere of a limited aesthetic. The creative power is part of existence itself, and the painting, as soon as it becomes truly symbolic, ceases to be a mere calculated rationalist concept. Hence my Prometheus is not to be interpreted like other individual artistic efforts. I was secretly helped by mankind in its creation, the very mankind that, hoist with its own petard, prepares in east and west for the journey to the moon.

On my Triptych, THERMOPYLAE

Written in the shadow of the death of my great friend Wilhelm Furtwängler, who was at my side throughout the creation of the painting.

Why did the Persian King allow the body of Leonidas to be mutilated and fastened to a cross? Was he not satisfied with the evidence of his eyes? All that was left of his opponent's manly bearing—bones, sinews, skin—rotting in the dust? The story of Leonidas, by human standards, should have ended with his death.

So, did it seem nobler for you, Spartans, to die than to allow me, Xerxes, to trample on your honour? Perhaps such thoughts ran through the barbarian monarch's mind and drove him to make an example of the man he had defeated. There is far more behind it than the simple black-and-white picture of history.

Eye-witnesses of the Persian war told their stories to Herodotus. Was it indeed the historian's intention to describe the ruler of the greatest kingdom in the known world, who commanded an army larger than that of any other ancient prince, and whose colossal power and superhuman opportunities caused the defeat of every people that withstood him, as nothing more than an inhuman chief of a Hunnish horde? Or did Herodotus, after the war, spitefully pour scorn on the King of Kings, like a servant humbled and dismissed his post?

The modern determination to defame and devalue everything that the past held sacred, our presumption in dismissing as nonsense anything that is not perceptible to our minds, leads us to try to read modern motives into Herodotus.

Why did the Persian despot mutilate the body of Leonidas? If the question is put thus baldly, the contrast between the Greeks and barbarians becomes clear, and with it the mind of Herodotus. A barbarian is a man without tradition and history; he therefore belongs to every period, our own included. For we live in a period when powerful emotions, love of freedom, and humanity are despised because the mass-mind is totally sterile. In totalitarian states men of such stamp are automatically liquidated. The Greek, Leonidas, and the barbarian, Xerxes, conjured up by Herodotus in the minds of his readers, are pictures of souls that penetrate the mind, and I choose the expression with care. Because modern art, which has spread throughout the world as never before, is surely a reflection of our urge to destroy, to deform, and to annihilate. The cynical pride of the West in its own destruction, and in seeing its image reflected by an art whose mission is the abnegation of everything honoured by tradition, reveals the condition of our soul. Now, neither war, nor crises, nor economic conditions are exclusively responsible for the sin of contempt for tradition. Modern art, considered as an image of the distracted condition of our minds, is in no way indebted to those peoples who have abandoned European society, or who never took any part in it. For even when a totalitarian régime determines human values only in so far as they are of use to the State, they still remain human values, although they only have the worth of a coin which the State mints at a fixed value regardless of its metal content.

Herodotus' description of the Barbarians reveals a historic truth which the Greeks, though unconsciously at first, discovered. It was borne in upon them, as it were, secretly; but truth arouses suspicion in those who do not find it for themselves, and Xerxes, to whom the spirit of truth was a stranger, was not prepared to cede the substance for the shadow. Undoubtedly Herodotus was concerned with the truth, which had triumphed over Xerxes. That explains the King's attempt to destroy the mystery—the noble soul, the love of freedom and justice, symbolized by Leonidas, even when he was no more than a corpse on a plain drenched with blood. What Herodotus could not foresee, however, was that the difference between humanity and barbarism would emerge victorious from every battlefield thereafter. This is the spirit of Western civilization, and it is as little limited by time as the idea of Europe by frontiers. Owing to the extraordinary nature of Greek art, of which the significance was not only aesthetic but also ethical, embracing both the State and the idea of a human community, we are able to discover a reflection of ourselves in both victor and vanquished.

The separation of the aesthetic from the moral was first discovered by the Sophists. Afterwards it seemed obvious to us, as did the separation of knowledge as a form of science from the vision of the inspired artist, and at last the extraction of the individual element from the human community. The criterion of judgement does not depend on individual estimation. Hence the thought never occurred to the citizens of Athens as they watched the drama of the defence of Thermopylae in the theatre that the play was a simple presentation of one or two decisive episodes of the war. Herodotus' history of the

Persian wars was not a straightforward report. The battles were not fought for the unification of the Greeks, nor for the prosecution of commercial interests, nor for an ideology. Quite different from modern wars which are caused and continued by lack of foresight, the Persian war was fought because of the difference between men and barbarians, as Herodotus makes clear.

Before he died Socrates was advised not to get excited by talking, otherwise it would be necessary for him to take two or even three draughts from the goblet before the poison took effect. 'Then the man who proferred the poison would have to do so twice or thrice', was his quiet answer as he rubbed the leg where the chain had been. For, like his pupils, he too had reason to be afraid that there would be no one left tomorrow capable of imparting what he knew—that there was something more than bones and sinews or whatever was to be buried under the name of Socrates, that the existence of a soul, the mystery behind the invisible, made it seem right to him not to fly to Megara or Boeotia, but to accept the penance determined by the Athenian people. And, even as he was dying, he remembered his debt to Aesculapius. Thus, Socrates preserved his reverence for the gods even though they did not exist.

Would it not, therefore, be better for us, wholly dedicated as we are to materialism, to reject altogether an art that no longer tries to conceal by beneficent illusion the dust and ashes—dust and ashes to which we have reduced the history of man, so that the living dead may never step beyond the frontiers of the future or the past?[14]

Every year Kokoschka visits London, and on each visit he paints a new view of this gigantic city, for the artist is especially attracted by the Thames. Kokoschka also painted further views of Hamburg and Lübeck, Stuttgart and Bremen. Landscapes, city views, portraits, and compositions were attacked afresh with the same zest and enthusiasm as ever. The tapestry of his imposing life-work is being completed. The graphic work, especially the lithographs, becomes ever more dominant—single motifs, often themes and variations on paintings (Homer), or series like the Apulian and Greek portfolios, and book illustrations for King Lear, the Odyssey, and the story of Saul and David. The polemical humanist writings sink into the background in favour of the poetic stories in the form of memoirs—*Ann Eliza Reed* and *A Sea Ringed with Visions*. A new artistic activity was offered when Wilhelm Furtwängler commissioned him to design the sets for *The Magic Flute* in Salzburg in 1955. This production was the first of an important series of theatrical designs, further evidence of his sure sense of style, his emotional engagement, his inventive scene-changing and original effects of colour and light. It was followed by Ferdinand Raimund's *Moisasur's Magic Curse* and the *Fettered Fantasy*, Shakespeare's *Midsummer Night's Dream*, Ibsen's *Rosmersholm*, Weber's *Oberon*, Verdi's *Masked Ball*, and *The Magic Flute* again. These productions for the theatre could not really be described as anything new, for we have already seen the youthful artist designing shadow-pictures for the 'Speckled Egg' in the Vienna cabaret called *Fledermaus*, apart from the designs for *Murder Hope of Women*, *Hiob*, and *The Burning Bush*. He had also produced several of his own works. But he developed a far wider interest in the course of his later activity in this field, especially within the framework of the Salzburg Festival, the Vienna State Opera, the Raimund theatre, the theatres of Florence, Genoa, and Chicago.

XIII

THE LABYRINTH OF THE WORLD

Kokoschka's faith in the survival of Austria died with his mother. In company with other small nations Austria had become a pawn in the hands of the great powers. When, before the second world war, the Austrian Ministry of Education had invited him to become Director of the School of Arts and Crafts, where he had begun his career, Kokoschka took advantage of it to publicize his ideas of the school as an *officina humanitatis*, and accepted only on the condition that the school would be reformed on these lines. He was well aware that he would soon have to leave Austria to save his life, his work, and his political liberty. The Ministry's formal refusal reached him in Prague, written on a postcard. Sarcastically he said that he particularly cherished public recognition, but the reform of the Volkschule lay close to his heart. It was his opinion that the greatest revolution in Europe had been the introduction of universal education. They ought to understand *that* in the land which had given birth to Comenius, the most enlightened teacher of all. Youth alone can save the world, and the only person he wanted to paint there in Prague was one who, like himself, believed in youth, a worthy follower of Comenius and a man who would not want to see the world in reverse. He was speaking of T. G. Masaryk, the first president of Czechoslovakia.

In a foreword to an essay on Prague and Vienna by Professor Hans Tietze, Kokoschka wrote: 'Vienna looks hopefully towards Prague, her sister city. It is not only the past but the future that binds related peoples together. Prague has been called the most westerly city of the east, and was far more a companion in destiny with Vienna than a rival for the prizes of beauty, intellect, and historical importance. Two beautiful sisters, each brilliant in her own way. They were heralds, moreover, of a common civilization which is the spiritual and intellectual exchange between West and East.'[1]

'During his stay in Prague,' wrote Dr Feigl in 1947, 'Kokoschka painted several large and one small view of the city for me. I was honoured with the duty of arranging permission for the artist to use certain standpoints for his landscapes. It was no easy task, especially when one remembers that Kokoschka took it into his head to invade some very unlikely places. Once it was the house of a bank manager's widow, and another time the balcony of the City Water Board near the Moldau, full of busy preoccupied officials; then a view from one of the windows in the Cloister of the Order of the Cross, and the Grand Master, with whom I was very friendly, actually arranged for the room Kokoschka picked to be cleaned and kept for the artist's sole use for three weeks. Once there was a distinctly uncomfortable climb on the cliffs called Vyšehrad, where we crawled about for a whole morning like mountain goats. Then, finally, the private garden of the American Embassy on the Kleinseite and the villa belonging to the retired and sick politican, Dr Karel Kramář, in its marvellously dominating position on the edge of the Prague Belevedere. The best thing about these expeditions was our success. No one refused permission, and Kokoschka was able to paint pictures from all the points I have mentioned. Only the view from the Vyšehrad did not come off. The best of all in my opinion is the painting from Dr Kramář's, with its view over the Kleinseite and the Cathedral of St Veit. It is now in the possession of the Prague architect, Dr Müller. It reached the highest price realized up to that time—I think Kč 68,000.'[2]

Altogether Kokoschka painted fifteen (or sixteen) views of Prague. One which I saw unfinished in Prague was a view from Dr Karl Klein's house on the Campa Island. The artist stayed at first in the Ambassador, and later in the Juliš Hotel on the Wenzelplatz. He was able to borrow a studio from friends on the top floor of a house on the quayside, near the mills of the Old Town. From there he overlooked the Hradschin and the Charles Bridge, the city's finest landmarks, and all the old buildings of the Kleinseite— the Strahover monastery, the Moldau flowing under the arches of the Carmelite cloister, and farther on the Clementinum on the right bank. All five views of the Moldau were painted there, and Kokoschka was often to be seen eating in the Café Slavia opposite the Czech National Theatre. It was not long before he had gathered the usual circle of admirers. They encouraged him to go to Mährisch-Ostrau, where he painted the city. He was working on figure compositions at the same time, and two of these were exhibited at the Mánes Jubilee Exhibition—IN THE GARDEN I and II. He also finished the portrait of Annie Kniže in Prague, begun when he was a young man in Vienna and continued in 1932. In 1934, using the same canvas, he altered the whole composition. The SELF-PORTRAIT WITH A HAT, painted shortly before he left Vienna for Prague, was rendered practically unaltered into the larger composition called SELF-PORTRAIT WITH A STICK. That was followed by a portrait of MARTHA HIRSCH WITH A BALLOON, and that of Dr K. B. Palkovský. An especially successful portrait was the one of the Viennese industrialist Ferdinand Bloch-Bauer as a huntsman. The NYMPH and study of a nude, with nude figures in the background, are closely related to the mysterious composition called THE FOUNTAIN or NYMPH AT THE SOURCE. In Mährisch-Ostrau, Kokoschka nearly died. There he painted the PORTRAIT OF A DEGENERATE ARTIST. Like the *Bach Cantata* it is an artistic testament of the time; it looks back into the experience of the past and forward to the future. Kokoschka was standing at the cross-roads between life and death, between reason, in which he believed, and the insanity overwhelming the world.

In 1935 Kokoschka met the woman who was to become his wife. From then onwards she stood by him until they escaped together in 1938, almost penniless, to England, while the Third Reich tightened its grip round the little country. Kokoschka stood high on the Nazi's list of people to be liquidated, and they would undoubtedly have made short work of him, because he had been singled out as one of the leaders of what they called 'degenerate art', and his work publicly denounced. During the war Olda Palkovská, a Doctor of Jurisprudence of the University of Prague, reminded me of Hendrijke, Rembrandt's wife, who saved his life and ensured years of peaceful creativity despite misfortune and despair. I saw Frau Olda's concern for the great artist's well-being and her untiring helpfulness, writing his letters, translating and editing his political work, and protecting him from people whom he did not want to see, but, above all, keeping him young through her own youth. Kokoschka admitted to me that, but for her, he would not be here, that he would have committed suicide. After one had accepted the fact that Kokoschka, most freedom-loving of men, the admirer of women, the traveller, was married, one came to understand that after his mother's death Frau Olda had become the only resting-place where he could find peace in the turbulence of world events. Even in the midst of the war she built a protective home for him, from which he could set out daily to work. It was touching to meet them in the street—the tall, boyish figure of the girl arm-in-arm with the artist, who was smaller, and often quite lost in the city; or at home, when he took off his shoes after a long day and lay down on the sofa with his head in her lap or when he was cross because he had meant to do the washing-up and she had done it already. He was always an attentive, smilingly polite and affectionate husband whose greatness she never forgot.

The city of Prague was anxious to honour the artist, and they offered him, like Thomas and Heinrich Mann, the Freedom of Czechoslovakia. This brought Kokoschka back to the land of his forefathers, the country which had given the world Comenius, Cheltschicky, Masaryk, Mendel, Loos and Husserl, Carnap, Wittgenstein, Freud, Mahler, Schönberg, Webern, Kafka, Kraus, Werfel, Rilke and Musil. He was standing on the soil of a country and in the city where the peoples merged and civilizations met, inspiring each other—where the ancient history of the place stalks the narrow alleys and strikes the tired wanderer with its oppressive burden; where, under the fretted lamps, the rationalists clashed with the gloomy vision of Dostoievsky; where religious wars have cast their bloody shadows; where Slav melancholy and Jewish Talmudism, Hussites and the Catholic Baroque, have etched the features of man. In this city Kokoschka met the man whom he had once described in these words: 'In this man, the individual who is dependent on the temporal, the transient, on personal destiny and old age, is overcome. One can also see all mankind behind such men. I think biological laws make an exception when they create genius.' He was, of course, speaking of T. G. Masaryk.

'The greatest experience of his stay in Prague', wrote Dr Feigl, 'was Kokoschka's meeting with the aging president of the Republic, Masaryk, and the completion of his portrait, which I sold to a collector in New York. Through the intervention of the Presidential Chancellery, and after a meeting with Dr Anna Masaryk, the art-historian and Masaryk's favourite granddaughter, at a dinner given by my wife, the artist's path to the president was smooth. Kokoschka was fascinated by Masaryk's personality. He returned to his hotel one day after a sitting and confessed to me that he had kissed the hand of the old man in an upsurge of admiration. An unusual relationship, profound admiration on the one side and a true sympathy and understanding on the other, appears

60 Sir Stanley Unwin, 1959

61 Chatin P. Sarachi 1959

62 J. P. Hodin, 1964

63 The Prometheus Saga. Left Panel, 1950

64 Thermopylae. Centre Panel, 1954

65 Head of Pallas (From Homer's
Odyssey), 1964
By Courtesy of the Ganymed
Original Editions and Marlborough
Fine Art, London

66 King Lear, 1963
By Courtesy of the Ganymed Original
Editions, London

to have developed between them. There can be no other reason for Masaryk's sending for Kokoschka so frequently afterwards to come to Laný, where they drank coffee and talked, and this weeks after the portrait was finished.'

Whenever Kokoschka spoke of Masaryk his voice became soft and gentle. The first time they met at Laný, Masaryk's daughter, Dr Alice, was present, but later Kokoschka was left alone with the President.

While the portrait was being painted Masaryk had two serious strokes, and Kokoschka had to wait until he was well before he could see him again. From the beginning Kokoschka acted perfectly naturally, breaking through the ice of convention. He sought and needed to be in human contact with Masaryk. The President grew accustomed to him and, Kokoschka thought, seemed somehow to need him. One knows the way such people are usually approached. At their second meeting Masaryk had embraced him. Kokoschka spent many hours with Masaryk, he told me, and he could still remember the old man saying, When will you come again?

The first plan was that Kokoschka should live in Laný while he was working on the portrait, and an apartment was set aside for his use. But he was restless. It was too quiet there, like a cloister, with not even an inn near by. He had to go back to the city. But that brought more problems, for Kokoschka cannot travel alone on a train. How, then, was he to get out to Laný? So the President sent his car to fetch him. Kokoschka used to smile at the Palace Guard standing stiffly to attention as the car with the number 1 came into sight.

When he was ready to begin, Kokoschka told me, the President sat down on the arm of a chair. Kokoschka did not want to paint a stiff, official portrait, so he talked about all kinds of different things to try to get him to forget that his portrait was being painted. In the end the President sat down in the comfortable chair, and Kokoschka said he would paint him like that.

How long will you need? Two or three sittings? Kokoschka replied that he did not know, was never able to say. In the end the portrait took two years.

He was not in the least impressed by the trappings of the President, he said, by the fact that he lived in Laný, or in the Hradschin castle. The elegance of this man in his old age appealed to his aesthetic sense. Masaryk was always well dressed. His personality, his thought, his surroundings, were in complete accord—something one rarely encounters. Kokoschka had seen it before the first world war in the old aristocracy, the Thurn and Taxis, Princess Lobkowitz. The tall, slightly brittle figure of the President made an extraordinarily subtle impression.

Kokoschka enjoys painting old men, especially if they are wise. T. G. Masaryk was a special case. He seemed to emanate an aura of perfection. In his conversations with Masaryk, Kokoschka broached humanist and political problems, but he also chatted cheerfully in his Viennese manner while he studied the President's changing expression. Kokoschka felt that he had a restful effect on him, and Masaryk, for his part, knew that Kokoschka admired him. He was also very interested in Kokoschka's views on Comenius and their application to the modern world. Kokoschka relates how the President authorized his Ministry to prepare a statement to the effect that the implementation of an international school reform would indeed represent the crowning of Masaryk's ideas. Kokoschka urged the President to broadcast his message to the world, but his illness prevented it. On Cheltschicky they had different views, the President acquiescing in the morality of self-defence and quoting Tolstoy in support. Kokoschka believed in Cheltschicky's pacifism—Gandhi's policy of non-violence. Kokoschka found Huss as boring as the burgomaster of Jičín. It was frightful, of course, that he was burned, but so were thousands of others. But Cheltschicky was a true Christian. At that time they knew nothing of Buddhism, and the question was whether the world could be altered without changing the nature of man. As to who was right, the Hussites or Cheltschicky and his critics—Masaryk believed in the Hussite philosophy. Kokoschka could not talk about such things for long, and as soon as he saw that the President was becoming excited he stopped, for Masaryk was already very old. After his stroke he had to hold his arm in a sling, and his sight was so bad that he had to bring things close to his eyes, which were blue and transparent, almost blind. When he began to recover Kokoschka sent him a telegram. The Post Office had just issued some new telegraph forms and Kokoschka chose one decorated with flowers. Masaryk was delighted and asked to have it described. Sometimes in discussions Masaryk would reply: But Kokoschka would say . . ., and he spoke also of Kokoschka shortly before his death.

Once Masaryk was returning from a drive, wrapped in rugs in a carriage drawn by two splendid horses. Kokoschka excused himself for coming too early. Masaryk was in the best of spirits and looked at him roguishly. You look like a boy who has been stealing apples, Kokoschka said. The President laughed happily, for few people spoke to him so freely. Masaryk loved the artist's easy warmth. So you never have black coffee after dinner? Kokoschka once asked. Never, only the decaffeinated kind. Kokoschka said he would have to have a cup of coffee, otherwise he could not work, so the President, thus encouraged, ordered coffee for himself as well, breaking all the rules. But it did him no harm.

Kokoschka made two sketches and then began to paint directly on to the canvas. The paint is applied thinly to the face, making it appear almost transparent, in the way Kokoschka saw him, as though he were already on the other side. The landscape of Prague is touched in with rare economy, and Comenius was already in the picture at Laný. Kokoschka said he wanted to paint the Masaryk who could still believe in progress. The tragedy in his career was that he had tried to translate the high ideals of true democracy into political reality—and they made him pay for it. But when Kokoschka knew him he was no longer the great statesman, only a gentle old man whose work was finished. Kokoschka hoped to capture something of the mysterious magnetism which radiated from this unique man. As he, an artist, had to perceive humanity as something palpable, so the politician, Masaryk, had to theorize to convince himself. Kokoschka had wanted to paint a modern symbolic portrait which would serve to explain the educational philosophies in which they both believed.[4]

The painting of T. G. Masaryk holds a special place in Kokoschka's portrait gallery.

It is the portrait not only of a leader but of his attitude to tradition and of his life's work. In the middle is the seated figure of the statesman, gazing, as it were, at a distant vision, seeing on his left the burning of John Huss as the antithesis of humanism. A metaphorical figure looms in the left foreground, the ethereal face of Comenius, the embodiment of humanist educational thinking, an imperious call to tradition holding the *Via Lucis* like a shield. The hands of Comenius—wonderfully painted—hold the book containing the message that man must trust his senses and thereby develop a natural judgement which will enable him to return to a reasonable way of living. Hence Kokoschka painted an eye, nose, mouth, ear, and hand on the book.[5] The hand can caress; it can also kill. Both aspects are represented, with the figure of Masaryk in the centre dividing and linking together, listening, as it were, with one side of his being to the voices of the past, whilst the other is turned to the present: to the view of Prague with the Karlsbrücke and the Hradschin and children playing happily by the Moldau. Liberty and humanism, the product of martyrdom and spiritual courage, are symbolized in this allegorical portrait of Masaryk. History and modern life, idealism and reality, are presented as dialectical opposites. The artist here presents a synthesis of portrait, allegory, and landscape.

Kokoschka often used to remember Masaryk, and found that he could see him more clearly after a lapse of time which allowed him to be objective. Regretfully Kokoschka thought Masaryk should have been a philosopher and avoided politics. They killed him in the end all the same. He had always had to deal with their petty squabbles instead of doing something for the people, for the world. He was almost a sage. But Kokoschka disagreed with him over Cheltschicky. Masaryk said: 'If someone attacks me here, at my desk, then I must defend myself.' But did Kokoschka defend himself when the Russian stuck his bayonet through his chest? The only possible peace programme for Kokoschka was to be found in the works of Comenius and Cheltschicky, but even the Czechs ignored them. Kokoschka once said that he thought he and Masaryk might have achieved something if they had met sooner.

On his arrival in London in 1938 Kokoschka lived in Hampstead, a district where many foreigners, especially Germans and Austrians, made their homes. Kokoschka found London much changed. After war was declared, life for him, as for all painters, became very difficult. He could not work outside, and he was cut off from the contact with nature which was essential to him. In Polperro, where he stayed from August 1939 to June 1940, interrupted only by a brief visit to London, he twice painted the harbour and began his series of political pictures with THE CRAB. Events made him extremely bitter. He had to leave Polperro because of defence regulations which prevented foreigners from living on the coast. When the air raids on London started he was standing at his easel in the studio of the house between Swiss Cottage and St John's Wood.[6]

Soon after his arrival in England he had painted from memory a picture of Prague with symbolic figures in the foreground into which he had poured all his sense of the glory of the past, his uncertain future, and his longing for the Continent and the countries where he had been recognized as an artist, and which were now submerged in a black cloud of hatred. It was a farewell to the past and to his faith in humanity, peace, and the nobility of learning and of art. Europe was crumbling into ruins. Kokoschka was living daily the death of European man, the end of the spirit of the Baroque in the world. European culture was being systematically destroyed. The artist often said then that it was a matter of indifference to him whether he lived or died.

At that time he painted many water-colours, and it was like a plant sinking its roots into a soil from which they had formerly taken nourishment. The water-colours drew him towards the small, true things of nature. It was a groping backwards, groping towards a deeper emotion so as to forget the face of the present. These water-colours linked him with the Oriental tradition of Japan—the last civilized people on earth, he used to say—whom he loved and admired as artists. Some of the water-colours he painted then were the equal of the finest Chinese and Japanese paintings, but they also contained something new—a brilliance of colour foreign to Oriental works, and a nervous tension that was European. Jewels of the art of water-colour, they were painted in England, a country renowned for this technique. I have already mentioned that Kokoschka made coloured drawings exemplifying the conviction, rooted deep in him, that art depends absolutely on the creation, not on the material, as he used to explain to the pupils who gathered round him to seek inspiration and wisdom from him as from a clear spring. He told me that he believed that modern oil-painting had become a kind of mechanical snobbism. But the simple wood-block print of Japan was an art of the people, and it was one of the sources from which the French Impressionists drew their inspiration. As the bombing attacks on London increased the small house in which the Kokoschkas were living began to collapse, and they moved therefore to a block of flats. The narrow claustrophobic atmosphere did nothing to alleviate the effect of the Blitz on his darkening mood. His friends cannot easily forget the tragic experience of those years. As his humanist faith faltered he was forced at last to change his earlier opinion, seeing State education now as a means to destruction because children learned only at second hand and never from experience, until at last they could not see at all, swallowing the propaganda meted out to them. But whilst he himself gave everything up for lost he wanted to enable others to face a future in which he no longer believed. He began to write feverishly, tirelessly. He addressed meetings, argued, and attacked.[7] When I recall his drawn, sallow face and the sad, lost expression in his eyes then I realize that this unique man would not admit that the deafening roar of bombs, the crumbling of cities and the din of propaganda were stronger than the range of his voice. He spoke only of humanity, lived only for the sake of repeating again and again a faith which he had begun to doubt.

Had he carried his humanist ideals through the labyrinth of the world only to find at last that he had been a fool, that everything he held sacred was nothing more than the crackling of thorns under a pot?

Although his friends loved, admired, and cared for him, there was none who could calm the troubled heart and clear the apocalyptic vision from his mind. Anxiety gnawed at his vitals; his relatives were in danger, his work in jeopardy, and in England he encountered indifference. Finally, there was the bombardment of Monte Cassino, Dresden, Vienna, Hiroshima. It was a barbarian creed—an eye for an eye, a tooth for a tooth—not

the democratic ideal for which millions of young men were dying. Even the end of the
war failed to break his mood, for he could see only too clearly that the main problems
remained unsolved. Peace, to him, was only a pause for breath. Sometimes, when he
could bear it no longer, he would go and stay in the country for a while, coming back
refreshed by his contact with nature and able to face the world more easily.

Kokoschka did succeed in rousing many people by his words, even if he sometimes
seemed to lack the strength to hold himself upright. I remember still a letter addressed
to Sir Donald Wolfit in which Kokoschka pointed out the importance of his performance
of Lear at the time, and the one he wrote to the Soviet Ambassador Lebedev discussing
the mass production of penicillin.

Kokoschka was an idealist and believed that truth and peace are indivisible. 'Truth
does not alter with the language of a people.'[8] He also pointed out the enmity between
power politics and culture.

'Power politics advance like a steam-roller, following a straight line—into nothing.
Culture on the other hand is like the circulation of the blood, it is a living symbol of
mental activity binding the people with a common heritage. When the circuit is
broken, the heart stops beating.'[9] Culture and humanism are one. Comenius understood
this when he turned to humanism for the foundation of education for the people.[10]

Kokoschka began to write once more to restore Comenius to the world's consciousness. He described him not as an historic figure but as a spiritual comforter, come to
bring healing to the mind,[11] and at an exhibition in London called *The War as Seen by
Children* in 1943 Kokoschka grasped the opportunity to ask: 'Who are right, adults or
children?[12]

Like François Mauriac, Kokoschka sees every new generation 'surgir dans l'arène
comme le taureau dont nous sommes surs qu'il sera tué'.[13] (Surge forward into the arena
like the bull, which we know will be killed.)

He found life very difficult. 'When I saw the rotten way one had to earn a living in
this world it was like a chill awakening . . . I was strong enough, I know how one does
it, but I will not soil my hands.' Then, with a sad little smile, he said: I have harmed the
rich people but never the poor. That is thieves' honour.

In addition to the destruction, the realization of the role played by science in the
tragedy of mankind seemed the final blow. Jacques Maritain wrote of science, 'it plays
such a majestic part in the legend of modern life, it has promised and denied everything,
it has explained the independent existence of things and produced the complacent self-
satisfaction in the human mind which has led so many people away from everlasting
truth into the poverty of modern existence.'[14]

The words could have been written by Kokoschka, and because he never expressed
anything that he had not directly experienced, either as an artist or as a writer, we are
struck by the candour of his work. He could say with Goethe: 'I was never affected in
my art. If the experience did not, as it were, burn my fingertips, then I let it
pass.'

After the war Kokoschka at last began to escape from his pessimism. He told me he had had a visit from the goddess again. She had reappeared quite unexpectedly and I felt the restorative effect on his mind.

For Kokoschka the most important postwar event was undoubtedly the great exhibition of his work which took place in Basel in March and April 1947. Works came from all over the world—oils, drawings, water-colours, pastels, lithographs—two hundred and sixty in all[15]—retrospection and reflection of a lifetime. Kokoschka was present, and spoke at the opening.

It was followed by some happy months spent in the Valais, in Sierre, Château Muzot, Sion, and Zermatt, when, absorbed in creation, his mind was healed. In July and August the exhibition went to Zürich, and subsequently, with some exceptions, to Amsterdam in November.[16] This exhibition was afterwards displayed in all the leading galleries and museums of the United States, and ensured his world position.[17] Previously, however, he had been honoured in Europe by the one-man show of sixteen of his paintings in the XXIVth Biennale in Venice in 1948. The postwar exhibitions were extremely important for him, but they also made a great impact on the artistic perception of the time. It was a new start on a broader, international footing. At a time of spiritual crisis Kokoschka appeared as the representative of a philosophy of art which was scarcely known in western Europe and the United States, but which had its roots in the oldest artistic tradition of Europe.

'Expressionism', wrote Kokoschka, 'is traceable as a living tradition back to Nordic chain-ornament, to the early Christian art of the Byzantine churches of the Slavs, to the splendid bookbindings of the Ottonian era in the tenth century, to Romanesque and Gothic religious art, to Grünewald, Hieronymus Bosch, Breughel, to folk printing, and finally, especially in the old Austrian civilization, to Baroque art. The tradition of German art was broken, but it received a new impulse from the French Revolution as exemplified by the romantic landscapes of Caspar David Friedrich and the humanist portraits of Runge and Waldmüller in Vienna, and it outlived the reactionary politics of Peel and Metternich. This tradition nearly perished in the industrialization of Germany; that culture is not entirely forgotten by the people is due to the artists.'[18]

To evaluate the work of Kokoschka in the period of the two world wars, and to appreciate its historical background, it is necessary to examine the facts of art history and art psychology.

If we compare the methods of modern science with those of modern art an extraordinary phenomenon emerges. In whatever land a scientist may be working, and whatever his nationality, the methods he uses are based on internationally recognized principles. The results affect the whole of mankind. In the Fine Arts, however, man's urge to self-expression has sought different routes and different methods of figuration. Modern art cannot reflect the mind and soul of modern man, because there is no such image.

Such a comparison between science and art would be unjustified if it were not for the appearance of a tendency to apply scientific methods even to art. Cubism is governed by rationalism, and in programmatic Surrealism and conscious Primitivism rationalism is dominant. Art is overshadowed in the first instance by psychoanalysis and in the second by the history of art. They express the artist's disquiet in the modern world. Gauguin escaped to the South Seas, but it was Freud who coined the concept of cultural malaise.[19] The most important event in the Impressionist period was the discovery of Japanese prints in Europe, not the physical nature of light. The Symbolists discovered primitive art, but the appearance of African and other primitive shapes in the work of Picasso and the *Brücke* group was more an intentional conscious action than a spontaneous reaction. The styles were quickly adopted and as quickly superseded. It was a restless search, and not a genuine orientation.

The unified development of science is proof that it concerns only one side of the material world, and this is successful only in a specific and very limited way. In other fields it must be admitted that scientific methods and modes of thought exert a straitening effect on spiritual possibilities. The analytical mind and the creative functions of the spirit are diametrically opposed.

When the question of the 'crisis' of modern art was raised, the crisis in question was generally understood to be the development of extremes represented by the School of Paris. In this connexion it is of interest to observe that the French artists generally followed the classic and harmonious line—Monet, Seurat, Cézanne, Matisse, Bonnard; whereas it was the Spaniards, Russians, Germans, Dutch, and Italians who invented the extremes of Cubism, Constructivism, Futurism, Abstract art, and Surrealism: Picasso, Malevich, Boccioni, Mondrian, Kandinsky, de Chirico, and Dali. In every one of these the rational-constructive element dominates, however irrational its gestures may sometimes seem.

Another rather different crisis threatens art. Modern art in comparison with that of former years suffers from a diminishing inspiration. A far-reaching change is taking place in the mind of man as a result of technical civilization. It seems as though we are the products of the adjustment of our minds to the mechanical world, and that we are suffering from a disengagement from the primitive forces of creation. This is not new. Ludwig Klages in his *Grundlegung der Wissenschaft vom Ausdruck*[20] writes: 'A victory of the will over impulse results in a disturbance of the mind's means of expression.' Fewer and fewer men are capable of mythical or artistic feeling. They outgrow their natural impulsive harmony by forcing the cultivation of the intellect till they pay the ultimate penalty in the collapse of civilization. Indirect proof of this is to be found in the child's natural expressive urge. Children are born with the whole potential of experience, but it narrows and is lost as they mature (Čižek).[21] The artistic urges of the mentally deficient should also be mentioned, in so far as their ability to express themselves relies on a surge of expression released by illness.[22] The schizophrenic Swedish painter, Ernst Josephson, produced significant Expressionist works after illness had liberated him from the limitations of tradition and contemporary taste. Henri Rousseau has his 'childlike art' to thank for the *naïveté* of his soul. Yet creative processes cannot depend on the recovery of a primitive simplicity which modern man has perforce lost. The problem is more complicated. Klee is a mystical, naïve, constructive mannerist who has escaped the tension of his nervous system by repetitive scrawling. Two large groups emerge from a stylistic analysis of the modern schools. In the one, formal laws are established by a conscious process of which the function can only be defined as scientific. This is exemplified in the Impressionists' theories of colour and light; Seurat's Pointillism; the geometrical theses of analytical Cubism and Futurism; de Chirico's architectural Surrealism; Mondrian's abstract Purism, and the figurative Purism of Jeanneret. Picasso often moves on the border between them. Liberation of the imagination from natural phenomena, which at first seemed such a revolutionary step, has finally produced a de-humanization of art (Ortéga y Gasset called it a great triumph; the Abbé de Brémont dubbed it the pure process of creation, and Malraux gave it a psychological foundation when he interpreted the origin of a work of art as the experience of another work of art, not as a natural response.[23] Such dehumanization of art implies defeat of the sources of imagery in man. Wilhelm Worringer defines it as the distinction between abstraction and empathy.[24] Where the artistic drive produces inorganic abstract forms there can be no question of involvement, but only a compulsive opposition to it, a tendency to suppress life. Worringer even describes abstraction as a flight from life, in the Freudian sense of a flight into neurosis. 'Abstract regular forms', writes C. G. Jung, 'are the best, indeed the only ones offering relief in the frightful confusion of the world scene.' Jung, agreeing here with Worringer, carries the idea of abstraction further: 'Abstraction is seen to be a function which resists the original "la participation mystique" (Levy-Brühl). It denies the subject in order to break the link with it. Empathy as a principle of artistic creation is founded on the magical significance of the subject which is possessed by a mystic identification with the object.'[25] Empathy is the method of the Expressionists.

Hence we can speak of two broad currents, Expressionist and intellectual-rational art, through which the modern formative will unfolds. Art is a language, and we can therefore detect two different though complementary types of man behind its utterances. The classification into romantic, classical, dynamic and harmonious temperaments is of long standing. Kretschmer added further subdivisions—asthenic, athletic, pyknic.[26] Jung coined the ideas of introvert and extrovert.[27] Yet all these scarcely solve our problem. The Expressionists are men who would regard it as a spiritual sin to produce something on cold and rational lines. Both Edvard Munch and Kokoschka have expressed these opinions.[28] On the other hand, some artists are rational and intuitive by turns. Only the true Expressionist can be an archetype in the Jungian sense. He has a collective subconscious whose content and function exhibit an archaic character. 'It is not a question of archaizing or imitating antique examples, but of qualities inherent in relics. Such qualities are defined by those psychological features which accord, in essentials, with the character of primitive mentality'.[29] The artist's images are, then, only archaic if they have unmistakable mythological parallels. The Expressionist artist is linked with the myth-building force, with the truly creative original power of the soul, whence flow the symbols which express the images of life. This power offers the only prospect for the regeneration and intensification of modern art. Expressionism is a matter of personality rather than a school. The relationship between personality and style becomes more apparent as the connexion with subconscious sources becomes clear. Max Dvořák, analysing the relationship between style and period, comprehends the history of art as the history of the spirit, and forcibly expresses the view that art history should not remain in the materialist and scientific sphere in which it has languished since the Renaissance. Dvořák describes the artist's feverish vision and the dreamlike unreal existence in the womb of his inner inspiration, which result in constructions and forms and colours that far outweigh his powers of observation.[30]

Expressionism is a style which appears only in times of acute spiritual stress. Alois Riegl indicated that one of its most important characteristics was a profound religious excitement.[31] Michelangelo's *Pietà*, formerly in the Rondanini Palace, or the *Descent from the Cross* in the cathedral of Florence, belong to this form of expression as much as the works of El Greco and the Baroque. It is a turbulent, conflicting, passionate art, exemplified in the work of van Gogh, Corinth, Munch, Ensor, Kokoschka, Rouault, Soutine and Yeats, in which the experience of the soul is at variance with the domination of mathematical thought, causality, and technical progress, in short, with the mechanization of culture.

The reason why Kokoschka was ordained to express the spiritual conflicts of the era is made clear by the development in his work. He was forced into it by the depths of his own suffering. The restless rhythms of his brushwork and his method of composition—which is dynamically constructed on emotional links—reveal his character. Kokoschka never abandoned the concept of space. Hence his art is the antithesis of the French School which advocated the concept of the two-dimensional picture. His perspective is not calculated; it is not constructed in the manner of the Renaissance (Alberti, Leonardo, Ucello), nor in the manner of Cubism or abstract art, but develops from the natural function of seeing. We have spoken of the penetrating faculty of Kokoschka's eye. It is interesting that his first portraits were done when Freud was making his first essays into psychoanalysis.

Kokoschka is deeply aware of man's link with eternity without which he could not live or create. He is a mystic with a transcendental understanding of the world. He recognizes man's communion with the created world and speaks of the penetration of hostile forces into the field of art. He defines art as 'a spontaneous creation, when the artist dedicates his ego to his work, like a mother devoting her life to her child, or like the child loving a doll, which is really nothing more than a piece of wood clad in rags. Art is the creation of a reality from the void by material means, a new order of things that can be seen, heard, and touched.'[32]

Kokoschka, the Expressionist, feels that he is formally and spiritually linked with the world of the Baroque. Baroque also moves with an endless feeling of space and eternity; it expresses spiritual tension and human nostalgia. It is the last cultural epoch of Europe and exhibits a common spiritual denominator which we have lost. Kokoschka had no alternative but 'to cling to the few roots which he bore within himself'. Inner creative processes always fascinated him. He needed the vision, the contact with eternity.

Returning to Jung's definition of a work of art we now realize that it embraces Kokoschka's idea of the Vision. Kokoschka's visions are archaic. Hence archaism is the psychological basis of Kokoschka's Expressionism.

SELF-PORTRAIT

Far from the ravaging events of the closing phases of the war, away from the appalling destruction menacing London, in the bleak Highlands of Scotland, Kokoschka told me the story of his life.[1] On a walk under rugged overhanging crags on the shore of Loch Achall, as we strode over the barren hillsides where eagles soared searching for a primeval forest, he brought the events of his life vividly before my eyes. Once we strolled through the long twilight, watching the moon rise above Loch Broom, and Kokoschka, who was making bitter remarks about the war, stopped and said suddenly: This is just as though we were guests of Munch, don't you see? Two Lonely People on the Sea-Shore? Another time we went to look for a thicket where herons were supposed to nest, but the artist's thoughts remained far away in the distant days of his early struggle for art and a significant faith. I realized how much better were those days when artists still had difficulties and opponents because a firmly entrenched *bourgeoisie* were the patrons of the arts, whereas the present is carried away by uncritical commercialism and is only enthusiastic about the sensational. All Kokoschka's youthful efforts to make his mark, to arouse interest in order to distinguish himself from the others, no longer had any meaning. The attempt to link revolution in art with the political and economic climate was a capital error which is now obvious.

Kokoschka spent a few weeks in the calm of Ullapool and then stayed with some Scottish friends, returning to London in the autumn. All through the following year, till the armistice after Hiroshima, Kokoschka was in despair. He also suffered from gout which had to be treated by painful injections. He told me that he had always had a good deal of physical pain and could scarcely remember a time when it was otherwise. In any case, he added, physical pain served to remind him that he was alive.

He used often to revert to the idea of an 'historical Ice Age' through which we are living. We only know that we are freezing, he would say, and memory, that extraordinary ability which allows us to forget the present in vivid remembrances of the past, is dying out. Man has lost his memory, otherwise he would beware. Kokoschka thought that Europeans had become like the masses of Asia, lacking experience and consciousness. Only the artist can rescue the mind of man. Our time had not produced the man who held his nose when confronted with death,[2] or a leader like Saul or David. These were human images and he thought the Greeks had come closer to truth because they looked at it from the human angle, which is far better than trying to be absolutely objective. The philosophy of the Church lulled us into accepting our tormentors.

Some truths cannot be ignored, but no one believes them until they are forced to. Many people, he thought, were sadists today, and a sadist is a feeble individual. Healthy, normal people have no such needs. Because Newton deposited the skeleton of materialism in the cupboard[3] we are condemned to live in an age of progress. The greatest possible misery for the greatest number of people is the real meaning of Bentham's philosophy.[4] What is progress?—Kokoschka asked. It is the lift which will destroy the white races. You rise higher and higher, fifty, sixty stories. Once there, you press a button and back again to the ground. Creatively the white race is finished. It was the same with the pug-dog. Then Kokoschka told me that when he was a boy he had to take the rent to a woman who owned a pug. The wretched creature yapped and struggled for breath. He hated it, and the woman, too, but he still had to go. One day the dog was gone. He had never been able to grasp the idea that things which were there could suddenly vanish like that. Now, he thought, the white race, the torch-bearer of civilization, would vanish too. Everything had its time, its ebb and flow. Man does not easily accept nature as his mentor, but he will have to learn how to do it. It is a law of nature that gregarious animals survive, whereas the solitary, ferocious beasts are exterminated. International politics have sunk to the level of those great beasts, and will undoubtedly be destroyed.[5] The herring swims in large shoals because it cannot defend itself, and a huge shark will be choked if it encounters such a shoal—they have often been caught in a trawl. Another example is offered by plants and trees. Some plants sink their roots very deep into the ground, others just beneath the surface, and together they form the kind of soil that enables a tree to grow roots and thrive. But systematic planning as in Canada, where all the forests were uprooted and wheat planted instead, causing the fertile top-soil to be washed away by the rains and leaving only a dust-bowl, destroyed everything. This is the fate of civilized human society. Nothing will remain but automata creeping and crawling on the earth like beasts with their eyes blinkered, whilst the leaders fly from place to place. Already now, in the atomic age, the world is governed by one or two politicians and scientists. All the rebellious fire of the spirit is extinguished, but it forged the history of Europe. Now it has to be destroyed, lest the memory of individual men, who were the antithesis of the mass, remain alive. Kokoschka was deeply disturbed, he declared, not for himself, but at his powerlessness.

In his studio, however, there was always an atmosphere of timelessness and meditation, a balance between the soul and the intellect, encouraging thought to spread and grasp the eternal problems. It was like being enclosed in a tower. Montaigne also lived in a time of insecurity, and he used to meditate in the tower on his estate, and we can profit by his words even now. Thus, while this tragic phase of history unfolded, wise words were spoken, unexpected links between thought and feeling were forged in the kingdom of Kokoschka's studio. Everything seemed to fit in to a mysterious and convincing pattern.

Kokoschka was not concerned with history.

History, he said, begins with Alexander. The Mediterranean civilization came before, and he was interested in that.

On the two easels there were compositions with motifs from Scotland; a third was propped against the wall. One depicted a thundery landscape with such depth as had not been painted since Rubens. On the left a rainstorm creates blue shadows; there is a sheep, mournful and impatient, while a rabbit crouches in a hole. The sheep looks inwards towards the distant sunshine, drawing the onlooker's gaze with it. The foreground depicts grouse and a still life of flowers lit by a strong light. Is there an allegorical message? What was extraordinary about the scene to inspire the artist? Only the beauty of the nature of everyday things, the longing of an animal. He had been wandering about rather lost, when a sheep suddenly stood before him panting. At first, he said, he did not know why, because he had not seen the lamb hidden by the mother. That was love; love, light, and space are all the same. Here the depth is most concentrated—and Kokoschka pointed to a place at the back of the picture—and it lifts the foreground. The focal point is not in the middle: he said he always put it to one side. He had done it, probably unconsciously, from the beginning, because he always approached things from the back. He had waited hours for the rabbit to appear; then, in the end, the animal knew he was there, and he became part of the scenery. That is important, too.

Then there were the Scottish hunters. They lived in a completely isolated house, and never ate bread. They shot rabbits for their dogs; the rest they ate themselves. The house was horrible—dogs everywhere and a foul smell. There were wires criss-crossed overhead like a factory, and the cupboards were full of empty cartridge-cases, nets, traps, and rubber-boots. They were perfectly happy there. The atmosphere was reminiscent of Ibsen's *Wild Duck*. One of the men was huge, a wild creature with pale eyes; the other was very quiet. The big one once tried to shoot the other in a fit of rage, but the bullet went into the mirror, which had never been mended. When they were not out rabbit-shooting they sat by the window and watched the peacock fanning its tail. It was beautiful. Kokoschka painted the scene, the room in pale pink and lilac tones like a pastel, the man with the gun seated on a chair before the mirror in which the room is reflected. A dog lies under the chair, and beyond is the window with the wood and the peacock. In the foreground is a stuffed animal, like a gargoyle. Painting this picture did Kokoschka good. He felt close to primitive life which puts death, and landscape and its beauty, into natural perspective. He experienced solitude and the calm of the forest far from wars and revolutions.

Then there was a picture of Ullapool, a small harbour huddling against the hills, and in front a little house and a garden. There was a dog, a cat, a bicycle, a bottle of milk, and a basket—a colourful poem of every day life. Creatures and things were fused by the artist's eye into a brilliant dream. Kokoschka had not experienced that full peaceful sense of summer, of calm stillness, since he had painted ZRÁNÍ (Summer 1938/40).

The naked girl in the foreground standing in the cool stream is composed with a marvellous play of blue shadow and hot sunlight. A figure sits in the sun with a dog and a basket, with another female figure in the shade. The painting is splendidly rich, like a tapestry. Kokoschka carried this picture with him from Prague and finished it during the Blitz, weaving into it his memories of happier times. CAPRICCIO, done in 1942/43, also has an intense feeling of summer and a breath of mystic wonder. The animals in Kokoschka's paintings always have an inexplicably magical effect—dogs, cats, goats, sheep, rabbits, and doves all tread softly in the steps of Pan. Kokoschka, like Dürer and Munch, is fascinated by natural forms; he paints the wordless presence of the beasts, and his pictures unveil the mystery hidden by tangible reality.

The DUCK SHOOT presents a woman wearing a red bathing-costume standing in a boat and leaning back, as if she were holding her breath: a shot from the tiny figure of the hunter in the background and the heavy duck hurtles to the ground. Life goes on around the dead falling bird, and the dog stands waiting, like Cerberus, in the water. The composition is a spatial triangle; the leaning woman, the hunter, the direction of the shot, and the falling duck.

Kokoschka is like Antaeus; he draws his life from his mother—the earth. Often, during the war, I would imagine Kokoschka to be like a forest tree, its roots deep underground and drawing the life-giving sap to the branches, and even in the ice-cold world about its crown bringing forth leaves, blossom, and fruit. A tree which grows straight and tall through storm and drought, casting cool shadows over the torrid heat of man's will to destroy. Such rhythm, such pulsating life, and quickening of the mind I have never before encountered. Few are so richly blessed with subtlety and clairvoyance, with a mind of lightning emotional energy, that can illumine whole eras of human history. In the shifting, restless ant-heap of the world he stands like an Indian sage, meditating and inwardly calm, and offers his friends the enduring experience of contact with human greatness. The story of Kokoschka's life and his philosophy may therefore be repeated in his self-portraits, so that we may comprehend it more fully.

Every age is characterized by a type of man cast in the mould of its own inherent laws; the Greeks by the Apollonian and Dionysiac ideals; the Jews by the God seekers and Prophets; the Middle Ages by the monks, martyrs, and mystics. The Renaissance saw its ideal in the *Uomo universale*—the Universal Man. It was still possible then to have a complete understanding of human learning. But our own time is ruled by the bleak specialization foreseen by Goethe when he wrote: 'Knowledge gets one nowhere today; one loses oneself in the attempt to understand everything.'

Goethe realized the danger which now hangs like a sword above the world. He understood the idea of the indivisibility of life, and he tried to merge art and science. He was fighting against the analytical-mechanical spirit of Newton, and he laid the foundations of the study of morphology. He saw a new ideal of humanity. Faust was still medieval, but Wilhelm Meister embodied the new socially-active man, whose principles, and this is important, were rooted deeply in tradition. Goethe realized that it was essential to oppose the increase in materialism by morality, lest new forces at the disposal of man should become a curse rather than a blessing. Work and renunciation alone would be the saving of man. Goethe found Rousseau's *Emile* too sentimental and blurred; he also rejected Winckelmann's Greek neo-classical ideal as inadequate, although it was fashionable at the time. Social man, in the best sense, was Goethe's ideal—the sublime character foreseen by the eighteenth century who made an appearance in the nineteenth to be immediately forgotten by the twentieth, Romantic man was as unreal an image as the neo-classical. He was pessimistic, unbalanced, and doctrinaire.

The young Kokoschka had instinctively rejected Rilke's and Hofmannsthal's *bourgeois* aesthetics. He sensed that art was dying of 'good taste', and felt the forces ranging deep and turbulent within his mind.

Modern man is rediscovering the primal contact with emotional life. Kokoschka retreated from the fog of decadence, the desert of mechanization, to his own roots. He felt nearer to neolithic man than to Swann or Emanuel Quint.

Reading Emerson's *Representative Men* it is at once obvious that there is no record of the intellectual types characteristic of our time: the rationalist scientist, the amoral materialist, the agnostic-progressive, the professional revolutionary, the rabid anarchist, the nihilist, and the existentialist—all are missing. However, the rare man of the present is also missing, the man who treads the lonely mystic path of that whole life which the Renaissance, by its devotion to the rational, tried to extinguish.

Missing, too, is the man who shuns the future, like Dante in the *Inferno*, but whose emotional life is still more fruitful than that of the scientist. Such men resemble the grain of wheat which, dormant for thousands of years in an Egyptian tomb, began to sprout when planted in fertile soil. The miraculous spark of life was not extinguished. Age-old wisdom is preserved in the hearts of such men, and their work is the germ that will out-live the long desert of sterility. They are stricken with reverence and awe before the mystery of life, as were the early mystics by their love of God. Like oracles they stammer the truth in riddles. They are men who err and suffer, not manipulators of the soul. But the disparity between the world of creation and the world of men is clear to them, and this knowledge enables them to break out from their own time into eternity.

Teeming with curiosity and longing and expectation, the young Kokoschka rushed headlong into life. His acute sensitivity meant that each disappointment left a deep scar, and he bore the marks of the decadence preceding the two world wars. He suffered the blows of harsh reality, yet still found courage to acknowledge the truth as he saw it.

In his SELF-PORTRAIT AT TWENTY-SIX Kokoschka painted himself as Saint Sebastian; he saw his wretchedness. He was afraid, but hoped that he would be able to escape his destiny. Women constructed cages of gold around him—of sensual desire, ecstasy, sybaritic luxury. Still he found no happiness and broke loose (DOUBLE POR-TRAIT, 1912). The Youth was now a man, but what of his ideals? Did he choose the easy path? Look at his portrait. One hand is clutched convulsively to his breast, whilst the other holds the brush gracefully like the young Dürer with the thistle. Soon he will point accusingly with his right hand to the beholder, or reflectively to heaven like Leonardo's John the Baptist. His lips will speak of the lyrical blue flower hidden in the heart of every young man, of the dreaming youth he had been. His face bears the lines of searching doubt, and his mind has experienced more than the sensibility and pain which he no longer fears. An experience which none of us today can afford to throw away—the archaic mother-goddess, the primeval response. His task is to bring the life-forces to the light, not to leave them in darkness as would those who try to stir primitive cultures and the soul of man from their long sleep by science and analysis. The time was 1914 and the young Kokoschka in the blue portrait stood at the cross-roads of life (SELF-PORTRAIT WITH BRUSH).

It is of interest to compare this face with the portrait painted also in Vienna, but in 1913. Decades of inner experience had been crowded into one short year, and there is horror and ghastly astonishment in his eyes, as though he had looked upon the head of Medusa. Greenish-yellow, his hand stands out from the warm red waistcoat, the first finger outstretched like a memory of the Kunstschau poster in 1908 in which he was pointing to his heart (SELF-PORTRAIT WITH HAND ON HIS BREAST). Disappointment has drawn down the corners of his mouth, and the line of his lips is determined and firm. The sweet idyllic dream is not for him, nor the smooth perfection of formal art his goal. His was the path of despair, of death and resurrection. At the turn of 1914 his portrait was that of a man concealing his secret worth, like the priest of a persecuted sect.

He seems to stand in a damp grotto holding his brush, and his face and form appear metallic under the eerie leaden light. The colours are muted: dark blue for the jacket, a neutral background, and a few warmer brownish-red tones on the hand, cheek, neck, and ear barely indicated. The facial expression, with its close-pressed mouth, fine-drawn nostrils and hunted eyes, is that of a man betrayed. And the emptiness hangs menacingly, an intolerable burden, advancing almost to the centre of the canvas (SELF-PORTRAIT WITH RAISED BRUSH, 1914).

The first war came and Kokoschka survived it, though wounded and close to death. The horror of the human predicament—*la condition humaine*—dawned on him. He had already developed emotionally, far beyond the point attained by most people only in a whole lifetime. Anxiety about his personal fate, even death itself, had been overcome, for he had looked death in the face. But he was mentally and psychologically unbalanced, verging on the insane. Gradually he pulled himself together, took up his brush, looked into his inmost being, and painted what he found. That is what you are; *tat tvam asi*. The background is nothing but a violently shifting darkness and light. Kokoschka did not look back; the past was dead. But the brush stormed across his canvas, broad violent strokes of an acid greenish-yellow—the colour of death. One hand points to his heart, the seat of his pain and his physical wound. The other holds an imaginary palette. This was Dresden, 1917. His eyes are wide, the dreams are banished from the gaze of his haggard face.

The moving portrait done six years later makes us realize how much the artist has suffered and how much still lay ahead. It is a study of isolation. The arms are pressed against his breast; suffering and melancholy sit in his eyes and upon his mouth, the too-large head rests on a thin body, enhancing the impression of helplessness. The rich surge of colour still could not silence the tragic side of his life. The hands droop from toil-worn arms, and we seem to hear the voice of Gilgamesh crying: 'I drank my fill at the fountain of suffering, and sorrow was my sustenance' (SELF-PORTRAIT WITH CROSSED ARMS).

67 Oskar Kokoschka in his Studio, 1962
Photo: Adelmann

68 The Artist's residence

69 Double Portrait (Oskar Kokoschka and his wife Olda), 1963–4

And the same cry echoes through the moving drawing inscribed by Kokoschka *Im 34 Jahre, Wien, Okt. 1920* (Aged 34, Vienna, Oct. 1920).[6]

PAINTER AND HIS MODEL II clearly reveals the advance Kokoschka had made between 1908 and 1924, the year in which it was done, in his development as both a man and an artist. The youthful Kokoschka of 1908, who pointed to his bleeding heart and whom the painter introduced into his canvas, was suffering the pains of the rebel against convention, the rebel who drank at the source of existence and his own experience. He was not curbed by his trials but accused and challenged. Now the undisciplined young rebel against the sterility and vulgarization of life, the mutinous artist, had developed into a mighty primitive. He stands with his arms outstretched like the chief of a tribe untouched by civilization, inhabitants of the primeval forest. He has more in common with the carvings of Easter Island than the decadent European. The woman, insignificant in the background, is almost extinguished by the brutal archaic force of this man. The first version describes him in the decisive Dresden years (1922–3), already on the way to the liberated mood of ecstatic, rapturous existence and Dionysiac self-immersion in the joy of living (PAINTER AND HIS MODEL, I).

Is there, then, nothing but a face bloated with wine and sensuality in the richly glowing colours of the portrait of LOT AND HIS DAUGHTERS? The percipient eye denies such an accusation. In another portrait he sits in the background like a man in a dream drunk with the presence of woman, the painter between two women. What is the end of life? Who is the woman in the centre and the woman on her right? We seem to hear the questions: Why am I painting this? What forces me to do it? (JACOB, RACHEL AND LEAH). As a young man he pointed bitterly to the wound inflicted on him metaphorically by cultural decadence and physically by the war (*Poster for the lecture on the Nature of Visions*). In THE EXILES he bade farewell to culture, with his friends.

Almost all Kokoschka's self-portraits, from the first, painted when he was twenty-six, to the latest ones, dating from just after the second world war, have a tragic melancholy undertone. He never painted his other face—cheerful, bold, and charming—those features, that Austrian gaiety, immortalized by Mozart in his letters to his cousin, which won countless friends for Kokoschka and helped him to prevail over a good many enemies. Kokoschka became the first artist in Germany, thus fulfilling Loos's prophecies. Where, then, was Vienna with its intrigues, hostility, and decadence? Far behind, with all his friends of former days and the woman who had caused him so much sorrow and almost destroyed him; nothing more than a pale shadow beyond the khaki landscape of the war.

Kokoschka looks in the glass again—at Nogent-sur-Marne in 1932. Here is the artist. Cap on head he stands and paints; his hand is heavy with creation, his gaze lost in a world of visions. The eyes are close together, as in PAINTER AND MODEL II, and his gaze seems to be drawn powerfully inward. On the canvas behind is the Baroque figure of a woman, the incarnation of his vision for which he lives and fights. Courage and endurance shape his mouth. He has sacrificed good fortune, which once more came near to seducing him (The Goddess), but he destroyed it with his own hands. He allowed riches to slip away, seeking life itself; he despised property and saved his life (SELF-PORTRAIT WITH A CAP). This portrait echoes through the one painted in Vienna in 1934, and the portrait of the following year with hat and stick done in Prague, though the head, leaning on the hand, is less sculptural, not so clear-cut or so determined. It is more a contemplative statement, almost a looking-back on the past, as though he wanted to remember. Throughout the humanist argument into which politics had driven him, had he perhaps overlooked something more significant?

In 1937 Kokoschka painted his portrait again, this time in Mährisch-Ostrau. It was a time of trial. The huge exhibition of degenerate art was on in Munich. Kokoschka stood in the pillory knowing that his life's work was about to be destroyed after filth and shame had been cast upon it. He saw ruin on every side, and no way of escape. His mother was dead, his sister was very ill, and he had no money to help her. In addition he fell ill and nearly died. The city was so dirty that he developed a dangerous ulcer. He collapsed one day in the street, and was brought back unconscious to his hotel. When the doctor at last brought him round he said: You are saved. If you had gone a day earlier into hospital you might not have survived.

In this distracted condition he painted the PORTRAIT OF A DEGENERATE ARTIST. Kokoschka turns the accusation inherent in the title into an ironic reprimand. His mother was dead, Germany's moral and intellectual background was poisoned, the surroundings natural to him, as well as his mother-tongue, were lost. So he had come to the end. He told me that for a long time he had carried a picture in his mind; he had tormented himself trying to paint it, but in the end it was spoiled. He yielded to despair. Then he painted himself on the same canvas. He wanted, so he told me, to tell his own story, to discover where he stood with the changes and the challenges of life.

In the background is his mother in her green Alpine landscape, and here the man, naked and exposed, and the stag—the hunted beast. The portrait has two faces, he explained, the sick and the sound. If you step back the face becomes poor, sallow, and thin—then it smiles again. Here—and he pointed to the left side of the face—you see how angry he is, whereas here, on the right side, he seems contemplative, almost sad. No one can paint the back of a head today. Yet the whole head is in this picture. The old masters had the knack of getting the eye of the portrait to follow the beholder; now here, the whole body turns. Usually only a sculptor can do this; Kokoschka told me he did it unconsciously. After a lapse of ten years he was looking at the picture again. Look, he said, it approaches from the left and leads away into the distance. The expression of the face is joyful and confident, sad and wondering. It is neither pretentious nor imposing; it is intimate.

The hand is dead, stony, but suddenly the dead man stirs. That was how it happened. Kokoschka had given himself up for lost, when he woke again to life. It was painted so that interest centred on the face to make you feel as if you could creep into the space behind the arms. The Baroque is three-dimensional, and the Flemish school also, but they did not paint like this. You can even feel the end of the nose in this portrait. The whole face is alive, every feature has suffered.

I knew that many others had substance but little expression. If one looks at this face, the violent brushwork, these strange hands, the lurid blue of the shirt against the green, then one can comprehend the confession of this man, who stands like a pillar asking: 'Who am I? Whence come I? Where am I going?'—You may remember the healing words of Jakob Böhme, 'The world will fall to dust. The earth will melt, and the cliffs and the elements; the Divine Will alone, for which the earth was created, shall abide.'[7] Then you realize that the man can only be saved who has faced death and the devil; man on the cross-roads of good and evil, wrestling with the angel. That man only will be rescued who has faith in his own rebirth.

Thus armed, Kokoschka braved the dreadful years of the second world war. We recognize in him shattered Expressionist man as the representative of our time 'who is blessed from above and below',[8] born to carry the torch through the darkening years of progress.

The man who survived a second world war throughout which he courageously stood up for his idea of truth—not the half-truths of the belligerents—and to whom the Allies did not seem so pure and innocent even in contrast with the black evil of those who openly subscribed to brutal satanism, painted, like Goya before him, in heroic isolation, their true portrait in the name of art, of culture, and of humanity. In 1948 he painted himself in Fiesole. A new life was ahead; the world was once more open and expectant. Exhibitions were held in the great cities. Kokoschka swung into renewed activity over the whole field of art, approaching his autobiographical stories with a smile, with rapture, and recreating a kaleidoscope of remarkable events. Honour was piled on honour, justifying a remark he once made to me, that as a young man he had always given, but now it was his turn to receive (SELF-PORTRAIT, FIESOLE).[9]

In the painting TESEUS AND ANTIOPE, he represents again the victory of the female principle, the legendary; and in HERODOTUS against a backcloth of war and peace he appears, himself a legend, symbolizing the Greek of antiquity who listens and observes, recording whatever life unfolds.

Now his life has come full circle. He has achieved what was in his power and his destiny. He has aroused love, stirred men from their torpor, and given youth a banner. He has been a strong river that purifies and unbinds the passions, undermining outworn decadence, flowing powerfully on. He has painted another self-portrait now with his wife (DOUBLE PORTRAIT, 1963-4). The long story is etched in his smiling, benevolent face. He has withstood life's ebb and flow; he has astonished, like an acrobat in a circus, with his antics; he has given happiness and joy like one of those clowns whom we love because their folly is old and wise, touching our hearts. Kokoschka loves the circus, especially the clowns and the acrobats, and all the colourful atmosphere that breaks with everyday monotony. If a circus is ever near you will find him there, drawing. Grock, whom Kokoschka much resembles, once said: My destiny is founded on two words which I often use—'Why' and 'Impossible'. If you ask me how I came to be a clown I can only answer 'Why?' If I tell you, you will certainly say 'Impossible'. Fate weaves with two strands—good fortune and ill, but in life man must be his own pilot.[10]

NOTES

1. The Three Faces of Kokoschka

[1] The Viennese architect Professor Josef Frank described this lecture to me in a letter written on the 7 September 1947. The lecture was couched in a difficult and archaic language with references to old biblical texts. 'Kokoschka gave a lecture in the Academic Union for Literature and Music on the 26 January 1912. It was entitled *On the Nature of Visions*. The room was packed. Kokoschka spoke only for about half an hour but most of it was quite incomprehensible and disconnected. . . . Adolf Loos and Kraus were among those at the front and they were invited to make a contribution. Kraus read aloud some of his aphorisms on Kokoschka—but he had never paid any attention to his paintings before. One of these was: "Kokoschka paints everyone as though they were dead. Once he was going to paint a corpse but the coffin was already closed", and there were several others equally pointless. Then Loos rose and spoke about Kokoschka's gift of second sight.' *Von der Natur der Gesichte*, first published in *Menschen*, Journal of New Art, 4 Year, Vol. I, 25 January 1921. Reprinted in *Oskar Kokoschkas Schriften*, English translation by Hedi Medlinger and John A. Thwaites in Edith Hoffmann: *Kokoschka, Life and Work*.

[2] *Disarmament of Children. Abrüstung der Kinder, als Programm einer demokratischen Volksschulfront, auf welches sich solche Regierungen verpflichten mögen, die sich von Diktaturen unterscheiden wissen wollen* (*A programme for a democratic method of education, suitable for governments which want to be distinct from those of dictators*). Published in London and read as a lecture at the exhibition *The War as Seen by Children*, January 1943, with the motto: 'The achievement of the Democratic Idea of Education would be the crowning of my ambition', T. G. Masaryk in *Conversations with the Artist*, Lány, 1936.

[3] *On the Nature of Vision*. Foreword to *Orbis Pictus*. First published in the Yearbook *Unser Weg* (*Our Path*), 1920. Extracts published in *Oskar Kokoschkas Schriften*, 1907–55.

[4] *On the Power of Virtue*. From:
Where there is true love and wisdom, there is neither fear nor ignorance.
Where humility consorts with happiness, there is neither greed nor envy.
Where there is serene faith in God, there is neither trouble nor indifference.

[5] The mother and child *motif* is frequent in Kokoschka's work.

[6] Jan Amos Comenius, Komenský in Czech, (1592–1670), the last bishop of the Bohemian Brotherhood, theologian, philosopher (*Pansophia*), pedagogue (*Didactica Magna*) and humanist (*The Labyrinth of the World*). He was the most persecuted person of the Thirty Years' War, an apostle of Peace (*Via Lucis, Angelus Pacis*), founder of the visual teaching method (*Orbis Pictus*) and of the idea of a universal school for the people. Kokoschka was familiar with *Orbis Pictus* while still a boy in Prague and in England he spent much time in research on Comenius (compare the portrait of T. G. Masaryk, the drama *Amos Comenius*, his English address *Via Lucis, A Study of the Origins of a Contemporary Mental and Material Crisis*, and the lecture given in the Prague Urania in 1936, when he read from his youthful autobiography and described his wounding during the First World War.

[7] Quoted from the typescript of the artist.

ii. *The Melancholy of the World*

[1] This refers to *A Petition from a Foreign Artist to the Righteous People of Great Britain for a Secure and Present Peace*. Humbly tendered and signed by Oskar Kokoschka, London, December 1945, and published in: *Kokoschka, Life and Work*, by Edith Hoffmann. The prefaces by Kokoschka were written for *Oils and Water-colours by Chatin Sarachi*, Redfern Gallery, May/June 1945.

Sarachi was a friend of Kokoschka and was his pupil in London. At that time about eight young artists were followers of Kokoschka, among them the gifted young Irish woman, Ishbel McWhirter and Philip Moysey, the commercial artist, who was doing pastels and water colours at the time and whom Kokoschka used to call 'Saint Philip' because he lived the life of an ascetic in a gypsy caravan.

Cats and Women was an exhibition of works by Edwin Smith in the Berkeley Galleries, London, 1944.

[2] Heinrich Wölfflin: *Die Kunst Albrecht Dürers*. E. Panofsky & F. Saxl: *Dürer's Kupferstich Melencolia I*.

[3] In the visitor's book of an exhibition of the work of the Austrian painter, Marie Louise Motesiczky, held in London in 1944 he wrote: Oskar Kokoschka, Europe.

[4] Stefan Zweig: *Der europäische Gedanke in seiner historischen Entwicklung*.

[5] From a letter to the author.

[6] When Gandhi began his fasts in 1945 in an attempt to bring about a reconciliation between the Hindus and Moslems, Kokoschka decided to go to India to paint him. He collected all the paper-cuttings he could find about Gandhi and was very moved when he learned of the embracing crowds, and, at the end of the fast, over the attempted assassination and Gandhi's astonishing words of forgiveness as he tried to understand and excuse the deed. Kokoschka had completed the formalities and was waiting to go to New Delhi when three shots in head and breast killed the Apostle of Pacifism. Gandhi's sacrifice disturbed Kokoschka deeply and he saw it as an evil omen for the future.

[7] The exhibition mentioned by the artist is the one held in Karlsbad in 1909.

[8] In May 1946 a letter from Kokoschka to Alfred Neumeyer was published in the *Magazine of Art* in Washington, in which among other things he said he wanted to raise £1,000 for the starving children of Vienna. 'Austria was the first and least heeded of Hitler's victims. The *Anschluss* was officially recognized by the Great Powers but the Austrian people was given no opportunity to express an opinion. It waits still in vain. I hope to get this £1,000 in the U.S.A. for a picture painted in 1943 with the title *What We Are Fighting For*. It is a large and impressive picture. Should you know anyone or any public institute which might be interested I will gladly send a photograph. . . .'

[9] In the foreword to the catalogue to the important Kokoschka exhibition in Basel in 1947 Dr Fritz Schmalenbach wrote: 'Anyone who criticizes these new pictures should not forget the courage and strength needed, against all today's rules of painting, to handle the themes which really occupy the present world, painting them relentlessly and explicitly on canvas.'

[10] *Anschluss—Alice in Wonderland, 1942*. The final version of the picture shows several different kinds of military helmets of the warring nations. The faces of the three figures are reminiscent of the leading politicians.

[11] Heinrich Wölfflin. *Renaissance und Barock*. Carl Justi described the Baroque engraver and architect G. B. Piranesi (1720–78) as a modern, passionate, even daemonic nature. Infinity, the mystery of the sublime, of space and power was his field. (*Winkelmann und seine Zeitgenossen*). The connexion with Kokoschka is clear, his dislike of the Renaissance understandable.

[12] Franz Anton Maulbertsch (1724–96) was the most important artist among the last Austrian Baroque painters. His work, influenced by Italian and South German art, developed

a dramatic-narrative, formal character similar to that shown by Schmidt of Krems. Allegory is subservient to history. With Maulbertsch one can speak of a Folk or Peasant Baroque. In 1960 Kokoschka wrote the preface to Klara Garas' work on the Austrian master, in which he characterizes the philosophy of life of the Baroque period—one of the finest essays he has written.

[13] Hermann Bahr: *Wien.*

[14] Oskar Kokoschka: *An Approach to the Baroque Art of Czechoslovakia.*

[15] This picture *Summer II (Zrání)* was begun in Prague in 1938 and finished in London in 1940. It is now in the collection of the National Gallery of Scotland, Edinburgh.

[16] This portrait commission was arranged by Dr Fred Uhlmann a lawyer and now a naivist painter, author and art-collector. With his wife, Diana, he organized the 'Artist's Refugee Committee' in his house, 47 Downshire Hill, London, N.W.3. Thirty to forty artists from Austria or Germany, who had been called 'the Kokoschka Group' (John Heartfield was one of them) were brought to England on the initiative and with the financial help of the Committee. Herr Uhlmann, who was introduced to Kokoschka around Christmas 1938, persuaded his brother-in-law, now Lord Croft, to let Kokoschka paint his portrait. This was done in 1939: *The Honourable Michael Croft.* Then followed the portrait *Posy Croft.*

[17] Nimptsch, Member of the Royal Academy of Arts in London and the Academy of Florence, was one of the close circle of Kokoschka's friends among them the picture-restorer and music-lover Sebastian Isepp, the diplomat and painter Chatin Sarachi, his friend, the poet, Fred Marnau, the publisher Walter Neurath, the author of this book and several others. It was in Nimptsch's studio, 409 Fulham Road, London S.W.10, that Kokoschka used to draw. Kokoschka did portraits between 1943 and 1946 of Countess Drogheda, 1947 Valerie Goulding, 1951 Isepp, 1953 Lady Strafford (*Galatea*), 1957 Sarachi, 1959 Pamela Hodin and Nimptsch. In 1958 the portrait drawing of Ernest Rathenau, 1960 that of Marnau and 1964 of the author.

[18] Oskar Kokoschka: *A Sea Ringed with Visions.*

[19] Frau Margareth Hinz, an acquaintance of Countess Drogheda had a house in Boundary Road, London N.W.8, opposite the second-hand bookshop belonging to Josef and Willy Suschitzky. The Kokoschkas lived there from June 1940 to February 1941. The house has been pulled down. In 1938 Kokoschka's first London address was 45a King Henry's Road, London N.W.3. In Polperro the Kokoschkas lived in Cliff End Cottage and before it was bombed they twice visited Plymouth with friends.

[20] Dr János Plesch published his memoirs *János, The Story of a Doctor.* They were originally written in German, although the German edition only appeared in 1949 in Munich published by Paul List with the title *Ein Arzt erzählt sein Leben.* The second edition was brought out by List with the title *János erzählt von Berlin.* In this book Dr Plesch wrote: 'Unfortunately I had few opportunities to meet any of the great French Impressionists. That made me pursue contemporary German art with even greater keenness—thanks to my initial acquaintance with Max Liebermann, Max Slevogt, Emil Orlik and Oskar Kokoschka. I possess valuable drawings by each one of them—proof of their art and their friendship.'

[21] *Polperro II,* 1939, *The Crab,* 1939/40.

[22] The catalogue, which has four illustrations, of the exhibition at the Leicester Gallery comprised the following works: *The Terrace, Richmond; Self-Portrait; Paris, Louvre; Lyon; Paris, Opéra; London, Waterloo Bridge; Portrait of Professor Kestenberg; The Thames from the Savoy; Portrait of a Boy; Biarritz, Beach; Mont Blanc; Venice, Santa Maria della Salute; Portrait of Herwarth Walden; Courmayeur and the Dent des Géants; Two African Girls; Portrait of Frau Else Kupfer; The Chase; Portrait of Herr Ebenstein; Exodus (Col de Sfa near Biskra; Aigues Mortes; Mandrill; Toledo; El Kantara; Biarritz II; Venice, Santa Maria della Salute, View Over Roofs; Lac Leman; Vernet-les-Bains; Portrait of Sidi Ahmet ben Tidjani Marabout of the Zaouira Tamelhat near Touggourt (Algeria); Dover; The Painter; Tom cat; Flowers; Portrait of Miss Adele Astaire; Tigon.* The foreword, which was Kokoschka's first introduction to

England was written by P. G. Konody and is important for the clear distinction it makes between Kokoschka and the German Expressionists.

²³ Kokoschka was unable to stand the damp in Boundary Road and moved to Mandeville Court which had central heating, and then again to 55 Park Lane, where he and his wife remained till September 1946. Then they took over 120 Eyre Court, Finchley Road, which had been occupied by Kokoschka's parents-in-law, Dr K. B. Palkovský and his wife, from September 1940 to 1946.

²⁴ *The Vision of Piers the Plowman*, by William Langland (1362–99); Johannes von Saaz, *Ackermann aus Böhmen*, 1401. Johannes von Saaz, or Tepl, was a Bohemian Early Humanist.

²⁵ On the back of the picture the words are written: 'A red egg for Manchester-Christianity, wishes kindly OK', London, 1939.

III. *Mir*

¹ The *Via Lucis of Amos Comenius*, in four acts and twelve scenes, was first conceived in Prague when Kokoschka was painting the portrait of T. G. Masaryk, the first President of the Czechoslovak Republic (1935–36). The figure of Comenius, who holds the *Via Lucis* like a shield before him is the embodiment of that tradition of humanism which the President tried to realize in his political life. The play was written in London and Polperro in 1938/39, and in that fateful year Kokoschka sent a copy to me in Stockholm with the request that I try to have it produced in the Dramatiska Theatern as a warning. It proved to be impossible because Swedish opinion at that time was favourably inclined towards the Third Reich. *The Merchant of Venice* was put on instead.

It was this first draft that Kokoschka worked on at Ullapool in 1944. Several scenes were re-written and some of the speeches made by the political leaders of the day were interpolated into the text to strengthen the connexion with our own time. Kokoschka's *Comenius* is not a historical play. It uses the historical ideas of Comenius and the chaos of the Thirty Years' War to point the miseries of our day. In the fourth act Comenius goes to visit Rembrandt, so that the wish of the Bohemian Brothers to have his portrait painted by the master should be fulfilled. In fact the portrait of Comenius was painted by one of Rembrandt's pupils, Jurriaen Ovens. Kokoschka depicts the artist painting *The Night Watch*, and inserting the mysterious figure of a small white-clad girl, as if in a trance. *The Night Watch*, however, was painted in 1642 and not at the end of Rembrandt's life. The imaginative significance of this problematical figure (Rembrandt may well have needed a point of light in that part of the composition, and the figure probably had no other meaning, although Kokoschka turned her into a small Jewish girl from the ghetto where Rembrandt lived) gave Kokoschka the chance to relate the confusion of the seventeenth century to the devastation of today. (See also: *Larenopfer*, in J. P. Hodin *Bekenntnis zu Kokoschka*, where this scene is closely analysed. Also see: *Oskar Kokoschka Schriften*.)

² James Burnham: *The Managerial Revolution*. Edward Bernstein: *Cromwell and Communism*. Lin Yutang: *The Importance of Living. Lettres complètes d'Héloïse et d'Abélard*.

³ Hanns Hörbiger and Philipp Fauth: *Glaziale Kosmogonie, eine neue Entwicklungsgeschichte des Weltalls und des Sonnensystems*.

² See also Oskar Kokoschka's unpublished manuscript: *A Civilising Story*, in which he discusses these ideas and his share in the search for oil. (London, 1947.)

⁵ Mount Ararat in Turkey, Assyrian *Uradhu*, where the Ark is supposed to have settled. *Ra* (*Re, Phra*), the Egyptian Sun God, creator and preserver of life. The Arabic word for lion is *'Asad*.

⁶ T. G. Masaryk: *Russland und Europa* (*Rusko a Evropa*).

⁷ The artist's father died in 1921.

IV. *Maria and the Bull*

[1] Oskar Kokoschka: *Aus meiner Jugendbiographie*, 1933.

[2] Pierre Briquet: *Traité clinique et thérapeutique de l'Hystérie*, Paris.

[3] Oskar Kokoschka: *Kinderkrankheit*, 1947. The style of the *Jugenderinnerungen* is quite different. There is an ironic element in the *Kinderkrankheit*, a greater objectivity of expression whereas *Aus meiner Jugendbiographie* is imbued with the emotional, mythical experiences of early childhood.

V. *Parents*

[1] Skye is the largest of the Western Isles of Scotland. The Celts were in Austria before the Romans. Hallstadt f.i. is an old Celtic settlement. The Germans came afterwards. This leads one to England which has the same mixture of peoples. Slavs and Avars were later arrivals.

[2] Mánes also painted Kokoschka's grandfather, who moved in the cultural circle of Navrátil, Smetana, Mánes. The portraits are in the Prováznik collection in Jaroměř and were reproduced in the Journal *Uměni*, published by Štenc. The portrait of his grandfather is now in the National Gallery of Prague.

[3] The first contract with the Berlin art-dealer Paul Cassirer was signed in 1910. Cassirer was to receive one picture a year. The contract was renewed in 1916. In 1925 the most important contract with Cassirer was agreed, by which the dealer financed Kokoschka's extensive journeys. The only condition was that he should paint good pictures.

[4] Kokoschka's sister married the General Dr Emil Patočka. She died, a widow in Prague, in 1960 just as Kokoschka was about to open an exhibition in London entitled: *Oskar Kokoschka in England and Scotland*, November/December, 1960.

[5] Karl Kraus, founder and sole publisher of *Die Fackel* (*The Torch*), was a political, social and literary critic, whose aggressively ironic ideas appeared regularly in his paper. He was a creative innovator and reformer of the German language, a poet and the author of several important books, for instance: *Pro domo et mundo*; *Die chinesische Mauer*; *Die letzten Tage der Menschheit*; *Der Untergang der Welt durch schwarze Magie*; *Die Sprache*, etc.

Adolf Loos, Viennese architect, was one of the four great innovators in architecture, with Perret, Wright and Behrens. Author of the books: *Ins Leere gesprochen*, 1897–1930, (*A Voice in the Wilderness*) and *Trotzdem*, 1900–30, (*Nevertheless*). He it was who discovered and encouraged Kokoschka in his artistic career.

Peter Altenberg (Richard Engländer), one of the most remarkable of the Viennese 'Bohemians', and a friend of Adolf Loos and Karl Kraus. Master of the aphorism, satirist and lover, whose home was in the Hotel Graben, he was also a permanent guest at the café Herrenhof. Author of: *Was der Tag mir zuträgt* (What the day brings); *Wie ich es sehe* (How I see it); *Prodromos*; *Neues-Altes* (*Old-New*); etc.

Felix Albrecht Harta, Viennese painter, who admired Kokoschka.

[6] From: *The Story of Our Daughter Virginia*, in *A Sea Ringed with Visions*, Oskar Kokoschka.

[7] The letter is dated 25/3/1936, Hotel Juliš, Prague.

[8] Dated: 12/9/1939, Cliff End Cottage, Polperro, Looe, Cornwall.

[9] Alluding to the exhibitions in Basel, Zürich and Amsterdam in 1947 and the exhibitions in America 1948/49.

[10] Kokoschka's mother died in 1934, his father in 1924.

[11] After the Second World War Kokoschka was honoured by his hometown Vienna with the Freedom of the City.

[12] The Communist régime of China saw its greatest enemy in the tradition of ancestor-worship and therefore has done its best to destroy it.

[13] Recorded by Dr Eugenie Schwarzwald in: *Wenn Kokoschka spricht* (*Kokoschka speaks*).

[14] Berta Patočková-Kokoschka: *Mein Lied* (*My Song*).

[15] Oskar Kokoschka: *Ich bin ein Seher* (*I am a Seer*).

VI. *The Foothills of Art*

[1] He took his school-leaving examination in 1904 at the *Realschule* (Technical High School) in Vienna, 18th district.

[2] Communicated by Dr Eugenie Schwarzwald.

[3] Josef Frank speaks of this period as the decline of arts and crafts in Vienna—'One can really scarcely call it art'. In a letter to the author of 7 September 1947.

[4] Berta Zuckerkandl-Szeps' memories of Gustav Klimt.

[5] *Ibid.*

[6] Kokoschka's teachers at the School of Arts and Crafts were: Anton R. von Kenner, Carl Otto Czeschka and between 1907 and 1909 Berthold Löffler.

[7] *Die träumenden Knaben* (*Dreaming Youths*), written in 1907 and published in 1908 by the *Wiener Werkstätten*. See Literary Sources, Chapter VI.

[8] Professor Josef Frank writes: 'I remember that Kokoschka was once a witness in court and when asked what his profession was, replied: painter, sculptor, actor, dancer and so on. He had indeed done all those things in the cabaret.' Letter dated 7 September 1947.

[9] Anton Romako, 1834–89, pupil of Kaulbach, was a famous portraitist, history, landscape and animal painter. He lived in Rome from 1857 to 1874 and when he returned to Vienna competed against Makart without success. He committed suicide.

[10] Franz Anton Maulbertsch (Marpertsch), 1724–96, painted innumerable ceilings in Austria, Hungary and Bohemian churches, castles and libraries. He developed and perfected the Austrian Baroque tradition. Kokoschka's tribute to his inspiration as a young man is contained in the preface to Klara Gara's book: *Franz Anton Maulbertsch*, written at Villeneuve in July 1960.

[11] Anton Faistauer *Neue Malerei in Österreich*. Reflections of a Painter.

[12] R. W. Emerson: *Plato, the Philosopher*. In *Representative Men*.

[13] Professor Josef Frank in his memoirs. Letter to the author of 7 September 1947.

[14] Clay model head of the dancer Grete Wiesenthal.

[15] Room 14 of the exhibition.

[16] Self-portrait—Warrior, painted clay bust. This head was rejected by the sculptors (especially Metzner) on the grounds that it was not plastic art. Kokoschka was asked to come and explain and he agreed that it was indeed not sculpture, but said that it presented sensations experienced under the skin. (Professor Josef Frank.)

[17] Kokoschka made another Self-portrait in 1908, a painted clay relief modelled on a portrait of Franz Liszt. It was acquired by Herwarth Walden for the *Sturm-Galerie* in Berlin in 1910.

[18] This appeared in 1908 with a title page and a vignette of a deer in moulded leather. Kokoschka also prepared fifteen coloured postcards in a style reminiscent of East European folk-art for the Vienna workshops, also eight designs for book-plates. Dr Hans Ankwicz-Kleehoven has described eight book-plates for: Frau Emma Bacher; Frau Mitzi and Dr Josef Binder; Lotte Franzos; Arthur Fürst; Robert Freund. *Austrian Yearbook*: *Ex Libris und Gebrauchsgraphik*.

[19] This small book was never printed; the illustrations are lost. It appeared in a new edition with twelve lithographs from 1913 under the title *Der gefesselte Kolumbus* and published by Fritz Gurlitt. For further editions and reprints, see Literary Sources Chap. VI.

[20] Dürer also said: 'The noblest sense of all is seeing.'

[21] The main theory of the Enlightenment was that ignorance and religious superstition were responsible for the cruelty and injustice of humanity.

[22] This name for Kokoschka intimates the 'female' side of the male, his 'anima'. See also: C. G. Jung: *Relations between the Ego and the Unconscious*. The liaison with the *anima* is psychologically of the same significance as the identification of the conscious with the unconscious. Kokoschka also speaks of *The Women in the Moon* (*Der Weisse Tiertöter*), instead of the more usual *Man in the Moon*. Perhaps it should be seen as the ideal, unattainable, unreal woman, although here there may be a deeper meaning in the sense of the 'mother-side' of life.

[23] Published in Oskar Kokoschka: *Dramen und Bilder* (*Plays and Pictures*).

[24] Oskar Kokoschka: *Hiob* (*Job*). See Literary Sources.

Hiob was produced: 1917 in the Albert Theatre, Dresden, with Kokoschka as producer and with two other dramas: *Mörder Hoffnung der Frauen* (*Murder Hope of Women*) and *Der brennende Dornbusch* (*The Burning Thornbush*). In 1919 by Max Reinhardt in the Kammerspiele of the *Deutsches Theater* in Berlin and in 1920 in the Neue Theater, Frankfurt am Main, together with *Mörder Hoffnung der Frauen*.

[25] The *coniunctio solis et lunae*, considered as the unification of opposing forces, was one of the mysteries of the alchemical art, *arcanum artis*. The marriage is a symbol of the oneness of man, superseding the division of the sexes and therefore only to be attained when the male and female principles are united. (C. G. Jung: *Psychology of the Transference*.)

[26] Now in the collection of the Musées Royaux des Beaux-Arts, Brussels.

[27] *Mörder Hoffnung der Frauen*, for printing history see Literary Sources, Chapter VI. Productions: First, 4 July 1909 in the Garden theatre of the *Kunstschau* in Vienna. During the First World War it was produced by the Dada theatre on 14 April 1917 together with *Sphinx und Strohmann* in Zürich. (Dada Galerie, Bahnhofstrasse, 19.) On 3 June 1917 it was produced in the Albert theatre Dresden and with *Hiob* and *Der brennende Dornbusch* in 1918. Käthe Richter and Ernst Deutsch played the chief parts, and Kokoschka produced. Heinrich Georg produced it in 1920 and 1921 in the Neue Theater, Frankfurt. Paul Hindemith set *Mörder Hoffnung der Frauen* to music and in this new musical form it appeared in 1921 in the Landestheater, Stuttgart and in 1922 in the State Opera House, Frankfurt.

[28] When Kokoschka led me through the great retrospective exhibition of his work mounted in the Tate Gallery, London, from 14 September to 11 November 1962, the aspect of his work on which he laid greatest stress was his conception of space.

[29] Kokoschka wrote down some of these memories of Reinhold in March 1935 in Prague and used it as a Life-Story for the preface to Ernest Rathenau's book *Kokoschka Handzeichnungen*. In writing these memories I have used a handwritten first draft of Kokoschka's manuscript for the description of Kew Gardens which was put at my disposal by his pupil Hilde Goldschmidt. The piece appears in unabridged form in my book *Bekenntnis zu Kokoschka*.

[30] Professor Josef Frank characterizes the first modern architecture of Central Europe: 'Of all the artists in this group Loos was certainly the most cultivated and with a settled philosophy of life. He was of course an aristocrat; the others always had a bad conscience about this and Kraus reacted to it like a pendulum. Kokoschka who belonged to the younger generation was able to free himself of it.' Letter to the author dated 7 September 1947 from Stockholm.

[31] Otto Kallir the art-dealer remembers the events which finally drove Kokoschka from Vienna to Paris. It happened through pressure from Loos and was not Kokoschka's wish at all. The cause was the slashing of a painting (*Children Playing*) in the Kokoschka exhibition being held at the time. (Letter dated 27 February 1963, New York.) It was on another occasion that the painter Sebastian Isepp went with Kokoschka to Paris.

[32] *In Memory of Adolf Loos*. A speech made in Vienna on 27 October 1933. Published in *Kokoschka Schriften*. Kokoschka also published a second memorial to Loos under the title

Ins Leere Gesprochen and in his recorded memories he speaks in detail of Loos. He also made possible the publication of the book *Der Architekt Adolf Loos* adding a sensitive and interesting preface.

33 Spring 1911. Kokoschka was represented by twenty-five paintings.

34 Comments from the press and his friends about Kokoschka's early days come from Ludwig Hevesy, Adolf Loos, Karl Kraus, Albert Ehrenstein, Else Lasker-Schüler. See Literary Sources: H. M. Wingler, *Oskar Kokoschka, ein Lebensbild in zeitgenössischen Dokumenten.*

35 Hermann Bahr: *Wien.*

36 Kraus recommended Altenberg to the S. Fischer Verlag, Berlin. The poet described it in his inimitable fashion in *Vita Ipsa* in 1918 and in the same work discussed the significance of Karl Kraus: 'If Karl Kraus had not been so upset, misunderstood and hurt when it happened, one would scarcely be able to credit the sincerity of his work.'

37 Alfred Polgar: *An den Rand geschrieben.*

38 Bruno Walter: *Theme and Variations.* See also Herta Singer: *Im Wiener Kaffeehaus.*

39 See also: Josef Hoffmann, *Die Anfänge Oskar Kokoschkas* in *Bekenntnis zu Kokoschka.*

40 Hermann Bahr: *Wien.*

41 When Kokoschka was forced to resign from his post as assistant in the School of Arts and Crafts he became for a short period (1912–13) the drawing master at the private school run by Dr Eugenie Schwarzwald. Kokoschka had met Hermann and Eugenie Schwarzwald through Loos in 1911. A former pupil of this establishment, Dr Hedwig Schleiffer, who now lives in the U.S.A., has described the new spirit of art which Kokoschka represented in this progressive school. *Kokoschka, Pioneer in Art Education.*

VII. *Nature Morte*

1 Callimachus.

2 This picture was dated 1909 by Paul Stefan, which is correct, although Paul Westheim dates it 1907, Edith Hoffmann 1907/8. There is no reason why this important work should not have been exhibited at the first and second *Kunstschau* if it were already in existence. Therefore all the evidence points to its having been finished after the Second *Kunstschau.*

3 F. Bodmer: *The Loom of Language.*

4 A. Tarski: *Der Wahrheitsbegriff in den formalistischen Sprachen.*

5 Marcus Fabius Quintilian: *De Institutione Oratoria.*

6 José Ortega y Gasset: *Le Dehumanización del Arte,* 1925.

7 Guillaume Apollinaire: *Les Peintres Cubistes,* Méditations Esthétiques.

8 Henri de Brémont: *La Poésie Pure.*

9 Henri Focillon: *Vie des Formes.*

10 The great exhibition of Old German art held in Schaffhausen in 1947 gave Kokoschka the opportunity to tell the world what the art and cultural traditions of Europe meant to him. His *Rückblick auf die Schaffhauser Ausstellung* appeared in *Atlantis.*

11 Kokoschka spoke at length on Kleist's *Amphitryon* after a performance of the play in the *Freier deutscher Kulturbund* in London. While still inspired by this performance Kokoschka wrote a letter to the producer which has since become famous and which was published in the FDKB news.

12 Peter Cheltschicky: *Das Netz des Glaubens.* In the Autumn of 1945 I sent Kokoschka the German edition of my essay, *J. A. Comenius and our Time,* and a study of Cheltschicky called *Die gewaltlose Gesellschaft.* He wrote to me from Ullapool on the 2nd October, 1945: 'The essay on Cheltschicky will become an historical document because, apart from us two, no one in England (and probably not more than a few people in the whole world) knows anything at all

of this prophet of the Dark Ages. I wish I could remove the beam from the eye of our times.'
[13] Gustave Flaubert: *Jules et Henri.*

VIII. *New Horizons*

[1] From J. P. Hodin: *Kokoschkas erste Schweizer Erinnerungen.*
A letter from the artist to the author runs: 'Winter 1908. First journey to Les Avants near Montreux with a commission from Adolf Loos to paint Bessie Loos. This journey also produced the winterlandscape *Vue sur la Dent du Midi*, the *Duchess* and *Count Montesquieu-Rohan* and *Verona*. In Spring 1929 when the hotels closed after the winter season I went to Munich (for the first time), where I painted Gustav Meyrinck and was rescued again by Loos (since I was stranded there) and sent back to Switzerland to paint the portrait of Auguste Forel in Sion. Please be sure to get these dates right because otherwise mistakes will arise.' In view of these dates the picture of Meyrinck must have been done before the portrait of Auguste Forel and all the works which were done in this first stay in Switzerland should be advanced in date by one year. The young artist did not remain long in Munich. The city did not have a great deal to offer and reminded him too much of Vienna. All the reactionary German painters were entrenched there. Gustav Meyrinck, who was at the height of his fame then, was friendly towards Loos's fledgling. But Kokoschka had only the slenderest means—he had to pawn his watch and even tried to escape from his *pension* by night by means of a rope from the window—and the young wanderer soon left Munich and turned for home.
[2] Heinrich Wölfflin: *Die Kunst Albrecht Dürers.*
[3] See J. P. Hodin, *Oskar Kokoschkas erste Schweizer Erinnerungen.*
[4] *Ibid.* Also: *The Story of our Daughter Virginia* in Oskar Kokoschka: *A Sea Ringed with Visions.*
[5] From J. P. Hodin: *Oskar Kokoschkas Schweizer Erinnerungen.* Auguste Forel, the scientist, wrote in his autobiography: 'In January 1910 the little-known, new-style painter came to me with the request that he be allowed to paint my portrait. I agreed on condition that I should not be constrained to buy the picture and that I could go on working at my desk while it was in progress. The young, modern artist watched me particularly from the side and behind but did not succeed in producing a likeness, only an expressive atmosphere. Actually when it was finished only one eye and the left (crippled) hand were clearly portrayed—according to the criticism of professionals. Herr Kokoschka also showed us some of his imaginative works which seemed to belong more to the realm of psychiatry than art as, in my opinion, do most of the Cubists, Impressionists, Anti-perspectivists, Anti-draftsmen, daubers and so on. I did not buy the portrait but Kokoschka reaped his reward! *Mundus vul decipi, ergo decipiatur.*'
[6] Kokoschka spent the time between the Spring of 1911 until the outbreak of war in Vienna, with the exception of a short journey with Alma Mahler to Italy in 1913. He was wounded and returned to Vienna in 1915 where he remained till Easter 1916. In 1924 Kokoschka returned to Vienna from Italy for some months when his father died. He spent another short period in Vienna between the journeys to Paris, Bordeaux, Biarritz and the French Riviera made in 1925. He also came back in the Spring of 1930. In 1931 when Kokoschka was already famous in Germany the socialist City Council of Vienna asked him to paint a view of the City. Before Easter 1932 Kokoschka left Vienna again to go to Paris, but he returned to his birthplace in the same year and remained there, with the exception of a short stay in Budapest till the middle of the year. Then followed the removal to Prague in the face of the growing menace of the *Anschluss.* It was only in 1949, after the years of his exile in England, that Kokoschka returned to the City of Vienna.
[7] Wilhelm Dilthey: *Weltanschauung und Analyse des Menschen seit der Renaissance und*

Reformation. Sigmund Freud: *Vorlesungen zur Einführung in die Psychoanalyse.* Alfred Adler: *Menschenkenntnis* (Individualpsychologie). C. G. Jung: *Wandlungen und Symbole der Libido.*

[8] Sigmund Freud: *Totem and Taboo.*

[9] Henri Bergson: *Creative Evolution.*

[10] Edmund Husserl: *Ideen zu einer reinen Phänomenologie und phänomenologischen Philosophie.*

[11] Hermann Cohen: *System der Philosophie.* Paul Natorp: *Philosophie, ihr Problem oder ihre Probleme.* Ernst Cassirer: *The Philosophy of Symbolic Forms.* Georg Simmel: *Soziologie.*

[12] Ferdinand Tönnies: *Gemeinschaft und Gesellschaft.* Oswald Spengler: *The Decline of the West.*

[13] Rudolf Eucken: *Die Lebensanschauung der grossen Denker.*

[14] Walther Rathenau: *Gesammelte Schriften.*

[15] Henri Bergson: *Creative Evolution.*

[16] Charles Pierre Péguy: *Note sur M. Bergson et la philosophie bergsonienne.*

[17] Emil Utitz: *Grundlegung der allgemeinen Kunstwissenschaft,* Katherine Gilbert and Helmut Kuhn: *A History of Esthetics.*

[18] Alois Riegl: *Gesammelte Aufsätze.*

[19] Max Dvořák: *Kunstgeschichte als Geistesgeschichte.*

[20] Wilhelm Worringer; *Abstraktion und Einfühlung (Abstraction and Empathy).*

[21] Kokoschka wrote in Autumn 1945: 'During my journey to Munich I conceived the idea of publishing with Herwarth Walden a progressive art-magazine for the *avant-garde* artists who were proscribed and derided. Thus *Der Sturm* became an international art-journal, whereas formerly it had been only a small pamphlet for which I had sent contributions already in 1908.'

[22] Kokoschka had sent reviews of circuses and variety-shows, as well as drawings of the circus, to *Der Sturm* from Vienna. His first acrobat and juggler drawings date from 1906/7.

[23] Nell Walden and Lothar Schreyer, *Der Sturm.* A Memorial to Herwarth Walden and the artists of the *Sturm*-circle.

[24] Albert Soergel: *Dichtung und Dichter der Zeit.*

[25] Oskar Kokoschka: *Menschenköpfe.*

[26] Kokoschka wrote this story with a few changes and during his stay in Switzerland in 1947 published it in the *Neue Zürcher Zeitung* of 2 July as *The Story of our Daughter Virginia.* It reappeared in *Oskar Kokoschka Schriften* and in the autobiographical work *A Sea Ringed with Visions.*

IX. *The Inner Image*

[1] Frau Alma Mahler, the daughter of the landscape painter Emil J. Schindler, wife of Gustav Mahler and after his death of Walter Gropius and Franz Werfel, describes the passionate relationship with Kokoschka in her autobiography, *And the Bridge is Love,* 1958. In a letter to the author (24 January 1956) she wrote: 'Frau Erica Tietze asked me whether I could contribute something about Kokoschka's methods of working, and I told her I would think about it. I shall try to write something about him from my heart, for I still regard him as one of the greatest artists.' Then on the 11 April 1956: 'I wrote earlier to you that I can still not write about Kokoschka. I have written it all down, but it is still too close for me to allow it to be published.'

[2] A water-colour (see ill. 19) and two charcoal sketches for this project have been preserved: *Entwurf zu einem Krematorium (Sketch plan for a crematorium), Architekturskizze für Stadtbaumeister Konrad Berg, Breslau*; and *Skizze des Querschnitts mit Freskoentwurf auf das Thema von Leben und Tod (Sketch of the transverse section with fresco design on the theme of life and death)* Both dated 1914. Compare E. Tietze-Conrat: *Ein Porträt und nachher* in J. P. Hodin: *Bekenntnis zu Kokoschka.*

[3] Kokoschka's first designs for frescoes were *The Dream Bearers,* 1908. The drawings com-

missioned by the city surveyor Berg for the crematorium in Breslau were later to have been used for a memorial to the art-historian Max Dvořák, which Kokoschka and Loos planned, but it came to nothing.

[4] Dr János Plesch: *The Story of a Doctor.*

[5] Oskar Kokoschka: *Rückblick auf die Schaffhauser Ausstellung.*

[6] In the first six years of his painting activity, that is to the beginning of the First World War, Kokoschka had painted seventy-five portraits including his Self-portraits. Between 1946 and 1956 he only painted twenty portraits. Later he continued to paint portraits but not so frequently as in his early career.

[7] Anton Faistauer: *Oskar Kokoschka*, in *Neue Malerei in Österreich.*

[8] Karl Kraus: *Sprüche und Widersprüche.*

[9] Quoted from: Alfred Polgar: *Peter Altenberg.*

[10] Oskar Kokoschka: *Variationen über ein Thema.* Italian ed. *Variazioni Su Un Tema.*

[11] Sir Edward describes his first meeting with Kokoschka in his autobiography, *Look back, look forward.*

[12] Professor J. D. Bernal, F.R.S.

[13] Professor Bernal did not in actual fact work on the atom bomb research, but on the highly-destructive material used for razing whole cities called *Blockbusters.*

[14] A letter from Dr W. R. Valentiner, at that time attached to the Los Angeles County Museum, explains: 'Kokoschka first intended to come to the States in 1927 and I had got the tickets for him and concluded all the formalities; then he let me down by not arriving on the steamer as planned. About six months later I received a postcard from him from Constantinople or Tunis making his apologies. After that it was not so easy to arrange for permission for him to come.' As the situation in Europe degenerated Kokoschka always held this plan to go to America in reserve. On 25.3.36 he wrote to Dr Valentiner from Prague: 'I was stupid not to have come to the States with you, for by now I would have been world-famous over there, whereas here in Europe the houses of cards collapse as soon as you build them. I recently painted Masaryk in Prague; it is an important composition (I studied him for a long time in person). I have done a couple of landscapes for local museums and now I am free again. Could one paint the President of the United States? I was invited by the Russians to go there, but I have heavy debts and a brother in Vienna and have to keep on sending money which is not allowed from Russia . . . so, my friend, if you come to fetch me in an aeroplane, this time, I shall certainly be there.'

Kokoschka was invited to go to the Mille College in California about that time but it proved impossible to get an entrance permit for him. The artist was very bitter. In March 1940 he wrote to me in Stockholm, from Polperro: 'Even if it were allowed I would not be very keen to go to America, I am not tough enough to push my way forward. I cannot begin again from the beginning after thirty years of hard work, so if it is my destiny to fall then I shall do so with resignation. I do not belong to those artists who carelessly change sides wearing the colours of their chosen patrons in turn. You see art is one thing and social life another. If there is no worthy person in the world who will lend an ear, quite apart from social considerations, then the laurels will remain for my post-mortem, for reasonable reward seems to be reserved only for those who handle my work commercially (not excluding the Third Reich).'

A letter written to Dr Valentiner on the 5 April 1941 has a bitter note: 'I must admit that I find it difficult to understand the bureaucratic methods of some American officials, for they are often the cause of martyrdom and even the death of those who are subject to the sadistic-religious mania which has spread from Germany and is unconsciously supported in neutral countries by officialdom. I understand the reasons for immigration control, but the small difficulties, caused perhaps to neighbouring countries, would be as nothing compared with what the refugees could expect at home . . . I was only a persecuted artist, an unwanted immigrant, even though the university of Chicago had invited me to come and teach . . . not only as the greatest artist of the time, but also as a man who wanted to initiate American youth into the mystery of true art. If I die during the war it will be thanks to the red handkerchief of Mr . . .'

Kokoschka came to America for the first time in 1949 in connexion with the exhibitions of his work: Institute of Contemporary Art, Boston, 16 October to 14 November; Phillips Memorial Gallery, Washington, 5 December to 17 January 1949; City Art Museum, St Louis, 21 February till 21 March 1949; Mr H. de Young Memorial Museum, San Francisco, 10 April to 15 May 1949; Society of the Fine Art Galleries, Wilmington (Del), 6 June to 3 July 1949; Museum of Modern Art, New York, 19 July to 4 October 1949; Feigl Gallery, New York, 9 February to 5 March 1949 (14 new water-colours). In January 1949 Kokoschka paid a visit to the Director of the Boston Institute, James Plaut, who had arranged the exhibitions. The artist gave a lecture to the students in the Boston Institute. The success of this first lecture was such that the Director of the Boston Museum of Fine Arts invited the artist to return in the summer of the same year as a 'visiting artist', and to give lectures at the Summer School held in Pittsfield (Mass.). Kokoschka travelled from Boston to New York (1–13 September) and on to Minneapolis at the invitation of the Director of the Minneapolis Museum, Richard S. Davis, where he stayed from November till Christmas. There he painted the Double Portrait of Mr and Mrs John Cowles. In 1952 he returned to Minneapolis once more on the invitation of Richard S. Davis and again in 1957 when he stayed from mid-October till the end of January. He painted five pictures in that city: apart from the Cowles Double Portrait, a portrait of Pete Gale (1952) and one of her husband Richard P. Gale (1957); the portrait of Putnam Dana Macmillan (1957) and a painting of the three children Richard, Margery and John Davis. Kokoschka also gave lectures in 1952 at the Minneapolis School of Art.

[15] Kokoschka wrote to me during the war explaining that he planned to put a stamp on the back of his paintings with the words: 'This name has never yet been misused.' He was very troubled about the appearance of faked 'Kokoschkas' which were being sold in Czechoslovakia and Hungary and brought over to America by refugees as their sole precious possession. Since then many fakes have been discovered and not only from those two countries.

[16] Oskar Kokoschka: *Rückblick auf die Schaffhauser Ausstellung* (*Reflections on the Schaffhauser Exhibition*).

[17] Oskar Kokoschka: *The Portrait in the Past and Present.*

x. *The Torment of the Heart*

[1] *Sphinx und Strohmann*. A one-act curiosity, 1907. *Mörder Hoffnung der Frauen*, 1908. *Schauspiel* or *Der brennende Dornbusch*, 1911. *Allos Makar*, poem. 1913. *Der gefesselte Kolumbus* and *Orpheus und Eurydike*, dramas, 1915/1918. *Hiob*, an enlarged and illustrated edition of *Sphinx und Strohmann*, 1917.

[2] See also: Memories of Kokoschka in Alma Mahler: *And the Bridge is Love.*

[3] Arthur Rimbaud: *Le bâteau ivre.*

[4] See Georg Schmidt: *Zu Kokoschkas Windsbraut* in J. P. Hodin: *Bekenntnis zu Kokoschka.*

[5] *Allos Makar*, in *Zeit-Echo*, a wartime diary of the artists.

[6] 'O Ewigkeit, du Donnerwort — so spanne meine Glieder aus.' Words of the cantata by J. S. Bach. Eleven lithographs by Oskar Kokoschka and the poem *Zueignung* (*Dedication*).

[7] J. E. Cirlot: *A dictionary of symbols, Diccionario de Simbolos tradicionales*. C. A. S. Williams: *Psychology of Chinese Symbolism and Art Motives*. Bernard Leach: *Drachen-Träume-Leben* (*Dragons, Dreams, Life*) in J. P. Hodin, *Bekenntnis zu Kokoschka.*

[8] The same attitude towards the Man-Woman-Death relationship is expressed in Kokoschka's illustrations to Karl Kraus's book *Die Chinesische Mauer.*

⁹ Dürer's engraving *Ritter, Tod und Teufel* took up once again the idea of the Christian knight (the *eques christianus* of Erasmus), an ancient mystical conception—c.f. King Arthur and the Round Table—which had often appeared in popular woodcuts. Life for the christian was service in the army of God. Fighting for his beliefs he feared neither death nor the devil. Kokoschka comes nearer to the early mystical approach than to that of Dürer and Erasmus. He handled this theme twice: *Knight, Death and the Angel I*, about 1909; *Knight, Death and the Angel II*, 1910. H. M. Wingler sees it as his first religious composition dedicated to his mother 'because he had refused a very advantageous position for the sake of his creative freedom'. But it is not a religious theme in the sense that *Flight into Egypt* (1911) is religious, and is described as the first religious picture by Bohuslav, the artist's brother. Nor in the sense of *Crucifixion* (1911), *Veronika with the Sudarium* (*c.* 1911); *the Annunciation* (1911); *the Visitation* (1911). Kokoschka never touched on the theme of Christianity again. The Crucifix appears in the left background of the *Prometheus* triptych, but only as a symbol. Themes from the Old Testament however still appear later on. A series of lithographs with the Passion as its theme was published in Cassirer's journal *Der Bildermann* in Berlin in 1916. *Der Bildermann* was published in only eighteen numbers with a supplement *Lieder des Bildermann* (*Songs of Bildermann*). The journal had a secondary title *Stone-drawings for the German people*. It was published by Leo Kestenberg. In the seventh issue Kokoschka's *Christ on the Mount of Olives* appeared with the title *Annunciation*; in the ninth issue *Christ crowned with Thorns*; number twelve *The Crucifixion*; number fourteen *The Resurrection*; in number sixteen *The Kiss of Judas* (*Gethsemane*); number seventeen *The Last Supper*; number eighteen *Rest on the Flight into Egypt*, with portraits of Käthe Richter and Dr Fritz Neuberger.

¹⁰ *Knight Errant, 1915*. Kokoschka described his wartime wounds in an autobiographical sketch of 1934 in Prague. In the chapter called *Jessica* of his book *A Sea Ringed with Visions* all his experiences in the war including the wounding are described, with some differences. Also on the gramophone record *Oskar Kokoschka erzählt aus seinem Leben*.

In the present work Kokoschka's war experiences are reproduced in the chapter *Knight, Death and the Angel* from the artist's own words told to the author during the Second World War (that is more than ten years before the final version by Kokoschka), and written down as he spoke. The spontaneity of this version will perhaps justify its inclusion. It must, however, be said that the artist often altered and reshaped published episodes from his life.

¹¹ *The Fountain*. (Jacob, Rachel and Leah.) Both the female figures are portraits in Kokoschka's picture, as also in the painting *Lot and his Daughters* and *Painter and his Model I* (1922/23). The theme of man between two women, common enough in life and literature, is here approached and fashioned anew. In the second version of *Painter and his Model II* (1924), which is less flat in colour, less like a tapestry, and much more strongly expressionist and reminiscent of negro art, one figure is replaced by the self-portrait for a poster which Kokoschka had done for his lecture in Vienna *On the Nature of Visions*. (*Akademischer Verband für Literatur und Musik, 26 Januar, 1912*, in the *Ingenieur- und Architekturverein, Wien I., Eschenbachgasse* 9). His 'wounded' condition of both before and after the war is expressed and the finger, which in the poster points to the symbolic wound in his chest, is replaced in the painting of 1924 by the artist's outstretched arm, signifying his attempt to defy the evil of the world through art.

The version of the picture done in 1932, like the one of 1922/23 which is only preserved in photographs, shows the same female figures with the left-hand seated figure clothed, the central figure, formerly clothed, is now naked and appearing more in the guise of Woman than any particular woman, a process, however, which had only got halfway, for the face remains individual. The face of the artist is reduced to a large size head nearer the version of *Painter and his Model II*, in other words, more primitive, more universal—Man. In the last version both female figures are nude, the one on the left seated in profile, the central figure composed as a diagonal.

Both have the features of his future wife. The painter in the right side of the composition, resting his hand on the central figure's knee, has his right arm outstretched with the hand close to the face of the figure on the left. The central figure has an aura behind and appears stiff as a sphinx both in face and body. This motif is related to the life-sized doll (Chapter X) which also reappears in the story *Ann Eliza Read*. The idea of *Nymph and Faun* might have been the origin of this motif. The figure on the left smiles. The movements of her hands and those of the central figure are erotically symbolic. All three figures are placed on a luxuriant background of plants, on the left a house and copulation scene, a dog between the two heads to the right, in the foreground a reptile and a goose which is sliding away between the legs of the left-hand figure. We are in the kingdom of the animals. The goose was a symbol of care and watchfulness to the Romans.

[12] Letters of Minona McEwen written in 1947/48, in the possession of the author.

[13] Oskar Kokoschka: *Dreaming Youths*.

[14] These events are recapitulated in a slightly different form in the chapter called *Easter on Cypress* in Kokoschka's book *A Sea Ringed with Visions*. The same remarks are relevant here as for note 10, as the story is here based on personal reminiscences communicated to the author about ten years before the artist published them.

[15] Kokoschka wrote to me about this contract: 'Paul Cassirer saw my work in Berlin and offered me a very considerable retainer for a beginner, with the proviso that I should paint no specific number of compositions, not even one if I did not feel like painting, but that whatever I should send him must not fall below the quality of the work he had already seen. It was the most unusual contract ever made in the art-trade.'

[16] I saw the photograph of this lady on the mantelpiece in Kokoschka's studio in the house he had built near Montreaux on the Lake of Geneva. It was the Goddess.

[17] This graphological examination was undertaken in London at my suggestion by a pupil of Jung, the graphologist, H. J. Jacoby.

[18] Henri Focillon: *Rembrandt*.

[19] Catalogue of the largest exhibition of his graphic work, the great retrospective exhibition held from May to July 1958 in the Vienna *Künstlerhaus*, section *Water-colours and Drawings* and *Graphic Works and Reprints from the Kokoschka-Archives* (Wolfgang Gurlitt), 517 entries. Although the most important works, and especially of the early period, were exhibited here, they by no means cover the whole graphic work of the artist. The number of drawings alone must be more than a thousand today.

The First *Internationale* of Drawing held in Darmstadt in 1964 was devoted to a special exhibition of Oskar Kokoschka. (Catalogue, pp. 270–311) with two commentaries by Carl Georg Heise and an introduction by H. M. Wingler. Fifty-seven catalogue entries. Another very important catalogue is the one to the exhibition: *Oskar Kokoschka*: Illustrations, Folios, Posters, Graphic contributions to Journals and Books. Poems, Dramas, Portraits and Theatre-sets. Pupils' work from the *School of Seeing*, Salzburg. Museum für Kunst und Gewerbe, Hamburg (29 April–20 June 1965).

The first list of graphic works is incomplete and partly incorrect in the catalogue: Oskar Kokoschka: *Aus seinem Schaffen* (1907–55). Wilhelm F. Arutz: *Das graphische Werk Kokoschkas*, 1908–49. It contains 163 entries.

Ernest Rathenau's work *Der Zeichner Kokoschka* (*Kokoschka the Draftsman*), with a preface by Paul Westheim, has 146 drawings. An earlier book by Ernest Rathenau includes 120 collotypes of examples differing from those in the later volume. This early book by Rathenau was at first provided with a preface by Westheim and a vigorous autobiography by Kokoschka himself, but Westheim had to leave before the war and the book was confiscated by the Nazis and destroyed with all the originals. Only very few examples were saved. A third volume is at present in preparation by Ernest Rathenau.

The book by Professor Michelangelo Masciotta, *Disegni di Kokoschka* was also confiscated by the Fascists. It contained thirty-four illustrations.

In the year 1954 a small book appeared called *Künstler und Poeten* (*Artists and Poets*)— portrait drawings by Oskar Kokoschka. It was published with an introduction by Hans Maria Wingler. Another little book of interest in this connexion is: *Oskar Kokoschka, Lithographien*. An introduction and discussion with the artist by Remigius Netzer.

[20] Ernest Rathenau: *Ein Kokoschka Buch*. cf. note 19.

[21] Oskar Kokoschka: *Olda*, with a foreword by Werner Hofmann.

XI. *Knight, Death and the Angel*

[1] A Kokoschka postcard also appears in *Der Sturm* Berlin as number 9 in the series *Sturm-künstler* (*Sturm-artists*).

[2] The singer later made a record of this melody for Kokoschka so that he could listen to it whenever he wanted to. See also *Letters from a Traveller in an Imaginary World*. Second letter from the Traveller, Dresden, Spring 1919.

[3] Countess Alexandrine Mensdorff-Dietrichstein. On his journey back from the Eastern front Kokoschka, a wounded soldier, spent some time in the Brünner military hospital.

[4] *Orpheus and Eurydice* appeared between 1915 and 1918. In 1923 Ernst Křenek set the piece to music. In 1956 the following sets were made to accompany a production of the drama. In coloured chalk: *Return of Orpheus, Furies in the Bedchamber, Orpheus sees Eurydice again in Hades, Orpheus and Eurydice return from Hades, Night on the Boat, Spirit of Eurydice in the Glow of the Fire, Morning Dream*.

[5] This event is described in the biographical tale *On the Nature of Visions* in the journal *Genius*, published in Munich, 1919.

[6] Oskar Kokoschka: *Der Fetisch* published in *Künstlerbekenntnisse* (*Confessions of an Artist*). Collected and published by Paul Westheim. Paul Westheim speaks naïvely of 'the child, the player in the artist' although it is in fact a question of a psycho-pathological nature. Kokoschka wanted more than a work of art. A woman of the Far East could perhaps have created this synthesis of a living presence and a stuffed model, after years of devoted work. He did not want to see any stitching so that he should not be unhappy when he remembered that the fetish was nothing but a sack of stuffing. And his words sound desperate: 'Do you not see that my life is passing in agony, while you are permitting the vicious, real things, cotton wool, stuff, thread, chiffon or whatever the horrible paraphernalia are called, to obtrude in all their worldly significance, while I see a being before my eyes that is two-faced, a dead and living spirit.'

[7] Kokoschka made 160 drawings for this picture most of which he destroyed. There is also an unfinished painting of the standing doll in a private collection in London.

[8] Alma Mahler-Werfel: *And the Bridge is Love*.

[9] These six fans were done between 1912 and 1914; the order is not known as only one, the large one with the battle-scene, is dated 1914. Water-colour on swan's parchment.

[10] On an original print by Arrhenius, Kokoschka wrote the following words: 'He is also a star-gazer and used to have a very pretty servant girl in those days. O.K.' On a print of Selma Lagerlöf are the words: 'She gave me an apple in Falun. O.K.'

[11] See also *A Sea Ringed with Visions*, First letter from my journey to Stockholm, Winter 1917.

[12] Ida Bienert, *Kleine Erinnerungen* in J. P. Hodin, *Bekenntnis zu Kokoschka*.

[13] F. K. Gotsch, *Kokoschka als Lehrer*, in J. P. Hodin, *Bekenntnis zu Kokoschka*.

[14] Published in *Weserkurier*, 7.2.1948. Reprinted in *Kokoschka Schriften*.

[15] Kokoschka painted Dr Wallerstein's portrait. It is one of the artist's finest water-colours.

He inscribed it as follows: 'Dresden, 14.11.23, to my dear friend Wallerstein. After a few days effort it came all by itself. I just painted it. O. Kokoschka.'

[16] These extracts are taken from the descriptions by Gitta Wallerstein (later Perl) who sent them to the author in 1948 from New York.

[17] See also: *A Sea Ringed with Visions*, Third letter from the Traveller, Dresden 1920.

[18] See also: *A Sea Ringed with Visions*, Second letter from the Traveller, Dresden, Spring 1919.

[19] Felix Emmel: *Das ekstatische Theater*.

[20] Successful production of *Sphinx und Strohmann* (14 April 1917) in the Dada-Galerie, Zürich by Hugo Ball, who played Firdusi, reviewed in his memoirs *Die Flucht aus der Zeit* (*Flight from our Times*), caused great interest in the drama. See also the foreword to *A Prelude to the Absurd* by Walter H. Sokel and the foreword by Karl Kerenyi to *Orpheus and Eurydike*.

[21] *Schrei und Bekenntnis* (*Cry and Confession*). Expressionist Theatre.

[22] Ludwig Rubiner, overture to *Die Gewaltlosen* (*The Helpless*), in the series *Der dramatische Wille* (*The dramatic Urge*).

[23] *Ahnung und Aufbruch* (*Apprehension and Uprising*). Expressionist Prose. *Von den Wegbereitern bis zum Dada*. (From the Pioneers to Dada). *Menscheitsdämmerung* (*Twilight of Mankind*).

[24] Albert Ehrenstein *Menschen und Affen* (*Men and Apes*).

[25] *Expressionismus, Literatur und Kunst*, 1910–23. An exhibition of the German Literary Archive in the Schiller National Museum, Marbach a. N. Catalogue published by Bernhard Zeller.

[26] See also: Walter H. Sokel, *A Prelude to the Absurd*.

[27] It was only after the Second World War and his journey to the United States that Kokoschka's world fame was assured. During these years Germany has done honour to Kokoschka as one of the greatest masters, and England followed later on.

[28] Kokoschka signed his first contract with Paul Cassirer in Berlin in 1910. According to it Cassirer received a painting every year. This contract was renewed in 1916. A third contract was drawn up in 1924/25. The news was brought to the artist by Professor Leo Kestenberg, who described it to the author: 'I remember the time when I came to tell him the news—in the *Sturm* building of Walden situated in the Potsdamer Strasse in Berlin, where he occupied a very small room—that Paul Cassirer had agreed to a yearly guaranteed salary of 30,000 marks, and how he received the news, half-unbelieving, half-ironical.' It was a very favourable contract which endowed the wide travels. In 1926 Paul Cassirer committed suicide and the business was taken over by Dr Walter Feilchenfeldt and Dr Grete Ring.

[29] See also: Georg Schmidt: *Zu Kokoschkas Windsbraut*, in J. P. Hodin: *Bekenntnis zu Kokoschka*. The political idea was also explained by Kokoschka in his retrospective essay, *Die Macht der Musik* written for the Journal of the Dutch Museums in 1955.

[30] A letter from Kokoschka to Minona McEwen runs: I had no musical education because there was never any money to spare at home when I was a boy. Nonetheless I learned to love music as much as if I had been trained although even now I cannot play any musical instrument.

[31] Leo Kestenberg: *Bewegte Zeiten, Musisch-musikantische Lebenserinnerungen*. See also: Leo Kestenberg: *Was mir Kokoschka bedeutet* in J. P. Hodin: *Bekenntnis zu Kokoschka*.

[32] *Oskar Kokoschka erzählt aus seinem Leben*. A self-portrait on a record.

XII. *Orbis Pictus*

[1] Oskar Kokoschka: *A Sea Ringed with Visions*.

[2] Thomas Mann on Kokoschka in *Der Wiener Kunstwanderer*.

[3] Denis Diderot: *L'essai sur la Peinture*.

[4] Kokoschka's first landscape—*The Hungarian Landscape*—was painted in 1908 on the estate

of Pudmaritz not far from Vienna, Slovakia today. It was the property of the patron of art Ernst von Lieben, a brother of Countess Henriette von Motesiczky, and a friend of Adolf Loos, who had built his house, and of Peter Altenberg and others.

[5] Taken from the unpublished *Memories of a Journey* by Dr J. H. F. Lütjens written at the request of the author in 1963. They contain the only authentic material on Kokoschka's journeys.

[6] Max Dvořák: *Über Greco und den Manierismus*, in *Kunstgeschichte als Geistesgeschichte*.

[7] Letter dated 4 September 1947 from New York, to the author.

[8] Letter dated 30 December 1947 from Tel Aviv, to the author. See also: Leo Kestenberg: *Was mir Kokoschka bedeutet* in J. P. Hodin: *Bekenntnis zu Kokoschka*.

[9] Dr Eugenie Schwarzwald: *Der Redner Kokoschka* (Kokoschka Speaks). Preface to the catalogue of the exhibition in Mannheim 1931.

[10] See also: Kurt Juhn, *Erlebnis mit einem Gesalbten*, Oskar Kokoschka erzählt, Zeit im Bild, Prague, January 1935.

[11] See also: Oskar Kokoschka: *Bemerkungen zum Kunstunterricht* (*Notes on Teaching Art*). Neue Zürcher Zeitung, 8 August 1953. Reprinted in H. M. Wingler, *Oskar Kokoschka*, and in the foreword to the catalogue of the exhibition held in the *Haus der Kunst*, Munich and in the *Künstlerhaus*, Vienna (both 1958).

[12] Tape recording by a student: Kokoschka's farewell speech to his students, given on the 11 August 1961 at the close of the Summer course.

[13] Goethe: *Dämon in Urworte, Orphisch*, 1817.

[14] See Lit Sources. Reprinted in H. M. Wingler, *Oskar Kokoschka Schriften*.

XIII. *The Labyrinth of the World*

[1] Hans Tietze: *Abriss einer Österreichischen Kunstgeschichte* (*A Summary of History of Art in Austria*). Preface by Kokoschka.

[2] Letter from New York, dated 4 September 1947.

[3] This painting is based, so far as the central group of mother and child is concerned, on one of the last done in Vienna before the departure for Prague—*Mutter und Kind* (*Im Garten*), *1934*. The face of Kokoschka can be seen on the right and in the left background the figure of a woman.

[4] The following document explains what is to be done with the money paid for this picture: 'Fursecroft, George St., London, W.1, 24 October 1944. I hereby authorize Dr Hugo Feigl, Owner of the Feigl Gallery, 601 Madison Avenue, New York, 22 N.Y., to pay the sum of $4,000 (£1,000), which Mr Oskar Kokoschka is expecting from the sale of his picture, *The Philosopher T. G. Masaryk*, to the Czechoslovakian consul in New York, so that it may be used in accordance with my wishes.

I will be personally responsible for this amount and will use it for a refugee organization which will be set up in the U.S.A. and which shall be known as "The Oskar Kokoschka Fund for War Orphans of all nationalities in Czechoslovakia." The organization will be run on the lines laid down by the Czech humanist J. A. Komenský. Signed Jan Masaryk.' (Quoted from a letter written by Dr Hugo Feigl from New York, 4 September 1947) See also: J. P. Hodin: *Kokoschka's Reminiscences of Masaryk*.

[5] In the first version it was *Orbis Pictus*. In the final version a small figure of death was added on the lower part of the book.

[6] The London addresses where Kokoschka stayed are listed in note 19 of Chapter II.

[7] In 1943 Kokoschka was president of the Free German League of Culture and in this capacity he tried to spread the idea among refugees and English people that German cultural values had nothing to do with contemporary political events. Important speeches were: *A*

great Task, given on the occasion of the opening of the theatre of the Free German League. Published in *Freie deutsche Kultur*, December/January 1943, London; *The Fifth Anniversary of the Free German League of Culture* held in the Bonnington Hotel, 19 December 1943; *Zum Amphitryon* an open letter on Kleist's immortal work, published in the FDKB *Nachrichten* (Free German League News Circular), London, May 1944; *Free German Artists*, foreword to a catalogue of an exhibition held at the Charlotte Street Centre, London, June 1944.

[8] *Freie Deutsche Kultur*, London. No. 2, February 1942.

[9] Foreword to Hans Tietze: *Abriss einer Österreichischen Kunstgeschichte*, London, Junges Österreich, 1945.

[10] Foreword to the catalogue *Free German Artists*, London, June 1944.

[11] Oskar Kokoschka: *Comenius, the English Revolution and our Present Plight*, in an anthology: *The Teacher of Nations*, Cambridge, 1942.

[12] Foreword to the catalogue: *The War as seen by Children*, London, January 1943.

[13] François Mauriac, *Le Jeune Homme*.

[14] Jacques Maritain: *The Dream of Descartes*.

[15] Catalogue to the exhibition held in the Kunsthalle Basel, 22 March–27 April 1947, 260 entries.

[16] Catalogue to the exhibition held in the Kunsthaus Zürich, 4 July–31 August 1947, 184 entries. Catalogue: *Oskar Kokoschka in het Stedelijk Museum, Amsterdam*, November–December 1947, 107 entries.

[17] The great exhibitions held in Vienna and Munich ten years later, and the ones which followed in Hamburg and London saw him at the height of his fame.

Catalogue: *Oskar Kokoschka, Haus der Kunst, München* 14 March–11 May 1958, 431 entries.

Catalogue: *Oskar Kokoschka, Künstlerhaus Wien*, 19 May–13 July 1958, 682 entries, the most comprehensive exhibition of his works ever held. (1–164 oil-paintings; 165–413 water-colours and drawings; 414–682 graphic work and book illustrations).

Catalogue: *Kokoschka, A retrospective Exhibition of Paintings, Drawings, Lithographs, Stage-designs and Books*, organized by the Arts Council of Great Britain. The Tate Gallery, London, 14 September–11 November 1962. 291 entries.

Catalogue: *Oskar Kokoschka, Ausstellung Kunstverein Hamburg*, 8 December–27 January 1963, 76 entries.

Catalogue: *Oskar Kokoschka*, Museum für Kunst und Gewerbe, Hamburg, 29 April–20 June 1965. Illustrations, Folios, Posters, Graphic contributions to journals and books, poems, plays, portraits and stage-designs, sculpture and wall-paintings. The new graphic series, Pupils' work from the *School of Seeing* in Salzburg, 348 entries.

[18] Oskar Kokoschka: *Zu einer Ausstellung*. Freie deutsche Kultur, London, May–June 1944.

[19] Sigmund Freud: *Civilization and its Discontents*.

[20] Ludwig Klages: *Grundlegung der Wissenschaft vom Ausdruck* (*Fundamentals of the Science of Expression*).

[21] See also Herbert Read: *Education Through Art*.

[22] Hans Prinzhorn: *Bildnerei der Geisteskranken* (*The Creative Activity of the Mentally Deranged*).

[23] José Ortega y Gasset, *La Dehumanizácion del Arte*—Abbé Henri Brémont, *La Poésie pure avec un débat sur la poésie pure*. André Malraux: *Psychologie de l'Art* (*The Psychology of Art*).

[24] Wilhelm Worringer: *Abstraction and Empathy*.

[25] C. G. Jung: *Psychologische Typen* (*Psychological Types*).

[26] F. Kretschmer: *Körperbau und Charakter* (*Physique and Character*).

[27] C. G. Jung: *Psychological Types*.

[28] J. P. Hodin, *Edvard Munch, der Genius des Nordens*. J. P. Hodin, *Oskar Kokoschka, Die Krise der Kunst und der Expressionismus*.

²⁹ C. G. Jung: *Seelenprobleme der Gegenwart* (*Modern Man in Search of a Soul*).

³⁰ Max Dvořák: *Kunstgeschichte als Geistegeschichte* (*The History of Art as the History of the Spirit*).

³¹ Alois Riegl: *Die Entstehung der Barockkunst in Rom* (*The Origin of Baroque Art in Rome*).

³² Foreword to the catalogue: *The War as Seen by Children*, London 1943.

xiv. *Self-Portrait*

¹ See also: Chapters III and IV.

² Reference to the figure of the rider in the fresco *Triumph of Death* in Pisa.

³ The skeleton in the cupboard. Jung also uses this metaphor to describe the profusion of primitive and unconscious influences on the mind. Kokoschka applies it here to the greatest superstition of our times—rationalism.

⁴ Philosopher and Politician, Jeremy Bentham (1748–1832), the founder of Utilitarianism, preached the theory of the greatest good to the greatest number: 'The greatest happiness of the greatest number is the foundation of morals and legislation.' (*The Commonplace Book*.)

⁵ It was Peter Kropotkin who called the attention of society to the fight against Darwin's theory.

⁶ Not all the artist's Self-portraits are discussed here, but only those which are essential to the development of the idea advanced in this chapter. The first Self-portraits, a painted plaster relief and a painted clay bust—*Warrior* (1908)—were exhibited at the first *Kunstschau*.

⁷ *The Works of* Jakob Böhme.

⁸ The Benediction of Jacob, which Thomas Mann applied to Kokoschka. See: *Der Wiener Kunstwanderer*, November 1933.

⁹ A coloured lithograph of 1956 displays the same spiritual attitude.

¹⁰ Dr Adrian Wettach (Grock): *Nicht mö-ö-öglich*, in *Artisten, Ernstes und heiteres Variété*, by Fred A. Colman and Walter Trier.

LITERARY SOURCES

CHAPTER I

HANS PLATSCHEK: *Oskar Kokoschka*, Editorial Poseidon, Buenos Aires, 1946.

EDITH HOFFMANN: *Kokoschka, Life and Work*, Faber & Faber, London, 1947.

MICHELANGELO MASCIOTTA: *Kokoschka*, Del Turco Editore, Florenz, 1949.

HANS MARIA WINGLER: *Oskar Kokoschka. The Work of the Painter* (trans. Frank S. C. Budgen), Galerie Welz, Salzburg, Faber & Faber, London, 1958.

J. P. HODIN: *Bekenntnis zu Kokoschka*, Florian Kupferberg Verlag, Mainz and Berlin, 1963.

ST FRANCIS OF ASSISI: *The Little Flowers of St Francis* (trans. Thomas Okey), Everyman's Library, Dent, London, 1963.

C. G. JUNG: *The Practice of Psychotherapy. Essays on the Psychology of the Transference and Other Subjects* (trans. by R. F. C. Hull), Routledge & Kegan Paul, New York, 1953. (Collected Works—Vol. 16, edited by Herbert Read, Michael Fordham, Gerhard Adler.)

L. LEVY-BRUHL: *How Natives Think* (trans. Lilian A. Clare), London, G. Allen & Unwin, 1926.

CHAPTER II

HEINRICH WÖLFFLIN: *Die Kunst Albrecht Dürers*, Verlagsanstalt F. Bruckmann, Munich, 1926.

ERWIN PANOFSKY: *The Life and Art of Albrecht Dürer*, Princeton University Press, Princeton, New Jersey, 1955.

E. PANOFSKY UND F. SAXL: *Dürers Kupferstich Melencolia I, Eine quellen- und typengeschichtliche Untersuchung* (Studien der Bibliothek Warburg II), Leipzig and Berlin, 1923.

STEFAN ZWEIG: 'Der Europäische Gedanke in seiner historischen Entwicklung', in *Zeit und Welt*, Gesammelte Aufsätze und Vorträge, 1904–40, Bermann-Fischer Vorlag, Stockholm, 1943.

HEINRICH WÖLFFLIN: *Renaissance und Barock*, Verlagsanstalt F. Bruckmann, Munich, 1888.

CARL JUSTI: *Winkelmann und seine Zeitgenossen*, Verlag F. C. W. Vogel, Leipzig, 3rd ed., 1923.

KLARA GARAS: *Franz Anton Maulbertsch*, Amalthea Verlag, Vienna, 1960.

HERMANN BAHR: *Wien*, C. Krabbe-E. Gussmann Verlag, Stuttgart, 1907.

OSKAR KOKOSCHKA: 'An Approach to the Baroque in Czechoslovakia', *Burlington Magazine*, No. 476, Vol. LXXXXI, London, November 1942. (In Czech trans.: České baroko', in *Obzor*, London, May/June 1943. A German version in the volume *Stimmen aus Böhmen*, London, 1945.)

OSKAR KOKOSCHKA: *A Sea Ringed With Visions*, Thames & Hudson, London, 1962. (*Spur im Treibsand*, Geschichten, Atlantis Verlag, Zürich, 1956.)

JÁNOS PLESCH: *The Story of a Doctor*, Victor Gollancz, London, 1947. (*Ein Arzt erzählt sein Leben*, Paul List Verlag, Munich, 1949.)

CHAPTER III

J. P. HODIN: 'Larenopfer', in *Bekenntnis zu Kokoschka*, Florian Kupferberg Verlag, Mainz and Berlin, 1963.

OSKAR KOKOSCHKA: *Schriften 1907–1955*, edited by H. M. Wingler, Albert Langen-Georg Müller Verlag, Munich, 1956.

JAMES BURNHAM: *The Managerial Revolution or What is Happening in the World Now*, New York, 1941.

EDWARD BERNSTEIN: *Cromwell and Communism. Socialism and Democracy in the Great English Revolution*, G. Allen & Unwin, London, 1930.

LIN YUTANG: *The Importance of Living*, Heinemann, London, 1938.

Lettres Complètes d'Abélard et d'Héloïse, Garnier Frères, Paris, 1908.

HANNS HÖRBINGER-PHILIPP FAUTH: *Glazial-Kosmogonie*, Hase & Koehler Verlag, Leipzig, 1913.

T. G. MASARYK: *Russland und Europa* (*Rusko a Evropa*), Jena, 1913.

CHAPTER IV

OSKAR KOKOSCHKA: 'Aus meiner Jugendbiographie,' *Der Wiener Kunstwanderer*, Jahrgang I, Nr. 10, Vienna, November 1933.

OSKAR KOKOSCHKA: 'Kinderkrankheit', *Neue Züriher Zeitung*, Zürich. I, 8 July 1947; II, 9 July 1947; III, 10 July 1947; IV, 13 July 1947; V, 13 July 1947.

PIERRE BRIQUET: *Traité clinique et thérapeutique de l'Hystérie*, Paris, 1859.

CHAPTER V

OSKAR KOKOSCHKA: *Dramen und Bilder* (Introduction, Paul Stefan), Kurt Wolff Verlag, Leipzig, 1913.

BOHUSLAV KOKOSCHKA: *Geh mach die Tür zu, es zieht*, 1925.

BOHUSLAV KOKOSCHKA: *Ketten in das Meer*, 1917.

DR EUGENIE SCHWARZWALD: 'Wenn Kokoschka spricht', in *Die Bühne*, Vienna, October 1934. (Reprinted in *Prager Tagblatt*, 1934.)

BERTA PATOČKOVÁ-KOKOSCHKA: *Mein Lied* (Ausgewählte Gedichte, mit 7 Lithographien von Oskar Kokoschka), Gurlitt Verlag, Vienna, Linz, Munich, 1952.

OSKAR KOKOSCHKA: *Variationen über ein Thema, mit einem Vorwort von Max Dvořák* (ed. Bohuslav Kokoschka), Verlag Richard Lanyi, Vienna, and Ed. Strache, Vienna—Prague—Leipzig, 1921. (Portfolio with ten plates in heliogravure.)

OSKAR KOKOSCHKA: 'Ich bin ein Seher' ('I am a Seer'), *Österreichisches Tagebuch*, Nr. 43, 2 Jahrgang, Vienna, 28 November 1947.

CHAPTER VI

OSKAR KOKOSCHKA: *Die träumenden Knaben* ('Dreaming Youths') was written in 1907 and published in 1908 by the Wiener Werkstätten. This small work consists of a poem, eight colour lithographs and two black-and-white illustrations and is provided with the following remark: This book was written and illustrated by Oskar Kokoschka, published by the Wiener Werkstätten, and printed by Berger & Chwala, 1908. The Kurt Wolff Verlag, Leipzig, published 275 numbered copies in 1917. Further reprints: *Das Kunstblatt*, Year 1, Vol. 10 (without illustrations); Oskar Kokoschka, *Schriften 1907–55*, Albert Langen-Georg Müller Verlag, Munich, 1956; in a smaller format in Oskar Kokoschka, *Die träumenden Knaben und andere Dichtungen* (Der Weisse Tiertöter, Spruch, 1911, Allos Makar, Zueignung, Lauschender), with a foreword by Hans Maria Wingler: *Kokoschkas Dichtungen*, Verlag Galerie Welz, Salzburg, 1959.

BERTA ZUCKERKANDL-SZEPS: *Erinnerungen an Gustav Klimt*, Die Bühne, Vienna, October 1934.

ANTON FAISTAUER: *Neue Malerei in Österreich. Betrachtungen eines Malers.* Amalthea Verlag, Vienna, 1923.

KRISTIAN SOTRIFFEN: *Modern Austrian Art. A Concise History*, Thames & Hudson, London, 1965.

R. W. EMERSON: 'Plato the Philosopher', in *Representative Men*, Blackie, London, 1923.

DR HANS ANKWICZ-KLEEHOVEN: 'Exlibris von Oskar Kokoschka', in *Österreichisches Jahrbuch für Exlibris und Gebrauchsgraphik*, Österreichisches Jahrbuch, Vol. 38, Vienna, 1949–51.

OSKAR KOKOSCHKA: *Der gefesselte Kolumbus* ('The Fettered Columbus'). The book mentioned in the text was never printed. It appeared with twelve lithographs from the year 1913 in a revised version with the title *Der gefesselte Kolumbus*, and published by Fritz Gurlitt Verlag, Berlin, 1916 and 1920, and in its final version, though without illustrations, in a special edition of the journal, *Die Gefährten*, Vienna, Leipzig, Year 3, Vol. 10. Reprinted in: *Das Kunstwerk*, Year 2, 1918; in the *Gurlitt Almanach* for the year 1920, and in the Gurlitt series, *Die neuen Bilderbücher*, 3, Series 21; in the Gurlitt series *Die Malerbücher*, 1921 in a small, popular edition, and in Oskar Kokoschka, *Schriften 1907–55*, op. cit., without illustrations.

ALBRECHT DÜRER: *Schriftlicher Nachlass* (ed. Ernst Heidrich; Introduction, Heinrich Wölfflin), Julius Bard Verlag, Berlin, 1910.

OSKAR KOKOSCHKA: *Hiob*, with fourteen lithographs, Paul Cassirer Verlag, Berlin, 1917. *Fritz Neuberger in herzlicher Freundschaft zugeeignet.* Also in *Vier Dramen*, Paul Cassirer Verlag, Berlin 1919. *Job* (a drama), 1917. Translated by Walter H. and Jacqueline Sokel in *An Anthology of German Expressionist Drama. A Prelude to the Absurd* (ed. Walter H. Sokel), Anchor Books, Doubleday & Co, New York, 1963.

C. G. JUNG: 'The Relations between the Ego and the Unconscious', in *The Collected Works of C. G. Jung*, Vol. 7, Two Essays on Analytical Psychology (trans. R. F. C. Hull), Routledge & Kegan Paul, London, 1953.

C. G. JUNG: 'The Practice of Psychotherapy', *Essays on the Psychology of the Transference and Other Subjects*, op. cit.

OSKAR KOKOSCHKA: *Hoffnung der Frauen* was published for the first time in 1909 with five line-engravings and music by Herwarth Walden by the Sturm Verlag in the form of a small book with red binding. A reprint appeared on 14 July 1910 in the revue *Der Sturm*, Year 1, Vol. 20, with the title 'Mörder Hoffnung der Frauen' (without a comma, Kokoschka emphasizes), and then in the book edited by Paul Stefan: *Oskar Kokoschka, Dramen und Bilder*, Kurt Wolff Verlag, Leipzig, 1913, but with the original title once more. In 1917 it appeared with *Der brennende Dornbusch* as No. 4 in the series called *Der jüngste Tag*, in the Kurt Wolff Verlag, Leipzig. In 1919 it was published again, in company with *Orpheus und Eurydike*, *Der Brennende Dornbusch* and *Hiob* under the title *Vier Dramen* and the dedication 'Dem treuen Freunde Adolf Loos gewidmet vom Verfasser', by Paul Cassirer, Berlin, and in 1920 with *Die Träumenden Knaben* and the poem *Allos Makar* (1915), a *Spruch* (1911), a *Rätsel* (1915), the preface to *Vom Bewusstsein der Gesichte*, and *Der Brennende Dornbusch* in the revue Die Gefährten, Year 3, Vol. 10, Vienna, Leipzig. In 1921 Paul Hindemith's *Drei Operneinakter* (Textbook) appeared, published by B. Schott & Söhne, Vienna and Leipzig, and *Mörder Hoffnung der Frauen*, text by Oskar Kokoschka, an abstract for the piano, published by B. Schott & Söhne, Mainz and Leipzig. *Murderer the Women's Hope*, 1907 (trans. Michael Hamburger) in *An Anthology of German Expressionist Drama, A Prelude to the Absurd*, op. cit.

OSKAR KOKOSCHKA: 'Lebensgeschichte', Preface to Ernest Rathenau, *Kokoschka Handzeichnungen*, Berlin, 1935. Reprinted in Oskar Kokoschka, *Schriften, 1907–1955*, under the title 'Vom Erleben'. See also: J. P. Hodin, *Bekenntnis zu Kokoschka*, op. cit.

LUDWIG MÜNZ AND GUSTAV KÜNSTLER: *Adolf Loos, Pioneer of Modern Architecture* (Introduction by Nikolaus Pevsner; Appreciation by Oskar Kokoschka), Thames & Hudson, London, 1966.

OSKAR KOKOSCHKA: 'Adolf Loos zum Gedächtnis', in *Der Wiener Kunstwanderer*, Vienna, Year 1, November 1933, No. 10.

OSKAR KOKOSCHKA: 'Ins Leere gesprochen, eine zweite Erinnerung an Adolf Loos', *Forum*, Vienna, Year IX, July/August 1962, No. 103/104.

OSKAR KOKOSCHKA: Tells his Life Story. An Autobiography on Record with an Introduction and Colour Reproductions of the Artist's Major Works, containing Explanatory Notes, (Hannes Reinhardt, Gottfried Sello; Deutsche Grammophon Gesellschaft, Hamburg, 1962.) See also: Adolf Loos (1870–1933), Catalogue of the Exhibition in the Galerie des Beaux Art Paris, November 1962.

HANS MARIA WINGLER: *Ein Lebensbild in zeigenössischen Dokumenten, zusammengestellt und herausgegeben zum 70. Geburtstag Oskar Kokoschkas*, Albert Langen—Georg Müller, Munich, 1956.

HERMANN BAHR: *Wien*, Vol. 6: 'Städte und Landschaften' (ed. Leo Greiner), C. Krabbe-E. Gussman Verlag, Stuttgart, 1907.

ALFRED POLGAR: *An den Rand geschrieben*, Ernst Rowohlt Verlag, Berlin, 1926.

BRUNO WALTER: *Theme and Variations*, New York and London, 1947. (*Thema und Variationen. Erinnerungen und Gedanken*, S. Fischer Verlag, 1960.)

STEFAN ZWEIG: 'Das Wien von gestern', in *Zeit und Welt*, Gesammelte Aufsätze und Vorträge, 1904–40, op. cit.

HERTA SINGER: *Im Wiener Kaffeehaus*, Verlag für Jugend und Volk, Vienna, 1959. (With Bibliography.)

LUDWIG PLAKOLB: *Kaffeehaus. Literarische Spezialitäten und amoröse Gusto—Stückeln aus Wien*, R. Piper Verlag, Munich, 1959 (with contributions by Altenberg, Polgar, Schnitzler, Fridell, Kuh, Weinheber, *et al.*)

JOSEF HOFFMANN: 'Die Anfänge Oskar Kokoschkas', in J. P. Hodin: *Bekenntnis zu Kokoschka, Erinnerungen und Deutungen*, op. cit.

DR HEDWIG SCHLEIFFER: 'Kokoschka, Pioneer in Art Education', *School Arts Educational Magazine*, New York, Vol. 59, 10, June 1960.

CHAPTER VII

The Works of Callimachus (trans. H. W. Tytler), T. Davison, London, 1793.

GIACOMO LEOPARDI: *Poems by Leopardi* (trans. John Heath-Stubbs), John Lehmann, London, 1945.

SØREN KIERKEGAARD: *Samlede Vaerker*, Copenhagen, 1962–4. (Particularly: *The Concept of Dread*, 1944; *Fear and Trembling*, 1939; *The Sickness unto Death*, 1941; *Either—Or*, 1944. All: Oxford University Press.)

FRANZ KAFKA: *The Trial* (trans. Willa and Edwin Muir), Secker & Warburg, London, 1956.

FRANZ KAFKA: *The Castle* (trans. Willa and Edwin Muir, with additional material trans. Eithne Wilkins and Ernst Kaiser), Secker & Warburg, London, 1953.

MARTIN HEIDEGGER: *Existence and Being* with an Introduction by Werner Brock (trans. Douglas Scott, R. F. C. Hull and Alan Crick), Vision, London, 1949.

JEAN PAUL SARTRE: *L'Étre et le Néant: Essai d'ontologie phénoménologique*, Librairie Gallimard, Paris, 1943.

CHARLES BAUDELAIRE: 'Les Litanies de Satan', in *Les Fleurs du Mal*, *1857/1861*, Les Editions G. Crès, Paris, 1911.

A. N. WHITEHEAD: *Science in the Modern World*, Cambridge University Press, 1945.

E. A. BURTT: *The Metaphysical Foundations of Modern Science, 1924/1932* Doubleday, New York, 1955.

J. W. GOETHE: *Theory of Colours* (trans. from the German with notes by C. L. Eastlake), London, 1840.

MAX PLANCK: *Das Weltbild der neuen Physik: Physikalische Abhandlungen und Vorträge aus Anlass des* 100, Geburtstages von Max Planck herausgegeben vom Max Planck Institut, Munich, Vieweg Verlag, Brunswick, 1958.

ALBERT EINSTEIN: *The World As I See It* (trans. Alan Harris), John Lane, London, 1935.

WERNER HEISENBERG: *The Physicist's Conception of Nature* (trans. Arnold J. Pomerans), Hutchinson & Co, London, 1958.

WERNER HEISENBERG: *Philosophic Problems of Nuclear Science*, eight Lectures, (trans. F. C. Hayes), Faber & Faber, London, 1952.

ERWIN SCHRÖDINGER: *Science and Humanism*, Cambridge University Press, Cambridge, 1951.

NIELS BOHR: *Atomic Physics and Human Knowledge*, John Wiley & Sons, New York, 1958.

MAX BORN: *Physics in My Generation*, Pergamon Press, London, 1956.

SIR CHARLES SHERRINGTON: *Man and His Nature*, Cambridge University Press, Cambridge, 1940 and 1950.

ADOLF PORTMAN: *Biologie und Geist*, Rhein Verlag, Zürich, 1956.

ADOLF PORTMAN: *Zoologie und das neue Bild des Menschen*, Rowohlt Verlag, Hamburg, 1956.

PIERRE TEILHARD DE CHARDIN: *The Phenomenon of Man* (Introduction by Julian Huxley), Collins, London, 1959; and other works.

ARTHUR STANLEY EDDINGTON: *Science and the Unseen World*, George Allen & Unwin, London, 1929.

NORBERT WIENER: *The Human Use of Human Beings: Cybernetics and Society*, Anchor Books, Doubleday & Co, New York, 1954.

ERWIN SCHRÖDINGER: *What Is Life? A Physicist's Approach to the Subject* (with an Epilogue on Determinism and Free Will), Cambridge University Press, Cambridge, 1944.

J. ROBERT OPPENHEIMER: *Science and the Common Understanding* (B.B.C. Reith Lectures, 1953), Oxford University Press, Oxford, 1954.

RABINDRANATH TAGORE: *The Religion of Man*, George Allen & Unwin, London, 1931.

S. RADHAKRISHNAN: *The Reign of Religion in Contemporary Philosophy*, Macmillan, London, 1920.

S. RADHAKRISHNAN: *Eastern Religion and Western Thought*, Oxford University Press, Oxford, 1939.

ALBERT SCHWEITZER: *Christianity and the Religions of the World*, Lectures, (trans. Johanna Powers, i.a.), Selly Oak Colleges, Central Council Publications, London, 1923.

JULIAN HUXLEY: *The Humanist Frame*, Allen & Unwin, London, 1961.

RUDOLF STEINER: *Die Rätsel der Philosophie*, Philosophisch-Antroposophische Bibliothek, Berlin, 1914.

P. D. OUSPENSKY: *In Search of the Miraculous: Fragments of an Unknown Teaching*, Routledge & Kegan Paul, London, 1950.

G. GURDJIEFF: *All and Everything*, Routledge & Kegan Paul, London, 1950.

H. P. BLAVATSKY: *The Secret Doctrine* (3 vols.), Theosophical Society, London, 1897–1905.

JACQUES MARITAIN: *Science et Sagesse*, Labergerie, Paris, 1947.

ALDOUS HUXLEY: *The Perennial Philosophy*, Chatto & Windus, London, 1947.

MARTIN BUBER: 'Das Problem des Menschen', in *Dialogisches Leben*, Georg Müller Verlag, Zürich, 1947.

NICOLAS BERDYAEV: *Works*, Geoffrey Bles, London, 1937–53.

J. HUIZINGA: *Parerga*, Pantheon Verlag, Amsterdam/Basle, 1945.

M. DE UNAMUNO: *The Tragic Sense of Life in Men and in Peoples* (trans. J. E. Crawford), Macmillan & Co, London, 1921.

PAUL VALÉRY: 'La Crise de L'esprit', in *Variété*, Gallimard, Paris, 1924.

PAUL VALÉRY: 'Notes sur la grandeur et decadence de l'Europe', in *Regards sur le Monde Actuel et autres essais*, Gallimard, Paris, 1946.

ALFRED WEBER: *Das Tragische und die Geschichte*, R. Piper Verlag, Munich, 1943.

ALFRED WEBER: *Kulturgeschichte als Kultursoziologie*, R. Piper Verlag, Munich, 1960.

KARL JASPERS: *The Origin and Goal of History* (trans. Michael Bullock), Routledge & Kegan Paul, London, 1953.

LEWIS MUMFORD: *The Transformation of Man*, Allan & Unwin, London, 1957.

EGON FRIEDELL: *A Cultural History of the Modern Age* (trans. Charles Francis Atkinson (3 vols), A. A. Knopf, New York, 1930–2.

W. Y. EVANS-WENTZ: *Tibetan Yoga and Secret Doctrines*, Oxford University Press, Oxford, 1935.

SIR JAMES JEANS: *The New Background of Science*, Cambridge University Press, Cambridge, 1933.

F. BODMER: *The Loom of Language* (ed. L. Hogben), Allen & Unwin, London, 1944.

A. TARSKI: *Introduction to Logic and the Methodology of Deductive Sciences*, Oxford University Press, New York, 1949.

RUDOLF CARNAP: *Foundations of Logic and Mathematics*, University of Chicago Press, Chicago, 1939. See also: Susanne K. Langer, *An Introduction to Symbolic Logic*, Diver Publications, New York, 1937.

MARCUS FABIUS QUINTILIAN (*c.* A.D. 35–95): *De Institutione Oratoria* (ed. N. Angelius), P. Juntae, Florence, 1515.

JOSÉ ORTEGA Y GASSET: *The Dehumanisation of Art and Other Writings on Art and Culture*, Anchor Books, Doubleday & Co, New York, 1956.

GUILLAUME APOLLINAIRE: *Les Peintres Cubistes : Méditations Esthétiques*, Eugène Figuière, Paris, 1913.

ABBÉ HENRI DE BRÉMONT: *La Poésie pure avec un débat sur la poésie pure*, B. Grasset, Paris, 1925.

HENRI FOCILLON: *The Life of Forms in Art* (trans. Charles Beecher Hogan and George Kubler), Yale Historical Publications, New Haven, 1942.

OSKAR KOKOSCHKA: 'Rückblick auf die Schaffhauser Ausstellung', in *Atlantis: Länder, Völker, Reisen*, XIX Year, No. 12, 1947.

PETER CHELTSCHICKY: *Das Netz des Glaubens* (*Siet Wiery*), Einhorn Verlag, Dachau, Munich, 1923.

KNUT HAMSUN: *Pan*, from Lieutenant Glahn's Papers (trans. James W. McFarlane), Artemis Press, London, 1955.

KNUT HAMSUN: *Paa Gjengrodde Stier*, Gyldendal Norsk Forlag, Oslo, 1949. (*Auf überwachsenen Pfaden*, Paul List Verlag, Munich, 1950.)

GUSTAVE FLAUBERT: *Sentimental Education* (Trans. with Introduction and Notes by Anthony Goldsmith), Everyman's Library, London, 1941.

CHAPTER VIII

J. P. HODIN: 'Oskar Kokoschkas erste Schweizer Erinnerungen', *Neue Zürcher Zeitung*, Zurich, 13 January 1964.

AUGUSTE FOREL: *Out of my Life and Work* (trans. Bernard Miall). G. Allen & Unwin, London, 1937.

PAUL WESTHEIM: *Oskar Kokoschka*, Gustav Kiepenheuer Verlag, Berlin, 1918; 2nd ed., Paul Cassirer Verlag, Berlin, 1925.

WILHELM DILTHEY: *Weltanschauung und Analyse des Menschen seit der Renaissance und Reformation*, II Vol. *Collected Works*, 5th ed., B. G. Teubner, Stuttgart, 1957.

SIGMUND FREUD: *Introductory Lectures on Psychoanalysis*, Works Vols. 15 and 16, Hogarth Press, London, 1963.

ALFRED ADLER: *The Neurotic Constitution: Outlines of a comparative Individualistic Psychology and Psychotherapy*, Kegan Paul, Trench, Trubner, London, 1918.

C. G. JUNG: *Psychology of the Unconscious: A Study of the Transformations and Symbolisms of the Libido: A Contribution to the History of the Evolution of Thought* . . . (authorized trans. with Introduction by Beatrice M. Hinkle), Moffat, Yard & Co, New York, 1960.

SIGMUND FREUD: *Totem and Taboo and other works*, Works Vol. 13, Hogarth Press, London, 1955.

HENRY BERGSON: *L'Evolution Créatrice*, Felix Alcan, Paris, 5th ed., 1908.

EDMUND HUSSERL: *Ideas: General Introduction to Pure Phenomenology* . . . (trans. W. R. Boyce Gibson), Allen & Unwin, London; Macmillan & Co., New York, 1931.

HERMANN COHEN: *System der Philosophie*, I–III, Bruno Cassirer Verlag, Berlin, 1902, 1907, 1912.

PAUL NATORP: *Philosophie, ihr Problem oder ihre Probleme*, Göttingen, 1921.

ERNST CASSIRER: *The Philosophy of Symbolic Forms* (trans. Ralph Manheim), Yale University Press, Newhaven, 1953.

GEORG SIMMEL: *Soziologie*, Untersuchungen über die Formen der Vergesellschaftung, Leipzig, 1908.

FERDINAND TÖNNIES: *Gemeinschaft und Gesellschaft*, Grundbegriffe der reinen Soziologie, Berlin, 7th ed., 1926.

OSWALD SPENGLER: *The Decline of the West* (2 vols), George Allen & Unwin, London, 1926/29.

RUDOLF EUCKEN: *Die Lebensanschauungen der grossen Denker: Eine Entwicklungsgeschichte des Lebensproblems der Menschheit von Plato bis zur Gegenwart*. Veit & Co., Leipzig, 3rd ed., 1899.

WALTER RATHENAU: *Gesammelte Schriften* (5 vols.), Berlin, 1918.

CHARLES PIERRE PÉGUY: *Note sur M Bergson et la philosophie bergsonienne*, Paris, 5th ed., 1935.

EMIL UTITZ: *Grundlegung der allgemeinen Kunstwissenschaft* (2 vols), Ferdinand Enke, Stuttgart, 1914/20.

KATHERINE GILBERT AND HELMUT KUHN: *A History of Esthetics*, New York/London, 1939.

ALOIS RIEGL: *Gesammelte Aufsätze*, Dr Benno Filser Verlag, Augsburg-Vienna, 1929.

MAX DVOŘÁK: *Kunstgeschichte als Geistesgeschichte: Studien zur abendländischen Kunstentwicklung*, R. Piper Verlag, Munich, 1924.

WILHELM WORRINGER: *Abstraction and Empathy: A Contribution to the Psychology of Style* (trans. Michael Bullock). Routledge & Kegan Paul, London, 1953.

NELL WALDEN AND LOTHAR SCHREYER: *Der Sturm: Ein Gedenkbuch an Herwarth Walden und die Künstler des Sturmkreises*, Woldemar Klein Verlag, Baden-Baden, 1954.

NELL WALDEN: *Herwarth Walden*, Florian Kupferberg Verlag, Berlin and Mainz, 1963.

NELL WALDEN: 'Kokoschka und der Sturmkreis', in J. P. Hodin: *Bekenntnis zu Kokoschka, Erinnerungen und Deutungen*, op. cit.

ALBERT SOERGEL: *Dichtung und Dichter der Zeit. Eine Schilderung der deutschen Literatur der letzten Jahrzehnte. Neue Folge: Im Banne des Expressionismus*, R. Voigtländer Verlag, Leipzig, 1925.

OSKAR KOKOSCHKA: Menschenköpfe, Verlag *Der Sturm*, Berlin, 1916.

CHAPTER IX

ALBERT EHRENSTEIN: *Tubutsch* (with twelve line-engravings by Oskar Kokoschka), Verlag Jahoda & Siegel, Vienna, 1911. (Reprinted in small format, *Inselbücherei*, Insel Verlag, Leipzig, 1919.)

KARL KRAUS: *Sprüche und Widersprüche*, Verlag der Fackel, Vienna-Leipzig, 1924.

KAREL ČAPEK: 'Karl Kraus als Lehrmeister', in *Stimmen über Karl Kraus zum 40. Geburtstag*, Richard Lanyi Verlag, Vienna, 1934.

ALFRED POLGAR: 'Peter Altenberg', Preface in *Der Nachlass von Peter Altenberg*, S. Fischer Verlag, Berlin, 1925.

RUTH LANDSHOFF-YORCK: *Klatsch, Ruhm und kleine Feuer. Biographische Impressionen. Kapitel: Litho Ruth* 3, Kiepenheuer & Witsch, Cologne-Berlin, 1963.

J. D. BERNAL, F.R.S.: *The Social Function of Science*, Routledge & Kegan Paul, London, 1939.

OSKAR KOKOSCHKA: 'The Portrait in the Past and Present', *Apropos*, No. 3, Portrait Painting, London, 1945.

CHAPTER X

OSKAR KOKOSCHKA: *Sphinx und Strohmann, ein Curiosum*, Einakter, 1907 (*Sphinx and Strawman, A one-act Curiosity*, 1907). *Mörder Hoffnung der Frauen*, 1907/9 (*Murderer The Women's Hope*, trans. Michael Hamburger in *An Anthology of Expressionist Drama*, op. cit.) *Schauspiel, oder Der brennende Dornbusch*, 1911. *Allos Makar*, Dichtung, 1913. *Orpheus und Eurydike*, Drama, 1915/18. *Der gefesselte Kolumbus*, 1916. *Hiob*, enlarged and illustrated version of *Sphinx and Strawman*, 1917 (*Job*, trans. Walter H. and Jacqueline Sokel, in *An Anthology of German Expressionist Drama*, op. cit.) All in Oskar Kokoschka: *Schriften 1907–1955* (ed. H. M. Wingler), op. cit. Cf. *Orpeus und Eurykike* with essays by Poliziano, Calderon, Gluck, Calzabigi, Offenbach-Crémieux, Kokoschka, Cocteau, Anouilh, in *Theater der Jahrhunderte* (Preface by Karl Kerenyi), Albert Langen-Georg Müller Verlag, Munich, 1963; see also Ann Eliza Reed: *Erzählungen und Lithographien by Oskar Kokoschka*, printed for the members of the Maximilian Society, Hamburg, 1952; *Spur im Treibsand* (*A Sea Ringed with Visions*), op cit.; also 'Erinnerungen an Kokoschka' in Alma Mahler: *And the Bridge is Love*, Hutchinson, London, New York, 1959 (*Mein Leben*, S. Fischer Verlag, Frankfurt a/Main, 1960).

ARTHUR RIMBAUD: *Poésies Complètes* (Preface by P. Verlaine), Léon Varnier, Paris, 1895.

GEORG SCHMIDT: 'Zu Kokoschkas Windsbraut', in J. P. Hodin: *Bekenntnis zu Kokoschka, Erinnerungen und Deutungen*, op. cit.

OSKAR KOKOSCHKA: 'Allos Makar', in *Zeit-Echo: Ein Kriegstagebuch der Künstler*, I Year, No. 20, Graphik Verlag, Munich, 1915. Reprinted in Oskar Kokoschka, *Schriften 1907–1955*.

PAUL BEKKER: 'Zu Kokoschkas Bachmappe: Offener Brief an den Herausgeber des "Kunstblattes" ', *Das Kunstblatt*, I Year, No. 10. Weimar, 1917.

OSKAR KOKOSCHKA: 'Zueignung', poem with eleven lithographs, in the series *Neue Bilderbücher*, 1, Fritz Gurlitt Verlag, Berlin, 1918. (The original edition of the portfolio published by Fritz Gurlitt Verlag, 1916 and 1917, without the text of the cantata and without the poem 'Zueignung', contains nine lithographs.)

J. E. CIRLOT: *A Dictionary of Symbols* (*Diccionario de Simbolos Tradicionales*), Routledge & Kegan Paul, London, 1962.

C. A. S. WILLIAMS: *Psychology of Chinese Symbolism and Art Motives*, The Julian Press, New York, 1960.

BERNARD LEACH: 'Drachen—Träume—Leben', in J. P. Hodin *Bekenntnis zu Kokoschka, Erinnerungen und Deutungen*, op. cit.

KARL KRAUS: *Die Chinesische Mauer*, Kurt Wolff Verlag, Leipzig, 1914 (with eight lithographs).

ERNEST RATHENAU: *Der Zeichner Kokoschka* (Preface by Paul Westheim), privately printed, New York, 1961.

MICHELANGELO MASCIOTTA: *Disegni di Kokoschka*, Parenti, Florence, 1942.

H. M. WINGLER: *Künstler und Poeten—Bildzeichnungen von Oskar Kokoschka*, Buchheim Verlag, Feldafing, 1954.

REMIGIUS NETZER: *Oskar Kokoschka, Lithographien: Einführung und Gespräch mit dem Künstler*, R. Piper Verlag, Munich, 1956.

OSKAR KOKOSCHKA: *Olda* (Preface by Werner Hofmann), Galerie Welz Verlag, Salzburg, 1956.

OSKAR KOKOSCHKA: Forty-eight Plates in Photogravure, Eight Plates in Colour. With two Original Lithographs. Edited and with Introduction by James S. Plaut and a Letter From the Artist. The Institute of Contemporary Art, Boston; Max Parrish, London, 1948.

CHAPTER XI

OSKAR KOKOSCHKA: *Orpheus und Eurydike*, 1915/18 (set to music in 1923 by Ernst Křenek), in *Vier Dramen*, Paul Cassirer Verlag, Berlin, 1919. Also: *Orpheus und Eurydike*, a play in three acts, with music by Ernst Křenek, Universal Edition, Vienna, New York, 1925. Extract scored for piano with text, 1925.

OSKAR KOKOSCHKA: 'On the Nature of Visions' (trans. Hedi Medlinger and John Thwaites), in *Kokoschka: Life and Work*, by Edith Hoffmann, op. cit.

OSKAR KOKOSCHKA: 'Vom Bewusstsein der Gesichte', in *Genius*, Munich, 1919.

OSKAR KOKOSCHKA: 'Der Fetisch', in *Künstlerbekenntnisse: Briefe, Tagebuchblätter, Betrachtungen heutiger Künstler* (collected and edited by Paul Westheim), Prophyläen Verlag, Berlin, 1925.

F. K. GOTSCH: 'Kokoschka als Lehrer', in J. P. Hodin: *Bekenntnis zu Kokoschka, Erinnerungen und Deutungen*, op. cit.

FELIX EMMEL: *Das ekstatische Theater*, Berlin, 1924.

KARL OTTEN: *Schrei und Bekenntnis: Expressionistisches Theater*, Hermann Luchterhand Verlag, Darmstadt, Berlin, 1959.

LUDWIG RUBINER: 'Vorspiel zu "Die Gewaltlosen" ', in the series *Der dramatische Wille*, Gustav Kiepenheuer Verlag, Potsdam, 1919.

KARL OTTEN: *Ahnung und Aufbruch, Expressionistische Prosa*, Hermann Luchterhand Verlag, Darmstadt, Berlin, 1957.

GOTTFRIED BENN: *Lyrik des expressionistischen Jahrzehnts: Von den Wegbereitern bis zum Dada*, Limes Verlag, Wiesbaden, 1955.

KURT PINTUS: *Menschheitsdämmerung*, ein Dokument des Expressionismus: Rowohlts Klassiker der Literatur und Wissenschaft', *Deutsche Literatur*, Vol. 4, Rowohlt Verlag, Hamburg, 1959 (1st ed., 1920).

ALBERT EHRENSTEIN: *Menschen und Affen, 1910–1925*, Ernst Rowohlt Verlag, Berlin, undated.

BERNHARD ZELLER: *Expressionismus, Literatur und Kunst, 1910–1923*. Austellung des deutschen Literaturarchivs im Schiller Nationalmuseum, Marbach a.N., 1960.

WALTER H. SOKEL: *An Anthology of German Expressionist Drama: A Prelude to the Absurd*, op. cit.

GEORGE SCHMIDT: 'Zu Kokoschkas Windsbraut', in J. P. Hodin: *Bekenntnis zu Kokoschka, Erinnerungen und Deutungen*, op. cit.

OSKAR KOKOSCHKA: 'Die Macht der Musik', in *Museumsjournal* (periodical of the Dutch Museums), Amsterdam, 1955.

LEO KESTENBERG: *Bewegte Zeiten, musisch-musikantische Lebenserinnerungen*, Möseler Verlag, Wolfenbuttel and Zürich, 1961.

LEO KESTENBERG: 'Was mir Kokoschka bedeutet', in J. P. Hodin: *Bekenntnis zu Kokoschka, Erinnerungen und Deutungen*, op. cit.

CHAPTER XII

SIR EDWARD BEDDINGTON-BEHRENS: *Look Back, Look Forward*, Macmillan, London, 1963.

J. W. GOETHE: 'Dämon', in *Urworte, Orphisch*, 1817.

J. P. HODIN: 'Mythos und Schicksal Europas', in *Bekenntnis zu Kokoschka, Erinnerungen und Deutungen*, op. cit.

OSKAR KOKOSCHKA UND WALTER KERN: 'Zu meinem Tryptichon "Die Thermopylen" ' in *Thermopylae: Ein Tryptichon*, (texts by Walter Kern and Oskar Kokoschka), BW-Presse, Winterthur, 1955. (Reprinted in Oskar Kokoschka *Schriften 1907–1955*, op. cit.)

OSKAR KOKOSCHKA: *Thermopylae 1954* (Introduction by Carl Georg Heise; contributions by Oskar Kokoschka und Bruno Snell), Philipp Reclam Jun. Verlag, Stuttgart, 1961.

OSKAR KOKOSCHKA: 'Die Prometheus-Saga', *Werk*, No. 7, July 1952. Italian Version: 'La Saga di Prometeo', in *La Biennale*, Venice, No. 10, September 1952. (Reprinted in Oskar Kokoschka *Schriften 1907–1955*, op. cit.)

FRIEDRICH NIETZSCHE: *The Will to Power* (trans. A. M. Ludovici). Vol. 14 of *Complete Works*, J. N. Foulis, Edinburgh and London, 1909.

THOMAS MANN: *Über Kokoschka*, in *Der Wiener Kunstwanderer*, Year I, No. 10, Vienna, November 1933.

DENIS DIDEROT: *Essais sur la peinture*, Fr. Buisson, Paris, 1795.

MAX DVOŘÁK: 'Über Greco und den Manierismus', in *Kunstgeschichte als Geistesgeschichte*, op. cit.

DR EUGENIE SCHWARZWALD: 'Der Redner Kokoschka' (Preface to the Catalogue of the exhibition in Mannheim, 1931). See also: H. M. Wingler: *Oskar Kokoschka, ein Lebensbild in zeitgenössischen Dokumenten*, op. cit.

KURT JUHN: *Erlebnis mit einem Gesalbten: Oskar Kokoschka erzählt*, Zeit im Bild, Prague, January 1935.

OSKAR KOKOSCHKA: 'Bemerkungen zum Kunstunterricht', *Neue Zürcher Zeitung*, Zurich, 8 August 1953. (Reprinted in H. M. Wingler, ed.) Oskar Kokoschka: *Schriften 1907–1955*, and in the Preface to the Catalogue of the Exhibition in the Haus der Kunst, Munich, 1958, and in the Künstlerhaus, Vienna, 1958.)

CHAPTER XIII

HANS TIETZE: *Abriss einer österreichischen Kunstgeschichte*, Junges Österreich, London, 1945. (Preface by Oskar Kokoschka.)

J. P. HODIN: 'Kokoschka's Reminiscences of Masaryk', in *The Central European Observer*, Vol. XXIII, No. 2. London, 18 January 1946.

OSKAR KOKOSCHKA: 'Comenius, the English Revolution and Our Present Plight', in *The Teacher of Nations*, Cambridge, 1942.

FRANÇOIS MAURIAC: *Le Jeune Homme*, Hachette, Paris, 1926.

JACQUES MARITAIN: *The Dream of Descartes*, Editions Poetry, London, January 1946.

SIGMUND FREUD: *Civilization and its Discontents* (trans. Joan Rivere), L. & V. Wolf, Inst. of Psycho-Analysis, London, 1930.

LUDWIG KLAGES: *Grundlegung der Wissenschaft vom Ausdruck*, Johann Ambrosius Barth, Leipzig, 1943.

HERBERT READ: *Education Through Art*, Faber & Faber, London, 1943.

HANS PRINZHORN: *Bildnerei der Geisterskranken*, Julius Springer Verlag, Berlin, 1923.

JOSÉ ORTEGA Y GASSET: *The Dehumanization of Art*, op. cit.

ABBÉ HENRI DE BREMONT: *La Poésie pure avec un débat sur la poésie pure*, op. cit.

ANDRÉ MALRAUX: *The Psychology of Art* (trans. Stuart Gilbert) (2 vols.), Zwemmer, London, 1949.

ANDRÉ MALRAUX: *The Voices of Silence* (trans. Stuart Gilbert), Secker & Warburg, London, 1954.

C. G. JUNG *Psychological Types; or The Psychology of Individuation . . .* (trans. H. Godwin Baynes), Library of Psychology, Philosophy and Scientific Method, London, 1923.

F. KRETCHMER: *Physique and Character* (2nd ed. revised with appendix by E. Miller, trans. W. J. H. Sprott), Kegan Paul & Co, London, 1936.

J. P. HODIN: *Edvard Munch, der Genius des Nordens*, Florian Kupferberg Verlag, Mainz-Berlin, 1963.

J. P. HODIN: 'Oskar Kokoschka, die Krise der Kunst und der Expressionismus', *Der Monat*, II Year, No. 18, Berlin, 1950.

C. G. JUNG: *Modern Man in Search of a Soul*, Routledge & Kegan Paul. London, 1961, also *Psychological Types*.

ALOIS RIEGL: *Die Entstehung der Barockkunst in Rom* (ed. A. Burda and Max Dvořák), Anton Schroll Verlag, Vienna, 1908.

CHAPTER XIV

JEREMY BENTHAM: *Economic Writings* (Critical Edition), George Allen & Unwin, London, 1952.

JAKOB BÖHME, *The Works of*, Vol. II (54 Epistles), D. Bryce & Son, Glasgow, 1886.

THOMAS MANN: *Über Kokoschka*, in Der Wiener Kunstwanderer, op. cit.

DR ADRIAN WETTACH: '(Grock) Nicht mö-ö-öglich', in *Artisten, ernstes und heiteres Variété*, by Fred A. Colman und Walter Trier, Paul Aretz Verlag, Dresden, 1928.

INDEX

(Major paintings by Kokoschka, excluding portraits, are in small capitals. Titles of his writings are in italics)